HENRIETTA MARIA

The Mordaunts

The Backstairs Dragon:
A Life of Robert Harley, Earl of Oxford

William's Mary:
A Biography of Mary II

HENRIETTA MARIA

by Elizabeth Hamilton

Coward, McCann & Geoghegan, Inc.

New York

Illustrations follow pages 34, 98, 162, and 226

First American Edition 1976

Copyright © 1976 by Elizabeth Hamilton

SBN: 698-10713-6

Library of Congress Cataloging in Publication Data

Hamilton, Elizabeth, Lady, 1928-
  Henrietta Maria.

  Bibliography: p. 261
  Includes index.
  1. Henrietta Maria, consort of Charles I,
King of Great Britain, 1609-1669.
DA396.A5H35   1976   941.06'2'0924   [B]   76-206

TO EPPIE

Contents

The publishers acknowledge the following for permission to reprint the photographs in this volume:

"Henry IV," by Frans Pourbus the Younger. Reproduced by gracious permission of Her Majesty the Queen. "Marie de Medici," portrait study by Sir Peter Paul Rubens. Crown copyright, Victoria and Albert Museum. "Henrietta Maria," *c.* 1611, by Frans Pourbus the Younger. Reproduced by permission of the Uffizi Gallery. "Louis XIII," by Frans Pourbus the Younger. From the collection at Parham Park, Sussex. "Scenes From The Ballet Armide," 1617. Engravings. Bibliothèque Nationale. "Charles I in 1628," by Gerrit van Honthorst. Reproduced by permission of the National Portrait Gallery. "Henrietta Maria and Lady Carlisle: Detail from Apollo and Diana," by Gerrit van Honthorst. Reproduced by gracious permission of Her Majesty the Queen. "The Duke of Buckingham and His Family." Artist unknown. Reproduced by gracious permission of Her Majesty the Queen. "Charles I, Henrietta Maria and Charles, Prince of Wales," by Hendrick Gerritsz Pot. Reproduced by gracious permission of Her Majesty the Queen. "Charles I and Henrietta Maria Departing for the Chase," by Daniel Mytens. Reproduced by gracious permission of Her Majesty the Queen. "Charles I and Henrietta Maria Dining in Public," by Gerard Houckgeest. Reproduced by gracious permission of Her Majesty the Queen. "Philip, 4th Earl of Pembroke, with His Family," by Sir Anthony van Dyck. Collection, the Earl of Pembroke, Wilton House. "The Five Eldest Children of Charles I," by Sir Anthony van Dyck. Reproduced by gracious permission of Her Majesty the Queen. "John Williams as Keeper of the Great Seal." In Westminster Abbey Library; signed, J. C. Reproduced by courtesy of the Dean and Chapter of Westminster. "Archbishop Laud" (detail), by Sir Anthony van Dyck. Reproduced by courtesy of the Archbishop of Canterbury. Copyright reserved by the Church Commissioners and the Courtauld Institute of Art. "William Prynne." Artist unknown. Reproduced by kind permission of the Treasurer and Masters of the Bench of Lincoln's Inn. "Charles I in Robes of State," by Sir Anthony van Dyck. Reproduced by gracious permission of Her Majesty the Queen. "Henrietta Maria in 1640," marble bust by François Dieussart. The Royal Collection of Rosenborg Castle, Copenhagen. "Designs for Masques," by Inigo Jones. Devonshire Collection, Chatsworth. Reproduced by permission of the Trustees of the Chatsworth Settlement. "Marie de Medici Arrives at St James's Palace," engraving from de la Serre's *Histoire de l'entrée de la reine mère dans la grande bretagne 1639.* Reproduced by permission of the Curators of the Bodleian Library. "Somerset House," engraving in L. Knyff's *Britannia illustrata.* The Royal Institute of British Architects, London. "The Trial of Strafford." Engraving reproduced by permission of the Trustees of the British Museum. "Henrietta Maria Greeted

Acknowledgments

My thanks are due to all those who have allowed me to consult and quote from documents and letters—Earl Fitzwilliam and his Trustees, and Mr John Bebbington, Director of the Sheffield City Libraries, Lord Spencer for kindly showing me account books and letters at Althorp, Mr T. Cottrell-Dormer for letting me quote from two letters written by Henrietta Maria to the Duke of Gloucester in 1660, Dr Levi Fox, Director of the Shakespeare Birthplace Trust, Stratford-on-Avon, who brought to my attention the accounts drawn up after the Queen's visit to the town in 1643, Mr A. G. Meecham of the Bath City Council Administrative and Legal Services Department, Mr N. Higson of the Brynmoor Jones Library, University of Hull, Mr O. S. Tomlinson of the North Yorkshire County Library, Mr K. D. Holt, Humberside County Archivist, Dr Margaret O'Sullivan of the Staffordshire County Record Office, and the many County Archivists who have supplied me with information concerning the royal progress in 1634, the Queen's journey from Bridlington to Oxford, and her flight to Exeter.

I have received courteous and patient help from Librarians and their staff at the Bibliothèque Nationale, the Bodleian Library, the British Library Manuscripts Room, the London Library, the National Register of Archives, the Shakespeare Centre, Stratford-on-Avon, the Warwickshire County Library, and from Mr Kenneth Timings and the staff of the Public Record Office.

In the search for illustrations, Sir Oliver Millar has given me much valuable advice, as has Mr L. J. van der Klooster of the Netherlands Institute for Art History at The Hague. I should like to thank Sir Robert Mackworth-Young, the Royal Librarian, and Miss Lowe, for their help, as well as Miss Evans of the National Portrait Gallery, and Mr T. S. Wragg, the Librarian at Chatsworth.

I owe a debt of gratitude to all those modern scholars whose work in recent years has thrown so much new light on the reign of Charles I, and to Henrietta Maria's biographers, particularly Miss Carola Oman and Professor Quentin Bone.

Mr Christopher Sinclair-Stevenson of Hamish Hamilton has as always given me much-needed help and encouragement, and I have had the usual support from everyone at home—I thank them all, young and old, for their tolerance, despite the all-pervasive sound of the typewriter. My husband once again deserves a particular vote of thanks for everything he has done, with a special mention of the days at the Bibliothèque Nationale spent transcribing, translating from the French and wrestling with Queen Henrietta Maria's erratic grammar, eccentric spelling and idiosyncratic handwriting which he has to admit he found even more difficult to decipher than his wife's.

NOTE

Events which took place in England during Henrietta Maria's lifetime are dated according to the Old Style which was ten days behind the New Style in use on the Continent.

Notes at the end of the book are given according to page references, and all abbreviations are explained in the bibliography.

HENRIETTA MARIA

Chapter 1

DAUGHTER OF FRANCE

TOWARDS THE end of November 1609, the Queen of France was preparing for the birth of her sixth child at the Palace of the Louvre. The midwife, who complained that she tended to lose other valuable clients as a result of waiting on the Queen in her many confinements, had already been in attendance for two months. To pacify her the King promised that if his wife produced a daughter he would pay her three hundred crowns, raising the sum to five hundred in the case of a son.

The Queen, Marie de Medici, was a woman of mediocre intelligence but considerable piety, and she had recently commissioned a wood-carver to make rosaries for some ladies in her train. His equipment was now cleared away from the little tower room where he had been working. The accouchement was to take place in the *grand cabinet* which was large enough to accommodate all those noblemen and ministers who felt it was their duty to be present at the birth. The small room adjoining, which was usually occupied by the Dauphin when he was not living in the royal nursery at Saint-Germain-en-Laye, had been made ready for the new arrival. One evening, the eight-year-old Prince Louis went into the room, climbed into the cradle and rocked himself to sleep with his little dog beside him.

Louis had been born in more congenial surroundings in the oval room at Fontainebleau, the charming house in the forest which was far more to the Queen's taste than the grime-encrusted Louvre. The Parisian palace, with its dark turrets often enveloped in the mists that rose from the Seine and its moat full of polluted water, had proved a poor substitute for the elegant *palazzi* of her native Florence. On first seeing it she had written home to her uncle describing it as 'half ruined, half built, half antique and half modern'. Though successive kings had done what they could to improve the fortress-like pile it was a grim relic of earlier times, inconvenient to live in and too small to accommodate the growing number of palace servants. For Henri the Louvre had unhappy associations. Over thirty years before, he had been held hostage there after the terrible massacre of the Protestants on the notorious night of Saint Bartholomew.

Although Marie de Medici had fulfilled her prime function of providing

I

her husband with five healthy children, three of them sons, there was little affection in the marriage of this ill-assorted pair. The Queen found it hard to resign herself to Henri's many infidelities, and the King despised the fat blonde Florentine he had married as his second wife for the sake of expediency.

The Queen felt her first labour pains in the evening of November 26, the feast of Saint Catherine. Soon after ten o'clock, a Princess was born and presented to her father under the eyes of the ministers and members of the Council. The King took the baby, embraced her and put her back into the arms of the royal governess, Madame de Montglat, who had received all the previous children in this way, and who was responsible for bringing up at Saint-Germain not only the legitimate children but also Henri's eight acknowledged bastards, the fruit of his liaisons with Gabrielle d'Estrées, Henriette d'Entragues, Jacqueline de Bueil and Charlotte des Essarts.

After the birth the Dauphin was allowed to see his mother, and later he visited his new sister. He took her hand and fondled it. 'Laugh at me, *ma sœur*, laugh little child,' he said, adding, 'look how she clasps and squeezes my hand.' She was a vigorous and pretty baby and the King took to her at once. But there was no public rejoicing at her birth. Not a single cannon was fired, and no Latin verses greeted her appearance. The King said that if his child had been a son, he would have wished to distribute a hundred thousand crowns, and the people of Paris were disappointed, believing that daughters increased the King's avariciousness. Marie de Medici, however, had realized their potential value, and she was already planning to turn them all into queens like herself.

The royal children were baptised privately soon after birth in a great copper font, embossed with silver, dating back to the ninth century. Although the public naming ceremony did not take place until much later, the new daughter was from the start called Henriette-Marie after both her parents. Like her brothers and sisters she was washed in wine and oil of red roses before being wrapped in swaddling clothes. After this first cleansing, baths were a rare occurrence, only to be indulged in on medical advice for water was scarce, particularly in Paris. In the narrow streets, which ran between high, ill-lit houses, the air was putrid with the stench of dung, rotting refuse and slops tipped into the gutter. Even in the palace the smell of candle-grease and ill-washed bodies was almost asphyxiating, and the situation was not improved by the courtiers who did not scruple to foul the courtyards and staircases. To sweeten the nursery, Madame de Montglat would remove the baby and burn juniper wood in the room. Marie de Medici covered herself in a strong-smelling scent which she manufactured personally—it was the only way she could bear the close proximity of her sweaty husband.

Henri IV was fifty-six years old at the time of his youngest daughter's birth. Courageous and full of vitality, with a fine crop of hair and a grizzled beard, good-looking though with the long nose of the Béarnais, he had brought political stability and economic recovery to a country rent by lengthy civil wars. The son of Antoine de Bourbon and Jeanne d'Albret, Henri had come to the throne only when the three effete sons of Henri II and Catherine de Medici had all died without producing an heir. He had married their sister Marguerite de Valois, but had hardly ever lived with her.

Through his fanatically Protestant mother, Henri had inherited the kingdom of Navarre, but the throne of France did not come to him without recourse to the sword. He was also obliged to change his religion, his much-quoted theory being that Paris was worth a mass. During his long struggle with the Catholic league he proved himself a military man of great ability and personal courage. Finally, by agreeing to become a Catholic, he had brought in an era of religious tolerance, and with the Edict of Nantes in 1598 recognized the great power wielded by the Protestant element in the south. The country had for too long been weakened by plague and faction; it was Henri's task to provide a strong central authority powerful enough to keep the feudal nobles in check. By building up a spirit of national unity, the King gave France the strength to oppose the Habsburg family which dominated Europe from Spain to Austria and the Netherlands. Unlike so many other monarchs, he knew how to choose his advisers wisely, and in particular he showed his wisdom by putting his financial affairs into the safe hands of the Duc de Sully. Thanks to Sully's fiscal policies he was able to bring greater prosperity to the country as a whole, and to build up a reserve of funds in the vaults of the Bastille. He relied on his own judgment and that of his closest advisers, refusing to summon the States-General, and ruling as a benign dictator.

Although Henri maintained a remarkable youthfulness and vitality in spite of the difficulties he had faced throughout his life, he was now racked with gout caused by over-indulgence and perhaps also by his extreme *fragilité* where women were concerned. He had become involved in many casual affairs, but at one time it had been thought that he would try to legitimate the sons of the beautiful Gabrielle d'Estrées, the one really lasting love of his life. The children of Henriette d'Entragues were brought up at Saint-Germain, where she herself was a frequent visitor, much resented by Louis who showed some loyalty for his mother and felt indignant about his father's infidelities.

Early in the year of Henriette's birth, Henri had fallen passionately in love yet again, this time with a fifteen-year-old girl, Charlotte de Montmorency, who had become engaged shortly after her arrival at court to

François de Bassompierre, one of the King's most faithful companions. Henri's eye first lighted on her when she was rehearsing for a ballet and, although he retired to bed at once with an acute attack of gout, he did not forget the striking-looking girl. Throughout his fortnight's illness he slept badly for, as Bassompierre put it, 'love and gout keep those they attack very wide awake'. Bassompierre was summoned to the bedside and the King outlined a plan to offer Charlotte to the Prince de Condé who was one of the King's closest relations. Since Condé loved the chase 'a hundred times better than women', Henri was sure that he would succumb to a generous bribe and agree to a marriage only in name. By keeping Charlotte in the family he hoped to be able to have her to himself as a comfort in his old age. Bassompierre, although upset, told his master that he was unable to think of any better way of demonstrating his loyalty than to give up an illustrious alliance with a perfect woman. The King embraced him and wept, promising to look after his fortunes in the future as if he were one of his own children.

The King's plan succeeded only up to a point. Condé was in favour of the marriage, but was less enthusiastic when Henri said that he would not put any obstacles in the way of a speedy divorce. The King was acting in a most undignified manner, hardly suitable for a great sovereign. On one occasion he disguised himself as a huntsman with a patch over one eye and blew kisses to Charlotte who was watching him from a window. All through the summer of 1609 Condé did his best to protect Charlotte from the advances of her elderly admirer. A few days after the birth of Henriette, when the King was at play, the news was brought by the officer of the watch that the Prince had fled the country taking his wife with him. The King at once left the card table, putting his silver in Bassompierre's care, and went to the Queen's bedroom. Marie de Medici had been very ill ever since the birth; she lay in her large canopied bed while her husband fulminated about the disappearance of the latest object of his lust. Soon he was surrounded by lords all giving him different advice, but at least before taking any action he had the good sense to wait until Sully could be summoned from the Arsenal. The Duc advised him to do nothing. '*Comment rien*, what do you mean, nothing?' the King demanded. Sully explained that if he pretended not to care, nobody would show any sympathy for Condé who would soon be asking to return. Unfortunately the King was too incensed to listen to this wise advice.

For the first few days of the new princess's life the palace resounded with violent quarrels between her mother who was ill and frantic with jealousy, and her father who was beside himself with frustrated passion. Beyond the palace too there was turmoil. The Catholics distrusted the King's foreign policy; they saw him aligning himself more and more openly with the Protestant powers and suspected that he was prepared to go to war on their behalf. Old hatreds revived and the Protestants in the capital were full of jubilation. There was a growing fear that at Christmas they would rise and massacre the Catholics in a long-awaited revenge for Saint Bartholomew's night. Soothsayers and astrologers were prophesying the King's early death. Many people were prepared to forget that he had done so much for his country, and were quick to complain about the heavy taxes, the unpopular edicts—particularly those aimed at curbing extravagance in dress. Henri's popularity had not unnaturally waned as a result of his endless infidelities, and it was insufferable that he had become infatuated again, and with such a young girl when he himself had begun to look like an old man, with his nose almost touching his chin.

Soon it became known that Condé had fled with his wife into the Low Countries and had put himself under the protection of the Archduke Albert who ruled there under the sovereignty of Spain. He later went on to Spanish-controlled Milan, leaving his wife in Brussels. The King threatened to retrieve the fugitive Princess at the head of fifty thousand men. Attempts were made to persuade Condé that he must part with his wife, and Henri himself sent innumerable messages.

But the departure of Charlotte, who was being compared to Helen of Troy, seemed to arouse his warlike instincts and deprive him of his normally more balanced outlook. In any case the army had been put on a war footing; he was a soldier at heart and it was a tempting prospect to see himself leading his troops into battle. A justification for the outbreak of hostilities was provided when the Duke of Cleves died without issue. The German Protestants feared that his lands would now fall into the hands of the Catholic Princes, and the Catholics were becoming increasingly apprehensive about the Holy League which had been formed among the Protestant states. The dead Duke's possessions were not extensive, but they were large enough to alter the balance of power should they fall into Catholic hands. When the Archduke Leopold seized Jülich, the Elector of Brandenburg retaliated by occupying Düsseldorf, at the same time inviting France to intervene in the dispute. Henri replied by sending troops to the frontier, and there were rumours that he intended to take the Duchy for himself.

During the first months of 1610, the King and Queen seemed at times to be reconciled, some thought on account of a mutual affection for their youngest child. The King was proverbially fond of his children, legitimate and illegitimate. He took a keen interest in their welfare, writing frequently to Madame de Montglat with detailed instructions about wet nurses or the need to fumigate the rooms where there had been infectious diseases. Anyone seeing him play with his sons and daughters, kissing and teasing them, might have thought he was an ordinary father and not a king. He allowed them to sit on his lap at meal-times while he fed them with titbits and sips of wine. Yet it was said that he was fonder of Henriette-Marie than he had been of all the other children, and the Queen, normally bereft of maternal feelings, showed some affection for her. She was to resemble her father, both in looks and temperament, inheriting his lean good looks and curly hair, his courage and vitality.

As the year went on, relations between Henri and his wife deteriorated again as she became increasingly angered by his alliance with the Protestants, and he showed his dislike of her plans to marry off her children to members of the Spanish royal family. The King was still determined to retrieve Charlotte and he even formulated a scheme to kidnap her and bring her back to Paris. The plan failed because in a moment of childish elation he told the Queen who passed on the details to the Papal Nuncio. Charlotte was making herself ill by drinking iced water and refusing all food. She was kept in virtual captivity and was missing the life of Paris. She wrote pathetically to the King, begging him to rescue her.

Marie de Medici was obsessed by the trappings of royalty, and she would not rest until she could persuade the King to have her formally crowned. He had always resisted the idea, but now he capitulated, ignoring the words of the soothsayer who prophesied that he would die at the hand of an assassin on the day after his Queen's coronation. He was planning to join his troops on May 17 and had made careful plans for a council of regency, making sure that no responsibility should rest with the Queen in his absence, for he knew too well that her lust for power was not matched by political acumen. To pacify her he allowed plans for the coronation to proceed. The astrologers were specifically predicting that he would meet his end on May 14, and as the date of the coronation had been fixed for May 13, Sully did his best to persuade the Queen that it would be wiser to cancel the arrangements for the time being. She could not agree with him; in her opinion she had waited too long already and was not to be put off when she was on the verge of fulfilling her ambition.

The King himself tended to ignore the prophets of doom; all the same he was undoubtedly in a nervous state and was suffering from nightmares. Bassompierre heard him talking of his early death and felt obliged to remind him that he was still in his prime and possessed everything to make life worth living—fine houses, healthy children and beautiful mistresses. One day, as the King drove through the streets where expensive preparations were being made for his wife's formal entry into the city, with allegories and triumphal arches, he saw a coat of arms of the Medici family carried out in black and surrounded by the emblems of widowhood. There were many other ill omens, but he was too busy conferring with Sully about the forthcoming war to bother about such trifles. He was planning to allow himself a day or two after the coronation to put his affairs in order before leaving for the front.

With his family, Louis, Elisabeth, Christine, the Duc d'Orléans, Gaston and Henriette-Marie who was carried to the ceremony in her nurse's arms, the King watched his wife in her hour of triumph somewhat cynically, making facetious remarks to those around him. The Queen, who looked radiant, was dressed in cloth of gold and as always was smothered in jewellery. After the ceremony the King returned to the Louvre with the children while the Queen remained at the abbey of Saint-Denis.

The next day the King's mind was understandably overshadowed by the sinister words of the soothsayers. To help chase away his melancholy he gave orders that Gaston and Henriette should be brought to his room. For a while he forgot his fears as he played with his children. He had made up his mind that in the afternoon he would visit Sully, who was ill. Outside, a huge red-haired Catholic from Angoulême, François Ravaillac, waited by a mounting block under the arches of the Louvre. Hidden by the porch and unnoticed by the Swiss Guards, he was able to watch for the King, and at about four o'clock when the heavy royal coach appeared he followed after it on foot. It was the time of day favoured by the nobility for visiting their friends or the fashionable shops, and the streets were choked with traffic. As the coach entered the Rue de la Ferronerie it was halted by two wagons, one loaded with wine barrels and the other with hay. Because of the congestion, the King's lackeys had taken a short cut through the charnel-house by the cemetery of Saint-Innocent, so that there was nobody guarding the coach. This gave Ravaillac his opportunity. The King was seated in the coach next to the Duc d'Epernon who was reading him a letter. His face was turned to the light; the assassin had no difficulty in identifying him. Ravaillac put his foot on a spoke of one of the wheels and stabbed the King, who cried out, 'I am wounded.' The second blow was mortal. Blood had begun to pour from the victim's mouth, and although he opened his eyes three times there was evidently little hope of survival. Ravaillac gave himself up without resistance. The Duc d'Epernon calmly told the gathering crowd that the King was not dead but only wounded; he drew the curtains of the coach and gave orders that it should return to the Louvre.

The Dauphin had gone out into the town to see the decorations and when the news of the assassination reached the Queen, she thought at first that it was he who had died. 'My son!' she cried, rather to everyone's surprise, for she had shown little affection for Louis—nobody, in fact, had seen her embrace him for at least seven years. When she arrived at the palace and saw her husband's body, she cried over him as loudly as she had quarrelled with him in the previous weeks; her wails could be heard all over the Louvre.

When the news spread through Paris there was at first a terrible silence.

Then people began weeping and the whole city seemed to be filled with groans and cries. Shops shut, the decorations were torn down, and many said they felt as if they had lost a father. They forgot now that the King's popularity had been on the wane, and he was remembered for his tolerance, his genuine love of the people, for the fact that he had restored the greatness and the power of France. Already they were calling him *Henri le Grand*.

For the King's closest companions the news was almost unbearable. Bassompierre began to run like a madman; he seized the first horse he could find and rode at full speed to the palace where he pushed past the Swiss Guards who stood with lowered pikes, and ran to the King's closet where he flung himself at his master's feet, crying bitterly. Sully received the news at the Arsenal where he had been sitting half-dressed waiting for the King to visit him. He went out at once and as he rode through the streets he was joined by other gentlemen who crowded round him asking what they should do. Nobody knew yet whether the King's death was the first stage in a well-planned coup; to be on the safe side Sully turned back without going to the palace and barricaded himself into the Bastille.

All that night at the Louvre there was panic and alarm. The Queen was told to stop weeping and to concentrate on her children's safety. They were all brought from their apartments and put into one room, watched over by guards with crossed halberds. Henriette-Marie, impervious to the commotion, slept on peacefully in the arms of her nurse Dondon.

By morning it was realized that the assassination was not after all the prelude to a general insurrection, but the work of an isolated madman intent on saving the Papacy from a King with Protestant leanings. Sully, who had bought up all the bread he could find and was preparing for a long siege, decided after all that it would be safe to go to the palace. 'The King is dead, the King is dead,' the Queen cried when she saw him, and he replied coldly that the Kings of France never died. He pointed to the nine-year-old Louis and said, 'Madame, there is the living King.'

Without delay the Queen Mother took her son to Parliament and demanded the Regency for herself, thus going against the careful plans made by her husband just before his death. The young Louis XIII rode to the Paris Parlement dressed in purple velvet, and spoke the words he had been told to say in a voice that was hardly audible. The Queen interrupted her own speech just at the right moment by bursting into tears. She showed no reluctance to make the most of her position, and lost no time in giving orders that her son should sleep in her room, so that she could keep an eye on him night and day.

In a moment, at the senseless whim of a fanatic, power had been transferred from a politically astute and experienced man to a nine-year-old boy and his unintelligent mother. Preparations for war ceased abruptly and many feared that the death of the King would turn out to be the prelude to another era of civil strife. To forestall trouble the Duc d'Epernon assembled all available troops, stationed a large guard round the Louvre, sent soldiers to the Pont-Neuf and made sure that nobody challenged the Queen Regent's authority. Bassompierre, always popular with the Paris crowds, rode about the streets begging people to be loyal. The nobles who were in Paris hastened to pay homage to the young monarch. The Queen Regent made it clear that she would continue her husband's tolerance towards the Protestants and would make use of his advisers. To Louis she said, when she presented Sully to him, 'My son, this is M. de Sully, you must love him well, for he is one of your father's best and most capable servants, and you must pray that he continues to serve you in the same.'

As soon as the Prince de Condé received the news of the death of the King, he left Milan and travelled to Brussels where he was reunited with Charlotte. The Prince, who had risked so much to remove his wife from the attentions of the *vert galant*, now cared little whether she came with him or stayed where she was, for his thoughts were directed towards the new opportunities for power and plunder which had opened up for him in France. As he crossed over into his own country he gathered round him a crowd of gentlemen, and more joined him as he neared the capital. As soon as he entered the city, however, those who were with him suddenly dispersed, and by the time he reached the palace they were all to be seen ranged loyally at the side of the King and his mother. He was later rewarded with a gift of the Hôtel de Gondy in Paris, with thirty thousand crowns for furnishings. Since many of the nobles had their own troops which they did not scruple to use if provoked, the Queen Regent felt that it was politic to distribute largesse among all those who indicated that they would only conform at a price. To please the nation in general, various taxes were revoked and for a while the government was in the happy position of taking little and dispensing benefits to all.

At the coronation which took place on October 17 in Rheims, Condé played an important part, presenting Louis to the Cardinal, fixing his spurs and removing his crown when it became too heavy—this was significant in the light of subsequent events. Ironically it was the beautiful Princesse de Condé, whose flight had caused Henri such distress at the time of his youngest child's birth, who now had the task of carrying Henriette at the ceremony.

The little Princess had made few public appearances since the death of her father. At the funeral she had travelled in the procession to Saint-Denis and had sprinkled water on the corpse from a *goupillon* which Madame de Montglat put into her hand, but during the summer months she had remained in the lugubrious rooms at the Louvre which were all draped in black. After the coronation it was thought unwise for the younger children to return to Paris where there was growing unrest as a result of the Queen Regent's policies. Although Louis had to stay in the capital with his mother, the younger children spent most of their time at Saint-Germain, the château built by François I only fifty years before on the site of an earlier castle. Set on a hill at the edge of a forest with a fine view over the valley towards Paris, it was in every way a more salubrious place than the Louvre. Louis often longed to be with his brothers and sisters, and on one occasion, when his mother would have liked him to attend to affairs of state, he insisted on going to visit them, setting off early in the morning. He told his mother that she could attend to affairs herself, since he was in any case too young to be bothered with them.

Although Madame de Montglat was obliged to issue orders forbidding courtiers to foul the main courtyard, the air at Saint-Germain was sweet, and as soon as he reached the suburbs of Paris, Louis always noticed the stench. Life at the château was easy and pleasant; lessons were not arduous and they seldom took place at set hours. During the summer the children spent much of their day in the gardens which had been built for their father by Tomaso Francini, with fountains and grottoes in shell-work and coral, and flower beds along the river's edge. Throughout the summer the patterns of colour remained constant owing to the gardener's ability to choose flowers that bloomed from spring to autumn 'like a knot of divers-coloured ribans, most pleasing and most rare'. Broad steps led down from the house to the Seine which wound placidly through the valley. 'It is impossible to imagine,' wrote the Papal Nuncio Bentivoglio, 'a more charming country than this, not like our hills, which are steep, barren and horrible in many places. These green hills of France preserve the lively colour of spring all the year round.'

As soon as they were out of swaddling clothes, all the royal children were dressed in long heavily-embroidered frocks and petticoats, with bibs to protect their fine satins and silks at meal-times, and pinafores when they went out to play. When they were small, leading strings were attached to their dresses to prevent them falling when they tripped over their long clothes, or stumbled on the steps. The day began early, with hair-brushing the most unpleasant part of the ritual, and washing kept to a minimum. When Louis had a bath it was enough of an event for his doctor, Héroard, to make a note of it in his diary. The young King loaded his toy boats with the rose petals that had been scattered on the water and said they were ships sailing from the Indies and Goa. Afterwards he was firmly put to bed to recover from the unusual experience. Each bedroom was furnished with a large four-poster bed, a small hand-basin and a *chaise-percée* of great elegance. Madame de Montglat's was covered with

crimson serge, and the royal variety was often under a canopy. It caused
no surprise if the great granted an audience when they were occupying
this particular throne.

The outer quadrangle at Saint-Germain housed the stables, storage
rooms, smithy, guardroom and kitchens. Madame de Montglat, in her
capacity as *gouvernante*, ruled over a large household of ushers, pages,
captains and soldiers of the guard, musicians, cradle-rockers, nurses,
gardeners and domestics. King Henri, having entrusted her with the
important task of watching over his children, expected her to make
everything else subordinate to this work. When she became a widow,
Henri told her that the Dauphin would take the place of a husband; she
was to be exempt from the usual period of mourning and he counselled
her to desist from wailing and crying. Mamanga, as the children affec-
tionately called her, was not above ensuring that her own family benefited
from her position, and she gave places in the household to several of her
relations, appointing her daughter, Jeanne de Saint-Georges, whom the
children nicknamed Mamie, as assistant governess.

Henri had given special thought to the Dauphin's upbringing and he
had counselled Madame de Montglat to discipline him severely to ensure
that he did not become spoilt. He was whipped far more often than any of
the other children and felt the injustice keenly, especially as the bastards
were treated far less harshly. When it came to the younger children
discipline had been relaxed and nobody took their upbringing too
seriously. The two elder Princesses, Elisabeth and Christine, were gay,
attractive girls, and the dark-skinned Gaston made a good playfellow
although he was not over-gifted with intelligence. All the children were
healthy and very active, with the exception of the little Duc d'Orléans,
who had been sickly from birth. As members of the royal family they
were given a life of luxury which was considered theirs by right. They had
the best of everything and there was always plenty of good food. It was
said that all the Bourbons enjoyed a good appetite even when they were
ill. A great variety of ingredients and recipes was available, egg soup with
lemon juice, cock's combs, chicken roasted and fried in breadcrumbs,
mutton, veal and pork, sometimes served with sauces. Oysters were
brought in barrels of sea-water from the coast. Fruit tarts were cooked as
a birthday treat, instead of the more normal jellies, apricots, preserved
cherries or comfits made with spices—aniseed, coriander, fennel, nutmeg,
cloves and cinnamon. In general vegetables were despised, although for
the grown-ups cabbage was sometimes recommended to prevent baldness
or to give milk to nursing mothers. In Lent the diet was limited to fish,
vegetable soup, egg dishes and cheese from nearby Brie. Breakfast was
frugal, and another small meal, *goûter*, was served during the afternoon—
in summer it was sometimes taken into the garden. Frequently the

children drank wine mixed with water, although Héroard disapproved of this habit. They ate their soup by dipping their bread into it; forks were unknown and in general fingers were used, a clean napkin being brought with every course. Once, when Louis was devouring a wing of chicken at half past eleven in the morning, the Spanish ambassador chose this moment to call, and Madame de Montglat had to wipe the Prince's hand before he could hold it out to be kissed.

In the summer time the court sometimes moved to Fontainebleau. Built in mellow brick and stone on the edge of a small town in the heart of the forest, the château was described by the Papal Nuncio as a jumble of architecture, but it was the most homely of the palaces, with little left of the old castle to remind the inmates that it had once been a military stronghold. Here the children could wander through the gilded rooms, or feed the ducks and swans on the great canal and throw bread to the carp. They could watch the exotic birds in the great aviary, trying to find resemblances to people at court, or they could look out from the ballroom and see in the oval courtyard below the tilting at the ring, the bear-baiting or foxcub-chasing that often went on there. Sometimes rabbits, squirrels or birds were brought in from the forest for the children to have as pets.

During their father's lifetime, the children had seen a good deal of their parents, who had often come down to Saint-Germain. There were many descriptions of the King hugging and kissing his children or taking them by the hand, bribing them with rose sweetmeats or letting them spray him with water from the fountains. After his death they were not only bereft of his affection but they also saw far less of their mother who was too preoccupied with state affairs to visit them. When Henriette was ill at Saint-Germain in October 1611, the Queen Regent did not go to see her, but sent a lackey to bring news of her progress. 'I have ascertained,' she wrote to Madame de Montglat '. . . that my little daughter is indisposed of the fever which has again seized her . . . Let me know exactly the state of her disease; I shall meanwhile give orders that the physician Paulin shall come to you to see her and assist her, at any time that you may let me know that it is necessary. Take care that my said daughter lacks nothing that might afford her any remedy or solace to her complaint, and send me word about her.'

The children were looked after by the best doctors but even the most eminent men resorted to bleeding, which had by the end of Henri's reign become the most fashionable remedy for every kind of complaint, with purging as the alternative panacea. Héroard did not believe in indiscriminate letting of blood, but there are accounts of the scenes which took place when Louis was forced to swallow nauseating infusions of cassia, senna, rhubarb, bugloss and agrimony. When the Duc d'Orléans fell ill with a lethargy followed by convulsive fits, there was little that anyone could do. He had always been delicate, with a large head and a small body, and had suffered from a succession of fevers which the doctors put down to teething. It was Louis, and not his mother, who insisted on visiting him. '*Bonsoir, mon petit papa*. You do me too much honour to take the trouble to come and see me,' said the four-year-old Duke when his brother arrived. The King began to cry. 'Is there no way of saving him?' he asked. The Duke died the same night, and as always with a member of the royal family there were rumours of poisoning. The doctors were blamed for letting a boil on his neck close up; they defended themselves, saying that they had applied caustic whereupon the little boy had cried out as if he was being stuck with thorns, a good enough proof, in their opinion, that the wound was open. To silence any criticism, the Queen Regent invited members of the court to visit the royal nursery and satisfy themselves that everything possible was being done to ensure the children's safety.

The corpulent Queen was already arousing hostility, caused mainly by the fact that she was allowing her Italian favourites, the Concini, to dominate her life. They were being blamed for her growing Catholic bias which Sully, like many other good Protestants, was sure could only lead to trouble. Sully found himself ignored in the inner councils—a clear case of sectarian discrimination, in his opinion. Louis experienced a feeling of revulsion whenever he saw his mother in the company of the handsome Concino Concini, and even more so when she was closeted with Concini's wife Leonora Galigäi, a small witch-like woman with a large nose and fang-like teeth. At night, when her husband went back to his house in the town, Leonora would stay with the Queen, playing soothing tunes on the guitar and suggesting the policies she should pursue. *La Concina* seldom appeared in public, for she was always afraid of falling down in a fit, but everyone knew that she wielded power secretly, behind the scenes.

During Henri's reign the Concini had limited their activities to amassing a fortune, but as they now came to dominate the Queen Regent more completely, fierce hatred was aroused among those who had been supplanted. Condé refused to sit at the same council table as Concini who had now become the Maréchal d'Ancre. There was restlessness among the powerful noblemen whom Henri had kept in check with his firm policies. The Queen quickly squandered the wealth and political stability bequeathed her by her husband. The cost of living was rising steeply and unemployment was on the increase. Her only hope of restoring the family fortunes seemed to her to lie in the possibility of marrying Louis and Elisabeth to members of the Spanish royal house, although her husband had never favoured such a move. His belief had been that the two countries were too far apart in every way for a match to cause anything but personal unhappiness without great diplomatic gain.

To offset her insecurity, and to demonstrate the solidarity of the Bourbon dynasty, the Queen Regent required her children to appear in public on every important occasion. Henriette's earliest experiences were calculated to imbue her with a sense of the sanctity of kingship, of a world full of scarlet velvet, of white satin embroidered with gold, of plumes and jewels, triumphal arches and pyramids decorated with allegorical devices, fireworks and the music of oboes and violins. Before long she was to observe the darker side of the royal vocation—the clashes of ambitious courtiers and noblemen, the jealousies and scandals, the brutality of people in high places, and the corruption of court life which has made many monarchs yearn for rusticity, and had prompted thinking men like Montaigne to see in the gentle savage the qualities which are so often lacking in civilized man.

Chapter 2

A ROYAL EDUCATION

WHEN IT was announced that Louis was to marry a Spanish princess and that Elisabeth had become engaged to the heir to the throne, Louis clapped his hands and ran about the palace, while Elisabeth thanked her mother for arranging that she should become a queen rather than a mere duchess. Many Frenchmen were less than pleased by the idea of the double marriage, but elaborate celebrations were planned to start on April 5, 1613 at a cost of more than two hundred thousand crowns. The Queen Regent was determined to surpass the Spaniards, which did not prove difficult since they were inclined to be miserly. The people of Paris were glad to celebrate after two years of mourning, and vast crowds saw the magnificent processions which at night were illuminated by thousands of lanterns. In the courtyard of the Palais Royal, Henriette and the other children watched tournaments from specially-constructed scaffolds. When all the excitement was over and the marriage contracts had been signed at the Louvre, the children returned to Saint-Germain where Elisabeth took some Spanish lessons and sometimes dressed up à l'espagnole. Louis appeared to put Spain out of his mind altogether; he was becoming increasingly addicted to the pleasures of the chase and sometimes sent his sisters trophies to prove his prowess—on one occasion he gave them two paws from a wolf. He had also become interested in tennis and in 1613 played for the first time in a covered court. Once, in July of this year, he cried when he did not win. 'The trouble is,' Héroard observed, 'that he does not like to be beaten.' The other children saw little of him at this time, but he sent them presents of porcelain and silver when he was on tour, and he wrote to them frequently, inquiring about their health and asking for news.

In 1614 Louis set off with his mother in the wake of troops sent to quell outbreaks of violence. The Huguenot princes were uniting against the crown and others were preparing to join Condé's banner. Before they left, the Queen Regent made arrangements for the public baptism of Gaston and Henriette-Marie who were now six and five years old. The ceremony took place on June 15, 1614 in the tower room which led off the Queen's antechamber. Henriette's godparents were her sister Elisabeth and the Cardinal de la Rochefoucauld. It was said that she received the names of both her parents because she resembled them in virtue and wisdom. Having been baptised privately at the time of their birth, the children were now anointed with oil and salt. It was a beautiful ceremony, and the ladies and gentlemen of the court who crowded to see it were sumptuously dressed. When it was all over the King played a game of tennis; he shot at little birds and chased the stags and hares which were kept in the Tuileries gardens for the purpose.

The King's tour turned out to be a great success and many people who had never seen him before were surprised to find that he was a normal and healthy-looking boy. At Amboise those who were guarding the town for the Prince de Condé came out with the keys of the city, and before long the Princes asked for a truce. On his return to Paris Louis was given an enthusiastic welcome, and both he and his mother were greeted as peace-makers. Soon afterwards, on September 20, he visited his brother and sisters at Saint-Germain, and they all returned to Paris to take part in the celebrations to mark his majority.

On reaching the age of thirteen, Louis was considered old enough to control his own destiny. The moment was opportune since the Princes, having patched up their quarrel, were glad of an opportunity to give public testimony of their loyalty. At the Palais Bourbon a glittering crowd of people watched the proceedings in the great gilded hall. The King sat on his *lit-de-justice* with his mother on one side and Gaston on the other. His sisters were seated just behind him with Madame de Montglat, and nobody was pleased when Leonora took her place beside them with what everyone thought was unbearable presumption. They heard Louis say his words firmly, assuring everyone that having reached the age of majority, he would do his best to govern with good counsel, piety and justice. His mother did obeisance to him and he thanked her, expressing the hope that she would continue to care for him and for his government.

After the ceremony the royal party returned to the Palace. The King was in a jubilant mood. He went to bed without any supper, asked for toys to play with, amused himself doing some painting and then went to sleep to the sound of music.

There was more ceremonial when the King went to open the States-General on October 26. The deputies processed to Notre-Dame, each one carrying a candle. This time the royal sisters sat with the eleven-year-old Comte de Soissons and the Prince de Condé, who was acknowledging everybody so graciously that he might have been the King himself. Louis, surrounded by all his family, was placed on the throne, and he promised, in the name of God, to lighten the burden of his people. In calling the Assembly, he had recognized the right of free discussion, and some were hopeful that the deputies would be able to use their power to put an end to internecine warfare. But by the time the deputies returned to the provinces the following March, they had done nothing except fritter away in petty feuds and intrigues the power that had been handed to them.

Louis too failed to make use of the power which was now his by right. The Queen Mother continued to run the country as if he had never come of age, and made no attempt to train him in the art of kingship. She encouraged him to devote his time to his pleasures. He continued to have lessons, but his tutors found it increasingly hard to keep him at his books, and Latin was an imposition which he avoided whenever possible. His real bent was for practical subjects; he liked to paint pictures and make toy carts, or traps to catch small birds which he hung out of the windows in winter. During the months after his coming of age he became absorbed in metalwork and made jewellery with rubies and other stones. He had a flair for cooking, his speciality being bacon omelette.

The other children continued their desultory education with lessons at irregular hours. Sometimes they were let off altogether as a reward for behaving well. They learnt to write by tracing over a copy-book and later wrote out texts, including a verse composed by Louis listing the virtues of various Kings:

For the love of truth, Pharamont I
For courage, Charlemagne I
  And for temperance, Charles V
  And Louis XIII will surpass all the Kings,
By the grace of God.

By the end of 1614, Gaston had progressed from long petticoats to doublet and hose; he was granted his own household, with servants dressed in a special livery. He and his sister shared a learned tutor, Monsieur de Brevis, but in later years Henriette regretted the inadequacy of her education. As far as her mother was concerned, all that mattered was that she should be brought up a good Catholic, and the Carmelites in Paris were entrusted with the responsibility for her religious instruction.

Henriette was taught to ride at an early age, and all the princesses were given regular dancing lessons—they joined in before they could walk, carried in the nurse's arms. Louis had from the first shown signs of musical talent, beating the drum taps on the dinner service at meals, and Henriette was gifted with an exceptionally attractive singing voice. All the children sang a great deal, learning none too suitable songs from the women who waited on them, and performing carols at Christmas. They learnt to dance the saraband, galliard and branle, and many simple ballets were performed by the royal family and their friends at Saint-Germain or Fontainebleau.

The great court ballets which were staged in Paris during the carnival season could only be afforded once a year. When asked to provide the money for one of these elaborate occasions, Sully had flown into a rage, writing at the bottom of the estimate, 'And as much again for the lace.' In the early years of the young King's reign, once Sully's restraining hand was removed, the ballets reached a crescendo of brilliance with no expense spared. To impress the Spanish, Marie de Medici planned a lavish entertainment in the new year of 1615 embodying the story of Minerva. There was great competition among the nobility to obtain the most coveted roles. Elisabeth was cast as Minerva with a supporting company of ladies, including several of her half-sisters. Tomaso Francini had devised some spectacular settings and machinery, including a seascape with waves that rose and fell, and a rock which appeared out of the ground bearing ten Sibyls. The poet Malherbe had written a brilliant libretto and also put in an appearance, leading a dance of the shepherds.

The tradition of the *ballet mascarade* had grown out of the carnival festivities of earlier times, making use of the spectacle, allegory, grotesque dancing and masqued performers of the more primitive carnival processions. Now that the entertainment had withdrawn entirely within the palace walls, the people of Paris still felt they had a right to partake in the celebrations, and crowds besieged every doorway trying to force a way in past the archers who guarded the entrances. The audience began to assemble early on the day before the performance and many people were disappointed. The main hall at the Hôtel de Bourbon was used as it could accommodate more people than the Louvre. Twelve hundred white wax candles in silver brackets made the room so bright that it was hard to tell day from night. Opposite the dais where the King was to sit under a canopy a stage had been constructed which sloped gently down into the hall where the floor was kept clear for the dancers, the spectators sitting on tiered scaffolds round the wall.

Each year the performances had grown more sophisticated and many Italian ideas had been absorbed into the tradition thanks to the two Medici queens. Choreographers imported from Milan introduced ingenious dance routines, and the musical score became increasingly elaborate. But the *grand ballet* at the end of the evening still remained at the heart of every performance—that breathtaking moment when the masqued dancers invaded the scene and invited members of the audience to partner them in complicated patterns of movement carried out to the sound of violins, lutes and singing voices.

After the performance there was the usual *collation* of biscuits, candied violets and other *confitures*. The spectators then dispersed, and within a few days the austere season of Lent had begun. After Easter many Princes of the Blood and noblemen left the capital and retired to their country estates, where their subsequent actions showed that they had not absorbed the message of unity and harmony embodied in the music, dancing and verse in the final scenes of *Le Triomphe de Minerve*. Condé published a manifesto giving the reasons for his opposition. As the summer wore on repeated attempts were made to appease him, all without success, and he began to draw to his side all those who had a grievance of any kind.

It had been decided that the Spanish marriages would take place when Louis had completed his fourteenth year at the end of September 1615, but the Spaniards, alarmed by the growing unrest in France, were urging the Queen Mother to leave without further delay. It was arranged that the brides would be exchanged on the frontier in the middle of the river Bidassoa, and Louis was to await his wife, Anne of Austria, at Bordeaux. Since the entire family and most of the court were going too, it was not possible to set out without lengthy preparations. There was Elisabeth's trousseau to be seen to; the King's twenty-four pages had to be fitted out with tunics of crimson and blue velvet with red silk stockings and black velvet shoes. The Queen's dwarf trainbearer had a special braided doublet and the twelve pages of the music also had their own costumes. The newly-made ceremonial cloak had to be embroidered with three thousand and ninety-four fleurs de lys. There were beds for everyone including the matrimonial four-poster with curtains of red damask, a special litter for anyone unfortunate enough to fall ill on the journey, and a bridge furnished with pictures and tapestries where the mid-river exchange was to take place.

In August, a few days before the departure, Marie de Medici boldly went to the Bastille with her son and withdrew from its vaults enough money to defray her expenses. This blatant act was not popular, for the extravagance of the court had already come in for criticism especially at a time when every resource was needed in the struggle to maintain law and order in the country. On August 16 Louis went to see all his sisters. Because of alterations being carried out at the Louvre they were staying in the luxurious House of Zamet, the scene of many of their father's amours. The next day he left Paris early, his mother following later with Henriette and Christine. Elisabeth went separately as it was laid down that when a daughter of France left the kingdom to be married, she must be led out of the capital by the provosts and the magistrates with an escort of the militia. Later all three parties linked up and began to head south. The King had brought such a large army that anyone would have thought he was going to the wars rather than travelling to meet his bride. The soldiers plundered rapaciously as they went along, growing more discontented the farther south they went, for they much preferred the northern provinces to the burnt-up lands of the Midi. At Poitiers

Elisabeth fell ill with smallpox and it was not until September 28 that the expedition was able to set off again. Further delays were caused when the royal party had to make detours in order to avoid armed groups of Protestant supporters. The danger was at times so great that the Queen Mother let fall tears of relief when she finally arrived safely at Bordeaux with her children.

On the night before Elisabeth left for the frontier, everybody began to dread her departure. She was only thirteen and a charming, lovable girl. The King rode with her out of the town and returned the same day in tears. That evening, thinking of their sister, all the royal children felt very sad. The Spanish were equally reluctant to part with their princess and a month went by before there was news of her arrival. Louis, however, did not show any sign of impatience. The Archbishop's palace had been made available for him and he lived comfortably, enjoying the presence of his favourite, Albert de Luynes, a young man of noble birth but little wealth who had originally attached himself to the King's hawking establishment. He also had his caged birds and his little arquebuses, and he was able to go hunting, play chess, watch comedies and raid the cupboard where Cardinal Sourdis kept his sweets, distributing the plunder among his gentlemen. For the rest of the court, Bordeaux in the rainy season offered few attractions, and although the countryside around was beautiful, they all agreed that there was only one Paris in the world. 'Paris is our nest' was how the Queen Mother put it.

At last the news came of the exchange of the two Queens. Initial reports of the Spanish bride were extremely promising. Anne had first been seen reclining on cushions among a large crowd of Spanish ladies, wearing a dress of green satin with hanging sleeves and a ruff in the Elizabethan fashion, her blonde hair set off to perfection by a green bonnet embellished with a dark heron's plume. The only fault anyone could find with her was that her nose was rather too long and aquiline; her clothes also seemed somewhat old-fashioned to Parisian eyes and before she arrived at Bordeaux she was fitted out in a more up-to-date outfit with a *fraise*—a light upstanding ruff of delicate lace of the kind made fashionable by Marie de Medici.

The marriage was blessed in the Cathedral at Bordeaux on November 25, and many people wondered what would happen once that ceremony was over. It was well known that when as a boy of ten Louis had been told about his engagement he had asked his mother how one made children. Nobody knew whether he had ever received a satisfactory answer. The story was that Marie de Medici, determined that the whole of Europe should know that the marriage had been consummated, now told him herself that there was more to being married than making polite conversation. To prove her point she put the King and Queen into the large bed which had been brought all the way from Paris for the purpose and left them together for two hours. After this the King returned to his room and the Queen to the little bed which she had brought in her luggage from Spain. The next morning Louis appeared to be unmoved by his experience of the night before and he subsequently showed more interest in his falcons than in his Queen.

The court finally left Bordeaux on December 17. The journey home was long remembered for its hardships. The roads were bad and the weather exceptionally cold. Coachmen fell from their coaches frozen to death and a third of the King's guards died of cold or fever—more than he would have expected to lose in a battle. Wherever they were the King paid a courtesy visit to his wife before indulging in his usual pastimes— hunting, playing with his caged birds or toy cannon, or making marzipan. Sometimes everyone played games, especially the ones common to both countries. The Queen Mother's household tried out an *olla podrida* and later the King cooked the dish for himself.

As they neared Paris at the beginning of May the Queen Mother went on ahead of the main party with her two younger daughters. They were greeted at Saint-Victor by a thousand bourgeois militia drawn up under their colonel in the Rue d'Orléans; afterwards they went on to inspect the magnificent palace which the Queen Mother was having built in the Luxembourg park. They were greeted by the sound of oboe music which the workmen had laid on for them, and the Queen Mother was delighted to find that the work had been proceeding well during her absence.

Marie de Medici was now at the height of her power. Having united the royal families of Spain and France she was receiving congratulations from all quarters—some more sincere than others. She felt strong enough to dispense with the Chancellor, de Sillery, who had been appointed eleven years before by her husband. The Prince de Condé was arrested and many other noblemen retired to the provinces. The Concini had become more imperious and insufferable than ever; people had heard Leonora calling Louis an idiot and the Queen Mother a country bumpkin. The King's dislike of the favourites had deepened and he seemed uneasy and melancholy. In October he had a convulsive fit and for a while it was feared that this might develop into a serious seizure. 'For these precious heads one fears everything,' Bassompierre wrote. The King's marriage had not brought him any happiness, and the presence of Anne and her train was soon causing friction. The Queen was surrounded by a crowd of proud Castilians—confessors, almoners, maids of honour, doctors, apothecaries, footmen. They taught her to look down on the French with their easy manners and love of ostentation and show.

Albert de Luynes had been appointed head of the gentlemen of the chamber, and in January 1617 he played the leading role in a ballet

La Délivrance de Renaud. The King took the part of a fire demon and the famous dancer Marais was also in the cast. The composer Guédron and the director of ballets, de Belleville, produced a score remarkable for its vigour and dramatic force, full of flowing rhythms and pathetic cadences. De Belleville himself led the troupe of demons, who appeared in the grotesque shapes of lobsters, tortoises and snails, until they cast off their shells and were metamorphosed into old men in medieval costume. For this great occasion Francini had surpassed himself, inventing an ingenious method of revolving *plaques* which enabled the scene to be changed in an instant.

Great precautions had been taken this time to admit only ticket-holders, but the people of Paris, anxious not to miss a performance in which the King himself was taking part, almost mobbed the palace, pushing up the great staircase to the marble-pillared door of the chamber. It is probable that too many tickets had been issued and in any case the problem of seating everybody was so acute that the performance could not start before two o'clock in the morning. Those who were admitted were able to appreciate the fact that de Luynes had now become the supreme figure at court, as he played the part of the 'superb Renaud, proud victor of Mars'. On April 24 both he and the King experienced another *délivrance*. They had for a long time wished to be free of the Queen Mother's favourite, but this was not easy, since d'Ancre was continually guarded by a crowd of gentlemen wearing his colours. However, in the narrow passage leading from the great gate at the Louvre into the courtyard he was for a while unprotected, and he was set upon and killed by a group of assassins who were lying in wait for him. The fifteen-year-old Louis looked out of the window at the scene below and called out, 'Thank you, my friends, now I am King.'

The mob dragged the favourite's corpse through the streets and hung him upside down at the end of the Pont-Neuf on the gibbet where ordinary criminals were executed. They cut off his ears and made passers-by salute him with cries of *vive le roi*. Leonora was arrested and shut up in a barred room at the top of the Louvre. Later she was tried on a charge of witch-craft and sentenced to death by burning. The King however was not yet content. So long as his mother was still at court he felt that he could trust nobody. After d'Ancre's death he had her watched and guarded. The situation was soon unbearable and it was considered expedient for all parties that the Queen should go into exile at Blois. She departed with a few retainers, and a request that she should be allowed her youngest daughter as a companion was brusquely dismissed.

Chapter 3

FAMILY CONFLICT

ENRIETTE-MARIE WAS seven years old when the favourites she had so frequently seen in her mother's company met with their horrible fate. The peaceful days when all the sisters had spent so much time in the schoolroom at Saint-Germain had now gone for ever; they were expected to pass much of their life at court, where they saw their brother surrounded by crowds of courtiers all jostling to catch his eye, and where there was nothing of the informality of life in the country. The family had split irrevocably, with the King and their mother alienated, and Elisabeth vanishing for ever over the Pyrenees. They had letters from their sister begging them to treat her as they always had done, without feeling that they must become ceremonious because she had married the heir to the Spanish throne. She wrote to Madame de Montglat—'Mamanga'—telling her to look after the sisters well; when Henriette sent her a little cornelian box and some baskets—'the prettiest and most beautiful imaginable'—she expressed delight and especially appreciated the letter written in her sister's childish hand.

Elisabeth pretended to be well and happy, but all too soon a sad tone began to permeate her letters. With a touch of bewilderment she reported that she was at a place called *el pardo*; she went out hunting every day, but neither her husband nor his father ever seemed to be there. News came from Spain that the Princess was frequently in tears. This was not surprising in view of the fact that her husband was small, blond and fat, always dressed sombrely in black and strangely detached from everything and everybody, including his wife. Her one pleasure lay in the links with home, and particularly with her sisters. She sent Henriette some little toys to use in the *toilette* of her dolls, imploring her sister to remember her when she played with them.

The unsatisfactory nature of the Spanish marriages might have made everyone chary of negotiating another foreign match. But the Queen Mother was not easily deflected from her determination to find a crowned head for each one of her daughters. She had contemplated an alliance for Christine with the handsome, promising Henry, Prince of Wales, to the consternation of the Papal Nuncio, who told her uncompromisingly that she should not entertain the idea of delivering her daughter to hell and the devil. Prince Henry had dreamed of bringing the French Princess to England at once to allow more time for converting her to his religion, but his premature death had put an end to the project as well as many other hopes. James I offered his second son Charles as a substitute, but the younger Prince had none of the civilized grace of his brother, and in France they talked contemptuously of his *férocité*.

In spite of her extreme youth, Henriette-Marie had already been named as a possible wife for the English Prince, but the King, freed from his mother's domination, encouraged an alliance with the Comte de Soissons for political reasons. The Count's mother, an astute and managing woman, had steered her son carefully through the treacherous currents into which he had been pitched after the death of his father in 1612. The old Count had been a worthy but somewhat bizarre character, always at the heart of every embroilment. He had disapproved of the Spanish marriages, and after the engagements were announced had asked permission to leave the Court. In the summer before his death he had joined with Condé, and as a result his son tended to be linked in people's minds with the rebel Prince's cause. The Countess, however, had cunningly maintained a friendship with the Queen Mother. Now that Louis favoured a more conciliatory policy towards the Princes, a match between Soissons and his sister fitted in well with his plans. The Count and Henriette had always been allowed to visit each other's houses as often as they liked and were on terms of considerable familiarity. The youthful romance was already causing some comment in Paris; 'Mamanga has told me all your little *amours* with the Comte de Soissons,' Elisabeth wrote from Spain.

In February 1619, Christine was married to the Prince of Piedmont, Victor Amadeus I of Savoy, who had originally intended to acquire Elisabeth for his wife. On hearing the news of the Spanish engagements he had fulminated against Marie de Medici and all 'these Florentine women, who in all the states where they occupy a prominent position, bring confusion and bad government'. He now seemed satisfied with the younger sister, and when he arrived in Paris he made a very good impression on all who saw him. The marriage, which took place in one of the tower rooms at the Louvre, was the signal for an outbreak of gaiety in the capital which lasted all through the *jours gras* until the beginning of Lent. There was another cause for rejoicing which had been awaited impatiently ever since the arrival of the Spanish Queen. Relations between Louis and his wife had become progressively strained and recently he had limited his contact with her to formal visits in the middle of the morning. He had taken against her Spanish attendants, particularly the widows who were always dressed in black and who to his eyes looked like nuns. He found them repulsive and besides they cost a lot to keep.

Recently he had sent some of them back to Spain and this had perhaps paved the way for the firm course of action taken by de Luynes on the night of January 25. The King had had a busy day, hearing Mass, presiding at the Council and attending a rehearsal for the ballet which was to take place in February. The favourite, who was now satisfactorily married to an heiress, a vivacious beauty with dark blue eyes and drooping lids, went to the King's room when Louis had already said his prayers and gone to bed. De Luynes began by trying to persuade him to sleep with the Queen, an idea which Louis resisted strongly, finally bursting into tears. At this de Luynes picked him up and carried him to the Queen's chamber by the light of a candle carried by Monsieur de Beringhen, who died three weeks later, perhaps from delayed shock. Louis emerged from his wife's apartments at two o'clock in the morning in a state of undress, went to his own bed and slept peacefully until half past nine the following day. When the news spread through the court there was universal excitement and the Nuncio and the Spanish ambassador were so delighted that they sent despatches to Rome and Madrid, where bonfires were lit to mark the occasion.

Everyone agreed that they had never before seen the King in such high spirits. He spent his nights with the Queen and his days rehearsing the ballet *L'aventure de Tancrède en la forêt enchantée*. Surrounded by script-writers, composers and designers, his *maître de danse* Bocan and all the costumiers, musicians, actors, buffoons and singers, he was entirely happy and in his element. On the evening of February 12 he had supper with de Luynes and then entertained all those who were taking part in the ballet. De Luynes had once again landed the principal part, the King was playing the knight-errant Godfrey, and Henriette's *innamorato*, de Soissons, now an extremely personable sixteen-year-old, was also taking part.

As usual there was a succession of magnificent settings—a thick forest, an amphitheatre, and a semi-circular tabernacle enriched with pyramids, palms and laurels. A slate-blue sky dotted with clouds at one point opened to reveal a crowd of angels on gauze-covered scaffolding. Twenty-eight musicians were wafted down on a cloud, a magician appeared out of the ground, blood gushed from a tree when it was struck. It was Horace Morel, master of the King's fireworks, who produced the most spectacular touch of all. The demon gods, with burning sceptres and flaming crowns, duelled with Tancred and his companions while thunder rolled and lightning flashed; the whole scene was then enveloped in a wall of flame which in its turn gave way to total darkness.

The court was in a mood for celebration and two ballets were mounted that season. The Queen, defying her Spanish confessors, had become addicted to the art, and could not wait to perform in one herself. Several days after *Tancrède* she replied with her own ballet, based on the fable of Psyche, which explicitly stated the theme of love and hymeneal bliss. In the opening scene Venus and Cupid appeared in a gilded car drawn by two enormous swans and carrying children dressed as gods of love. The second set represented Love's Palace, and later, doors opened in the heavens, revealing the Queen among a crowd of goddesses all dressed in white and scarlet satin glittering with jewels and tinsel streamers.

The two ballets performed by the King and Queen in the new year of 1619 marked the highest point of the French court masque, which was never again to achieve such perfection of style, such dramatic intensity or such magnificence and artistic unity. In later years a decadence began to set in and subsequent ballets never to the same extent satisfied the French love of expressive dance and theatrical effect. The plots became weaker and the décor simpler as Louis spent more money on his armies and less on his court entertainments.

In February 1619 the Queen Mother had written a friendly letter to her son expressing her pleasure at Christine's marriage, but not long afterwards news was brought that she had escaped from the castle at Blois. It had been a tight squeeze easing her out of the window, and her companions had pushed her over the ramparts ignominiously tied up in a cloak. However undignified the method of her escape, she had reached freedom and was now likely to act as a magnet for all the King's enemies. When Louis sent representatives to Angoulême to treat with her, she refused to talk of terms and would not 'unbosom herself any otherwise than by lamentable complaints' as Bentivoglio put it. It was some time before any progress was made, but at last Louis agreed to meet his mother at Tours. Christine and her husband, as well as Henriette, joined the Court when it journeyed south, to be reunited with the mother they had not seen for two years. The meeting took place a few miles from the city, and on seeing her son the Queen could only exclaim, 'How you have grown', before bursting into tears. Bentivoglio found the whole interlude enchanting, with family peace restored, and the countryside around of exceptional beauty—'so smoothly glides that lovely river called the Loire, so delightful are its banks, so abounding with fruits'.

When the ten days had passed, the King and Henriette accompanied Christine as far as Amboise on her way to Piedmont. The Queen Mother decided to go her own way to Chinon. As long as she remained in the provinces she was likely to constitute a threat, and Louis was anxious to counteract her influence by establishing an amicable relationship with the Princes of the Blood. Condé had been released from captivity and the King hoped he would stay loyal out of gratitude. De Soissons, it was agreed, could best be secured by a marriage with Henriette. At the end of 1619 the matter had virtually been settled, and Louis sent an envoy to his mother asking her approval of a number of marriages including Henriette's, and Gaston's to Mademoiselle de Montpensier. Marie de Medici replied that although she did not disapprove of the other marriages, she hoped that when it was a question of her own children, Louis would desist from any final decision until her return to Court.

The news that she was to marry a Frenchman had increased Henriette's popularity. She had always been a favourite with the Paris crowds on account of her likeness to her father of hallowed memory. With her waif-like face and sparkling eyes she was an appealing child, already very self-possessed. Altogether she was attracting, at the age of eleven, far more attention than was good for her. Courted by the dazzling Comte de Soissons, and, as the youngest, tending to be spoilt by all the family, she was growing up expecting to have her own way on all occasions. Regular visits to her spiritual mentor, Mother Madeleine de Saint-Joseph of the Carmelites, helped to breed in her a genuine religious fervour, without providing an easy road to virtue for a wayward girl. 'I cannot be good all at once though I will do all I can to make you happy,' she wrote to Mamanga in a letter apologizing for a fit of temper.

Condé was less inclined than some to welcome Henriette's match. He could not view with complacency the prospect of de Soissons becoming the King's brother-in-law for he was quick to resent any threat to his own supremacy among the Princes of the Blood. Quarrels soon broke out between the cousins about matters of etiquette, and the Court began to take sides. The climax came when there was an argument revolving round the vital question of the napkin. Some thought that Condé had the right to hand it to the King, others supported de Soissons.

The Queen Mother's continued absence from the court was keeping everyone in suspense. When some of the more powerful noblemen left for their estates it was feared that they were planning to make trouble. Finally, to use Bentivoglio's image, the imposthume broke. The Comte de Soissons left the Court suddenly on June 30 and, with his mother in attendance, went off to join Marie de Medici who had become involved with the rebels now declaring their hostile intentions in many provinces. The King took a firm line and before long he set out with a large force to restore order.

For Henriette the situation was far from comfortable in that wet, unhealthy summer. The young man she had been on the verge of marrying had vanished to take up arms against her brother, who for his part had marched away to fight their estranged mother and half-brother, the Duc de Vendôme, who had turned his coat—not for the first time.

The King's military ardour was now aroused. He organized his campaign with as much care and enthusiasm as he had always expended on the ballets at court. Impressed by such a determined show of force, those along his route declared for his cause as he marched towards Normandy. On August 7 his armies were ranged in front of the Queen Mother's stronghold, the Ponts-de-Cé, which surrendered with surprising ease. Its loss was an irreparable blow for Marie de Medici, whose supporters, all at heart self-orientated, had already begun to quarrel among themselves. Before long she was seeking terms and in September she returned to Paris. When the King came back late in the year after a triumphal tour of the south, arriving on horseback in a buoyant mood, he found his mother, his wife and Henriette all at the Louvre to welcome him. The family was reunited at last, and Louis returned a hero, having brought peace to his country almost without bloodshed.

Soon after the King's return the Duchesse de Luynes gave birth to a son, but there was still no sign of the hoped-for royal heir. 'What is the Dauphin doing? Now that your Majesty is a wife, when will you become a mother?' Bentivoglio had the temerity to ask some time during the hopeful spring of 1619. The Queen blushed and said nothing. Now the King's love for her had cooled again and he was showing far more interest in the Duchesse de Luynes than he had ever manifested for his own wife. In any event by the spring of 1621 he was on the march again, setting out to quell what appeared to be a general Protestant uprising. Encouraged by the rapid subjugation of his mother's allies, Louis put a large army in the field and seemed all set to repeat his success of the year before. From Saint-Foy on May 25 he wrote Henriette a confident letter telling her about the new conquests he had made, but it was not long before he found that the Huguenots were a far tougher proposition than the quarrelsome nobles who had come together temporarily under the Queen Mother's banner. They formed a close-knit, efficient league, linked by strong religious ties and the discipline of a minority group.

Louis was encumbered with the usual quota of courtiers, as well as a contingent of his female relations. During the siege of Clérac, awnings of leaves had to be made to shelter the Queen and her ladies from the heat of the sun. In July Anne left her husband and made her way to Bordeaux, while the Queen Mother returned to Tours, where Henriette had come south to meet her. Part of the royal army was sent to invest La Rochelle and a large number of soldiers laid siege to Montaubon. The King's generals were confident of success, and the Duc de Schomberg was so sure Montaubon would fall that he invited Bassompierre to dine with him in the city next day. Bassompierre replied with his usual humour that since the next day was Friday, *jour de poisson*, it would be better to wait until Sunday and have a more expensive celebration. As it turned out several assaults failed to reduce the garrison, and as they waited outside the walls, camping out in the worsening weather, the King's forces were decimated by fever. On November 2 the siege was raised; six thousand men were left in the vicinity of the town but the rest were marched away to tilt at less obstinate targets. Three days later Louis, still in camp at Montaubon, wrote an affectionate letter to his sister saying that he often thought of her though he did not have time to write very frequently.

The King returned to Paris in January 1622. For the first time for years he was without de Luynes, who had succumbed to purple fever the previous December. Louis had already begun to tire of the favourite, whose death was something of a relief. He soon found the excuse he needed to eliminate the Duchesse from the Queen's household. One evening in Lent the Queen, who was thought to be six months pregnant, had spent an evening with Henriette. She left her sister-in-law's apartments with a crowd of ladies just after midnight, and as she crossed the Grande Salle, the Duchesse de Luynes seized her by the arm and made her run. She tripped and fell against the stage which had been set up ready for the ballet. The shock of the fall caused the loss of the last hope of motherhood she was to have until the birth over twenty years later of the son who would become Louis XIV. It was easy to find a scapegoat and the Duchesse was dismissed forthwith.

The Queen's accident cast a shadow over the festivities which had been lavish enough considering the state of the country. Bassompierre recalled that there had been many comedies and ballets and that everything had been very beautiful including the ladies—for him a very important point. The King's mind was on more vital matters. Although he had covered a great deal of ground on his previous campaign and had been granted the satisfaction of seeing many small towns surrender to him, the Protestants were still unsubdued, and La Rochelle, Montaubon and Royan still remained in their hands. In spite of the fact that many people advised him against it, he was determined to continue the war; his mother was equally determined to go with him for, as Richelieu put it, she thought that once anyone had spent a few months with her, they would then find that they could not do without her. It had been seriously suggested that the fourteen-year-old Gaston should lead the army, but wisdom prevailed and the sole heir to the throne was told that he must stay at home. Suddenly, on March 24, before the winter was properly over, and without having adequately prepared for the new campaign, Louis departed, by a back door, as if he had been carried off, with his mother in close pursuit. Richelieu observed that it looked as if he was going on a hunting trip rather than setting out to be a conquering hero. He embarked on a wearisome, unrewarding campaign which kept him away from Paris for nearly a year.

Chapter 4

MADAME HENRIETTE

WHEN LOUIS returned early in 1623 the Queen and his sister were busy with preparations for the ballet which was to be staged at the Louvre at the beginning of March. Every evening crowds of courtiers pushed their way into the Grande Salle to watch the rehearsals. Henriette, who was playing the part of Iris, was already arousing a great deal of admiration. Despite the fact that she was small for her age and her figure was childish, the Princess could dance 'rarely well' and her singing voice was outstanding. The highlight was a special solo addressed to her mother in which she tactfully asserted that like Iris she borrowed her colouring from the sun which shone on her.

One evening two Englishmen entered the Louvre and mingled with the courtiers. They were soberly dressed although they were wearing outsize periwigs. As they stood in one of the galleries watching the King 'solacing himself with familiar pleasures', they overheard two gentlemen discussing the masque and decided to push their way into the Grande Salle where the rehearsal was taking place. The Queen's Lord Chamberlain let them through 'out of humanity to strangers', and they were able to have a good view of the royal performers. The visitors left Paris next day and headed south, and it was a few days before everyone realized their true identity. The two men were in fact Charles, Prince of Wales, and the royal favourite, Buckingham, who were on their way to Spain to negotiate a marriage with the Infanta.

Both the King of England and his son were anxious to acquire the Spanish bride. Charles had fallen in love with her romantically from a distance and had made up his mind to woo her in person. James I was mainly motivated by the hope that the Spanish King might intercede on his behalf with the Catholic powers to arrange for the restitution to his son-in-law, the Elector Palatine, of the lands which had been taken from him as a reprisal for accepting the crown of Bohemia. Negotiations had been dragging on for years, and the possibility of bringing affairs to a speedy conclusion had persuaded him to part with his son and his 'dear Steenie'.

Charles told his father that they had taken the risk of visiting the French court because they had 'a great tickling to add it to the history of our adventures' and also because he wanted to see the Queen, who was his beloved Infanta's sister. They had been rewarded for their audacity by their glimpse of nineteen 'fair dancing ladies' among whom, in his opinion, the Queen was easily the handsomest.

The British Ambassador in Paris, Lord Herbert of Cherbury, advised the Prince and his party to head for the border as quickly as possible, making sure that they did not treat with any Huguenots on the way. They were dressed in riding coats all of the same colour 'in a kind of noble simplicity', but they had difficulty in refusing the invitations of noblemen whose houses lay along their route and who suspected that they were more important than their appearance suggested. It was by now well into Lent and they could not buy meat at any of the inns where they lodged, but their journey was on the whole uneventful, and they crossed over into Spain where they were 'the braveliest received that ever men were'.

Charles's love for the Infanta intensified as soon as he saw her. She was as fair as her sister, the Queen of France, and she had a delicate pink-and-white complexion. The Spanish saw to it that he was never alone with her, which was discouraging, but he was better qualified to worship from afar, being unlettered in the art of courtship. He had shown no interest in any ladies at the English court, and his affections had so far centred on Buckingham, who had cleverly guaranteed his own future by insinuating himself into the favour of the heir to the throne just as thoroughly as he had captured the mind and heart of the reigning king. As for the Infanta herself, she remained unaffected by the ardent admiration of her Anglo-Saxon suitor. On one occasion the Queen of Spain whispered in the Prince's ear that he would be well advised to give up his suit and woo her sister, Henriette.

Predictably the Spaniards began to stiffen their terms as soon as they had Charles in their power. Tempers began to rise in the unbearable August heat of the Spanish capital. Buckingham succumbed to what would probably now be called a virus infection. He had already fallen out with Olivares, Philip IV's chief minister. The Papal Nuncio was doing what he could to hinder matters, although as Buckingham told the King 'he receives such rude answers that we hope he will soon weary on't'. Attempts were made to convert the Prince to the Catholic faith, and Buckingham even told James that if he were to join the Roman church the whole matter could be expedited, to which the King replied that he was not 'a Monsieur who can shift his religion as easily as he can shift his shirt when he comes in from tennis'. The Spanish King was happy enough to treat with the English, giving vague assurances about the Elector

Palatine and demanding far from vague concessions for the English Catholics.

The Spanish refused to conclude any agreement until a dispensation arrived from Pope Urban VIII, who in his turn demanded terms which James could not accept. Charles, however, was growing desperate, and he had reached the point where he was ready to make dangerous concessions in order to complete his espousal. There had been several rumours that the dispensation, expiating the Infanta from the venial sin of marrying a heretic, was already on the way, but each time there was a further delay, and the exasperated Buckingham reported that it had been 'clogged with some new condition'.

At the French court Charles's proceedings in Madrid were watched with some interest. Henriette's future was still unsettled, and although the persistent de Soissons was still in the field, it was now unlikely that the Queen Mother would bestow her one remaining unmarried daughter on a mere nobleman of France until the possibility of a richer prize had been explored. The advantages of a union between the Prince of Wales and Henriette had been in people's minds for some time. Before his death de Luynes had already despatched an unofficial ambassador to England to sound out the King but had received little encouragement. Now, however, the outlook seemed slightly more promising, as reports from Spain suggested that a rupture was imminent. The Queen Mother had grounds for hoping that she might one day add another Queen to the family collection. As for Henriette herself, she had remarked, on hearing about Charles's journey to Spain in search of a wife, that he 'might have had one nearer hand, and saved himself a great part of the labour'. It was evident that Charles had not particularly noticed the diminutive French Princess when he visited the Court, but in the standard recipe for royal marriages, love at first sight was the least important ingredient.

The Comte de Soissons had distinguished himself in action at La Rochelle, and it was his opinion that he could claim Henriette as a reward for good service. The Queen Mother thought differently, and Henriette herself was by no means dedicated to the cause of her childhood suitor. The Cardinal de la Rochefoucauld, her godfather, took it upon himself to tell the Count's mother that she was mistaken if she believed that she might one day have the Princess for a daughter-in-law, 'the King being minded to bestow his sister the best way for her honour, and the Crown's advantage'.

When Charles left Madrid without having accomplished the mission he had so quixotically undertaken, an English Franciscan friar arrived in Paris, where he told the Queen Mother that the time was ripe to initiate negotiations for an English match. She consulted Richelieu, who gave the unorthodox ambassador a favourable hearing and sent him to

England 'with a full purse and a heart full of hope'. He went straight to Buckingham who was likely to be interested in any scheme which would spite the Spaniards. The Comte de Tillières, France's official Ambassador in London, remarked acidly that the favourite apparently preferred to deal with an ignorant monk and a mother infatuated with her daughter rather than a more prudent and knowledgeable intermediary.

In January 1624 it was still difficult for the French to make out whether the English were finally cured of their *maladie espagnole*; the Queen Mother's messenger found the Prince of Wales evasive when he had the temerity to raise the subject. The friar reminded Charles that Spanish good-will tended to be impressive in its outward manifestations, though small in its practical effect. Plenty of people were ready to go down on their knees, he said, and kiss the hem of one's garment, but when it came to opening the purse, that was something one could not expect of a Spaniard. De Tillières was of the opinion that the Prince treated the monkish minister as something of a joke, and he himself was inclined to approach the whole affair with caution. He had been in England long enough to understand the depths of feeling aroused by religious matters. It was his duty to warn the French King against the danger of believing that the English would be more ready to grant concessions to the Catholics if these were demanded by Paris rather than by Madrid. It was true that they felt more amicably disposed towards France than they did towards the country which had despatched the Armada and that they might be more willing to accept Henriette, daughter of the admired *Henri le Grand*, than a Spanish Infanta. De Tillières felt that anyone who knew the Puritans as well as he did was bound to view the possibility of an English match for a French princess with some trepidation, even though it might do something to check the expansionist policy of Spain. He was concerned about the safety of Madame's soul if she were to be brought into an alien world full of militant Protestants. In fact the more de Tillières thought about the subject, the more he found it alarmingly thorny. With the growing lack of accord between King and Parliament, he foresaw that England could rapidly become a country without leaders, troops or money.

In France nobody paid much attention to the Ambassador's warnings. Although there was no certainty that James had entirely given up all hope of a Spanish match, it seemed that he was willing to send an envoy, Lord Kensington, who would explore the possibility of promoting an alliance between the crowns of France and England. In Paris they awaited with some impatience the arrival of 'M. Quinsinton' who, it was rumoured, was coming to pay his court to the Princess. He put in his first appearance on the night when everyone was getting ready to go to the court ballet, and with his outstanding good looks and charming manner he immediately created a good impression. He went first to the apartments of the Duc and Duchesse de Chevreuse, and the Duchesse, who was the widow of de Luynes, immediately fell deeply in love with him. He for his part was amazed by the richness of the clothes everyone was wearing. 'I shall never be a beholder of the like worn by subjects,' he wrote in a letter to the Duke of Buckingham. After he had been there about an hour, the Queen Mother arrived with Henriette. Nobody had ever seen the Princess look so cheerful, and when the ballet was over, Kensington went to his lodgings and wrote enthusiastically, 'My Lord, I protest to God, she is a lovely, sweet young creature. Her growth is not great yet, but her shape is perfect, and they all swear that her sister, the Princess of Piedmont (who is now grown a tall and goodly lady) was not taller than she is, at her age.'

Kensington quickly decided that his best policy as a 'wooing ambassador' was to ingratiate himself with the ladies of the royal family, a task which was very much his speciality. The Queen, cold-shouldered by her husband and starved of love, soon blossomed in the company of this good-looking man, and persuaded him to let her see Prince Charles's miniature. The Queen Mother, although at first a trifle hesitant of leaving her daughter alone with the English Adonis, now said that she would allow him to court the Princess on his master's behalf provided he would give her a précis of what he intended to say. 'I obey my Prince's command,' he told her, 'in presenting to your fair and royal daughter his service, not now out of mere compliment, but, prompted by passion and affection, which both her outward and inward beauties have so kindled in him, that he was resolved to contribute the uttermost he could to the alliance in question, and would think success therein the greatest success in the world.' The Queen Mother was reassured. '*Allez, allez*, there is no great danger in that. *Je me fie en vous*—I trust you,' she replied.

When he repeated the speech to Henriette, he later told the Prince, 'she drank it down with joy and with a low curtsey, made her acknowledgments, adding that she was extremely obliged to my prince, and would think herself happy in the occasion that would be presented of meriting a place in the affections of his good grace'. He told her that the Prince now had her miniature which he looked at several times a day. She herself was not officially allowed to see the Prince's picture until a formal proposal had been made, but Kensington arranged for her to have an illicit look at his miniature, which she gazed at for a full hour, blushing with shame because she was unable to hide her feelings.

Soon Kensington was allowed to talk to Henriette whenever he wished. On one occasion they had a conversation which lasted for two hours. 'She is a lady of as much beauty and sweetness to deserve your affections as any woman under heaven can be,' Kensington told the Prince; 'in truth she is the sweetest creature in France, and the loveliest thing in

Henri IV

Marie de Medici

Henrietta Maria c.1611

Louis XIII

Scenes from the Ballet *Armide* 1617

Photograph Collection Viollet

ARMIDE APPELLE A SON SECOURS LES
DEMONS QUI PRENNENT DES FORMES
TOUTES CONTRAIRES A SES DESSEINS.

Charles I in 1628

Henrietta Maria and Lady Carlisle: Detail from *Apollo and Diana*

nature. Her growth is little short of her age, and her wisdom infinitely beyond it. I heard her, the other day, discourse with her mother and the ladies about her, with extraordinary discretion and quickness. She dances—the which I am witness of—as well as ever I saw anyone; they say she sings most sweetly; I am sure she looks as if she did.' A few days later he heard the voice for himself and was astonished by its beauty. 'Neither her singing master, nor any man or woman either in France or Europe sings so admirably as she doth' ran his eulogy. 'Her voice is beyond imagination, and that is all I will say of it.'

A little later Henriette received letters from King James and the Prince. After dutifully asking her mother's permission, she put the King's in her cabinet, but lodged the Prince's in her bosom. When this was told to the old King, he was pleased, for he thought it indicated that 'she would trust him, and love his son', though he was ready to declare war on her for not reading his letter without her mother's consent.

The Queen let it be known that she was much impressed by the Prince's good looks which she had observed in his miniature, and at Court the progress already made was causing considerable satisfaction. Kensington met with universal friendliness, although de Soissons was understandably cool. 'I encountered him the other day,' Kensington reported, 'and gave him the due that belonged to his rank but instead of returning me my salute, he disdainfully turned back his head.' The Count's friends advised him to hide his feelings, but he told them that this was impossible, adding that if Kensington had not been representing such an important prince, he would gladly have cut his throat. The Spanish Ambassador, too, looked on with disapproval. 'How!' he was heard to exclaim. 'Does the Prince of Wales, then, mean to wed two wives, since he is nearly married to our Infanta?'

When the break with Spain was officially announced, Kensington's advice was that the English should fall 'speedily on a treaty' and so avoid the delays that had bedevilled the Spanish negotiations. He was sure that the moment was particularly favourable as the Marquis de Vieuville had just superseded Chancellor de Sillery in the King's councils after a long struggle for power. The English marriage provided de Vieuville with a chance to gain prestige and consolidate his position. Kensington believed that he would not be as demanding as the Spanish.

By mid-April the situation looked promising. Although marriage was primarily a business arrangement where affection, if it featured at all, was expected to develop after the ceremony and not before, Kensington had seen to it that in this case desire had been aroused well in advance of the event. As far as Henriette was concerned, Prince Charles was 'the most complete young Prince and person in the world'. There was some degree of truth in this, for the heir to the throne had in recent years improved out of all recognition. It was true that the Spanish journey had been a fiasco, but it had helped the Prince to stand on his own feet, and he was no longer the weakling who had been forced into prominence on the death of his brother Henry. He had gained bodily strength through rigorous exercises, and his moral behaviour was exemplary. It is probable that at this stage nobody was stressing the point that Prince Charles was still shy and withdrawn and that he tended to stutter when nervous. He was religious by nature and meticulous when it came to attending prayers and services. Since this was the case it would be Henriette's duty to lead him towards the true Church. She was not worried by the fact that the Prince was treating openly with that ill-defined body of people so disliked by de Tillières, *les Puritans*. As far as she was concerned, there was nothing to stop her being united as soon as possible with the young man who had been painted for her in such attractive colours. However, being a royal princess she was destined to wait for many tedious months while the countries involved struggled to gain the maximum advantage for themselves before the 'indissoluble knot' was tied.

It had not been part of Kensington's brief to tell the Princess that the balance of power in Europe could be critically altered by her marriage with an English prince. The endless ramifications of the situation would in any case have been difficult to explain, for more was involved than a simple clash of Protestant and Catholic ideologies. The French feared above all the growing menace of Spain, for Philip IV could wield great influence through his relations among the German princes; and now he had acquired easy access to the Spanish Netherlands through the Palatinate which had been conferred on the Catholic Duke of Bavaria. The Spanish were also likely to gain the right to send supplies through the narrow sixty-mile-long pass of the Valtelline which formed a small state inhabited by a Catholic population but ruled over by the Grisons, a league of Protestant mountain-dwellers. The valley had been occupied by papal forces in 1623, but now the Pope found the task of manning the forts along the pass too onerous and seemed ready to grant the right of passage to Spanish troops. If France were to oppose the Spaniards in this area, she risked offending the Pope; in the same way, if she promised to help James in the Palatinate as part of the marriage treaty, she might find herself fighting with a Protestant army against German Catholics—a confrontation hardly calculated to meet with unqualified approval in the Holy See.

The situation was made more difficult by the delicate state of the English King's health. James I was now frail and petulant; he was frequently in agony with gout and indigestion. The French feared what they described as his *légèreté* and they sometimes wondered whether he was capable of carrying on negotiations at all. He had been in a depressed state of mind ever since the breakdown of the Spanish marriage, and the situation was exacerbated by a growing alienation from his son. Not so long ago he had wept tears of joy when Charles and Buckingham returned from Spain. Now, afraid that they were trying to usurp his power, he was tormented by jealousy and he resorted to petty ruses in order to outwit them. This had the effect of driving them into the arms of the Puritans. For once in his life Charles found himself in sympathy with Parliament, and when he appeared before the two Houses which assembled at Whitehall in March, he expressed with great confidence Buckingham's view that the marriage treaty with Spain was untenable and that war must be declared at once on England's traditional enemy. The Lord Treasurer, Sir Lionel Cranfield, was prepared to stand by the King, to the annoyance of Charles and Buckingham. De Tillières reported that they were determined 'to pull this thorn out of their foot'. Enjoying their transient alliance with Parliament they succeeded in procuring Cranfield's impeachment, and it was in this connection that James uttered his famous and prophetic remark that his son would live 'to have his bellyful of Parliaments'.

De Tillières was advised to make as much capital as possible out of the friction between the Prince and his father. He did this to the best of his ability, not without wondering how Charles and Buckingham managed to reconcile their anti-Catholic standpoint with the prospect of an alliance with France. The Ambassador was also told to play down for the time being the question of concessions for the Catholics, since the truth had by now percolated through to Paris that James was finding it hard enough to stem the tide of Protestant feeling without having to put forward proposals alleviating the sufferings of the papists. An 'obnoxious petition' describing the Catholic clergy as the professed engines of Spain, and calling for the enforcement and strengthening of the laws against the Catholics, had been withdrawn after a struggle. While assuring everybody that any increase in popery was 'as thorns in his eyes and pricks in his sides', James had substituted a simple prayer for the execution of statutes already in existence. He had always regarded himself as the great European peacemaker and now he found himself out of sympathy with the warlike mood of his son and his Parliament. His natural timidity prevented him from taking a firm line, and he was being pulled along, not so much *'de bonne volonté, comme par necessité'* as de Tillières put it. The Ambassador reported that he had even heard the King say privately that he knew he would eventually have to pass the patent against the Catholics, otherwise he would not have any money.

In view of the troubled situation in England, the French were anxious that James should send an official ambassador who would follow up Kensington's mission. The English too felt the need for a shrewder and more experienced diplomat. The choice fell on the Earl of Carlisle, who had already visited Paris on three assignments and was well known for his anti-Spanish standpoint. His arrival was awaited with some impatience. There were the usual incomprehensible delays and de Tillières described the members of the delegation sitting 'with their arms folded, doing nothing, to their great displeasure'. It was the end of May before Carlisle finally arrived bearing a portrait of the Prince which Henriette was now allowed to gaze at openly.

Carlisle had been told to proceed on the lines of a treaty that had once been prepared for a possible marriage between the Prince and Henriette's sister Christine. De Vieuville seemed ready to agree to more limited concessions for the Catholics, but de Tillières wrote urgently stressing that if care were not taken the plight of the Catholics might be overlooked altogether. The Ambassador had been in England since 1619 and knew what he was talking about, but in spite of his experience, in July he was suddenly recalled. An English observer reported that he had left in a hurry, being too 'jesuited' for the match. It was also his misfortune to be a brother-in-law of Bassompierre who was out of favour with the de Vieuville administration. His place was taken by the Marquis d'Effiat, who was known to be a persuasive negotiator. When the new Ambassador left for London he carried an assurance that Louis had no wish to change the state of affairs in England but only wanted to be satisfied about his sister's conscience.

Philip IV had expected the English to accept exemption for the Catholics from the Oath of Supremacy which acknowledged the King as sole arbiter of religious and temporal matters, as well as from the Oath of Allegiance, which made all subjects accept the King's supremacy. The French only asked that the Catholics should not be penalized for their religious convictions provided they acted as loyal subjects, but this was far-reaching enough in the present circumstances. De Vieuville agreed that the more difficult clauses of the treaty should not be published but contained in a secret letter.

Carlisle and Kensington visited the two Queens and Henriette every day, sometimes at Court, or in the evenings in the field where they took the air. Meetings with the French Commissioners were held every Monday, and throughout the month of July both sides worked hard at the council table. Carlisle hoped to extract a promise of help in the Palatinate and the French seemed prepared to make a limited undertaking in this connection. In August, 1624, however, the situation changed dramatically. During the summer months, Cardinal Richelieu had been quietly working himself into the forefront of the French King's councils. Louis, tired of the irresolute and fussy de Vieuville, had shown an increasing respect for Richelieu's superior intelligence and relentless determination to oppose the Spanish on every front. One day de Vieuville was arrested as he left the King's presence. Richelieu was given an official post as Secretary of State for Commerce and Marine; in reality he became the King's first minister.

News of the shake-up caused consternation in England. Although Richelieu's intentions could only be surmised, everyone was sure that he meant to drive a far harder bargain than the ineffective de Vieuville. James feared that the French would now 'take up the fashion of Spain . . . to spin time and expectations unprofitably'. D'Effiat foresaw endless difficulties and begged to be recalled although he had been in England for such a short time. In Paris the English Ambassadors were nonplussed by the suddenness of the *coup*. They had no time to ask whether they should offer the hand to the Cardinal—the best solution to this problem seemed to be for Richelieu to receive them in bed until they had been sent their instructions from London. There were rumours in Paris that Richelieu wished to end the negotiations simply because his predecessor had initiated them. When the Papal Nuncio asked him if this was true, he replied that it would be absurd to abandon something advantageous for such a trivial reason. He was just as well aware as everybody else of the advisability of an alliance with England—'*cette île étant comme un boule-vard sur ce royaume*' as he put it. At the same time he did not wish to make the Spanish mistake of asking too much. 'One must demand what one can obtain,' he said.

Early in September Carlisle and Kensington were presented with a proposal that a document should be drawn up separately from the main treaty, its purpose to ensure that Catholics would be allowed to worship privately without molestation provided they still swore allegiance to the King. Richelieu insisted that it would be little more than a formality, its main purpose being to placate the Pope. As the messengers went to and fro across the Channel with proposals and counter-proposals, the weeks began to slip by and nothing was decided. The Princess grew increasingly melancholy as each new obstacle occurred. It was difficult for her to understand why there should be so much concern about her conscience, about the question of whether her chapel should be public or private, or whether she should have charge of her purely hypothetical children until they were twelve or thirteen years of age.

In spite of the English King's obvious reluctance, Richelieu began to press harder for the Catholic clauses. Cynically enough he accepted the fact that James would never be able to honour his promises, but hoped that he would make them all the same in order to speed up the dispensation. It was part of the Cardinal's scheme to promote the quarrel between King and Parliament in the interest of reducing England to such a state of weakness and confusion that she would not be able to intervene on behalf of Protestants on the Continent. The question of Henriette's soul did not concern him unduly, and he was inclined to use the coldly impersonal argument that it was legitimate to jeopardize one of the faithful for the sake of saving a hundred others.

The Pope, with greater humanity, seemed to feel a genuine responsibility for Henriette's future. Although Father Bérulle was sent from France to expedite matters, Urban remained hesitant. He believed that marriage with a heretic prince could only bring her unhappiness, for if her husband or father-in-law should decide to persecute the Catholics she would be miserable; equally, if the penalties were relaxed the Protestants would vent their anger on her. It seemed probable that James was only interested in the alliance because he hoped it might help his son-in-law's cause in the Palatinate. The English King, for his part, was sure that all this 'flying back' from their original promises proved that the French were motivated by selfish considerations and not with the idea of bestowing the Princess to her best advantage.

Richelieu now decided that the time for procrastination was over. Unless some definite conclusion could be reached he feared that Gondomar would be back in England with renewed offers from Spain. Many people believed that Spanish trouble-making lay behind the Pope's reluctance—the Queen Mother herself had told Kensington that if the dispensation were granted 'the King of Spain would march with an army to Rome and sack it'. Richelieu certainly felt that the Holy See was asking too much and would have preferred to leave such questions as the nature of the chapels in England to the Princess's own discretion. He was resolved to go ahead with the signing of the treaty, dispensation or no dispensation. The Ambassadors were summoned and they agreed to sign without further argument. France gave a verbal assurance that she would support an English expedition to the Palatinate and would allow English troops to disembark on French soil.

The ceremony took place on November 20 and that night there was great public rejoicing in Paris. A few days later the French Secretary of State left for England. He was Henri-Auguste de Loménie de la Ville-aux-Clercs, later to be known by the more manageable appellation of the Comte de Brienne. He took with him the treaty for ratification, the secret letter and a very large train. Sixteen coaches met him at Dover and his arrival in London was greeted with salvoes of gunfire, bell-ringing and bonfires. It was the general belief that Henriette would be in England by the end of January.

Richelieu's sudden move forced the Pope into sending the dispensation. It was delivered to the Nuncio in Paris with instructions that it should not be handed over until the English King had made public a policy of religious toleration. Henriette received a copy and a congratulatory letter from Urban himself in which he compared her to the early English Queen Aldiberga who had first taken the Christian religion to England. He saw her as the Esther of an oppressed people, or the Clothilde of earlier times who converted her husband to Christianity.

Perhaps more welcome and certainly less daunting was the letter which came from Prince Charles. It was only the second he had ever written to her. 'I have not dared to take the liberty of testifying to you, by a single line,' it ran, 'the great impatience with which my spirit has been tormented, during my long waiting for the happy accomplishment of this treaty, until I received good tidings of it.' He referred to the occasion when he had briefly glimpsed her during his clandestine visit to Paris:

... my happiness has been completed by the honour which I have already had of seeing your person, although unknown to you; which sight has completely satisfied me that the exterior of your person in no degree belies the lustre of your virtues. But I cannot, by writing, express the passion of my soul to have the honour of being esteemed, Yours etc.

In her reply, Henriette expressed pleasure at the impatience he had shown, which provided proof of his good will:

The King my brother and the Queen my mother being willing that I should receive these testimonies of your affection, I will only say that if that has not an assured foundation in all the good which it makes you imagine in me, at least you will find a readiness to show you that you will not oblige an ungrateful person, and that I am, and shall always be, Your very humble and very affectionate servant Henrietta Maria.

Charles, encouraged by this formal note, sent her a present of some jewellery. 'Although it is totally unworthy of you,' ran the letter which accompanied the present, 'yet I hope you will receive it in good part, as coming from him who will be very glad to risk his life in your service, wishing nothing more than to be honoured with your commands, and to have some opportunity of showing by deeds, how much I am, Madam, Yours.'

It seemed that there was little left now to do except complete the trousseau and await the fleet which already had its orders to bring over Madame Henriette 'with honour and safety'.

Chapter 5

THE LITTLE BRIDE

IN ENGLAND hasty preparations had been made to accommodate the French Secretary of State. The more prudent counsellors
suggested that the money set aside for his entertainment should be
limited to eighty pounds a day in view of the King's penuriousness.
Neither James nor his son was in London; they had been spending some
weeks at Newmarket and it was arranged that they would travel to
Cambridge, staying at Trinity College for talks with the French. Most of
the Privy Council had assembled in the town, but the ceremony of
ratification was carried out quietly in the presence of the King, the
Prince, the Duke of Buckingham and one of the Secretaries of State.
The secret letter, which had been drawn up and dated November 18,
1624, was also signed. In it the King promised that for the sake of his
very dear son and Madame, sister of the Most Christian King, he would
allow his Catholic subjects even more liberty than they had been granted
under the Spanish treaty, provided that they used their privileges
discreetly and rendered the obeisance that true subjects owed to their
King.

Before returning to London the Ambassadors attended a dinner given
in their honour. Orations and a philosophy act were performed and the
King 'slept it out patiently' but retired to his room before the meal. He
was suffering from a severe attack of gout brought on by too much
conviviality at Newmarket; his hands were so swollen that he found it
difficult to hold a pen at the signing ceremony. The Prince took his
father's place at the magnificent feast which followed; the King drank to
Louis in his room and the cup was then brought to the Prince who handed
it to de la Ville-aux-Clercs and d'Effiat. Afterwards they all went to the
King's room and he made polite remarks about the forthcoming match,
followed by even more appreciative comments about the help he hoped to
receive for his expedition to the Palatinate.

De la Ville-aux-Clercs celebrated Christmas in London. The Lord
Keeper, John Williams, Bishop of Lincoln, had invited the Frenchmen
to spend an evening with him in the Jerusalem Chamber at Westminster.
As they went in at the north gate, which was brightly lit with torches, the

characterful Welsh bishop stood at the door and inveigled them into the Abbey 'assuring them that nothing should be done that might be in the least offensive to them'. They found themselves sitting in the stalls with all their train, unable to escape for half an hour while the choristers in their richest habits sang three anthems. Everyone stood uncovered, except de la Ville-aux-Clercs, who ignored all the unfamiliar psalms, hymns and motets and remained firmly on his knees, telling his beads. During one of the verses the Bishop presented them with copies of the Anglican liturgy translated into French, saying as he did so that their Lordships might 'at their leisure read in the book, in what form of holiness our Prince worshipped God; wherein he durst say, nothing savoured of any corruption of doctrine, much less of heresy, which he hoped would be so reported to the Lady Princess Henrietta'. De la Ville-aux-Clercs was overcome with embarrassment at the whole episode, and carefully left his copy of the liturgy in the pew, only to have it 'brought after him as if he had forgot it'.

At Christmas the King wrote to the Archbishops of Canterbury and York ordering the stay of all executions and proceedings against Catholics in ecclesiastical courts, 'and further, that our said subjects, Roman Catholics, be not in any way molested for the penalty of twelve pence imposed upon them by statute every Sunday they go not to church'. A number of Catholics were also to be released from prison, but de la Ville-aux-Clercs suspected that those in charge were delaying the release until after he had left England, intending to forget conveniently to do anything about it.

The Ambassadors were entertained lavishly in London, and the Duke of Buckingham, whose dinners were legendary, eclipsed everyone else with the splendour of his hospitality. He provided an ostentatious feast followed by a ball *à la française*.

In view of all this generosity de la Ville-aux-Clercs experienced further embarrassment when he heard that Richelieu had withdrawn his permission for troops to land on French soil. It seemed that the Cardinal wished to placate the Pope who was now demanding that James should sign yet another document in Latin demanding a chapel for Henriette in all the royal houses outside London. De la Ville-aux-Clercs could understand the need for caution especially as the dispensation remained in the Nuncio's hands in Paris, but to explain the difficulty to the English was not so easy. When de la Ville-aux-Clercs went to see Buckingham he took d'Effiat with him, hoping that the Ambassador would be able to exercise some of his famous diplomatic flair. The favourite was predictably angry; troops were already being levied all over the country, and the trumpets were sounding to draw in horses at twenty-nine shillings a week. The Count of Mansfeld, who was to command the army, had recently arrived in England and was proving a great draw for the London crowds. He had tactfully paid a visit to an English church to prove that he was neither a papist nor an infidel. Now he was going on to Dover to await the arrival of his troops. It would be enough of a shock for him to see the unwilling rabble which was all the English could provide by way of an army, without being told that he would not be allowed to disembark them in France. Buckingham remarked icily that he realized, of course, that his country had no power to dictate to the French, but at least it had the right to complain about broken promises.

Soon it became evident that the cavalry promised by France was likely to fall far short of the number originally agreed. Early in the new year Huguenot resentment flared up in Languedoc and La Rochelle, and although nobody could tell at that stage how serious the rising would prove to be, the Cardinal was less likely to dissipate his forces in supporting the English expedition. De la Ville-aux-Clercs told Mansfeld that he was a fool to accept the command. He asked the hardened mercenary whether he really believed he would be able to regain the Palatinate in the six months which was the maximum time the English Parliament had agreed to support the troops. Mansfeld replied that it was hardly the work of a day, and was then advised to throw in his lot with Richelieu, who was much less biased against foreigners and more able to pay those who worked for him.

It was well known that the English King's finances were precarious, because of his dependence on Parliament and his partiality for favourites. There was 'an extremity of want' in the Exchequer and it was unlikely that the King would be able to pay his daughter, Elizabeth of Bohemia, her allowance and the five hundred pounds he had promised her for her lying-in. This was all very ironical in view of the fact that the Prince had lately given Buckingham twenty thousand pounds as a gift—or so it was believed. The forty thousand pounds that had been set aside for the Duke's expenses if he should be called upon to fetch Henriette from France seemed over-generous, especially when the provision of horses, transport and ammunition for Mansfeld's army was so inadequate. The men who had been pressed into service were nothing more than 'a rabble of raw poor rascals' and, as one observer put it, it was 'lamentable to see the heavy countenances, and hear the farewells of the pressed men, who are most unwilling to go on account of the bad season, the uncertainty of the employment and the ill terms on which they serve'.

In Paris Carlisle was growing impatient. 'These perfidious monsters', as he had come to call the French, were still imposing alterations and additions to the treaty, sheltering all the time behind the Pope's authority. 'I can endure it no longer,' he told Buckingham. On March 30, 1625, however, he was summoned by Richelieu and received a written promise that the marriage would take place in thirty days' time. De Soissons had been given the task—which he was unlikely to appreciate—of sending officers to Calais to meet the Duke of Buckingham. Madame's future was settled at last. She wrote to her brother, to the Pope and the English King, confirming that she intended to carry out all that was expected of her, and thanking the Pope for all the good care he had taken to ensure the safety of her conscience, which she particularly appreciated, 'having nothing in the world which is so dear to me . . . as a result of the good upbringing and instruction I have received from the Queen my mother'.

A despatch arrived from d'Effiat which contained disturbing news. Buckingham had dined at the Ambassador's lodgings and had told him that the King was suffering from a fever which seemed to recur every three days with mounting ferocity. The Duke was afraid that, unless the King's health improved, he would be unable to leave for France as planned. A few days later rumours were circulating in Paris that James was dead. D'Effiat reported that the doctors held out little hope. The King held his hands in cold water and drank a great deal of small beer, but neither these eccentric remedies nor those suggested by his medical advisers produced any improvement. The question of his son's marriage was much on his mind. He was worried about the French King's insistence that the proxy must be received within thirty days, fearing that any delay might jeopardize 'that excellent lady and that happy match'. One afternoon he talked for some time about Henriette's good qualities, recalling how she had put his letter in the cabinet and the Prince's in her bosom, 'intimating thereby that she should rely upon me [for counsel] and lodge my son in her heart'. On the day before he died the King appeared to gain a little strength. He took some broth and received the sacrament, calling for the Bishop of Lincoln, whom, d'Effiat pointed out, 'M. de la Ville-aux-Clercs knows well'. A little before dawn he sent for his son who came to the room in his nightgown. It seemed that the King had something important to say; he tried to raise himself on his pillows, but his words were inaudible and soon afterwards he died.

Letters of condolence were sent immediately, and the new King wrote explaining that Buckingham would not be able to leave at once. He suggested that the Duc de Chevreuse, who was closely related to the English royal family, should be appointed his proxy. Louis was glad that Charles was not making his father's death an excuse for further delay; he thought that it was as well to wipe away all tears as soon as possible for the good of the kingdom, since over-indulgence in sorrow could be interpreted as a sign of weakness. As for his sister, Louis was sure that she could only be happy in the hands of so great a King.

The engagement ceremony took place on May 8 at five o'clock in the evening. The King's chamber was closed from dawn onwards. Carlisle

and Kensington, now created Earl of Holland in recognition of his good
services, were fetched from the Faubourg Saint-Germain in one of the
King's coaches drawn by six horses. The Ambassadors cast off their
mourning clothes for the occasion and their footmen were dressed in
tan-coloured liveries enriched with gold lace. Their wives and all their
suite followed in a procession of coaches. At the main door of the Louvre
the lieutenant of the gate stood on guard with his archers. The coach
crossed the courtyard and deposited its occupants at the foot of the
Henri II staircase. They were led to the ante-room on the ground floor
overlooking the Seine where ambassadors always went when awaiting an
audience.

Meanwhile the King had entered the audience chamber with his
brother and various lords, all magnificently dressed. A throne had been
put ready for him under a dais which was draped with crimson velvet
trimmed with gold. The Queen and the Queen Mother had gone down
earlier to the Princess's apartments, which were on the ground floor
overlooking the Jardin de l'Infante. From there they walked to the first
floor and were led through the King's closet to avoid the crowd. The
Queen Mother went first into the chamber which was packed with
courtiers. As usual she was dramatically dressed in black with a great veil
of crêpe, a collar of large pearls and a huge cross encrusted with diamonds.
Anne of Austria was in rose-pink satin embroidered with silver, and the
tiny bride, led by her equerry, wore a white satin dress with hanging
sleeves which touched the ground, all so thickly embroidered with gold
and precious stones that the white could hardly be seen. The heavy train
was carried by Mamie de Saint-Georges and by Mademoiselle de
Bourbon, but they were unable to manage it between them and had to be
helped by the equerry.

Careful arrangements had been made to control all the people who
wished to be present at the ceremony, and it was remarkably orderly
considering the smallness of the space. All the same Henriette had some
difficulty in making her way to the chair which had been reserved for her
on the King's right hand. Once everyone was settled the King commanded
the captain of the guard to fetch the Ambassadors. They came in procession through the ranks of the archers who were drawn up in the antechamber with their halberds—their presence there being bitterly resented
by the *valets de chambre* who complained that as the King's bed had been
moved into the room for the occasion, the guards, by a strict rule of the
household, had no right to be there at all. When the procession reached
the threshold of the audience chamber, the two Englishmen made a
deep obeisance. Everyone rose to their feet, even the Kings and the
two Queens; the Ambassadors came forward, made another bow and
then, advancing into the enclosure which was divided by a balustrade

from the rest of the room, made the third bow prescribed by tradition. They remained standing in front of the King with their heads still covered, and said a few words in a low voice which nobody else was able to hear.

In ringing tones the King then ordered de la Ville-aux-Clercs to read the text of the marriage contract. It was a long and turgid document, but everyone was relieved to hear it at last, after all the interminable delays, the political complications, the differences of opinion over religious questions and the conflicting claims of France, England and Rome. When he had finished reading, de la Ville-aux-Clercs placed the document on the table, open at the last page, and presented a pen to Louis who signed in the large, thin, regular hand affected by all French monarchs right down to the Revolution. The Queen Mother was determined to sign too, if possible before her younger son, and the Queen, equally anxious not to be left out, added her signature alongside her husband's. This was considered quite unnecessary, a Queen being only a 'mean creature'. The Duc de Chevreuse then appeared in another grand procession, bringing the procuration in a rich casket, and taking the part of the fiancé at the engagement ceremony. When it was over he left the room, followed by the Ambassadors, but many people lingered hoping for a chance to congratulate the Princess. The crush was so great that many brocade dresses, specially made for the occasion, became crumpled and spoilt.

The days before the wedding were marred by a controversy which had developed between Cardinal de la Rochefoucauld, the Grand Almoner, and the Archbishop of Paris who thought he had a right to perform the wedding ceremonies as they were to take place in his church. The Archbishop summoned all the prelates in the city and a humble remonstrance was sent to the King pointing out that it was the Cardinal's duty to stay by the monarch's side. Louis remained immune to this argument and conferred the honour on his Almoner, causing the Archbishop to retire to the country in a temper. There were also countless controversies about precedence, and the Princesses of the Blood were up in arms because they were expected to share a bench with ladies of lesser importance. The Dean and a number of other clergy had decided not to appear at all out of sympathy for the absent Archbishop.

At three o'clock on the morning of Sunday, May 11, the captain of the guard with his archers went to Notre-Dame and placed his men in position, guarding the platform which had been set up at the great west door under an awning of cloth of gold. The awning had been intended to shade the participants from the sun, but as it transpired it served a different purpose for the rain never stopped all day. At six o'clock more guards appeared and the stands were soon full of people. Large crowds lined the streets and stood patiently waiting in the rain, watching the coaches of the Ambassadors arriving and the Rector of the University, the President of the Parlement, the Mayor of Paris and many other dignitaries in magnificent robes and furred cloaks.

At two o'clock Henriette left the Louvre and went to the Archbishop's palace. She had spent the day before praying and meditating at the house of the Carmelites. By the time Louis arrived she was already dressed; he had left the Louvre at five o'clock accompanied by a hundred Swiss Guards and ten archers. The Queen came in another coach with the Princesses of the Blood. When everyone had arrived the procession formed up and they all stepped out of a window onto a specially constructed gallery which sloped down to the platform outside the church. The Swiss Guards were lined up on either side of the gallery with standards unfurled; and, as the procession came into view at the door of the church, it was greeted by a resounding fanfare from the King's drums, trumpets and oboes. The heralds came first with members of the nobility four deep and followed by Holland and Carlisle, who had arrived in velvet-lined coaches emblazoned with their own arms and drawn by eight horses. The Ambassadors were dressed in silver cloaks and hats which were decorated with quantities of diamonds, their footmen wearing short jackets à l'anglaise. Henriette followed the proxy bridegroom, de Chevreuse, with the King and Gaston. She was wearing the royal cloak of tan-coloured velvet embroidered with fleurs de lys and lined with ermine; her crown was encrusted with diamonds and from it hung a large pear-shaped pearl of immense value. The Princesses de Conti and de Condé with the Comtesse de Soissons had been allotted the doubtful honour of carrying the train, which proved to be so heavy that they had commandeered one of the Conti gentlemen-in-waiting to walk underneath it and take some of the weight on his head. In the circumstances the Comte de Soissons had been excused attending the ceremony and had retired to the country to nurse his disappointed hopes in solitude.

The Cardinal de la Rochefoucauld stood waiting on the dais and a short ceremony was performed. Afterwards the English Ambassadors fell on their knees before their new Queen, and Colonel Sir George Goring, who had been standing nearby, mounted and rode off at a gallop, his task to tell King Charles that he was now a married man. The main party then moved into the church, the Ambassadors staying outside with the Duc de Chevreuse, who had become a Protestant for the afternoon.

When everyone was settled in the chancel, the heralds threw down pieces of silver from high in the scaffolding. Each coin had the heads of Charles and his Queen on one side and on the reverse a cupid scattering lilies. After the Mass, the Ambassadors and de Chevreuse came to the door of the chancel and led the Queen to the Archbishop's palace for the wedding feast. The best royal dinner service had been laid out ready and the room was decorated with the King's tapestries and a large number of chandeliers. The Queen Mother presented the napkin to the King who refused it three times before washing. He was sitting in the middle of a long table under a canopy next to his sister who was still wearing her crown and cloak. Every course arrived in procession headed by the Grand Prior followed by all the *maîtres d'hôtel* and finally the servants bearing the food. There was an abundance of everything, but nobody ate very much. Afterwards, at about eleven o'clock, the royal party returned to the Louvre, where they promptly ordered supper.

The celebrations and excitements continued for several days. Fireworks went up from a boat in the middle of the Seine and from almost every street in Paris. A number of cannons had been brought and set up along the quay below the gallery of the palace and these added their noise to the proceedings. It was all rather too much for Louis who retired to bed and was unable to partake of the superb collation of *confitures* in the great gallery at the Luxembourg palace which was graced by the three Queens. The palace had been lavishly decorated and the guests were entertained with a programme of songs and instrumental music, while outside in the gardens a firework display was mounted, the most spectacular that anyone had seen in Paris for years.

Marie de Medici was glad of an excuse to show off her palace, where the walls were adorned with the Rubens cycle of pictures depicting the highlights of her life. But the main centre of attraction was the Duke of Buckingham who had arrived in Paris rather unexpectedly. When he had intended to come as proxy bridegroom he had ordered a trousseau of twenty embroidered suits, and liveries for an army of attendants including sky-blue outfits embroidered with anchors for his twenty-two watermen. As it was, his clothes were already the talk of the town. The ladies of the Court were transfixed by his startling good looks—his curled moustache and his opulent hair, his strange dark eyes, his pointed Spanish beard and his graceful physique. It was said that the pearls on his tunic were attached with such calculated carelessness that they fell off in dozens every time he moved, and when they were swept up and handed to him, he looked at them with indifference and refused to take them back. The men of the Court were less impressed than the ladies. Rubens commented unfavourably on the Duke's 'caprice and arrogance'. The King and his ministers found it hard to hide their pleasure in being able to snub such a pretentious visitor. To his disappointment, Buckingham found that he could extract nothing more from the sphinx-like Richelieu than a promise to continue financial aid to Mansfeld's army at least for a while, and to send a messenger to the Huguenots offering to enter into peace negotiations.

Richelieu was unlikely to give Buckingham too much encouragement owing to the presence in Paris of Cardinal Francesco Barberini, Pope Urban's twenty-seven-year-old nephew. His official mission was to hand over the dispensation and he had appeared on the left bank riding a white colt in traditional imitation of Christ entering Jerusalem. Pious women crowded round him eager to kiss his toe, but his un-Christlike scarlet robes had provoked a demonstration staged by the students of the Sorbonne who were suspicious of papal intervention. Gaston was thrown from his horse as he went to meet the legate, and the students made off with the white colt, leaving Barberini to retreat ignominiously into Notre-Dame.

Charles hoped that at least Buckingham would be able to hasten the departure of his Queen whom he was naturally anxious to meet. 'I find the delay in her journey too insupportable to bear,' he wrote to Louis, adding that her arrival was 'a pre-occupation only to be understood by those who have fixed their desires upon things at once the most perfect and the most dear'. Henriette's trousseau was taking time to assemble; she had a dozen dresses fantastically worked, one with gold and silver embroidery on a background of black, another in grey satin, another in white with a long train, and the great royal robe in violet velvet embroidered with fleurs de lys and edged with arabesques. Four dozen nightdresses, a dozen nightcaps, five dozen handkerchiefs and three dozen face-cloths went into her luggage, as well as the great bed with yards of red velvet embroidered with silver, Turkey carpets, a dressing table, a large silver mirror, perfume pans, vinegar jugs and sugar basins. There were four sets of plate for celebrating the Mass, with crucifix, chandeliers, chasubles, stoles and altar furnishings.

The new Queen's train included laundresses and linen-maids, her chamberlain and secretary, gentlemen ushers and pages—all fitted out with crimson tunics and plumed hats—not to mention the *officiers ecclésiastiques*, the Grand Almoner, the *confesseur ordinaire*, the chaplain, the clerk of the chapel, the priest of the oratory. This was a list calculated to raise the blood pressure of any English Puritan.

When the baggage train was finally loaded and Louis was well enough to travel, the procession set off for Compiègne. Henriette was carried in a red velvet litter and was escorted by the city archers, the militia, the guilds and the trumpeters. After staying for two days at Compiègne the King left for Fontainebleau and the rest of the party went on to Amiens, where the Queen Mother fell ill and caused a further delay. Charles began to send urgent messages; Parliament had already been convened and he would be unable to leave London once it had assembled. Wild rumours were beginning to circulate in England about the cause of the delay; some said that the Papal Legate had imposed a fifteen days' penance on the Queen for marrying before the dispensation was delivered. Buckingham was urging the Queen Mother to rise from her bed, much to the annoyance of de la Ville-aux-Clercs who thought it quite wrong that she should be expected to jeopardize her health, even her life, for the sake of the English and their Parliament. His advice, which she took, was to remain at Amiens with Queen Anne, and to allow her daughter to proceed, accompanied by Gaston.

The parting took place on June 16, a little way out of Amiens. Some reports said that Buckingham was weeping openly as he took his leave of Anne. Henriette on the other hand apparently displayed little emotion. She went on her way full of confidence, still surrounded by her countrymen and by her beloved Mamie de Saint-Georges. Marie de Medici presented her, before she left, with a lengthy letter written with more than a little help from Father Bérulle. It contained detailed instructions as to how she was to behave towards her husband, his subjects, her retainers and towards God. Morning and evening in her chapel she was to remember that without God she would be nothing, and that she had been placed in the world to do a great and glorious task, giving thanks daily that she had been born a Christian and a Catholic. She must remember that she had been sent into a foreign country expressly to help the Catholics who had suffered for so long. After God and religion her first duty was to her husband—she was, it is a comfort to note, to love him as such, and to honour him as a king, while praying each day for his conversion. She was to care for her husband's subjects, since she was bound inextricably to them by marriage, and to foster good relations between England and France. Excellent advice was offered to her concerning the care of her servants; she was to treat them all equally, without favouritism, except where merit demanded special recognition. As for herself, she was to be an example of honour, virtue and modesty, and she would have to use great discretion in view of the liberty which the English way of life afforded to women—a liberty which was as pronounced in England as restraint was in other countries. 'Adieu, *ma fille*, I leave you, and deliver you into the care of God and his angels.'

As soon as Charles heard that his wife had left Amiens, he despatched part of his fleet to fetch her. Naval captains, busy provisioning their ships for other voyages, were told to put aside their plans and to devote themselves to the task of 'wafting over the Queen'. Several ladies arrived at Boulogne to kiss Henriette's hand on the King's behalf; they included Buckingham's mother, his sister, the Countess of Denbigh and his niece, the Marchioness of Hamilton. In the French contingent, there was much talk of the Duke's behaviour with Queen Anne; it seemed that he had been somewhat indiscreet behind a hedge in a moonlit garden at Amiens and had paid a final visit to the royal bedroom, falling on his knees before the Queen and covering the counterpane with kisses.

The English were surprised to find their new Queen more mature and taller than they had expected. She seemed self-assured, and ready to talk vivaciously in her native tongue to anyone who cared to listen. Sir Toby Matthew, a recent convert to the Catholic faith, thought her 'a most sweet, lovely creature', full of wit, and sitting already on 'the very skirts of womanhood'. Seeing the sea for the first time, she went out on to the sandy shore to stare at the waves and was so lost in wonder that she let a particularly big breaker kiss her feet—as a naval observer euphemistically put it.

The weather worsened soon after Henriette's arrival at the coast, but on the first day that dawned fair she embarked and set sail with twenty ships in attendance. The sea was still very rough and the crossing took twenty-eight hours, but she finally arrived off Dover at about seven o'clock in the evening of Trinity Sunday—June 23 according to the French calendar, and June 13 in the old style still used by the English. It was a wet and dreary evening and few people had turned out to greet the fifteen-year-old Queen. She was carried in a chair up to the grim fortress of Dover Castle which had hastily been provided with some royal furniture. After supper she went straight to bed, leaving her retinue to explore the town. The French were already complaining of the inadequate welcome afforded to a daughter of France, and it had come as something of a shock to Henriette to find herself lodged in such mournful apartments and to be expected to sleep in a bed which in France would not have been considered fit for the servants. This was not the England that Holland and Carlisle, with their glowing descriptions of their native land, had talked about.

Next morning the King arrived when Henriette was only half-way through her breakfast. She went down into the hall at once and saw him standing there with only a few attendants, a small, neat figure, wearing the pointed Spanish beard which both he and Buckingham had affected since their trip to Madrid. He met her at the foot of the stairs, and she fell on her knees in front of him, trying to kiss his hand, and showing signs of emotion at last. Charles was reticent and seemed embarrassed by her tears; he tried to lift her to her feet, telling her that he had been in great distress, fearing for her safety at sea. After he had embraced her, Henriette saw her husband glance down at her feet, and she assured him that she was not wearing high-heeled shoes. 'I have no helps by art,' she told him.

The couple retired for half an hour's private conversation, and when they emerged Henriette introduced all her servants 'by quality and name in order'. That day at dinner the King carved venison and pheasant and the Queen ate a large helping although her confessor, who stayed close by her side, warned her severely that it was a fast day, the eve of St John the

Baptist. The next morning the King and Queen set out for Canterbury, having already experienced the first quarrel of their married life. Although Henriette's first words to her husband had been 'I have come into this country of your Majesty's to be used and commanded by you', it seemed that she had quickly forgotten her good intentions. In France the royal ladies always expected to be accompanied by one of their attendants and Mamie had automatically entered the coach and sat down beside her mistress. Charles considered this presumptuous and had planned to seat his wife between Buckingham's mother and sister, but his diminutive Queen flew into a rage at once, and her retainers supported her, pointing out that she was bewildered and far from home. When the difficulty was finally sorted out, the party proceeded to Canterbury, where the Queen retired to bed early. She was later joined by the King, who bolted all the doors of the room—there were seven of them—and afterwards locked out the only two gentlemen of the bedchamber who had been allowed to supervise the undressing ceremony. 'The next morning,' it was reported, 'he lay till seven of the clock, and was pleasant with the Lords that had beguiled them, and hath ever since been very jocund.'

At Canterbury there was another wedding ceremony, and after a day's stay the royal party set off for London, accompanied by the entire court and the staff of the Chapel Royal with its vestments, books and ornaments.

The road to Gravesend was lined with people, and first impressions of the Queen were favourable. She had asked the King not to be angry with her 'for her faults of ignorance before he had first instructed her to eschew them', and she now looked happier. 'She is nimble and quiet,' ran one report, 'black-eyed, brown-haired, and, in a word, a brave lady, though perhaps a little touched with the green sickness.' James Howell, who first saw her at the Bowling Green on Barham Downs with her ladies, considered that she far outshone the long-wooed Infanta, who had fading flaxen hair, was big-lipped and heavy-eyed. By contrast, he thought, 'this youngest branch of Bourbon . . . is of a more lovely and lasting complexion, a dark brown; she hath eyes that sparkle like stars, and for her physiognomy she may be said to be a mirror of perfection'. Her ladies, drawn up in two rows, seemed to Howell to shine like constellations.

At Gravesend the King and Queen embarked on a barge of state. The fleet was lying in order on both sides of the river and a volley of fifteen hundred great shot greeted the Queen's appearance. As the barge went up-river it was joined by hundreds of small craft which made a fine show as they passed under London Bridge. There was such a peal of cannon from the Tower that the Queen had 'never before heard the like'. The banks were lined with people, and more had packed into houses, ships and lighters along the route. Although there was a heavy shower as the royal pair reached Westminster, the windows of their barge were left open so that they could be more easily seen. They were both dressed in green and the Queen was waving to the cheering crowds.

Henriette spent her first night at Somerset House, once the home of the King's mother, Anne of Denmark. Again the bed set aside for her use caused much dissatisfaction. It had belonged to Queen Elizabeth and the French had never seen anything so old-fashioned. Outside, the streets were full of bonfires and the bells went on ringing until midnight. The people of London were pleased with their new Queen. It was said that when someone had asked her whether she could abide Huguenots, she had replied, 'Why not? was not my father one?' She was pretty, vivacious, not so small as everyone had feared and perhaps, after all, not so irrevocably Catholic.

Chapter 6

QUEEN OF ENGLAND

IN NORMAL times the Queen would have entered the capital along a route decorated with triumphal arches, but all plans for a state entry had been abandoned despite the large crowds which poured into London hoping to see the new King and his bride. The City had looked magnificent enough to the French when they viewed it for the first time from the river, but on closer acquaintance this vast commercial centre turned out to be a maze of dark and putrid streets, a perfect breeding ground for the virulent sickness which was spreading rapidly from parish to parish. It was thought wiser for the Queen to spend her first days at Whitehall without appearing in public. At a ceremony held in the palace, she was formally declared Queen in the presence of the French Ambassador and a large gathering of the English nobility. At the same time her marriage was confirmed and declared to be lawfully and fully consummated. In the evening the King dined in public and afterwards there was a ball. The Queen danced well, never once losing the dignity that was to be expected of a monarch. During the next few days there was much feasting and jousting, and the dinner given by the de Chevreuses was almost as fine as the King's. The Duke of Buckingham as usual did his best to outdo everybody with the lavishness of his entertainment, and one participant at least began to feel that 'the excessive bravery on both sides breeds a surfeit'. Some people looked on with disapproval, believing that so much festivity was out of keeping when money was scarce and the plague continued to rage. Others, remembering another Catholic Queen of that name, expressed apprehension when the King called his wife Mary. For this reason many preferred to style her Queen Henrietta Maria.

On June 18 the Queen went with her husband to Parliament, and sat by his side on a stool during the opening ceremony. The French who accompanied her found the tense atmosphere of the English Parliament very dramatic. The newly elected Members had come hurrying up to London in spite of the danger of infection and had been vying with each other for seats in the crowded Upper House. They were all anxious to see the new King of whom so much was expected, and to hear what effect his marriage would have on the Catholics of the realm. 'Love and ambition gave them wings,' wrote one of the Members, Sir John Eliot, adding, 'he that was first seemed happiest.'

The proceedings began with a solemn procession of peers headed by the Earl Marshal, the Lord Chamberlain and the Lord Treasurer, each carrying the gold or white staff of his office, and the prelates and officers of the Household. Rather to everyone's surprise, as the coronation had not yet taken place, Charles affected his crown and sceptre and wore a red velvet cloak lined with ermine. He seemed to be deliberately building up the concept of kingship as he took the crown and the royal sword from the officers of state, as well as a globe representing the supremacy which, as one Frenchman put it, the English liked to think they possessed on the high seas. When this ceremony was finished, Charles asked one of the Bishops to say prayers, having already given an order for the doors to be shut, leaving no escape route for the French, 'some whereof kneeled down, some stood upright, and one did nothing but cross himself'.

The King made a short speech, which was a relief to Members who had grown tired of the 'long, rambling quaint orations' of the late monarch. He reassured them by his recognition of their anxieties in matters of religion, and they were not too disturbed by references to the military undertakings set on foot by his father which he trusted the Commons would give him the means to continue.

On the first day of the session there was much applause for the King's policies, but it was not long before Parliament began to 'mutter' about religion. The Queen and her household did nothing to allay the widespread fear that the King had entered into an agreement to free English Catholics from all restraint. There were rumours that the Court was pullulating with priests, twenty-nine of them, who were walking about openly in their habits and frequenting the Queen's private chamber. She herself went to Mass every morning, communicated frequently and travelled down to Somerset House on festival days for vespers and a sermon. On one occasion she had been seen coming out of her bedchamber in her petticoat, leaning on the arm of her Lord Chamberlain, the Comte de Tillières, followed by six ladies who all went in to Mass. The priests complained persistently about the King's failure to provide his wife with a chapel, and Charles was said to have told them that if her closet was not large enough, they could try the Great Chamber, 'and if the Great Chamber were not wide enough, they might use the garden; and if the garden would not serve their turn, then was the park the fittest place'.

It was impossible for Charles to be honest either with his wife or with his Parliament. On one side the French were watching him closely to see whether he would carry out promises made to their King, while on the other the English were pressing him to impose the very penalties which should have been relaxed as a result of his marriage. Fortunately, at present, the English seemed ready to overlook his faults—the remoteness that went with dignity, the inhumanity sometimes a concomitant of virtue, and the stubbornness for which he had been notorious in child-hood and which now remained like *une sombre obstination*, as Maurois has put it with Gallic succinctness. It was not only the terseness of his opening speech in Parliament which made men reflect that he was preferable to his father. He was orderly—'order being indeed the very soul of outward things', in the words of Sir Benjamin Rudyerd speaking in the House. He was also admirably punctilious in his religion. The old King had provided a repulsive spectacle for anyone who cared to view him, senile, half-crippled, drooling, surrounded by 'fools and bawds, mimics and catamites'. By contrast Charles was dignified, temperate and chaste. Within a few weeks of his father's death he had begun to make great changes at Court. It seemed that there would be a return to the more systematic and formal regime of Elizabethan times with everybody taking their place according to rank. From now on the only way to gain access to the royal presence would be by way of the public rooms on set days of the week. Even the nobility and members of the Privy Council must await their summons and nobody would be allowed to enter by the backstairs or through private doors.

In all this there was only a single flaw. Though the King had made it clear that he wished to remain aloof from the majority, there was one man who slept in a room next to his own, and who had in his keeping the golden key which could open any door to the King's favour. The King seemed mesmerized by the hypnotic charm of the favourite he had inherited from his father. All his schemes to regularize the Household were in a sense cancelled out by the fact that he had received the Duke into 'an admired intimacy and dearness'. Although still not much over thirty, Buckingham had worked himself into a position of unprecedented power, surrounding himself with a regular army of relations, servants and hangers-on. The only threat to his extraordinary dominance over the King came from the Queen who was showing an alarming tendency to charm her husband. Buckingham, unrivalled and at the height of his power, was not prepared to accept a threat from this fifteen-year-old girl. To neutralize her influence, he was determined to surround her with his own female relations and to make all the trouble he could for her French entourage. This was not difficult, since there was already universal disapproval for her priests, and Madame de Saint-Georges was despised for her lack of breeding. 'The Queen's train, poor pitiful women, not worth looking after. The Duchess of Chevreuse fair, but paints foully,' ran one disparaging comment. The expense of feeding and housing so many foreigners was not appreciated at a time when money was scarce and the King's debts so many that 'one man's arithmetic could not number them'.

Since nobody had taken the trouble to teach the Queen even a few words of English, she sometimes appeared to be sullen and unforthcoming except with her own attendants. Few people made any attempt to converse with her in her own tongue, with the exception of Bishop Williams who for the past three months had kept a French servant continually at his elbow, in an attempt to make himself expert in that 'quaint and voluble language'. He delighted the Queen and her train by making a speech in French when he introduced his fellow Bishops. As a result the French greatly preferred him to the overbearing Buckingham, with whom de la Ville-aux-Clercs had found himself *en froideur* from the start.

Many Englishmen also disliked the favourite and held him responsible for the quixotic schemes which were gradually emerging. While ready to applaud the King and to acknowledge what seemed to be 'the innate sweetness of his nature', they felt uneasy about certain aspects of the new reign and about the policies so lightly sketched in by the King and his spokesman at the opening of Parliament. Already there were signs that Buckingham was callow in his diplomatic dealings, proud when it came to accepting advice, always convinced that any scheme must be worth pursuing and would be bound to succeed because his own brilliant mind had formulated it. His intention of establishing Britain as the greatest European power was conceived with a total disregard for the empty Exchequer. His schemes were apparently to be financed from the proceeds of the Spanish treasure fleet, which he had already captured in his mind's eye with an embryonic navy he had at present no hope of paying for, from an enemy on whom he had not yet declared war. None of the King's advisers had an exact brief to give the Commons a realistic estimate of the cost of his aggressive policies. The Lord Keeper, Bishop Williams, told members of his House that Charles had embarked on an undertaking 'whereby Europe would be stirred as the Pool of Bethesda by the angel', and bluntly added that the maintenance of Mansfeld's army and the fitting out of the navy had already used up money voted by the last Parliament of James's reign. It was now the duty of Members to give the King whatever money he needed to fulfil the plans forged in his father's time. Members were anxious for a sum to be settled at once as most of them would have left for the country weeks before if the opening of Parliament had not been postponed until after the Queen's arrival. They quickly voted two subsidies amounting to £140,000, a fraction of what was needed, and by the end of the first week in July no more than sixty Members were left in the capital.

Everyone who could fled to the country as quickly as possible. Those who had to remain made sure that all correspondence was fumigated and that coins were disinfected in tubs of water. Lord Keeper Williams, who was in the habit of dining at Westminster School, decamped hastily when one of the King's scholars became a victim. Lord Russell had the unpleasant experience of seeing his shoemaker fall dead at his feet just as he was pulling his shoes on. There was great concern in the Household when the King's baker died, and all the bread he had baked that day was given away to anyone prepared to accept such a lethal gift. Hasty preparations were made to remove to Hampton Court, and arrangements were put in hand to accommodate the French Ambassadors at Richmond.

It was not long before the plague began to spread to the country and soon it was rife in the Kingston area. The King sent a message from Oatlands, his Surrey palace, where he had gone for a few days' hunting, to tell his wife that she must move again, this time to Windsor. Just as she was leaving, the King arrived, if only to ensure that the Marchioness of Hamilton should take Mamie's place in the coach. De Tillières described how he came down the steps at Hampton Court with the Queen on his arm, and saw *le Buckingham* standing there with the King, asserting his authority as usual and talking very loudly, as Englishmen tend to do in the presence of foreigners.

The Court had not been at Windsor very long when sickness broke out among the priests, who were banished at once and told to stay in isolation in one of the tower rooms at Hampton Court. When a member of the King's guard fell ill and died it was decided that yet another move was necessary. The King went to Oatlands and the Queen to Nonesuch, where Charles visited her from time to time. The French noticed that whenever he came to see her he had some complaint, prompted, they were sure, by Buckingham and Carlisle. They found it sad to see the twenty-four-year-old King under the spell of these evil men. They urged the Queen to assert herself, and when a deputation arrived from the Privy Council to instruct her about the regulations to be observed in her household, she said tartly, 'I hope I shall have leave to order my house as I list myself.' Charles reprimanded her in private for this reply, but her answer was so rude that he did not care to repeat it, even to her mother. A side to her character was appearing which the English did not much care for. A Mr Mordant recorded that the Queen was pleasing to look at—but only if she was pleased. He had observed her expression when too many people had crowded into an overheated room at dinner. 'I suppose none but a Queen could have cast such a scowl,' was how he put it. On one occasion she went so far as to speak to her husband on the question of the Catholics, 'with what result is not known,' wrote Amerigo Salvetti, who represented the Grand Duke of Tuscany at the English court, 'except to cause upon his part some ill humour with the Duke of Buckingham who as usual governs everything'.

The French Ambassadors had spent much of their time in England lodging complaints about the treatment of Catholics, and the King had given them nothing but evasive answers. However, when the time came for d'Effiat, de la Ville-aux-Clercs and de Chevreuse to return to France he agreed to allow some released Catholic prisoners to go with them. It seemed obvious to Salvetti that the sooner these people returned to France the better the English would be pleased, especially as 'this French troop' had been costing the King over two hundred pounds a day. The financial situation had become acute; it was difficult to acquire even everyday provisions, and Buckingham was convinced that the King would have to demand another grant from Parliament. Experienced Members, who understood the temper of the House, advised him against it. They believed that it was unwise to press for funds to equip a fleet when nobody knew who the enemy was. 'The din of preparation is heard, but where is the thunderbolt to fall?' Salvetti enquired. Since the majority of Members had 'slunk home' and the rest were anxious to be gone, it would look like a political ruse to persuade those who remained to shoulder the responsibility for a further grant. With characteristic good sense Lord Keeper Williams advised the King against a move which would create bad feeling so early in the reign. He favoured an adjournment until Christmas, by which time the memory of the first grant would have faded and war plans would have had a chance to mature.

Buckingham's counsels prevailed and on July 11 both Houses were informed that Parliament would be adjourned to meet again almost immediately at Oxford. The King promised that he would then deal with the petition he had received concerning the execution of the penal laws against 'the wicked generation of Jesuits, seminary priests, and incendiaries, ever lying in wait to blow the coals of contention'. Almost simultaneously he issued pardons for the priests who were to return to France with the Ambassadors.

Towards the end of July the Court set off for Woodstock. At Oxford, Masters, Fellows and undergraduates had all been ordered to leave the town to make way for the Members of Parliament, who congregated on August 1 in the Divinity School for the first session. The mood of the House was not benign. Many Members had been forced to leave home almost as soon as they arrived, travelling long distances and risking infection at the inns along their way. During their brief stay in the provinces some had seen pardons, issued under the Great Seal, for Jesuit priests.

Members had another cause for complaint. During their absence the King had appointed as his chaplain Richard Montague, an Anglican clergyman whose views, in the opinion of the House, veered dangerously in the direction of Rome. He had made his name with a work entitled

New Gag for an Old Goose which had originally been written to counter the Catholic treatise *A Gag for the New Gospel*. Many Members, however, thought that his views seemed more Catholic than Protestant. His doctrine embraced an assertion of the divine right inherent in monarchy, and advocated confession and absolution, the doctrine of the real presence, the use of images, the sign of the cross and the efficacy of the saints. The Puritans he described as a faction, their divines 'bible-bearing and hypocritical'. Good Protestants, of whom there were many in Parliament, found such theories unacceptable. Montague was brought to the bar of the House where he received censure and was committed to the custody of the Serjeant. But Charles's favourite prelate, the small, austere Bishop of St David's, William Laud, had different ideas. On his list of clerics he had marked Montague with an approving 'O' for orthodox, and acting with Buckingham's sanction he had described Montague's theories as 'the settled doctrine of the church'. By appointing Montague his chaplain, the King had set the seal of respectability on Arminianism, the near-Romish doctrine which some saw as a serious threat to Calvinism on the Continent. Although the King released Montague from custody, Members agreed that he was not free of the bond imposed by the House and demanded that he should be brought to the bar of the House again. He pleaded sickness and said he was too weak to travel.

The first two days of August were spent discussing the growing menace of Catholicism—'this dangerous disease'—and the question of Montague's appointment. The third day Members kept as a fast in view of the dangers which surrounded them. On August 4 the King went into Oxford from Woodstock and summoned the House to the old hall at Christ Church. He spoke briefly, almost curtly, mentioning the necessity of fitting out the fleet and putting it on the high seas, but he made no attempt to come out with any honest assessment of his overall needs. Sir John Coke, Buckingham's mouthpiece, tried in a measured speech to give good reasons for the shortage of funds. But his talents lay in the field of administration rather than in oratory and he could not stand up to the eloquence of opposing speakers. The temperature of the House continued to rise and complaints multiplied. Not only had the King extended his protection to an Anglican whose opinions sailed dangerously close to popery, he had given hope to Catholics in general by reversing judgments of the local magistrates, thus making them more 'proud and insolent' than ever. His marriage treaty caused disquiet on account of the 'invisible' clauses which most certainly existed. The raising of the fleet—'so unnecessary a preparation and expense'—had been undertaken without any kind of consultation, as had the French alliance and the expedition to the Palatinate. Since this was so, responsibility for the success or failure of any enterprise must rest with those who planned the action. No names were mentioned but many veiled references pointed to Buckingham. As one powerful speech followed another, the King and his supporters grew uneasy. Criticism of their competency was 'no good music in their ears'. Gradually they realized that the House would not contemplate voting further supplies unless it could be given more share in the management of affairs, and unless the King agreed to put the penal laws into operation. Not that Buckingham despaired. On Sunday, August 7, he gathered round him a selection of what were variously described as his privadoes, creatures and parasites, and between them they framed an answer to the petition requesting that all necessary measures should be taken to suppress the spread of popery. The Commons, summoned to Christ Church the following morning, were amazed to find that all their requests had been granted. Buckingham then went on to suggest that in return enough money should be voted to cover the cost of Mansfeld's army, various subsidies to European powers and the fitting out of ships. 'Make my master chief of this war,' he told them, asking, 'What is it for his allies to scratch with the King of Spain, to win a battle today and lose one on the morrow, and to get or lose a town by snatches?' This sudden *volte-face* did not, however, bring Buckingham the support he had expected. Members were sure he was breaking promises made to the French and this only confirmed the general opinion that he was not a man to be trusted.

When the news of Buckingham's speech reached Woodstock the French were outraged. Everything secretly promised to their King had been jettisoned and it seemed that the agreement signed at Cambridge after so many months of deliberation had been no more than a scrap of paper to be torn up at the first convenient moment. Not content with enforcing existing laws against the Catholics, the perfidious Buckingham had even gone so far as to suggest new ones. Carlisle, exercising what Richelieu described as 'that spirit of falsehood which never left him', commented openly that the French and his ministers had in any case only put their signature to the secret articles in order to pacify the Pope. Bérulle, who was about to leave for France, said he would have a thing or two to report to his King, but Buckingham asked him not to put a worse colour than necessary on what was unavoidable. 'If you mean,' said Bérulle, 'to put the laws into execution, I neither can nor will endure it, whatever sauce you may be pleased to add.'

The disgust felt by the French at Woodstock was shared by Members of Parliament. It seemed preposterous the way the Duke had set himself up as the King's spokesman, standing there exuding self-confidence, arrogant and unbending as if he were the King and the government all rolled into one. His presumption knew no bounds. Reminding Members that the plague was still spreading and that nobody wanted to wait about for decisions, he demanded an immediate answer to his call for funds.

Buckingham's behaviour prompted Sir John Eliot, in a fine speech, to look back with nostalgia to the time of Cecil and Somerset, to statesmen bred by Queen Elizabeth, to the days when Crown debts were not excessive, when trade flourished, pensions were few, laws were executed, papists restrained and punished. In those days the council table had still held its ancient dignity, and no one man could gain transcendent power. There was something unhealthy in the present state of affairs which could not be cured until the King was prepared to redress the wrongs to be put before him in a formal remonstrance.

The King and his favourite tried to defend their actions by declaring that no step had been taken without the approval of the Council, but Sir Robert Mansel, one of its members, revealed that he for one had opposed Buckingham's scheme, and had never been consulted. To add to the Duke's discomfiture news came from the west of England that Turkish privateers had been marauding along the coast. The ships that might have beaten them off proved too leaky for the task, and their crews were sick, lacking clothes, and vinegar to wash between the decks. The pirates had captured eight hundred Englishmen only eight leagues from Penzance, which led people to wonder whether the Duke might not be better defending his own shores than fabricating schemes for foreign conquest. Sir Edward Seymour now felt confident enough to mention the favourite by name. 'Let us lay the fault where it is,' he said. 'The Duke of Buckingham is trusted, and it must needs be either in him or his agents.' It was decided that a petition be drawn up pointing out to the King that in the opinion of the House it was not fit 'to repose the safety of the kingdom upon those that have not parts answerable to their places'.

Although it was late when the House rose, the King called his Council and told them that he would not countenance any further debates. Parliament was aiming at a transference of sovereignty; as a King ruling by divine right he could not sit by while the power was snatched from his hands. The next day the House met and went into committee to prepare its protest, with Black Rod already knocking at the door. Only when the Remonstrance had been drawn up, put to the vote and sent to the King, was Black Rod admitted to summon the Commons to the Upper House for the dissolution. This bitter and dramatic scene provided a sad finish to the session which had begun in such a spirit of enthusiasm. Many doubts remained in Members' minds as they set off for their homes the second time that summer. The Catholics too felt disheartened, fearing that their future looked darker now than before the King's marriage.

After the dissolution of August 14 the Privy Council met at Woodstock. A decision was taken to raise a forced loan, a method usually resorted to only at times of grave crisis. The present state of emergency seemed to many people too nebulous to justify such an unpopular step. A proclamation promising that the laws against popish priests would be put into execution did little to placate those men of 'known wealth and ability' who would be called upon to contribute anything from ten to thirty pounds, sums which, in the King's opinion, 'few would deny to a friend'.

Relations were rapidly deteriorating between the English and the French. In England the French marriage was viewed with growing disapproval, while across the Channel there was anger at the treatment being meted out to Catholics. Discord and uncertainty were making the everyday business of government almost impossible, and as yet nobody had managed to work out the details of the Queen's household. The plague had not abated although the infected people in the city had been sent out to live in tents and cabins in the fields. A return to London was out of the question and it was evident that the Court would be on the move for some time to come. The number of courtiers was reduced to make it easier to move from place to place.

When the Queen was installed at Titchfield on the Earl of Southampton's estate, the King stayed at Beaulieu and devoted his days to hunting in the New Forest. He visited his wife fairly frequently, sometimes staying overnight. His visits were not always a success and on one occasion, when she tried to plead illness as an excuse for not seeing him, he showed his resentment, telling her that Buckingham would have demanded his rights more frequently had the Queen been his wife. Since she was ill, he would have to wait for another opportunity to tackle the matter; the Queen replied that there was no time like the present. After this scene, the King did not visit Titchfield again, but Buckingham continued to plague her with his presence, delighting to lecture her about her behaviour. Unless she changed, he told her, she would no longer be treated as a Queen but as the silly little girl she was. As her confidential servant he strongly advised her to put her house in order. She replied with her usual coolness that she had not intended to do anything unworthy of a daughter of France; she was not aware of any fault on her side, and she certainly had no desire in the world to annoy her husband. However, if the King really was dissatisfied, there was nothing, in her opinion, to prevent him from telling her so himself.

Buckingham's sister, the Countess of Denbigh, had arranged for Protestant services to be held at Titchfield. The Queen one day entered the room when a sermon was in progress accompanied by a crowd of ladies and dogs, all of them uttering 'the loud cries usual in chasing hares'. The local clergyman was convinced that as he was sitting in his garden one afternoon innocently sunning himself, two Frenchmen fired some shots at him from a nearby orchard; he believed that they were having their revenge as he had complained to the King about the unwarranted interruption of his sermon. The Frenchmen maintained that they had gone out to shoot at little birds and not at off-duty ministers of the church. One of their arquebuses had gone off by mistake and in any case they could not possibly have taken aim as the garden was surrounded by bushes. De Tillières went so far as to examine the bench where the clergyman had been sitting; he compared the alleged shot-marks with the vicar's portly frame and decided that if the story were true the gentleman would most certainly be dead.

On September 15 the King went to Plymouth to review the army and inspect the fleet. It was hoped that his presence might hasten the departure of the expedition before the autumn gales began. The people of Plymouth felt that they were unable to bear the burden of billeting troops much longer. Many had already turned their unwelcome lodgers out into the streets. The soldiers arrived in rags, and no clothes awaited them in Plymouth, although it had originally been intended to issue every man with a 'great coat of military shape'. Many of the ships they were to sail in were old and leaky, with sails that had seen service in the time of Queen Elizabeth. Eight hundred casks of meat were unfit for consumption, and money due to be sent from London had never materialized. Adverse winds coupled with financial shortages combined to keep the fleet in port and after waiting for ten days the King lost patience and left for Salisbury, telling the Queen to join him there.

Early in October the leaky armada set out. After four days it was 'encountered with a furious storm'; the ships were scattered but the majority went back into Plymouth Sound where they lay in great disorder buffeted by high winds. Somewhat chastened by this experience, eighty ships, including ten royal galleons, set out again on October 8. Nobody knew exactly where they were heading, but it was said that they were taking the general direction of Spain. Within a few days Buckingham arrived at Salisbury. While retaining for himself the title of Generalissimo he had delegated to Sir Edward Cecil the onerous work and hardship of the expedition. Cecil had served with some distinction as a soldier in the Low Countries, but the Earl of Denbigh who was appointed Rear-Admiral had no qualifications either nautical or military—he was, however, married to Buckingham's sister.

The King had been forced to issue a special edict making legal tender the quarter-crown pieces in which some of the Queen's dowry had been paid. No money was coming in from any source, and it was likely that the fleet would have time to go to Spain and back before the sums levied by the forced loan could be wrested from unwilling lenders. Buckingham, who had been entrusted with the task of negotiating a treaty with Denmark, was intending to pawn the crown jewels in Holland on the way, but to lay his hands on these at short notice was not so easy as he had anticipated. He spent some days in London trying to extract them from the custody of Lord Brooke, who was 'a prisoner to age and indisposition of body' and who also felt, like many others, that the decision to remove the jewels should not be taken without the sanction of the Council.

When Buckingham was still in London he received a message recalling him to Salisbury for a meeting with Blainville, the new French Ambassador. His embassy was officially to smooth over the differences which had arisen between the French and English courts, but Buckingham was warned that he had really come 'to frame cabals and factions, whereunto he is esteemed very proper, being characterized with the marks of a most subtile, prying, penetrating and dangerous man'. The French who were already in England did not feel that they could expect much satisfaction from Blainville's visit which in any case had come too late to do any good. The relationship between the King and Queen was more strained than ever, the English were in a sour mood and the French were 'full to the throat with disgust'. Blainville began badly by demanding concessions for the Catholics without first dangling the bait of military aid. The King replied that he had only promised to help the Catholics if they behaved with moderation. Since he had been receiving information about 'the bold and impudent speeches used by so many Romish Catholics . . . through the instigation of Jesuited priests . . . to raise stirs and tumults', he had given order that all recusants should at once be divested of any arms they might possess.

After a brief interview with Blainville, Buckingham took leave of his Duchess and set off for Holland with his two nephews; their expenses at Ipswich alone came to three hundred and seventy pounds. At Harwich six large and well-armed merchant ships stood ready to protect them from the Dunkirk privateers, but it had not been easy to find any craft not in the vicinity of Spain. The Duke had brought some of his own jewels to add to the rather meagre royal collection, in the hopes of extracting some much-needed money from the merchants of Amsterdam. In Denmark he blandly agreed that King Christian should be paid subsidies of thirty thousand pounds as a reward for entering into a treaty.

At Salisbury the situation deteriorated after the Duke's departure. The King complained continually about what he described as 'the maliciousness of the monsieurs'. He would have liked to 'cashier' the whole contingent, and only held back for fear of offending the Queen Mother. It was rumoured that forty of the Queen's retainers were to be sent back to France in the hope that the remainder would feel so ill at ease that they would 'make themselves suitors to be gone'. The French were certainly becoming more discontented every day; they were appalled by rumours that Buckingham's female relations were to be given all the appointments in the Queen's Household, imagining them whispering in her ear 'how dear she would be to the King her husband, how plausible and powerful among the people, how beloved of all, if she would change her religion'. In particular they suspected that there was an English plot to 'disnestle' Madame de Saint-Georges—it was their opinion that 'the world was come to a bad pass, if reason of state descended so low as her'.

The dismissal of Lord Keeper Williams caused further disquiet among the French. They had always trusted him and he had made many friends in the Queen's entourage. But the Bishop had aroused 'the causeless displeasure' of the Duke. It was true that he had advised the King to rule through his Council, but in doing so he had meant him to imitate Kings who 'intended not to turn Dukes of Venice, but (as they proved indeed) great and mighty monarchs at home and abroad'. The old King had charged the Duke and the Bishop 'to unite and work friendly for his service', but in the new reign Williams had found himself cold-shouldered in committee and kept out of the inner counsels. This, in the opinion of Archbishop Abbott, was typical of Buckingham's behaviour, for 'so my young Lord changed his friends as men do flowers—he liked a scent no longer than it was fresh'. Bishop Laud, seeing 'no man in the prospect of likelihood but this one, to carry the highest mitre from him', was also working for the Lord Keeper's downfall. It was useless for Williams to plead; the Duke had obtained an 'irrevocable sentence' before leaving for Holland. Williams was summoned to Salisbury and at a post-prandial interview he was told that he must deliver up his Seal. Williams made various requests, did what he could to salvage some financial benefits, and the King, 'with a sweet countenance, gave him his hand to kiss with a gracious valediction'.

After signing the treaty with Denmark at The Hague, Buckingham intended to continue his triumphal progress into France. News was received in England that new horses and liveries would be sent ahead for him, but his plans met with a check when the French Ambassador told him frankly that he would not be welcome. Friends in Paris wrote to warn him of possible dangers, and it was a fact that Louis felt a great repugnance for *cet anglois*—he certainly had no intention of allowing him near the Queen.

In England there was still an unsettled air about the court. The plague had not shown any sign of abating and the city of London was now so deserted that grass had begun to grow in the streets, while the value of property in the country continued to rise. As John Taylor, the water-poet, put it:

A Country Cottage, that but lately went
At four marks, or at three pounds yearly rent,
A Citizen, whose meer necessity
Doth force him now into the country fly,
Is glad to hire two chambers of a carter,
And pray and pay five pounds a quarter.

The disease was still raging at Windsor, but Hampton Court was considered relatively safe, and early in December the Queen celebrated her birthday there. For the first time since her marriage there was something of a festive atmosphere at court, and the King began to hope that his wife was mellowing. 'My wife begins to mend her manners,' he told Buckingham. When it was finally decided that the long-awaited return to Whitehall could take place immediately after Christmas, the Queen and her ladies made plans to present a pastoral at Somerset House. The Queen was cast in a principal speaking role, a prospect which the King viewed with some apprehension. His mother had danced in several masques and nobody had objected, but he feared that there might well be criticism if his wife held forth on the stage like any common player. Buckingham, however, was urging caution and had even advised the King to employ 'kind usages' in his treatment of the Queen. He was anxious now to gain French support in his struggle against Spain.

The King might be trying hard, at Buckingham's instigation, to pacify his wife, but beyond the palace walls stories of her capricious ways and her blatant Catholicism did nothing to improve her reputation. Opinion hardened when at Christmas time a young Englishman she had entertained at her Court declared himself a convert and made plans for an immediate departure to Rome. The French on their side thought the King, prompted by Carlisle, was showing signs of coming out more openly against the Catholics, as if, in Richelieu's words, 'it had been a question of gaining an empire rather than humiliating a young princess'. Marie de Medici saw to it that her daughter bore in mind the task imposed on her by the Pope, and wrote, on at least one occasion, 'a very sharp letter full of good lessons and instructions'.

During the long months of exile in the country few English people had found a chance to see the Queen, and when the opportunity came for her to appear in public, her behaviour only confirmed the bad impression that many people had already received. The King's coronation was to take place at Candlemas, a day set aside by the Catholic Church for enjoyment and festivity. The French ladies had planned to hold a ball that evening and did not wish to become involved in the solemn ritual of crowning a Protestant king. The Queen announced her intention of absenting herself from the ceremony and took up her position in the Gothic gatehouse of the palace so that she could watch the procession going to and from the Abbey. The pageantry of the occasion had been strictly curtailed, 'it being resolved from motives of economy, to save three hundred thousand crowns for better purposes', and the Queen showed little respect for what there was. Her curtained chair, which had been specially prepared for her at the Abbey, remained empty, and she was observed 'frisking and dancing' with her ladies at the window of the gatehouse.

The King was dressed in white—the symbol, some said, of the virgin purity in which he came as a bridegroom to meet his people, though the more cynical attributed his choice to a shortage of purple cloth. As he returned from the Abbey, he saw his wife and saluted her, lifting his crown slightly with both hands, showing a grudging respect for the un-crowned Queen, which few of his subjects felt inclined to share.

Chapter 7

PETITE RÉPUBLIQUE PARTICULIÈRE

ONCE THE plague had subsided, life in London soon returned to normal. The playhouses opened again after eight months, and a new company, Queen Henrietta's men, started performances at the Cockpit early in 1626 with two plays by James Shirley. The Court reassembled at Whitehall and Members of Parliament began arriving for another important session.

The French had decided that Henrietta should watch the procession for the state opening of Parliament from a window in the palace, but the King arranged for her to take her place on a balcony at the house of Buckingham's mother, where he believed she would see and be seen far better. The French saw this change of plan as another attempt to draw the Queen into the Buckingham orbit, but she herself appeared to acquiesce, until, on the day, she suddenly changed her mind as she passed through the King's antechamber. She announced that as it had begun to rain, she did not wish to walk across the damp garden and spoil her hair which had been so carefully dressed. The King thought that she was making an unnecessary fuss and sent Buckingham to tell her so. This the Duke did in his most imperious style, which made her more determined than ever to have her own way. It was Blainville who finally persuaded her to ignore the rain, take Buckingham's arm and go across the street with him to his mother's house. The King took offence when he heard that she had submitted to the French Ambassador and not to himself. He ordered her to come down from the window which until recently he had been so anxious for her to occupy. She refused, he lost his temper and threatened to have nothing more to do with her if she disobeyed him. Finally she returned to her apartments, and the King went on his way to Parliament to assert his authority there.

The assembly which the King had to face was, as one observer put it, an 'ill-faced Parliament', in spite of the fact that the King had disqualified the principal trouble-makers at Oxford by ensuring that they were pricked for sheriffs. Since the previous session, the King had achieved nothing that was likely to endear him to his Commons. It was difficult to present the expedition to Spain as anything but a disaster. Arriving off

Cadiz, the English had surprised a number of Spanish ships lying peacefully in the bay, but had lost their advantage by failing to attack at once.
It was decided to land troops at Puntal for the march on Cadiz, but as the
men proceeded across the salt marshes in the blazing sun, it was realized
that nobody had remembered to put food into their knapsacks. By
evening they were nearly mad with hunger and thirst. The place chosen
for the night's bivouac was near some houses whose occupants had fled
in a hurry, leaving behind in their cellars a store of new wine destined for
export to the West Indies. Out of humanity Cecil ordered a butt of wine
to be served to each regiment, but the soldiers began to force open more
casks and, drinking heavily on empty stomachs, they were soon in a hopeless state of inebriation, shooting each other and threatening their
officers. 'I never saw such beastliness, they knew not what they said, or
did,' wrote one member of the expedition. Cadiz had by now been
reinforced and could only be taken by siege, an operation quite beyond the
capabilities of the untrained troops, many of whom Cecil had described
as 'lame, impotent and unable'. Retreat was the only solution, with as
many men as possible, leaving behind those who had fallen dead drunk
into the ditches. Meanwhile the Spanish treasure fleet, laden with riches
from the Indies and the River Plate, crept back into harbour. The English
fleet had no alternative but to sail 'scatteringly home', the ships' crews by
now so decimated by sickness that there were scarcely enough men to
keep the watches.

It was not surprising that even before Parliament met there were
'murmurs' about the management of the expedition; further discontent
was caused by the forced loan, and the tactless seizure by the government
of French vessels thought to be carrying supplies for the Spanish in the
Netherlands. At the opening of the session, the Speaker, Sir Heneage
Finch, asserted that monarchy was 'the nearest resemblance unto Divine
Majesty which earth affords'. But there were many Members in the
House that day who believed that the King's record was less than divine.
It was soon clear that Parliament intended to be very 'stern' against the
Duke. Not that Buckingham himself seemed disturbed; he arrived at the
House carried on men's shoulders in a Spanish chair, as confident as ever,
and full of schemes for further naval activities all costing money which he
expected Parliament to provide. Neither he nor the King could be
accused of laziness, but the Duke was arrogant and the King obstinate, a
combination of faults rendering them unable to admit that they had
made mistakes in the past which they would be wise to avoid in the
future.

When Buckingham visited Henrietta after the quarrel on the opening
day of Parliament and told her that she was forbidden to receive Blainville any more into her presence, she said she was sorry that her husband,

who had so many other enemies, now faced the added disadvantage of a quarrel with the French. She told Buckingham that she would rather die than shut out her brother's Ambassador. Blainville retired to a house in Greenwich and awaited his instructions from France. He was in any case an unpleasant, cantankerous man, and even the French were beginning to feel that they would be glad to see the back of him.

For a few days Buckingham busied himself carrying messages between the King and the Queen which were not altogether polite in tone. Henrietta told Charles that if he could prove that she was in the wrong, she would be only too ready to go on her knees to ask forgiveness. When she finally requested an interview, Charles received her coldly. She asked him what her offence had been and he replied with simplicity, 'You told me it rained when it did not.' The Queen said that this hardly constituted an offence, but she added more submissively, 'If you believe it to be so, I will do the same.' Then she begged her husband to think no more about it. Delighted with this sudden reconciliation, the King kissed her and led her away to his room. The Venetian Ambassador was able to inform the Doge that the royal pair had resumed sleeping together, after a separation of several days.

The King had been noticeably depressed but now for a while he was in high spirits and he watched with great enjoyment his wife's performance in the pastoral play, Racan's *Arténice*. It was probable that the Queen had seen the play when it was performed at the French court six years before, and that she was able to explain to Inigo Jones the method of staging used in Paris. Although Jones had provided the settings for many masques in the previous reign, he now modified his technique to suit the French pastoral tradition, introducing such innovations as a proscenium arch, perspective scenery and a change in the weather from clear moonlight to dark clouds with thunder and lightning. The sets included a village scene where thatched cottages stood alongside Italianate villas, as well as a representation of Somerset House and the Thames, which brought the whole pastoral fantasy down to the level of real life. In Inigo Jones the Queen had found a designer capable of rivalling the great Francini; the costumes were brilliant and she herself had spent weeks training twelve *demoiselles* to execute the dances. The foreign envoys in the carefully-selected audience were much impressed by the whole performance; they thought that the Queen possessed considerable acting ability and far outshone the other ladies. Like her brother, the Queen was in her element in the world of music and the dance, and she moved at ease through a pastoral scene peopled with figures she knew and understood. Here, language was no longer a barrier, for the romantic spirit of d'Urfé's *L'Astrée* which had caught the imagination of the *beau monde* in the Paris of her childhood could be expressed through moving pictures and dances.

Mythological figures, well known to cultured people throughout Europe, their stereotyped appearance carefully defined in such works as Ripa's *Iconologia*, were as easily recognizable in London as they were in Paris, and as clear to the Venetian Ambassador as they were to the English King.

The King did not allow the publication of the script after the performance, and his caution in limiting the audience was justified. In general the English found the Queen's participation rather scandalous, and more shocking still was the fact that some of the ladies appeared in men's apparel. Henrietta's excessive piety during the Lenten season also came in for criticism. On Holy Thursday she walked with her ladies all the way from Somerset House to the chapel at St James's. Her husband's Protestant subjects would have preferred her to take her exercise in other ways. At Easter time a long gallery at Somerset House was divided up and fitted with cells, a refectory and an oratory, where the Queen and her train spent their time singing the hours of the Virgin.

On February 26 Blainville came up from Greenwich to attend a service at Durham House, part of which was used by the French Embassy. On this occasion constables had been stationed outside, charged with the task of arresting English Catholics who were in the habit of attending the Mass. Trouble broke out when some of the Ambassador's men drew their swords, not without directing blows at the officers and pursuivants, two of whom were injured. The local inhabitants, attracted by the noise, 'came in heaps . . . with bills and clubs' to support the officers. By good fortune, the Bishop of Durham, returning from Court at this moment, was able to avert further trouble by sending the French back into the inner court, and the constables with the gathering crowd into the road. It was said that throughout the disturbance Blainville looked on from an upper window without making any attempt to check his servants. In April he was recalled to France, but he lingered on in England enjoying the shooting at his country house. His intention, Salvetti reported, was 'to annoy powerful persons whose only wish regarding him is that he should be out of sight'. When he finally took his leave, he appeared amicable, although everyone believed that underneath he felt very differently.

While the Queen lived like a nun with her ladies at Somerset House, the King wrestled with his Parliament. Every day the temperature of the House continued to rise. 'Sulphurious vapour' flew from the mouth of Mr Clement Coke in a speech which contained the aphorism that it was 'better to die by a foreign enemy, than to be destroyed at home'. Sir John Eliot launched a fierce attack on Buckingham—who had once been his friend—accusing him of assuming the supreme command on land and sea without ever going into action himself. It would have been easy for the King to let the Commons blame his favourite, to plead his own youth and inexperience, and the bad counsels he had received, as an excuse for all his mistakes. But he stood by his friend with a consistent loyalty that was part of his nature. He insisted that Buckingham had proceeded with caution in all his dealings, had foregone his pleasures, devoting his life slavishly to the business of state. If the Commons insisted on attacking the Duke they would strike too at the King who had given him his trust, and they would be dealing a blow at the very concept of kingship. He announced that he 'would not have the House to question my servants, much less one that is so near me'.

Many felt that it was useless to talk of accusing and even of impeaching the Duke so long as the King was determined to protect him, but a powerful speech delivered by Eliot on March 27, the anniversary of the King's accession, stiffened the resolve of the majority to bring 'the great delinquent' to book. The King wrote messages, termed loving, but full of complaints of Members' impudence. He made it clear that he would not make any concessions or surrender a morsel of the prerogative handed on to him by his father with the Crown. 'Remember,' he said, in an ominous warning which filled the listening Members with apprehension, 'that Parliaments are altogether in my power for their calling, sitting and dissolution; therefore, as I find the fruits of them good or evil, they are to continue, or not to be.'

In spite of the King's intransigence, the House was determined to proceed to an impeachment. If the ordered universe was in some way out of tune, there was nobody to blame but the man who had moved away from his rightful place in the firmament. When the articles of impeachment were placed before the House on May 8, Glanville compared the Commons to the earth, the Lords to the planets, the King to the sun, the clergy to the fire, the judges and magistrates to the air. All these played their rightful part in the divine order; it was Buckingham, the 'prodigious comet', who had no place in this system.

To everyone's surprise, Buckingham appeared in the Lords on the day the articles were presented and laughed openly at his accusers. 'My Lord, do you jeer me?' the Speaker enquired. Both the King and the Duke listened urbanely to the catalogue of the Duke's offences, his 'superfluous feasts, his magnificent buildings, his riots, his excesses'. The King believed that if at times his favourite was over-generous, the fault too often lay with the receiver rather than the giver. It was true that he had 'engrossed' many appointments, that he was Lord High Admiral, Master of the Horse, Lord Warden of the Cinque Ports, Chief Justice in Eyre south of the Trent, Gentleman of the King's Bedchamber and Chief Clerk of the King's Bench, but all this was a testimony to his tireless energy and not to his ambition. Rather than let this public-spirited man be so unjustly accused, the King decided to take the initiative by issuing an order 'for the punishment of some insolent speeches lately spoken'. That same morning, the two chief orators, Eliot and Digges, were called from their places. At the door a warrant was shown to them by two of the King's messengers and they were taken to the Tower. When this became known there was great agitation in the House, which rose at once and postponed all business until the following day.

As the session drew to its close, the King became increasingly at odds with his Parliament. He was obliged to release Eliot and Digges when the peers decided that there was nothing treasonable in their speeches. Sir Dudley Carleton added to the general uneasiness with a strong warning about the dangers of arbitrary power. 'I beseech you, gentlemen,' he said, 'move not his Majesty with trenching upon his prerogatives, lest you bring him out of love with Parliaments.' He had recently returned from Paris, and his knowledge of foreign states was extensive. He had seen the misery of people in other countries, 'being nothing but skin and bones . . . and wearing only wooden shoes on their feet', unable to afford meat or clothes because of the taxes levied by Kings who were not answerable to a Parliament.

Many Members felt a deep sense of foreboding, and some were pointing to ill omens and prophesying famine and disaster. On June 13 there was a spectacular storm and at Whitehall the Court saw the river rise up in a misty whirlpool, almost engulfing a sculler whose boat was spun round six times before he was able to take refuge among the willows. Up-river, Members of the Commons hurried to the windows to watch the storm sweeping down towards Buckingham's home, York House, beating against the wall and the river stairs, but finally moving away, leaving his property, symbolically enough, unscathed.

Rather than expose his favourite to any further danger, the King ordered a dissolution, and Members returned, uneasy and dissatisfied, to their homes, without having voted the King the money he so urgently needed. The King tried to solve the immediate problem with an appeal for free gifts, but at a meeting in Westminster Hall only about thirty people gave without complaint and they were all in the service of the King. The rest demurred and joined in the general cry of, 'A Parliament! a Parliament!' Letters were sent out in July to all Justices of the Peace suggesting that since the subsidies needed for defence had been willingly agreed, they should 'lovingly, freely and voluntarily' supply what might have been levied by law if the Act had been passed. Attempts were made to economize at Court with the abolition of free meals provided at the royal cost. Immediately there was opposition from those who had always benefited from these and other perquisites. Equally unpopular were schemes to cancel many of the pensions which were putting a strain on the royal purse. Attempts to run the King's estates more productively proved less controversial but were not enough on their own to solve Charles's financial problems.

The economy was still suffering from the after-effects of the plague and uncertainties on the Continent, and there was every sign that a bad harvest would add to everyone's problems. Since the great storm in June there had been nearly six weeks of incessant rain. The hay crop was rotting in the fields and much of the corn was laid. The situation was so serious that the King ordered a day of public fasting. Foreigners found the ceremonies somewhat bizarre; throughout the country there were services with specially-written prayers and lengthy sermons beseeching the Almighty to preserve the country from its enemies. It had to be admitted that the air cleared the next day and fine weather prevailed for several weeks afterwards.

News from the Continent was not encouraging. The Danish Ambassador, arriving at Gravesend early in July, reported that Protestant forces were desperate for money. The Danish King was clamouring for the thirty thousand pounds a month so airily promised him, and his soldiers, levied on the security of English help, were threatening to disperse if their pay did not materialize. Holland and Carleton had worked hard earlier in the year to achieve good relations with France, and had even extracted a promise of joint action in Germany, but Charles had allowed a dispute about the captured French ships to drag on, refusing to admit that his idea of the law of prize could be wrong. Richelieu's patience evaporated when he found that Charles was planning to send help to the Protestants besieged at La Rochelle; on April 30 he signed a treaty with the Spanish at Barcelona. While Charles, for all his promises, was unable to find enough money to equip ships and men to protect his own shores, the Catholic armies on the Continent advanced like a torrent, winning a succession of victories.

It had been decided that the King's summer progress would be short and that he would stay as near London as possible, which was thought to be 'an argument of dangerous times'. In mid-July he left for the country with the Queen, but a week later Henrietta was back, in considerable pain with toothache; it was reported that she was sometimes to be seen writhing on the floor in agony. If this was the case the King was singularly unsympathetic; he told her that she was making too much fuss and accused her of weakness.

Released from the pressures put on him by Parliament, Buckingham now concentrated his efforts on his campaign to insinuate his relations into the Queen's Household. There were times when he appeared excessively friendly, but de Tillières was of the opinion that this was when he was at his most dangerous. When he approached Mamie, asking her to explain to the Queen the need to be more forthcoming in the bedroom, she replied prudently that she never meddled in *ces affaires-là*. The French were all uneasily aware that a crisis was approaching and they advised the Queen to proceed with caution. It was agreed that to pacify the King and Buckingham, she should admit two English ladies into her train, but Charles still insisted that she should accept the three he had chosen for her—the Countesses of Denbigh and Carlisle and the Marchioness of Hamilton. The Queen disliked Lady Carlisle and would have preferred the Duchess of Buckingham who at least was known to be virtuous. She reminded the King that his mother, Anne of Denmark, had only appointed two ladies-in-waiting, but he replied that a Princess of Denmark had more right to regulate her household than a daughter of France who was not nearly such *grande chose*. When Henrietta suggested that she should give the principal charge of her estate to the Bishop of Mende, who was only thirty years old and a close relation of Richelieu's, her husband was so angry that he walked out of the room and refused to discuss the matter.

One evening, when the King had already retired to bed, the Queen handed him a paper on which was written a list of the officials she had chosen to administer her revenue. He took it, telling her that he would attend to it in the morning, and warning her that he would confirm only the English appointments. She insisted that everyone mentioned on the paper had a brevet either from herself or her mother. The mention of his mother-in-law did nothing to placate the King, who pointed out that it was not in Marie de Medici's power to admit anybody without his permission. These cold exchanges continued until the Queen finally lost her temper and told her husband that if she had no power to administer the estates he had given her, then he could keep them for himself. Struggling to maintain the dignity of a reigning King even though he was in the bedroom, Charles suggested that his wife should remember whom she was talking to. She broke down then, telling him how unhappy she was, how shorn of power, how continually crossed. She considered that he was treating her as if she were of 'base quality' and not a Queen at all. But the King refused to listen to her complaints, for in his opinion she had no right to make them.

On July 12 Sir Dudley Carleton left for France furnished with instructions to warn Louis that the King would not be able to tolerate 'the cause and fomenters' of his wife's moods much longer. The King was anxious to justify the dismissal of the French retainers if this should prove necessary. He listed all the 'unkindnesses and distastes' which he had suffered; the 'little negatives' were too numerous to describe, but there were enough serious causes for complaint which had to be mentioned—the Queen's reluctance to be in his company, her failure to learn the English language, her refusal to respect the customs of his country. Her behaviour could only be explained by the fact that she was following 'the ill crafty counsels of her servants'. He was sure that she would never on her own initiative have walked—barefoot according to some accounts—across the park to Tyburn, falling on her knees in the company of the Bishop of Mende and others, and offering up prayers for the Catholics who had died there for their faith. This episode proved better than all the others that the marriage had proved a disaster, largely owing to the machinations of the Queen's French companions.

The situation was certainly becoming untenable. Sir John Finett, whose task it was to make arrangements for newly-arrived Ambassadors, never knew whom to approach. Everyone was anxious to kiss the young Queen's hand, and the Danish Ambassador was so pressing that he displayed what Finett described as 'an over-nice curiosity'. Diplomatic protocol was tortuous at the best of times, but the enmity between the French and the English created almost insoluble problems. With the help of the Bishop of Mende and Madame de Saint-Georges, Finett managed to arrange an audience with the Queen for the two Commissioners from Hamburg on July 30, but no sooner was this fixed than he was summoned by the King who told him that he was to let the Commissioners know 'without any noise' that the Queen was unwell and could not receive them. Finett spent an hour seeking out the Commissioners in the still-yard where they were staying, but no sooner had they cancelled their coaches than another message came from the King saying that the audience was to go ahead as originally planned. They were hurried into the presence without waiting in the chapel closet as was the normal practice. The Queen was waiting in the Privy Gallery with her ladies, ready to receive her visitors as if nothing had happened.

The next day the King and Queen dined together at Whitehall. After a good meal, they both seemed 'very merry'. The King, following his wife to her own apartments, found her with two of her ladies, 'curving and dancing'—two activities in which she indulged far too much for his liking. He told her that he had something he wished to say to her in his own room, and she answered with customary lack of respect that she could just as well hear him where she was. He then dismissed the ladies, locked the doors and broke it to her that all her servants, priests, attendants, male and female, must go.

To say that Henrietta made a scene is an understatement. She flung herself at her husband's feet, embracing his knees and kissing him, pleading with him to change his mind. When these tactics proved unsuccessful she broke out into sobs and groans loud enough to split the rocks, to use Richelieu's metaphor—and certainly audible to courtiers several rooms away. She reminded him of the promises so solemnly made in the marriage contract, and asked that if all the others had to go, then at least she should be allowed to keep Mamie. But the King was inexorable and refused all her requests.

The French meanwhile had been informed of their dismissal by Secretary Conway, who entered the room where they were having their meal. They had been expecting this to happen for months, but the finality and suddenness of the order took them by surprise and at first they were stunned and silent. The women then began to howl and lament as if they had been going to their execution, and the Yeomen of the Guard were forced to clear the room. The move to Somerset House began at once, but those who remained at Whitehall, hearing Henrietta's frantic cries from the room where she was incarcerated with her husband, crowded into the courtyard below. The Queen appeared at the window and shattered some of the panes of glass in a demented attempt to reach her banished friends, but the King pulled her roughly away. Her hands were bleeding and her dress was torn, but she calmed down eventually, rather more from exhaustion than resignation. For the next few days she went on a hunger strike and asked constantly to see her confessor.

It was Lady Denbigh who interceded on the Queen's behalf, with a request that she be permitted to keep her nurse, who was under orders to leave with all the rest. 'Brother,' she wrote to Buckingham, 'if you did but see and hear her it would grieve your heart to the soul. We have spoken with the King but he will not hear us.' In the end the Queen was allowed her nurse, Madame de Vantelet, who dressed her, a cook, a pantler and a tailor. The priest who was chosen to stay with her, Father Philip, was, in the opinion of the English, 'the silliest of them all'.

The French did not depart without some show of resistance. In spite of all the coaches, carts and barges drawn up outside Somerset House ready to take them away on the day after the great scene, they 'contumaciously refused to go' until certain debts had been paid. In their belief, the English would be unable to scrape up enough money to give them the back pay that was owing, let alone an apothecary's bill for £800 and the Bishop of Mende's estimate of £1,500 for what the English described as his unholy water. In the end they decided to accept the usual parting present of pendant ear-rings instead of wages, and the Queen had to admit that some of the debts had been invented for the occasion.

When the King heard that the French were refusing to leave, he sent down the captain of the Guard with some competent yeomen who threatened to drag them out by the heads and shoulders if they did not go of their own accord. At this their courage began to evaporate and they agreed to leave by the next tide. The Bishop of Mende asked permission to stay until midnight so that he might go away 'private and cool'; this was allowed and the whole contingent was soon on its way to Dover. All devout Protestants hoped that there would be a fair wind ready to waft them over to France, and the King told Buckingham that there was to be no more procrastination. They were to be driven away, if necessary, like so many wild beasts—'and so the devil go with them,' he added.

The majority of English people felt that the King was entirely justified in dismissing the expensive foreigners, and particularly the priests who were described variously as 'hypocritical dogs', 'bawdy knaves' and other even less complimentary names. It was said that at confession they would make Henrietta tell them how often in a night the King had kissed her. All the same there was some apprehension about the effect the dismissal might have on England's already strained relations with France. Louis wrote to Charles expressing his astonishment, but he promised to send a special envoy to look into allegations that the French retainers had formed a faction within the state like *une petite république particulière*. The French King's choice for this delicate task was the Maréchal de Bassompierre who had known Henrietta from childhood. He was courtly and convivial and diplomatic enough, it was hoped, to undo some of the harm effected by the disagreeable Blainville.

The French King and Richelieu had other matters on their mind, since a plot had been discovered, 'aiming at no less than taking the crown off the king's head, and so put it on Monsieur's'. The news that trouble was splitting her own family did nothing to cheer Henrietta's spirits. She wrote miserably home to her mother, begging for help and pity, without which she felt that she would reach the point of total despair.

Chapter 8

THE GREAT DELINQUENT

THE QUEEN passed most of the summer at Somerset House, but the King was often away, either enjoying his country pursuits or making plans to gather together a fleet capable of harassing Spanish shipping in the Biscay harbours. He also spent much of his time at the council table discussing ways of raising money. There were two sales of the King's plate and desultory attempts at economy continued. In mid-September news was received of a serious defeat of the Danes at Lutter. Charles came hurrying up to London from Theobalds and spent four hours debating ways and means of helping his uncle. A decision to sell yet more plate was arrived at, but all other methods of assisting the Danes could only be of academic interest owing to the chronic shortage of funds, which had not been improved by the expense of paying off the French household.

Four Catholics had been included in the Queen's new establishment— the Earl of Rutland, her Lord Chamberlain, Sir Thomas Savage, her Chancellor, the Countess of Buckingham and Lady Savage. A chapel was being hastily fitted up on the ground floor at Somerset House to show Bassompierre that there was no deficiency in this respect. The Maréchal arrived in England towards the end of September. The Queen's barge was waiting for him at Rochester and the King's coaches met him at Tower Wharf, but there was no official ceremony and he drove straight to the lodgings hired for him by his harbinger in Leadenhall Street at fifty pounds a week. At first it seemed that he would be no more successful than his predecessor. The King did not summon him to an audience for several days, guessing that the first thing he would do would be to ask for the restoration of the Queen's French priests.

At the public audience Bassompierre handed over his letters of credence to the King who was sitting on a raised platform with the Queen beside him. A few days later he was allowed to see the Queen. Buckingham arrived at his lodgings on his first night in London. Since his manner was clandestine and he was not even illuminated by the light of torches, he was refused admittance at first, but he returned later and stayed for an hour, airing his complaints about France and about 'certain people'. The Duke was soon calling on the Ambassador every day and they often went out together in a coach. When Bassompierre visited York House he was much impressed by the furnishings which were as fine as anything he had seen in all his travels. The King put off his plans to go hunting and concentrated on the proposals brought by Bassompierre, making the usual vague promises about the English Catholics, and undertaking to complete the chapel begun at St James's for the Infanta. Bassompierre worked very hard, attending many sessions at the council table with the ten Commissioners who had been appointed to treat with him. Buckingham told him to take no notice of the Council; what mattered was that he had the favourite on his side.

One day Bassompierre went to see the Queen, taking Buckingham with him. He made the two talk amicably to each other, but he was less successful when he tried to bring about a reconciliation between the King and the Queen. Whenever he saw them they quarrelled violently. One day the King appeared to make it up and treated his wife with great tenderness, but the next time he saw them they had another quarrel. Bassompierre thought that Henrietta often behaved provocatively, and he told her that unless she mended her ways, he would return to France without completing his business. What was more, he would tell the Queen Mother that many of the problems he was trying to solve had arisen as a result of her daughter's childish and temperamental behaviour.

When Bassompierre went back to his house after this frank interview, he was angered to find that his chaplain already had the Queen's version of the story. Next day when she sent for him he refused to see her. He had almost reached the end of his strength; the strain of the negotiations, coupled with the damp London weather, was making him ill and he had completely lost his voice. Within a few days, however, he was better, and he had the satisfaction of telling the Queen that the treaty was finished. Thanks to his own hard work and Buckingham's backing, he had extracted a promise from the King that his wife might be allowed twelve priests and a Bishop. This news put the Queen into a better mood. She accompanied the Duke and the Ambassador to Cheapside where they watched the Lord Mayor's procession which, Bassompierre thought, must be the finest ceremony for the reception of an officer to be seen anywhere in the world.

To mark the amicable conclusion of the negotiations the Duke mounted an entertainment at York House. Before supper there were musical performances and a complete ballet was presented between each course. The food appeared magically from above, let down in a sheet, 'no man seeing how it came', and the sweet water, said to cost two hundred pounds, appeared 'as a shower from heaven'. When the feast was over, the guests rested for a while before moving into the room where the masque was to take place. Bassompierre was impressed by the *tour*, an ingenious turnstile which admitted the audience one at a time, like the wooden turntables set in the walls of foundling hospitals where a mother could deposit an unwanted child without risk of detection. The device prevented the crush and confusion which were features of any performance in Paris. The masque embodied the theme of education, so fascinating to the Renaissance man, taking the story of Gargantua and the three tutors who sought to instil all the courtly virtues into their large and uncouth pupil. The Duke himself played one of the tutors and his performance called forth admiration. He had always danced superbly, and in the days of the late King had been able to soothe his choleric master by 'cutting a score of lofty and very minute capers'.

The coming of peace, that ideal state, was represented by a breathtaking scene in which Marie de Medici appeared enthroned among the clouds above the Channel, beckoning to the King and Queen of Spain, the Prince and Princess Palatine, the Duke of Piedmont and his wife, all so true to life as to be easily recognizable. The Queen Mother was inviting them to join her among the gods and so put an end to all the discords then raging so unprofitably in the Christian world.

It was four o'clock in the morning before all the dancing was over. The guests moved into vaulted rooms where a five-course dinner was served— 'a splendid refection of sweetmeats'. The King and Queen remained at York House for what was left of the night and the King seemed 'very jocund and merry'. There was some criticism of the part played by Buckingham, 'which many thought too histrionical to become him', and there was also disapproval, among the older and more reactionary members of the community, of the other Privy Councillors who took part.

Bassompierre had intended to leave for France immediately the masque was over, but the King persuaded him to stay and see the entertainment which the Queen was preparing for her own birthday. This was followed by another banquet and the next day Bassompierre took his leave. Carlisle came to fetch him with the King's best coach and the King and Queen received him in the Banqueting House with all the ladies ranged in order of rank on one side and all the lords and gentlemen on the other. While he waited at Dover for the weather to improve, Buckingham despatched a messenger to announce that he had decided to embark on a peace mission to France and wished to know whether such a visit would be well received.

The Ambassador admitted himself that Buckingham 'had stopped his mouth with a feast' and his countrymen received him without enthusiasm; they believed he had been too conciliatory because he had succumbed to Buckingham's charms. As for the Duke's projected visit, there was little problem about that; the French would not allow it, and made no effort to hide the fact. In spite of all Bassompierre's efforts the French and the

English continued to regard each other with animosity. An ill-equipped English fleet which set out to harass shipping 'returned presently again without doing of anything' except to capture a few French ships. There was a predictable backlash when the French seized a number of English vessels which had gone to Bordeaux to collect a cargo of wine; this provoked an immediate outcry and the English clamoured for revenge.

Once again penury made the King powerless. Every method of raising money had by now been tried. Members of the Privy Council had themselves been out in the provinces trying to persuade the gentry to part with their money. 'Refusers' included peers, gentlemen and even judges. In spite of assurances that the present method of asking aid from his 'loving subjects' did not mean that the King was creating a precedent, and that he would call a Parliament 'as soon as may be', many were reluctant to contribute, disliking the principle of the loan and fearing that any funds raised would be squandered by the King's favourite.

In the new year of 1627 the general situation deteriorated. Trade was falling into confusion, there was exasperation among the merchants, the pilots at Dover were on strike, complaining that they had never been paid for a variety of services, including their work in bringing the Queen over from France nearly two years before. In the capital the City trained bands had to be stationed near Buckingham's house to protect him from the sailors who were clamouring for pay. The King, attempting to frighten his subjects into providing money, was building up discontent as he packed the prisons with 'loan recusants'. Freeholders who had refused to contribute were consigned to the artillery yard as a punishment and others were sent into custody as far from their homes as possible.

A close watch was kept on all the Queen's servants travelling between London and Paris, and all her remaining French retainers were under suspicion as the two countries drifted into war. Just before Christmas she bought a lute and began to take lessons from a famous French performer, Monsieur Gouttier. The King and the Duke disapproved of the gentleman from the start, and the Queen's musical venture came to a sudden end when her teacher was arrested and imprisoned in the Tower, accused of talking about 'persons far above him in a manner which is intolerable'. He was examined in secret and later two more servants in the Queen's Household were taken into custody.

The Queen left Hampton Court immediately after Christmas 1626 to make preparations for the masque which was to be staged on Twelfth Night at Whitehall. In spite of the financial crisis no expense was spared, for an evening of fine spectacle could bring worthwhile prestige to a country even though it was on the verge of bankruptcy. It was rumoured that a thousand pounds' worth of taffeta and satin had been supplied, and the Queen's embroiderer was paid £913 10s for his work. The deployment of the diplomats was, as always, a delicate operation, the Venetian Ambassador, like his predecessors in King James's reign, insisting on a place under the canopy with the King. On the night, the Ambassadors arrived at the Great Gate at six in the evening. They had been asked to limit their train as much as possible because of the scarcity of places. The Dutch Ambassador had brought his wife and daughters who were 'thrust up in a corner without respects'.

The King showed great interest in the performance, carefully 'placing the ladies' gentlewomen with his own hand'. The masque ended in the usual way when the masquers invited members of the audience to dance in the grand finale, the King and fourteen noblemen and knights partnering the Queen and her ladies. Later in the year at York House, Buckingham presented another masque for the King and Queen. He was planning a naval expedition and had collected up a force of 'serviceable men' furnished with buff jackets, swords, daggers and cases of pistols, and he himself was to be seen strutting about in a military costume with an immense collar and an outsize plume of feathers in his cap. A great collier ship had been commandeered to accommodate the Duke's own 'living store' of provisions, and carpenters were already aboard making coops for the poultry as well as stalls for two goats, two milch cows and four fat oxen. The masque provided an ideal representation of the Duke's departure from the island of Britain. He was seen with Fame and Truth, pursued by Envy 'with divers open-mouthed dogs' heads representing the people's barking'. The Duke's friends feasted him every day and one evening he entertained the Queen at Chelsea.

The French were naturally alarmed by all the activity on the English coast, and a messenger from France tried to find out where the fleet was intended for—'whether for Spain, or some of the French coasts or other where?' Many Englishmen were apprehensive, knowing that for all the Duke's confidence the fleet was in a bad state and inclined to be mutinous, with fifty men dying a day and boys being sent to fetch the corpses and bury them at Stepney. There was something amounting to panic when a great fleet was sighted early in June off the Isle of Wight. The Duke set off at speed for the Downs, to embark and chase away what he believed to be Spaniards; they turned out to be nothing more menacing than some Hamburghers and Hollanders laden with salt.

In June 1627 the King visited the fleet at Portsmouth. He took a meticulous interest in all the preparations by sea and land—counted the men, pointed out defective arms and visited ships to urge people on. The Queen played her part by dining on board the Earl of Warwick's ship, the *Neptune*, at Blackwall. She went by boat to Greenwich and rode back to Somerset House accompanied by the Earl and forty others, all bareheaded. The Queen's priests wore skull caps and her ladies had little beaver hats, while the Queen herself sported a cap with a 'fair white feather'.

The Duke was extraordinarily sanguine. His equipment included carriages and saddle horse designed for use in a triumphal entry into a foreign town as yet unnamed. He slipped away without any leave-takings, and it was his sister who noticed the empty chair beside the King in chapel. The Duke's mother thought that he ought at least to have seen his wife before he left; they had lost their only son in the spring and now it was believed that she was pregnant again—'my lady pukes a little, which makes us hope she is with child'.

During the Duke's absence, the King 'knit himself up close to business' and instead of his usual summer progress he made what were termed 'hovering journeys' close to London. Buckingham's relations kept a close watch on the Queen, reporting on all her moods and assuring him in their letters that they thought he could rely on her. She had remarked, when Lady Carlisle handed her a letter from the Duke, that 'she hoped in the end this action would gain him the hearts of many'. It had been decided that she should travel to Wellingborough in Northamptonshire where she and her ladies camped in tents round the Red Well. The waters, rich in iron, were thought to promote fertility. While she was there the Queen found herself 'much incommodated for want of money' and she complained to the Lord Treasurer that she was unable to pay her servants' wages. Nor were members of the local aristocracy over-eager to entertain her, if Lord Spencer of Althorp can be considered a fair example. Although it was the middle of summer and Lord Spencer was by no means an old man, he pleaded ill health and cold weather as an excuse for failing to pay his respects. 'It hath pleased God to visit [him] with such a sickness of the palsy that he is not able to perform that duty which he oweth unto her Majesty' wrote his son, Sir William Spencer, to the Earl of Carlisle '. . . he now being under the physician's hands and not able to stir out of his own doors, the air and cold being forbidden him.' His daughter-in-law was in childbed, which provided another good excuse, but Carlisle was promised the best buck that the park at Althorp could provide, which at least gave some help towards the housekeeping. The King's advice was sought when it was time for the Queen to return, but he found it difficult to suggest a route, knowing as he did the uncertainty 'in women's determinations'.

By mid-August it was generally known that the Duke had landed on the Île de Rhé with the intention of taking aid to the besieged Huguenots at La Rochelle. The English gained a foothold and captured two out of three forts on the island. The Duke had shown considerable courage, standing in the bows of his boat with a drawn sword in his hand, and urging on the troops when they were driven back into the sea. By the end of August there was some hope that the last fort would not be able to hold out much longer as the occupants were reduced to one loaf a day and had nothing but 'puddle water' for all their needs. Soon, however, there were disturbing rumours that some ships had managed to win through with supplies for the besieged, and all the time the French army was receiving reinforcements. Louis had been lying ill with a tertian ague at Villeroy, and Henrietta had received permission to write to him with enquiries about his health and condolences for Gaston whose wife had died after disappointing everybody by giving birth to a daughter. The Comte de Soissons was planning to take up arms against the Crown, and with danger threatening from Lorraine and Savoy, Richelieu was said to be tearing his beard—what there was of it. De Soissons, however, was still in search of a wife, and refused to move unless he was rewarded with a daughter of the Elector Palatine; Lorraine did nothing and Savoy refused to move until English aid actually materialized. Louis made a good recovery and in October both he and Gaston had arrived to take charge of the besieging armies.

Anxiety in England grew as the days went by and no news came. Delay could only be serious with winter coming on as it was unlikely that the English troops could survive on the island in cold weather. The fleet under the Earl of Holland which was to have gone out with reinforcements was slow in preparation, and contrary winds prevented it setting out when at last it was ready. After making an attempt on the fort with inadequate equipment including ladders which were too short, the Duke's army was unable to resist a strong French attack. As the main body of English troops passed along a narrow passage across salt pits filled with water, the cavalry covering their retreat were forced back on to the causeway, crushing the foot soldiers or pushing them over the edge.

There was consternation in England when news of the defeat came through. One writer expressed the common feeling when he wrote that it was 'the greatest and shamefullest overthrow' the English had received since they lost Normandy, and Buckingham was more unpopular than ever. The King did not blame his favourite so much as those who had failed to keep the expedition supplied, and on the whole he was inclined to regard it as a blow of fortune 'who strikes inconstantly, sometimes here, sometimes there'. When the Duke arrived at Plymouth, the Lord Chamberlain was sent to greet him, bearing a rich jewel and an affectionate letter from the King.

That Christmas, nobody had time to prepare elaborate entertainments, and plans to mount a 'running masque' were cancelled after only a week's rehearsal. The one bright feature was the arrival of a Christmas present to the Queen from her brother, in the shape of Lord Mountjoy and other English prisoners taken on the island of Rhé. The Privy Council was meeting every day of the week—'so strictly doth the King tire them, and himself'—and a Shrovetide masque involving over a hundred actors was abandoned, though not before six hundred pounds had already been spent. The King would have been wise to curtail all expenses, for there had been much murmuring when it was learned that he had persuaded his banker to use funds urgently needed by the army at Rhé to buy up the Duke of Mantua's priceless art collection, outbidding Cardinal Richelieu and the Queen Mother.

In February 1628 the King went to Wallingford House for the christening of the Duke's newborn son, wearing for the occasion a long soldier's coat covered in gold lace, and his hair in a new style—'all gaufred and frizzled'. It was noted that the Queen, although a godmother, did not attend, and in March there were rumours that she was with child.

Although Buckingham's relations would have liked to dissuade him from embarking on another dangerous expedition, the King and his favourite were still determined to relieve the Rochellois. Since they had no alternative source of funds they were forced to call a Parliament. In his opening speech the King told Members that if they behaved like good subjects he would forget the offence given by the last Parliament. At first debates went well and the King was quickly voted five subsidies, but before long many experienced Parliamentarians were eloquently airing their grievances. They complained about arbitrary taxation, imprisonment without trial as well as the hardships caused by the billeting of troops—'murthers, rapes, robberies, burglaries, getting of bastards.' Members expressed concern that the young King was still supporting the Romish party and clergymen such as Cosin who, it appeared, was so blind that at evensong 'he could not read prayers in the Minster without three hundred and forty candles, whereof sixty he caused to be placed about the high altar'.

To placate his critics the King promised that he would confirm all the privileges of the subject contained either in Magna Carta or elsewhere, but he felt that the current crisis called for practical remedies rather than long-winded debates about ancient liberties. 'Now is the time for action, so I will not multiply words,' he told his Parliament. The Easter recess was cancelled, and on Easter eve he reminded Members of 'the pressing occasions of the time'. But in spite of his promises the more conservative element in Parliament remained uneasy, afraid that the King and his young advisers would continue to introduce innovations which would undermine the settled traditions of Church and State. It was decided that a Petition of Right should be drawn up in which all grievances would be clearly stated and which the King would be required to answer without evasions. More moderate Members suggested amendments allowing the King to take special powers in times of real emergency, but the majority feared that any compromise would give the King a chance to override the law as he had done in the previous months. When he returned an indefinite answer to the Petition, Members turned accusingly on the Duke, blaming him for the unwise administration of the King's affairs. A Remonstrance was then prepared complaining about the present state of affairs and mentioning both Buckingham and Laud by name, but the King stood by his friends and ordered a prorogation.

Once he was free from his struggle with Parliament, the King turned his attention to the naval expedition which the starving Rochellois had been expecting for so long. The most favourable moment for relieving the city, when the moon was full, the tides at their highest and the mole submerged, had already passed, but the King and Buckingham were undeterred. They were both staying at Portsmouth so that they could superintend the fitting-out of the fleet, and the King was planning a journey to Scotland in September for his coronation. The Queen was paying a second visit to Wellingborough. The waters proved to be of little value since they had been diluted by recent rains, but she enjoyed herself watching 'the dances of the peasantry'. She was short of money as usual and to prove her point she had asked her husband for twenty-one pounds to give to a poor Frenchwoman. When he insisted on knowing who was to be the object of his charity, she replied, 'I, sire, am the penniless pauper.'

Every day the Queen might have expected to hear that Buckingham had sailed for La Rochelle, but when a letter came, it was from Sir Dudley Carleton and not from the King, and it contained the news that the Duke was dead. Carleton told the Queen how Buckingham had come down into the parlour of the house where he was staying in Portsmouth, accompanied by his colonels, captains and many servants. He was on his way to visit the King at Southwick and his coach was already waiting outside. As one of the gentlemen bent forward to kiss his hand, an army officer named John Felton stepped forward and stabbed him. The Duke staggered, gasped out 'Villain'—the last word he spoke—and fell against a table. At first nobody realized what had happened; some thought that the Duke had fainted until they saw the blood gushing from the wound and from his mouth. There was pandemonium at once. 'Madam,' wrote Carleton, 'you may easily guess what outcries were then made by us that were commanders and officers there present when we saw him thus dead in a moment and slain by an unknown hand.' People crowded into the room, pressing round the Duke's body and doing what they could to resuscitate him. Meanwhile the murderer passed quickly through the crowd and stood in the kitchen of the house. When people started crying out, 'Where is the villain, where is the butcher?', he stepped forward and said with biblical simplicity, 'I am he.'

The Duchess, who had only just risen, came out on to the balcony above the hall when she heard the noise. She was joined by other ladies, and when they saw their lord lying dead below they broke out into spontaneous lamentation. 'Such was their screeching,' wrote Carleton, 'that I never in my life heard the like before, and hope never to hear the like again.'

The King was at prayers when they brought him the news that his favourite was dead; he said nothing and when the service was over he went to his room and did not reappear for two days. This brilliant, handsome man, only thirty-six years old, had engrossed so much of the business of government that for a while it seemed that life stood still. Plans for the relief of La Rochelle were shelved, the King's journey was cancelled, and nobody knew who would succeed to the dead favourite's place.

In the country as a whole there was much rejoicing when Felton's 'great good service' to the country became known. People had hated the Duke for his insufferable pride, the airs he assumed and the power he annexed. Fears that the assassination could have been part of a Popish plot were dissipated by Felton himself. He had thoughtfully hidden a message in the lining of his hat avowing that he had acted, after reading the Remonstrance, according to his own religious promptings, in order to save the country from the Duke against whom he had a personal grudge ever since he had been passed over for promotion. But for this message it is possible that Felton, had he been slain after the murder, might have been accused of acting in the pay of the French and this could have had serious consequences for the Queen. As it was, nobody could connect her name with Felton's. When she heard the news of Buckingham's death she hurried south immediately and was reunited with the King at Farnham. Stricken with grief as he was at the loss of his favourite, he turned to her for comfort and she consoled him, stepping effortlessly into the place which the Duke had occupied for so long.

Chapter 9

A NEW ORDER

THE DUKE'S funeral was a modest affair with no more than a hundred mourners in attendance. The streets were lined with armed burgesses for fear of public demonstrations, but there were no disturbances and what little noise there was sounded more like an expression of joy than of grief. In Paris they ascribed the fatal event to the Grace of Heaven.

The Queen visited the Buckingham relations personally and offered her condolences. The King rallied quickly and began to carry on the business left unfinished by the Duke. It was said that he did more in a fortnight than his favourite had achieved in several months. By mid-September he had despatched the much-delayed fleet, making a gracious speech on its departure, with a promise that all wages would be paid. The Rochellois were by now living on boiled cowhides, having devoured all available dogs, cats, mice and frogs.

Anyone less obstinate that King Charles I might well have decided that the time had come to give up the struggle and treat with the French. The Venetian Ambassador Contarini pressed him so hard on one occasion about the wisdom of an immediate peace that he took off his hat and said warmly, 'It is all true but my honour matters to me even more. My forces are to succour La Rochelle not to treat.'

But on October 18, 1628, within sight of the English fleet, La Rochelle capitulated. The survivors, who looked more like ghosts than men, were treated tolerantly, and Richelieu granted almost everything that Charles had demanded for them. Had he been prepared to negotiate earlier, many thousands of lives might have been saved and much suffering, endured in the hope of English help, avoided. Yet still the King refused to be daunted, and gave the Duc de Rohan a promise of further aid in spite of what he lightly termed 'the late mis-accident at Rochelle'.

In his determination to continue the war Charles received little encouragement from those around him. It was not necessary to be a mathematical genius to see that in any case the English King was in no position to wage war on anybody. This fact was distressingly evident to the Lord Treasurer, Richard Weston, who was anxious to preserve the

meagre funds deposited in his care and so favoured a policy of peace in
the interests of economy. The Venetian Ambassador was to be seen every
day at Court working for a truce, and he recognized in Henrietta Maria a
more powerful ally than all the other pacific groups combined. It was in
her interest to promote peace between her husband and brother, and since
she now wielded great influence over the King, she was likely to prove
an effective instrument. In Salvetti's opinion if she had not been so
young and so easily 'carried away by her companionships', she would not
have found it difficult to make the King do whatever she pleased. Contarini reported that she greeted him with evident pleasure when he told
her he had come on an errand of peace, and she promised to speak to the
King about it that night. It was reported that she broached the subject
tactfully to her husband, stressing that she did not wish to interfere.

The Queen was in excellent health. Although hopes that she was
pregnant the previous spring had been disappointed, there were now
growing rumours that she was 'breeding child'. A report that half the
town had been out searching for mussels to satisfy a sudden fancy seemed
to confirm the theory. The possibility gave courage to the peace-makers
who were sure that a reconciliation might come about more quickly if the
Queen were to produce an heir. Certainly the Queen Mother appeared
to be much better disposed towards the English as soon as she heard the
news. The King was overjoyed when he knew that his wife was to bear
him a child—his satisfaction, Contarini reported, defied exaggeration,
and it was hoped that he would be more likely than ever to be led by her
into a treaty with France.

A settlement might have been reached within a few months of Buckingham's death if the French had not continued to insist that Charles
should honour the promises made at the time of his marriage. This,
however, was totally 'obnoxious to the opinions and feelings of the King'.
He had fallen in love with his young wife at last and understandably had
no wish to risk reviving old jealousies and bitterness. The Queen herself
had grown to like her English attendants; she was waited on with great
care and treated with respect, and an influx of foreigners might well
threaten this new-found happiness. Although Charles was ready to accept
the eight or even ten Capuchins the French now wished to send in place
of the two Oratorians who had remained after the great exodus, he
adamantly refused to accept another Bishop in her Household, remembering the troubles caused by Mende. In all this Henrietta supported him.

What with Charles's tenacity and French punctilio, Contarini sometimes despaired. Every small point seemed to cause trouble, and as soon
as anything was agreed another equally delicate problem would arise.
The French, for example, were now insisting that the Queen Mother
should be granted precedence over her daughter, but Charles refused to

accept this condition, imagining all manner of difficulties. Marie de Medici was quite capable of using it as an excuse to dominate her daughter from a distance.

On January 16, 1629, just before the opening of a new session of Parliament, there was a petition from both Houses for a fast, with a prayer for union between the King and all the estates of the realm. It was the general hope that now the favourite had been removed, the King and Parliament would be able to work without rancour. Contarini felt sure that there was a universal desire for peace; he believed that Members would be well disposed towards a treaty, but he had been in England too long to expect them to achieve anything practical, or to alter their habit of arguing endlessly about religion and the prerogative.

The King had been forced to call a Parliament for the usual reason. His coffers were empty; all salaries had been suspended and the fleet which had come back from La Rochelle, badly battered by storms, had been quickly dispersed—the troops and sailors being sent home to save expense. As usual the Commons were not prepared to grant any subsidies until the King had heard their grievances. As Contarini had prophesied, his religious policies were soon under scrutiny. It was true that he had tried to pacify the Puritans by turning out some Catholic servants and imposing heavy fines on a few recusants, but the appointment of High Churchmen was causing much concern. The removal of Mountain, the Bishop of London, to Durham, had given rise to a multitude of puns, as well as a great deal of disapproval, his place at Fulham having been filled by William Laud. Laud laid much stress on the Church's authority and expected the laity to accept without question the form of service laid down by those in exalted positions. In his battle to keep the 'lawless, kneeless, schismatical Puritan' in check, Laud wished to eliminate discussion and individual theorizing. All 'curious search' had now been forbidden by royal proclamation, and the Bishop seemed to think he even had a right to dictate to Parliament. 'The upper house of Parliament did much distaste the Bishop of London, for that he had thrown down a book of articles at his first coming in,' wrote Thomas Rous in his diary.

Members worried less about the need to put the economy on a firm basis than they did about the position of the altar in church—whether it should be placed at the east end with or without candles, whether anybody should bow to it, or even whether it should be called an altar at all. Many saw it as a table placed among the people, allowing them to partake of the Lord's supper on equal terms with their minister. Unless the King could give some satisfaction on these all-important matters, he was unlikely to receive the money he needed. He argued in vain that his father had received automatically the duties levied on imported goods and known as tonnage and poundage; the merchants naturally agreed with Parliament that they were only doing their duty in refusing to pay impositions which they believed to be illegal and bad for trade.

Many Members were well-meaning and anxious to do the best for their country. But they were inclined to become excited to the point of hysteria, being led into destructive attacks on individuals whom the King himself felt bound to support. Buckingham, the universal scapegoat, was dead; Members were still reluctant to attack the King himself, their thinking tempered by the *Basilikon Doron*, the late monarch's standard work expressing the divine right of Kings to rule as God's unchallengeable deputy on earth. They found in Lord Treasurer Weston a satisfactory substitute. After the Duke's death Weston had been 'on the sudden wonderfully elated'. Lacking Buckingham's more exotic qualities, but powered by a strong desire to become the new sole favourite, Weston had inherited not only the King's favour but also the general dislike that went with it. 'I find him,' Eliot thundered, 'building upon the old grounds and foundations which were built by the Duke of Buckingham his great master.' Weston was married to a recusant; several of his children had been brought up in the Catholic faith, and it was easy enough to imagine that he was a crypto-papist eager to encourage High Church trends. His parsimonious economic policies also came in for criticism and it was easy to hold him responsible for inciting the King to claim tonnage and poundage illegally, 'without the gift of Parliament'.

By early March the familiar pattern had emerged. No progress had been made in the financial field, no satisfaction had been given over religious matters, the King's principal adviser had been singled out for criticism, and there were already rumours of a dissolution. Leading men in the Commons tried to formulate their grievances before it was too late. The King countered with a message ordering the House to adjourn before the protest could be read, but the Speaker was held down in his chair so that Members might not 'be turned off like scattered sheep' until all the points had been made. The protest branded as an enemy to the State anyone who sought to bring in popery, Arminianism or other opinions disagreeing with the true and orthodox Church—'as Bishop Laud, said one, as my Lord Treasurer, said another, everyone particularizing whom they thought fit'. The King sent several messengers who were all unable to obtain an entrance, but finally the door was opened, and the sergeant-at-arms was seen standing there ready to enter. The House voted its own adjournment which was to last for eleven years. Wearing his crown and royal robes, the King sat in the Lords to hear the announcement of the dissolution. 'I never came here upon so unpleasant an occasion,' he told the Lords, putting the blame on the lower house, and confessing that he felt 'justly distasted with their proceedings'.

On his return from the Lords the King seemed pleased, as if he had at last freed himself from a yoke which he had borne unwillingly for years. Now he had made it clear that he would not allow his ministers to be arraigned by the House of Commons. He would make Eliot and others who had spoken out frankly, suffer for their folly; they were sent to the Tower and the King made no secret of the fact that he intended to punish them harshly.

Not long after the dissolution, bonfires were lighted throughout the country to celebrate the confirmation of the Queen's pregnancy. All the Ambassadors came to bring their congratulations. Nurses were being engaged, and many ladies were offering themselves, although it was thought that the Queen would only accept those who were Catholic. It was believed that a representative from France would have to be present at the birth, and there were even rumours that mariners were being pressed to serve in 'the bringing over of the Queen Mother'. Marie de Medici had been in a quandary on hearing that two of her hitherto unproductive daughters, Henrietta and Christine, had both conceived for the first time and were both due to give birth in July of that year. She would have liked each of them to be attended by Madame de Péronne, in her opinion the best midwife in France, but as she had to make a choice, she characteristically decided that her youngest daughter should be given precedence, since it was her duty to bring forth a future King.

The certainty that the Queen was with child helped to accelerate the peace negotiations. For this and other reasons Charles was now determined to avoid expensive involvement on the Continent. Since his elected assembly had challenged his right to rule, raise money and deal with foreign affairs, he had decided to see whether he could ignore its existence. Rather than surrender a fraction of his sovereignty at home he was prepared to withdraw from the international scene, leaving his sister, the Princess Palatine, to fend for herself. The Protestants of Europe, the 'Common Cause', would have to look elsewhere for support, and Charles was to remain detached from the Thirty Years War with all its suffering and waste of resources, living in an isolated paradise on a limited budget.

At Susa a treaty was signed putting an end to the war between France and England. No definite claims were made either for the Catholics in England or for the Huguenots in France. By insisting that she was satisfied and well treated, Henrietta Maria had shown her brother the futility of holding out for the original terms of the marriage treaty, and she was commended for the part she had played. Naturally she was delighted with the outcome, and when Contarini visited her at Greenwich he found her in excellent health. They discussed the question of celebrations to mark the announcement of the peace and the Queen expressed her approval of bonfires, although the King was cautious, reminding her that there was so far only a reconciliation and not a full-scale peace settlement.

The public news of the treaty was released on Sunday, May 10 when the Court was still at Greenwich. The next day the Queen travelled up to Somerset House where a Te Deum was sung in her chapel. She returned to Greenwich by water and with characteristic impetuosity stood up in the barge before it reached the landing-stage. The shock of the impact threw her backwards, and caused her considerable pain which persisted during the next two days. It then became evident that although her child was not due for another six weeks, she had already fallen into labour. The town midwife was hastily sent for, but was so appalled when she discovered the identity of her patient that she fainted at once and had to be carried out of the room, leaving the surgeon, who did not pretend to be an obstetric expert, to do what he could. The Queen was in great pain, and there were fears for her life; the child was lying 'athwart her belly', and at one time there was a question of whether the Queen or the child would be saved. The King, who stayed constantly at her bedside, showed his love for her by putting her life before the child's. He would rather, he said, save the mould than the cast.

At last a prince was born and christened immediately by the name of Charles. He lived for only a few hours and the next day he was taken to Westminster Abbey, his small coffin being carried by six baron's sons, and attended by noblemen, bishops, judges and gentlemen. He was laid to rest by the side of his grandfather King James.

There was great distress at Court and in the city. Many feared that the Queen might miscarry again and prove incapable of bearing a living child. It was remembered, however, that a few days before the birth she had been frightened by a disturbance in the gallery at Greenwich, when Lord Dorchester's dog had rushed at her and seized her dress. Others attributed the catastrophe to the fact that she had taken too much exercise, sometimes walking uphill which was considered most unwise.

The Princess of Piedmont was more fortunate than her sister. Christine's pregnancy ran its full term and in July she gave birth to a daughter. Henrietta experienced some moments of jealousy, but she was still able to say that she was the happiest princess in the world. Immediately after her miscarriage she had fallen into a deep sleep and had quickly regained her health. It was considered miraculous that she herself had suffered so little harm, and this at least augured well for the future. In a generous letter to her brother-in-law, Henrietta wrote, 'As to my loss, I wish to forget it, in order to participate with you in the pleasure which my sister's happy *accouchement* has caused you.' The secret of the Queen's contentment lay in her husband's blatant affection, which had increased even more since he had so nearly lost her. The French Ambassador

Extraordinary, the Marquis de Châteauneuf, was amazed to see the King kiss his wife again and again. 'You do not see that at Turin,' he wrote, 'nor at Paris either.'

Towards the end of July the pair were separated when the uxorious King went to Theobalds and the Queen to Tunbridge Wells for what was intended to be a long course of the waters. Henrietta soon found that the spa could not offer enough distractions to take her mind off her husband, so, as Cottington told Wentworth, 'she is suddenly come from thence, and by great journeys meets with the King this night at Oatlands, whither he also returns to pay her in the same coin'.

Châteauneuf, who was an arch-intriguer, at first hoped to make capital out of the King's affection, using the Queen to steer him in ways profitable to the French. But he soon found out that Henrietta was too young and frivolous to care much about international politics, and Charles was aware of the dangers that might arise 'if a woman were to busy herself with matters of government'. He discovered a more fruitful sphere for trouble-making in the Household, by exploiting the Queen's one complaint that she did not receive enough money to look after herself or her dependents. Charles was inclined to think, as husbands so often do, that she was extravagant, and had complained to her in public that she was a bad housekeeper. He expected her to understand that like everybody else in those hard times she would have to economize, remembering that no money had been voted by Parliament and that the merchants were reluctant to pay any dues for fear of jeering crowds round the Customs House denouncing them as traitors. Weston, naturally tight-fisted, could see no solution short of making cuts in every department. His frugal, cantankerous nature appealed more to the King than to his wife, and Châteauneuf did not scruple to encourage the Queen in her dislike of the Lord Treasurer.

In the field of foreign diplomacy the Queen's preferences were more consistent than her husband's. On the one hand Charles would offer help to Christian of Denmark, make friendly overtures to the Dutch and to Gustavus of Sweden. On the other he extended a friendly welcome to Rubens, the painter-diplomat who had come over on a mission from Spain, and he sent Sir Francis Cottington off to Madrid. The Queen never veered from her disapproval of these Spanish dealings. She told Cottington frankly that she did not wish to have anything to do with Spain or with anybody there; when the King told her she could expect another Spanish Ambassador in September or October, she replied that the Spaniards would only deceive him again, to which he retorted that this was only her opinion.

Although there were some people of the Puritan persuasion who would have preferred the Queen to remain barren so that the succession could be settled on the Protestant offspring of the Princess Palatine, prayers were offered up that summer both in England and Scotland, beseeching God to make the Queen 'a happy mother of successful children'. In November there were confident reports that she was with child and in January 1630 a thanksgiving service was arranged. Laud fussily complained to Lord Dorchester that this could not be done at a moment's notice. A special prayer had to be concocted, nothing must be left to chance or inspiration, Bishops would have to be summoned for a conference and the King's approval sought. By February plans were well in hand for the lying-in; the Countess of Denbigh had handed in a warrant for two thousand pounds to cover the extraordinary provision of linen for the event, and over six hundred pounds were spent on the embroidery for the Queen's bed. Marie de Medici sent her daughter a beautiful chaise 'to deliver her from the danger of coaches', as well as a small heart to wear round her neck. 'I fancy it brings me such good fortune that I am always afraid when I am without it,' Henrietta wrote, promising that she would take all possible care of herself, in the hope that this time she would go to the end of her term. Charles also wrote to the Queen Mother confirming that his wife was behaving wisely: 'The only dispute that exists between us is that of conquering each other by affection, both esteeming ourselves victorious in following the will of each.'

In the new year the Queen had to overcome her dislike of all things Spanish when she received the new Ambassador, Don Carlos de Colonna, who came up to her apartments, his way flanked by 'a beautiful line of ladies'. Later he brought her letters from her sister Elisabeth, now Queen of Spain, who like Christine had the previous year given birth to her first child. Having prepared the way for Colonna, Rubens was now about to leave; the King gave him a jewel from his own finger and bestowed on him the honour of a knighthood. During his stay the painter had executed several works, including a picture of 'the history of St. George, wherein (if it be possible) he hath exceeded himself', as one contemporary put it. The Saint and the Princess he has recently rescued, who slightly resemble Charles and Henrietta, stand in a brilliantly-lit English landscape of the type Rubens admired so much, with cherubs soaring overhead, and in the background, tactfully, the riverside Palace of Lambeth.

Charles disliked Châteauneuf as much as he liked Rubens, and when the French sent a new Ambassador, Fontenay-Mareuil, he made it clear that he did not wish Châteauneuf to stay a moment longer than necessary. At the end of February, the Capuchin friars arrived in London, but although the Queen had bought up houses between Somerset House and the Mitre Tavern to make lodgings for them, and was planning to turn the tennis court into a chapel, work had hardly begun on the conversion.

The Duke of Buckingham with his family.   The Duke is seated with, on his right, his wife and his sister, Susan, Countess of Denbigh, and on his left his mother, the Countess of Buckingham and his two brothers. In front are his two eldest children, Lady Mary Villiers and a son, who died young

Charles I, Henrietta Maria and Charles, Prince of Wales.   The Queen and the child hold sprigs of olive symbolizing peace; the sprigs of laurel on the table symbolize war

Charles I and Henrietta Maria departing for the chase

Charles I and Henrietta Maria dining in public

Philip, 4th Earl of Pembroke with his family.   On the Earl's left are his wife, his daughter Sophia and her husband Dormer, Earl of Carnarvon.   On his right are his five sons, Charles, Lord Herbert, and his wife Mary Villiers, and Philip, William, James and John

The five eldest children of Charles I.   From the left, Princess Mary, Prince James, Prince Charles, Princess Elizabeth and Princess Anne

John Williams as Keeper of the Great Seal

Archbishop Laud

William Prynne

This did not surprise the new Venetian Ambassador, who had already noticed that the English were slow about everything, particularly where the Catholics were concerned. Châteauneuf had worked tirelessly to ensure the introduction of the Capuchins, and had tried even harder to establish a Bishop as their leader. Many people viewed the arrival of the friars with great suspicion, and wondered how the King would find the means to pay for them, but according to one of their number, Father Cyprien of Gamache, Charles and Henrietta Maria greeted them 'with strong demonstration of affection'. The King had been impressed with the members of their order he had met in Madrid, but he still refused to allow a Bishop in the Household.

The French King had presented the friars with a set of new cassocks, but very soon they asked permission to wear the patched brown habits which were the uniform of their order. On the third Sunday in Lent, they celebrated Mass, and Father Aimé preached on the theme of the deaf and dumb man in the Scripture, whom he compared to the Queen. If, he said, since the dismissal of the French, she had not been able to hear any preachers, it would be true to say that the Holy Ghost, the greatest preacher of them all, had spoken to her heart.

In France the Capuchins, with their simple way of life and genuine charity, had converted large numbers of Protestants, and when people in London began flocking to the Mass openly in great crowds, the King realized the need for firm action. He issued a proclamation for restraint, stating that anybody coming out of the Mass would be apprehended and brought before the Lords of the Council. Pursuivants were stationed outside the houses of the Catholic Ambassadors, and many people who went to Mass that morning were removed to dismal prisons, 'to be confined among persons of various classes', as Father Cyprien put it. It was reported that the wife of one of the Queen's officers, a woman of exemplary virtue, was prematurely delivered of her child owing to the rough treatment she received. Outside the Queen's Chapel the pursuivants warned worshippers as they went in that if they were English they would be wise to turn back, but some were arrested at their homes the following day, the more well-off being released on bail.

Prompted by Châteauneuf, the Queen complained to her husband, but Charles replied succinctly, 'I permit you your religion with your Capuchins and others. I permit Ambassadors and their retinue, but the rest of my subjects I will have them live in the religion that I profess and my father before me.' At his wife's insistence the King agreed to grant Châteauneuf an interview. The Frenchman hinted at reprisals against the Huguenots and advised the King to act more moderately. 'You cannot prevent me from concerning myself in what touches the honour and conscience of the Queen,' he said, 'as she is the sister of my King and we gave her on such conditions.' The King, expressing the opinion that it was not wise at this stage to excite the Queen's feelings, refused to discuss the matter, but Châteauneuf, during his last weeks in England, did all the damage he could—'using stimulants', was how Soranzo put it. The Queen refused to see the Lords of the Council for several days, and showed her disapproval of Weston, who was supposed to be sympathetic towards Catholics and yet had allowed such things to happen. It was the common belief among recusants that he had authorized and even suggested the arrests, in order to ingratiate himself with the Puritans and to raise some much-needed money by imposing fines.

The Capuchins were sure that it was due to Châteauneuf's undesirable influence over the Queen that she now refused to part with the two Oratorians, one of them her confessor, Father Philip, who were to have left as soon as the Capuchins arrived. Father Léonard was so disgusted that he threatened to return straight to France, taking all the other friars with him, but he was reminded that he had a mission and was obliged to stay in England to convert as many Protestants as possible. The departure of Châteauneuf eased the tension. At the Queen's insistence he was allowed to take back with him a number of priests, and after his show of strength the King allowed the Catholics to enjoy what Father Cyprien described as 'a sweet and agreeable peace'.

Plans were going ahead for the Queen's confinement. The King had given permission for Madame de Péronne to attend her. The midwife arrived in good time after an adventurous journey in which she had been captured by the Dunkirkers, in company with the Queen's favourite dwarf, her dancing master, and, it was rumoured, a contingent of twelve nuns. The King promised that once the Queen was brought to bed none of the nurses or rockers would be Catholics, and he refused to admit a French physician sent over by the Queen Mother. He insisted that the doctor should go back to France, 'with intimation he should do it speedily'. Fontenay thought that he should at least be allowed to kiss the Queen's hand, but the King, suspecting that Châteauneuf was behind the move, remained firm.

It was decided that St James's, surrounded by its extensive park, might prove to be the safest refuge from the plague. The Queen was allowed to have two of her Capuchins with her. May passed uneventfully, and on the 29th, in the early hours, she fell into labour, which lasted until the sun was high and she brought forth 'a new sun for all Great Britain'. The child, a prince—'a most grateful pledge sent to secure the succession' —was born between two eclipses, one of the moon on May 16, and the other of the sun on May 31; it was said that on the day of his birth a brilliant star was seen shining in the east at noonday by observers standing in St Paul's churchyard.

A few of the King's subjects made some outspoken comments, and one Perkins who threw doubt on the Prince's parentage was hung, drawn and quartered for his pains. But in general the infant's reception was favourable:

Welcome blest babe whom God thy father sent
To make him rich without a Parliament

was how one versifier expressed it. In both town and country there was the usual outbreak of bonfires, and the day after the birth the King went in solemn procession with the Lords of the Council and many others to St Paul's where he took the sacrament and gave thanks to God. Laud, who had the happiness of seeing the royal infant in the first hour of his birth, was asked to compose the official prayer of thanksgiving.

Although Madame de Péronne was sent back to France in July, the King caused offence by appointing the Countess of Roxburgh as the Prince's governess. Since the Countess had played an important part in drawing the infant's grandmother, Anne of Denmark, into the Catholic faith, the King was persuaded to substitute the Protestant Lady Dorset, causing his wife some annoyance in the process. 'He obliges no one, either in deed or word' was the comment of the Venetian Ambassador, Soranzo. Charles did, however, make sure that the Prince's christening should take place before the French King had time to lodge any objections. The Capuchins were informed that they would not be required to officiate as the King was making all the arrangements himself. Although one of the main clauses in the marriage treaty had stipulated that all the Queen's children should be brought up in the Catholic faith until they reached the age of fourteen, the Prince was baptised into the Anglican faith. Laud officiated, as Archbishop Abbott was considered too infirm. All the other spiritual lords were invited, with the exception of Bishop Williams, 'which troubled him mightily, that in a day of public rejoicing, when his Majesty's brow was clear to everybody, it should frown upon him alone'.

The Court kept free of the plague which raged all through the hot dry summer of 1630, and the Prince thrived. Twice the King broke off his progress and joined the Queen to visit their son who was large for his age and dark to the point of swarthiness. 'If my son knew how to talk,' the Queen wrote to Mamie, 'I think he would send you his compliments; he is so fat and so tall, that he is taken for a year old, and he is only four months; his teeth are already beginning to come; I will send you his portrait as soon as he is a little fairer for at present he is so dark that I am ashamed of him.' In July a strange fever swept through the Household and the Prince's nurse fell sick, but the child escaped and continued to flourish. In August and throughout the autumn there were rumours that the Queen was pregnant again. As the colder weather came, the plague died out and life returned to normal. The playhouses opened on November 12 after seven months of enforced idleness and new liveries were issued to the Queen's players. Henrietta made several visits to the theatre, which some of her husband's subjects found shocking.

The King's love for the Queen showed no sign of diminishing and the departure of Châteauneuf had removed one last source of friction. Tranquillity and a feeling of ordered calm were the King's greatest needs. In his foreign relations he was now trying to establish himself everywhere as a man of peace, and in his own Household he strove to cultivate an atmosphere that was civilized and lacking what he and his contemporaries described as 'jars'. In January 1631 he issued orders for the reformation of irregularities which stressed the need to observe due precedence, order and respect. His court was to be purged of uncivilized behaviour; nobody was to 'wait upon the King to Chapel in boots and spurs, or enter booted into the presence or the privy chamber'. Ladies about the Queen were reminded that they should keep to their places as strictly as the lords. It was stressed that nobody under the rank of baron should be allowed to enter the inner closet or set foot on the steps of the dais where the royal chairs were placed. When the King and Queen ate in public nobody was permitted to go too near, and all courtiers were expected 'to use great distance and respect to the royal persons, as also civility to one another'.

It was easier for the King to carry out his role as God's deputy on earth if in his everyday life he was set apart, a dignified and distant figure, never jostled by a crowd of ordinary mortals, many of whom were taller than he was. Artists were encouraged to propagate the legend, to paint the King, preferably on horseback, in attitudes that were splendid and remote. The King chose as his closest advisers efficient austere men like Weston, Wentworth and Laud, who dedicated themselves to the task of imposing the divine order on a people shut out from the highest mysteries by the palace walls and the altar rail. He was prepared to lavish large sums on entertainments at Court which embodied in words, music, dance and scenic effect the underlying theme of order and harmony.

As the year of 1630 drew to its close the scene-painters and carpenters were already at work on the cut-outs, cloud borders, scenes of relieve, backcloths. The embroiderers were busy stitching the costumes with patterns of silver and gold, and sewing on the sequins which would reflect the light from hundreds of lamps and candles. Inigo Jones worked tirelessly, consulting the source-books and emblem-books—Ripa's *Iconologia*, Callot's handbook of *commedia dell'arte* figures—which provided the basis for innumerable costume designs. For the Queen who was to take the part of Chloris, goddess of the flowers, Jones made at least eight different designs with alternative sleeve and skirt details. 'This design I conceive to be fit for the invention,' he wrote on the page he finally submitted to Henrietta, adding that if she wished to alter anything, she was to send her commands by the bearer. 'The colours are also in her Majesty's choice,' he added, 'but my opinion is that general fresh greens mixed with gold and silver will be most proper.'

Although he was in bad health now, having suffered two strokes, Ben Jonson had been engaged to write the scripts for the two masques which were to be performed in the new year of 1631.

The Queen's masque, *Chlorydia*, took place at Shrovetide, six weeks after the King's. The evidence suggests that during the preparations the Queen worked closely with Inigo Jones, who was ready to assimilate ideas and suggestions which she contributed, drawing on her memory of the ballets in Paris. The overall effect of the masque was warmer and less cerebral than the King's, and the sets and costumes expressed the spring-like theme in every detail down to the fresh greens recommended by Jones for the Queen's costume. Jupiter, wishing to create harmony between heaven and earth, had decided to strew the world with flowers, which would shine like the constellations in the skies:

All emulation cease, and jars,
Jove will have Earth to have her stars
And lights no less than heaven.

For the first time Jones startled the audience by drawing the curtain up rather than letting it fall to the ground, and the effect was intensified by the beauty of the pastoral setting which was revealed. For a moment there was a pause while the spectators had a chance to take in the gentle hills planted with trees, the slopes adorned with flowers, the fountains gliding out of the hollows. Then a luminous cloud appeared bringing a plump zephyr and Spring herself in a green and white dress wrought with flowers and a garland in her hair.

All this rural peace was threatened by a quarrel which had developed between Cupid and the gods. Believing himself 'slightly passed by as a child', Cupid had gone off in a rage to create chaos in hell. All the normal infernal routines had been upset; the furies were to be seen playing nine-pins, Tantalus had at last begun to eat the fruit which had eluded him for so long, and Sisyphus, instead of eternally rolling his ball, had become 'Mr Bowler . . . upon Tityus his breast, that, for six of the nine acres, is counted the subtlest bowling green in all Tartary'.

Ben Jonson was not partial to foreign innovations, but he had been persuaded to divide the anti-masque into eight clearly-defined *entrées* in the French manner. After a grotesque dance by the dwarf, Geoffrey Hudson, with six infernal spirits, the sky darkened, a sophisticated effect not easy to achieve in the days when lamps and candles could not be dimmed at the touch of a switch. The ensuing storm gave way as quickly to a sudden calm; the scene changed, revealing the Queen in a bower, surrounded by fourteen nymphs all played by ladies of her Household. The heavens then opened, and Juno and Iris, attended by many aerial spirits, appeared on clouds, while a three-dimensional mountain, large enough to support four people and topped by the figure of Fame on a globe, appeared from under the stage. Fame then took wing and flew up into the clouds, her wings actually moving, while a full chorus sang a song in honour of Chloris.

The hill sank back into the ground, the heavens closed and the masquers came down from the stage, out of the frame into the dancing place, where they chose their partners from the watching lords in a symbolic union of the real and the imaginary.

Chapter 10

THE TRIUMPH OF PEACE

L OOKING AT life from his own particular vantage point it was
easy for the King of England, in the spring of 1631, to feel a
certain satisfaction. His domestic life was peaceful, he had avoided
foreign entanglements, silenced his Parliament and set on foot a policy
of unification within the Church. His art collection was increasing, and
many foreign artists were coming to London, drawn by the air of stability
and the prospect of royal patronage. The English had struck Rubens as
'a people rich and happy in the lap of peace', and he had been impressed
by 'the incredible quantity of excellent pictures, statues and ancient
inscriptions' to be seen at the Court. The King had at least temporarily
solved his financial problems by cutting down on pensions, board wages,
free tables and expensive commitments abroad, but for his under-
privileged subjects the situation was rather less hopeful; to many it
seemed that the economy, as economies so often are, was altogether out
of control and a prey to unpredictable circumstances.

It had been a hard winter for 'the poorer sort' after the drought and
plague of the previous summer. Scarcity of wheat coupled with a decline
in trade and particularly the wool trade had brought many to the brink
of starvation. The Privy Council had been receiving pleas for help from
all parts of the country, and Justices of the Peace had been ordered to take
measures for controlling the price of wheat and for dealing with hungry
mobs. The King, however, did not hear the daily prayers to the overseers
for relief, and it was easy for him, as it was also for Bishop Laud, to
ignore the feelings of those who lived outside his own safe circle.

Reassured continually by the favour and friendship of the monarch,
Laud laboured to carry out his mission of unifying the Church, paying
little regard to the difficulties of clergy in parishes that had been going
their own way for years. 'If I had suddenly and hastily fallen upon the
strict practice of conformity,' one clergyman complained, 'I had undone
myself and broken the town to pieces.' The sight of a clergyman bowing
deeply to an altar which had been moved from its accustomed place in
the nave could cause the kind of resentment which prompted men to
leave all they had and set off for New England. The irritation aroused in

some parishes when incumbents were called upon to provide candles for altar lights or, worse still, tapers in front of images, was summed up succinctly by one churchwarden who wrote in the margin of an account for the payment of wax, 'W. Grace is a fool to pay, but some have no sense.' The moderate Bishop Williams recommended that Puritans should be wooed with 'fair entreaties'; it was his policy to introduce at first only such ceremonies as were palatable, waiting 'till their queasy stomachs would digest the rest'. But Laud did not believe in forbearance; he worked ruthlessly to save congregations from non-conformity and churches from decay. In January 1631 he appeared in Leadenhall Street in full regalia for the consecration of the rebuilt church of St Catherine Cree. He knelt in the doorway, visited different parts of the church, and bowed low on every possible occasion.

Bishop Williams believed that a rigid suppression of non-conformist opinions could make the zealots more rebellious than ever, so that in the end 'it would in all probability turn to a general combustion'. Such prophecies did not trouble the King. He never doubted that he was in the right. His wife had submitted to his will, and his own secure position compared favourably with his brother-in-law's, for Louis had fallen out with his mother who was now confined in the château at Compiègne. She had connived with the Spanish Ambassador, backed Michel de Marillac as Richelieu's successor, and spoken offensively to the King and the Cardinal on several occasions. Gaston had gone off in the direction of Orléans and it seemed likely that he would try to raise a revolt. Marillac had been arrested after the 'day of the dupes', and his place taken by Châteauneuf, who had not yet abandoned his attempts to make trouble in England.

One of the Queen's companions, the witty, sociable Chevalier de Jars, had gained a small foothold in her favour, and the King did not appear to resent the Frenchman's presence—perhaps because he was capable of giving him a good game of tennis. It was Fontenay who first suggested that the aptly-named de Jars could be acting as the agent of Châteauneuf who had come to the fore in France after the arrest of Marillac, without abandoning his attempts to make trouble in England. De Jars employed a house-breaker to climb through the window in the Chevalier's house and instructed him to carry off any correspondence to be found in the cabinet. The letters discovered were in the main from Châteauneuf to de Jars, but there were also three written by the Queen. In one of them she inadvisedly stated that she thought Châteauneuf would make a better first minister than Richelieu.

The Queen was not pleased when she heard about the break-in. She appealed to her husband to bring the thief to justice, but he did not listen to her, being anxious, no doubt, to show her that she meddled in dangerous intrigues at her peril. She had never liked Fontenay and now she felt less well disposed towards him than ever. She complained to him about the treatment her mother had received and showed some sympathy for Gaston, her childhood companion. In May, when her new Grand Almoner, the Abbé Péronne, arrived in England, the Queen pleaded indisposition and refused to receive him. Fontenay told her that she would now have to part with her confessor, Father Philip, and this she refused to do. Louis at once complained to Charles; the matter was important to him, for Father Philip was a member of the Oratory, a follower of Bérulle, who had ended his life in opposition to Richelieu. The Queen told Fontenay that she did not wish to be dependent on anything but her own good pleasure in what touched her Household; it was not the first time that she had been obliged to remind her brother that she was no longer a child, and she uttered some 'resentful expressions' which, it was thought, would certainly show the French King that she would not appreciate any further meddling.

Charles appreciated the danger of being drawn into a conflict with his brother-in-law, and he refused to let Marie de Medici threaten his hard-won domestic serenity, making it quite clear that he did not intend to offer her asylum in England. Henrietta was pregnant again and he did not want her upset, but he let her take an active interest in building projects and artistic matters, which were less dangerous, if at times more expensive to dabble in than politics. There was little enough in the Exchequer when it came to large-scale ventures. The King could only afford to improve existing property, and to complete the Queen's House at Greenwich, which had remained half-finished at the death of Anne of Denmark. At Michaelmas 1631, Inigo Jones was appointed Surveyor of the Queen's works, and at Somerset House and Greenwich, French craftsmen were employed to give the rooms that Gallic flavour which the Queen still preferred in clothes, gardens and interior design. When her old 'petticoat waist' had grown shabby after two years' wear, she asked Mamie to send over a French tailor to take her measurements for new ones. She had despatched a man to Paris especially to buy fruit-trees and flowers, and French designers had been in charge of the interior of the New Cabinet Room which had been built on to Somerset House opposite the Water Gate.

In the early hours of November 4 the Queen gave birth to a daughter, Mary, who was christened at once, some said because the baby was weak, although others guessed that it was to save the expense of a public occasion. On the same day the King went to see the Queen with her illegitimate brother, the Duc de Vendôme, who was in England for a few days' hunting. She made a quick recovery and was soon making plans for the masques that were to be presented in the new year.

Inigo Jones had ended his partnership with Ben Jonson. The final break had come after the printing of the texts the previous year. Collaboration had never been easy in all the thirty years that they had worked together, and Jonson had for some time been envious of the acclaim afforded to the man who was in his opinion a mere craftsman. He exploded into anger on seeing the architect's name placed before his on the title page.

Jonson had summed up his partner, as early as 1612, as a time-server and a flatterer, but the quarrel was more than a clash of personalities. Jonson was expressing a common humanistic view when he talked of the settings of a masque as the body or carcass, and the poetry as the soul or spirit. On the other hand there was a tendency, particularly among architects themselves, to elevate architecture above the level of a craft. They believed that by virtue of his intellectual ability and his understanding of architectural theory, the architect can become more than a builder whose edifices grow haphazardly dominated by the requirements of practical necessity and without any artistic discipline. For Jones, architecture was an extension of Plato's theory of harmony based on numbers, and it was his belief that every feature of a building—window, door, architrave, rustication—was subservient to the overall design. He had embodied his theories in the Whitehall Banqueting House, which stood out from the rambling buildings of the rest of the palace by the controlled and classical simplicity of its outline and detail. In the same way, the masques which were staged in its fine and lofty interior should, Jones thought, be the product of a single mastermind, with poetry, music, dance, costumes and sets all mirroring the central theme. In the text of *Chlorydia*, after the fable or story had been described, it was stated that 'upon this hinge the whole invention moved', and it was his desire to make every element subordinate to the whole which made Jones work so assiduously, turning out dozens of sketches for costumes and leaving as little of the actual designing as possible to his minions. Although he graciously gave the Queen a chance to alter the shade of her dress, he would probably have been none too pleased if she had exercised her prerogative and chosen a discordant colour out of keeping with the general theme.

By the new year of 1632 Inigo Jones was as secure in the Queen's favour as he had become some years before in the King's, and he felt confident enough to annex the position of the guiding spirit whose mind could dominate and direct the whole performance. 'He'll do't alone, Sir,' was how Jonson put it:

> . . . he will join with no man,
> Though he be a joiner; in design he calls it,
> He must be sole inventor.

Released from the restraining hand which his crusty companion had laid on him for so many years, Jones planned a succession of sets for the two masques of 1632 which would prove his supremacy for all time and establish the form as 'nothing else but pictures with light and motion'. In Aurelian Townshend he found a poet who was suitably self-effacing— 'as loath to be brought upon the stage as an unhandsome man is to see himself in a great glass'. Dozens of torches were ordered and the lights for the King's masque were scheduled for delivery on the first Monday in the new year. The King's masque, *Albion's Triumph*, performed on January 8, gave Jones an opportunity to display his classical virtuosity in a succession of Roman settings, and it also enabled him to project a heroic picture of the King, all-conquering through the power of love, bringing prosperity to his country through peace rather than war.

The Queen's masque, *Tempe Restored*, was to have followed a week later, but it was postponed until Shrove Tuesday as the Queen was suffering from a soreness of the eyes. The story was taken, most likely at the Queen's suggestion, from a French masque, the *Ballet Comique de la Reine*. The curtain went up to reveal a fresh rural scene with statues and fountains spouting water into vases, as well as some slender trees, 'whose leaves seemed to move with a gentle breeze coming from the far-off hills'. Tempe, who had been living with Circe 'in all sensual delights', had been turned into a wild beast by his enchantress who now pursued him across the stage, a furious figure in the form of the professional singer Madame Coniacke. The bestial elements were represented in the anti-masque by a succession of Indians and barbarians—there were no gentle savages in this world—and the higher qualities were introduced in the shape of fourteen Influences of the Stars, all played by children, who included Buckingham's daughter, Lady Mary Villiers, and his niece Lady Elizabeth Feilding. They danced a sarabande before taking their places among the lords and ladies of the audience.

By now the Queen had such faith in Inigo Jones that she was prepared to trust her royal person to one of his cloud machines. A calm sea under an orient sky, bordered by cliffs with a castle and trees, formed the background for one of the most spectacular effects ever achieved at Whitehall. First appeared the eight spheres seated on a cloud, all played by musicians with Nicholas Lanier, the composer, at their head. Two more clouds brought eight stars down to earth, followed by five more, and finally the Queen herself as Divine Beauty in a golden chariot studded with jewels. She was wearing a dress of watchet blue embossed with stars, her head haloed with light.

Everyone descended in due order, the Queen stepped out of her chariot and the clouds went into reverse, returning like a great chain linking earth to heaven. The 'apparitions'—those who had appeared from the sky—joined the chorus in a great tableau of blue and silver, with at least fifty people on the stage. After the main dance, the King and Queen sat together and saw yet another breathtaking effect when Jove appeared on an eagle 'with a glory behind him', and Cupid, suspended on a wire, flew about the stage, turning and soaring in the air, while thirty-five musicians stood below to assist them with a song in honour of 'this matchless pair'.

It was agreed that everyone, including the Queen, had excelled themselves, demonstrating by their efforts the magnificence of the Court of England. Divine Beauty, deigning to descend from the skies, had shown that man was 'only a mind using the body and affections as instruments', while corporeal beauty, 'shining in the Queen's majesty', had provided the embodiment of the ideal which the King wished to see throughout his Court and country.

As soon as the masque was over the King and Queen went away on a visit to Royston, Cambridge and Newmarket, which, as one of their subjects put it, 'with this year's double masques still increase the charge'. In the opinion of some there were better ways of demonstrating a country's strength than by expending money on masquing habits with doublets of white satin, carnation-coloured breeches, cloaks lined with plush, silk stockings, white shoes with carnation roses, hats and feathers, bands of lace in the newest fashion, gloves, girdles and points. Many people would have preferred to see the King giving active help to the Protestant cause under the banner of the magnificent Swede, Gustavus Adolphus. Charles, however, took little notice of his critics. He said openly that he was afraid to jeopardize his 'settled, quiet state'. He liked to spend his summers enjoying the pleasures of the chase, sitting for portrait painters, and enjoying that mirror of Divine Beauty, his wife, rather than marching from one dusty battlefield to another.

At Newmarket the Queen joined in the King's country pursuits with such enthusiasm that she overtired herself and had only just recovered in time to accompany him when he entered London. They stayed in the capital for only a short time before moving on to Greenwich. The King had invited Van Dyck to England, establishing him as Painter-in-Ordinary, and that summer he worked on portraits of the King and Queen as well as a family group with the Prince of Wales and the Princess Royal. Convinced that this was the best way to spend a summer, the King issued a proclamation directing all gentlemen to leave London and return to their country houses, where they could practise good husbandry and save the money which would otherwise be spent in ordinaries and dicing-houses. Believing that he had a right to impose regulations which promoted the cause of order and economy, the King ignored the feelings of men who might resent the measure as an intrusion into their private lives—and of their wives denied the pleasure of dressing up and parading about in Hyde Park under a summer sun. The heavy fines imposed on offenders were a useful source of revenue, and one unfortunate gentleman had to pay a thousand pounds for staying in London, although he pleaded that he was a bachelor and that his only country house had been destroyed by fire.

The King knew that if his subjects congregated in London taverns they would criticize his policies, and particularly his inactivity in the Protestant cause. Few Protestants could remain unmoved when they heard that Gustavus had won a succession of victories which had a heroic ring about them like stories out of the Book of Joshua. Almost unaided the Swede had made the papist 'hang his head like a bulrush', and Charles was content to let him continue the good work on his own. Gustavus had rejected a niggardly offer of financial help, and expressed his unwillingness to make any effort on behalf of the Palatinate in return for empty promises. He would not have refused a contingent made up of eight regiments of foot and three hundred horse, preferably with the unmilitary Charles in command, but he had long ago despaired of receiving any effective help. A suggestion that the long-delayed payment of the second half of Henrietta's dowry should be handed over direct to him also came to nothing, as he might have expected.

It was a cold summer—'the coldest June clean through that was ever felt in my memory,' wrote Laud in his diary—but a good harvest brought comparative prosperity after the drought and famine of the previous year. The King could look about him with satisfaction as he travelled through a fruitful countryside which had not suffered the ravages of war. While his brother-in-law struggled to quell Gaston's rebel forces which were under the leadership of the dashing Montmorency, Charles had time to spare for more creative tasks:

Temples and Towns by thy stayed hand.
First learn to rise, and then to stand.

Such had been the words of the apparitions hovering on a cloud above Whitehall in *Albion's Triumph*.

Plans were going ahead well for the construction of the Queen's chapel at Somerset House, and in September 1632 Henrietta laid the foundation stone in the Tennis Courtyard. A plot of ground had been fitted up with walls of tapestry and the floor was strewn with sweet-smelling flowers. The altar was furnished with enough chandeliers and vases in silver gilt to invite comparison with Solomon's temple. A large crowd gathered for the ceremony—it was as if the whole of London had turned out. Father Péronne celebrated High Mass and afterwards granted some indulgences 'while harmonious music ravished the heart'. The French Ambassador then led the Queen to the stone where she took mortar from a silver basin with a trowel fringed with velvet, and threw it three times on to the stone 'with a grace which imparted devotion to the people'. A silver plate carried a Latin inscription with an engraving of the royal couple on one side and of the Capuchins on the other. Gifts which the Queen presented to the workmen far surpassed their expectation and there were deafening shouts of *Long Live the Queen.*

That autumn orders were issued for regulating the Queen's Household —'to establish government and order in our Court on the side of our dearest consort the Queen, which from thence may be spread through all parts of our kingdoms'. It was stressed that everybody must keep their place in the system—no servant except a Duchess's 'chief woman' was to go beyond the Guard Chamber, the two gentlemen ushers on duty were allowed as far as the gallery door and no further; the grooms of the Privy Chamber, always correctly dressed in doublet and hose without cloaks, had to wait at the withdrawing room door 'to make fires and do other services as they shall be commanded'. The pages of the backstairs were to ensure that no unauthorized person was admitted, and they were on no account to employ a deputy unless they were sick and had been granted leave of absence by the Lord Chamberlain. The maids of honour were strictly disciplined, their day lasting from prayers at eleven until supper time with an hour off for lunch, 'and when they shall be retired into their chamber, they admit of no man to come there'. They were not allowed out of the palace without special leave, and if the mother of the maids found any 'refractoriness' in any of them, she was obliged to acquaint the Lord Chamberlain or his deputy.

The year ended well for the King and Queen and events seemed to confirm the wisdom of their way of life. Gaston's rebellion had been crushed; Montmorency had lost his life on the scaffold, while the great Gustavus had been found lying dead among the common soldiery on the battlefield of Lützen, shorn of his clothes, his plumes and his regalia. Charles, on the other hand, having lived through nothing more dangerous than a mild attack of smallpox, could look forward to another year of peace, pleasure and nuptial bliss.

Ever since their return from the country, the Queen and her ladies had been rehearsing a pastoral, *The Shepherd's Paradise* by Walter Montagu, who was a close friend of the Queen. It was hoped that the play would help to improve the Queen's English. Rehearsals were held every day, and it was reported that Taylor, a leading actor at the Globe, was going regularly to the palace 'to teach them action'. It was unfortunate, in this context, that William Prynne's *Histrio-Mastix or the Player's Scourge* should have first appeared in the autumn of 1632. It was a weighty tome running into a thousand pages, which attacked equally fiercely the evils of boys playing women's parts or of women acting in stage plays. It was Laud's chaplain, Heylyn, studying the book with meticulous care, who discovered that in the index women actors were described as 'notorious whores'. He also unearthed some criticism of dancing—the Queen's favourite pastime—and a comment that Nero's murder was well-deserved as he had been in the habit of frequenting plays. Since both the King and the Queen had their own players and were known to be devotees of the theatre, such remarks were not likely to meet with royal approval, and the suggestion that the chaste Henrietta could be classed as a whore was enough to justify, in the King's eyes, Prynne's immediate committal to the Tower.

Preparations for the pastoral went on, unaffected by Prynne's strictures. In the new year five men were paid the modest sum of sixteen shillings between them for working day and night on the construction of the theatre. The Lord Chamberlain issued strict directives as to who should be admitted—no great lady would be kept out, it was rumoured, even if she had 'mean apparel and a worse face', and no inferior lady would be admitted unless she wore 'extreme brave apparel' and a better face. Inigo Jones had designed some fine costumes and 'perspective' settings. Even Prynne would have been hard put to it to find a trace of immorality in the turgidly neo-Platonic dialogue of *The Shepherd's Paradise*, and it was as well that provision had been made for 'close-stools against the Queen's pastoral' since the performance lasted for eight hours; Lady Hamilton's part alone, it was reported, was 'as long as an ordinary play', and one feels for any chambermaid intrepid enough to see it through, as those of her rank were admitted only if they were prepared to sit 'cross-legged on the top of a bulk'.

The King was evidently impressed, as he ordered another showing for Candlemas. His affection for the Queen showed no sign of lessening, and she had demonstrated her devotion by staying at his side throughout his attack of smallpox. In the spring, however, Charles was put in a difficult position, not for the first time, by his wife's indiscretion. If the royal pair disagreed about anything it was about each other's friends; Henrietta had never grown to like Weston, and Charles sometimes found that her agreeable but over-ebullient companions were inclined to over-step the bounds of strict conformity. In March 1633, Jerome Weston, the Lord Treasurer's son, returning to England from Paris, intercepted letters to Châteauneuf from Lord Holland and the Queen. This seemed to confirm suspicions that Holland had been meddling in dangerous intrigues involving the Queen Mother, and that the Queen was inter-ceding on behalf of her old friends Châteauneuf and de Jars who had been imprisoned on a charge of plotting against the Cardinal. In spite of his wife's involvement, the King did not flinch from defending the Lord

Treasurer and his son, and when Holland challenged Jerome Weston to a duel the King had him arrested, as well as Henry Jermyn, another of the Queen's favourites, who had carried the challenge. The rift between the two Households became more clear-cut than ever before as the Queen's friends all began to visit Holland who was confined to his own house in Kensington, in open defiance of the King and Weston, who had now been created Earl of Portland.

Jermyn was banished from the Court; Holland was officially reprimanded although he was allowed to keep all his offices. The Queen was pregnant again, and it was hard for the King to resist her when she pleaded for her favourite. He was making preparations for his departure to Scotland where his long-postponed coronation was to take place on June 18. During his absence the Queen was described as 'a perfect mourning turtle', but her light-hearted companions did all they could to distract her. On one occasion, when she had gone up the river from Greenwich with a large crowd of courtiers to visit Buckingham's widow, she challenged Goring to a boat race on a long stretch of the Thames. The stakes were high, and crowds of ladies and gentlemen followed behind in small boats to watch the outcome. The royal barque finished in the lead, and the Queen netted a total of five hundred crowns.

On July 18, 1633, the King left Edinburgh, travelling ahead of his retinue and reaching London from Berwick in only four days in order to be with his wife the sooner. Her child was due in October and she told Mamie that she was much 'incommoded' by her size. The rest of the King's train followed more slowly, including Laud who had been at his side during the coronation ceremony, bowing and backing in front of an altar furnished with books, basin and chandeliers, in a manner that seemed to many altogether too 'haughty and pontifical'. The Archbishop of Canterbury had been ill for some time, and news of his death reached the Court soon after the return from Scotland. When Laud next put in an appearance, the King said to him, 'My Lord's Grace of Canterbury, you are very welcome.' Laud's own comment in his diary was unemotional. 'September 19 Thursday. I was translated to the Archbishopric of Canterbury. The Lord make me able etc.'

One of Laud's first tasks after taking up his appointment was to christen the King's second son, James, who was born on November 14. The usual rejoicing for a male child was slightly tempered by the fact that his health was precarious, due, the Puritans thought, to the presence of a papist nurse who refused to take the Oath of Allegiance. The Queen made such a scene when she was told to change her nurse that in the end she was allowed to have her way and the child survived in spite of the proximity of a Catholic. The succession was now well-established and the future looked serene. 'Never was there private family more at full peace nor was well qualified to fill. He was to tell the Scots that they must accept the service book or expect trouble, and this was not an easy message for a Scotsman whose estates lay in that stormy country.

Mary Hamilton died a Protestant, mildly resisting to the end the blandishments of the Catholics who hoped for a last-minute conversion. She passed away serenely, in the certainty that she would receive salvation from the hands of a non-sectarian God. As the Queen mourned the loss of one old friend, she saw the arrival of another—Madame de Chevreuse, who had fled from France after the discovery of Queen Anne's correspondence with Spain. There were few intrigues in which this expensive visitor had not dabbled. Although her presence in England was likely to jeopardize friendly relations with France, the Queen sent coaches to meet her, and the King decreed that she should be treated in the French fashion, easily and without formality, to avoid difficulties over protocol. 'Easy' was a word that could be used of the Duchess with impunity. Her violet eyes with their famous lids began to exert their attraction all over again—Lord Holland, it seemed, took up with her just where he had left off. Her original plan had been to stay for only a short while before going on to visit the Queen Mother, but it was evident that she was enjoying herself far too much to move off quickly. The King and Queen allowed her to sit in their presence, which caused some jealousy among the ladies at Court, and displeased the French Ambassador, not to mention his wife.

In May it was announced that Sir John Winter was to become the Queen's Secretary. It was a surprise appointment as many more familiar names had been in people's minds—Henry Jermyn, now restored to favour, Walter Montagu, Sir Kenelm Digby. Winter, a nephew of the Earl of Worcester, was a Catholic industrialist who owned iron mines in the Forest of Dean and coal-mines in Wales which with skilful management had turned him into one of the richest men in the kingdom. His wealth and natural resources were likely to prove of more value to the Crown than courtly virtues, and the King was not to regret the appointment, but inevitably criticism was aroused among those who feared the much overrated growth of Catholic influence in the country.

The Prince's household was also set up in May and at the end of the month the nine-year-old boy was installed as a member of the Order of the Garter. After the ceremony the Prince returned as usual to Richmond and the King and Queen went back to London before going down to Greenwich. As always the capital emptied during the summer months in spite of the crisis, a state of affairs that continued until the following October, to the surprise of the new Venetian Ambassador, Giustinian, who complained of the 'chronic sterility' of the Court. There were many disappointed men who returned to the country for good that summer. Three or four hundred had solicited for places in the Prince's household and tranquillity than in this glorious kingdom,' wrote Goring, 'for we hear not of the least disorder therein from one end thereof to the other.' Now that Laud was at Lambeth all seemed well with the world. At last he could really mould the Church to his liking and impose his influence on parishes throughout the land. He re-issued the *Book of Liberty on Sabbath Days*, better known as the *Book of Sports*, and ordered all churchwardens to buy a copy together with a new book of Articles and *A Prayer for the Queen's Safe Delivery*.

In every department the King sought to influence the life of his subjects, moulding the pattern of their Sundays, imposing a standard of morality and stressing the sanctity of marriage. Both he and Laud believed that on the sabbath 'the meaner sort' should be allowed their traditional recreations to refresh their spirits after the hard week's work. Morris dances, archery, leaping, vaulting, May games and Whit-ales were all useful outlets without which the working man might be tempted to resort to the tippling-houses. 'There is . . . a declaration in print,' wrote Sir Francis Cottington, 'by his Majesty's commandment in favour of Wakes and May-poles, which is as hardly digested by the Puritans as the putting down of lectures, a thing which the Archbishop endeavours much.' In the moral sphere, both King and Archbishop were anxious that the upper classes should be as severely punished as their poorer brethren. When Sir Giles Alington was brought before a panel of eight Bishops and severely penalized for incestuously marrying his niece, Laud, who had not himself considered the merits of marrying anybody, let alone his niece, was stern in his censure. Alington was fined £12,000 which was granted to the Queen, providing her with some useful extra income.

Although many of the King's decrees and proclamations were issued with the intention of benefiting the community and increasing public order, some of his subjects considered them an intrusion into their private lives. When Goring declared that he had not heard of any disorder from one end of the kingdom to the other, he was bearing witness less to an actual state of tranquillity than to the extreme isolation of the Court. The plebeian in *Albion's Triumph* had suggested that from his study window the patrician could see nothing but the sky, and it sometimes seemed that the King understood more about divine mysteries than he did about the thoughts and feelings of his people. It was difficult for the King, and even more so for the Queen, who was given to enjoying herself in her Catholic way on a Sunday after the Mass was over, to comprehend that a Puritan resented labourers disporting themselves and disturbing the long concentration of a non-conformist Sunday.

The King had managed to revive the practice of selling monopolies, made illegal in 1624, in a different form, finding it a useful means of

raising revenue. In 1633 he allowed the formation of a company of
gentlemen soap-makers, but quite failed to take into account the feelings
of housewives whose hands came out in blisters, or even of his Queen
who had always had her linen washed with fine Castile soap according to
the old recipe. Considerable apprehension was experienced by members
of the legal profession as they saw the King lay down arbitrary laws which
it would be their responsibility to enforce. The King for his part knew
how essential it was to have a loyal judiciary and he had been disturbed
by the fact that Prynne was a barrister of Lincoln's Inn and had
dedicated *Histrio-Mastix* to his fellow lawyers. To test the loyalty of
the legal profession the King invited the Inns of Court to present him
with a masque, thus giving them an opportunity of demonstrating that
they did not subscribe to Prynne's theories about dramatic shows.

The invitation was accepted with alacrity. Inigo Jones was enlisted to
design the sets, and James Shirley provided a text entitled *The Triumph
of Peace*. Men worked for ten days and nights without ceasing, preparing
the Banqueting House for the occasion. It was said that the cost might add
up to twenty thousand pounds, but this did not seem too high a price to
pay for the chance to project, in symbolism that the King would understand, a guarded criticism of the royal policies. On the evening of
Candlemas the Templars left the Inns of Court and processed through
the streets to Whitehall, giving the populace a touch of the pageantry that
had been seen in earlier times before entertainment had disappeared
behind the palace walls for the benefit of ticket-holders only. A hundred
gentlemen paraded by, gloriously furnished, each attended by a groom
and two pages; there were Roman chariots with charioteers, and horse
and foot soldiers to restrain 'the rudeness of the people'. The onlookers
particularly appreciated the anti-masquers as they moved past 'in
ridiculous shows and postures'.

As the procession passed through the London crowds, the audience
was assembling in the Banqueting House. There was such a crush that
the King and Queen had some difficulty in reaching their seats. The
proscenium was decorated with symbols of Peace, Justice and Law, and
the anti-masquers were all characters who offended against the law—
bawds, wenches and wanton gamesters, as well as a group of 'projectors',
whose schemes were as impractical as the soap-boilers' new recipe:

> He'll undertake to build a most strong castle
> On Goodwin sands, to melt huge rocks to jelly,
> And cut them out like sweetmeats with his keel.

The grotesques were sharply distinguished from a group of everyday
people, painters and carpenters, as well as the wives of the feather-maker
and the embroiderer. Some were heard crying out for admission, and they

appeared after there was a loud crack as if some of the machinery were falling. To discover the significance of the intruders there was no need to look in Ripa's *Iconologia*. These were the technicians without whom the masque could never be brought to life. 'We are Christians in these clothes,' said the embroiderer's wife, 'and the King's subjects, God bless us.' The painter pointed out the scenery he had decorated, and the property man's wife showed the audience an owl and a hobby horse she had helped to make. Their arrival served as a reminder of the world beyond the Palace walls, and in the final scene, set against a moonlit landscape of cultivated champaign country the masquers were called from their revels by Amphiluche, forerunner of the morning:

> Come away, away, away,
> See the dawning of the day . . .

With these words the masquers went out into the world of reality and into the harsh light of day, leaving the King and Queen safely within their palace walls.

The variety of sets and the richness of clothes impressed everybody, including the King and Queen, who this time had the satisfaction of knowing that there would be no bills to meet. The Queen said she had 'never seen a masque more noble'. A week later there was a second performance at the Merchant Taylors' Hall, and the Lord Mayor, though a sick man, gave the King an entertainment more lavish than any he had experienced in Scotland or on his way there:

> The grave aldermen would have presented a purse with two thousand pounds in gold to the Queen, but my Lord Chamberlain with a little sharpness described the gift as not a fitting present from such a body, so it was not given, but within two days they sent the Queen a diamond which cost them £4,000 which was well accepted.

The 'riding show' through the streets was even more magnificent on that night when for the second time the King was shown that he had no mandate to rule alone, that his subjects must not be excluded from his world, and that projects like the soap monopoly should be banished to the land of farce. But it seemed that for a second time the King missed the meaning. He intended peace to triumph, but he wished to establish it by his own prerogative, as he himself thought fit. The outside world had invaded his palace for an evening, but he did not repeat the experiment. For his own masque which took place on Shrove Tuesday, turnstiles were installed to admit 'none but such as have their tickets sent them beforehand'.

Chapter 11

THE TEMPLE OF LOVE

THE KING's Shrovetide masque, *Cœlum Britannicum*, written by the poet Thomas Carew, was performed at Whitehall on February 18, 1634. It opened with a scene set in a ruined city, and ended with a vision of Religion, Truth, Concord and other virtues poised on a cloud above Windsor Castle. The King, installed at the head of his Knights of the Garter, was presented as the latest and greatest of all the island's monarchs, his reign the highest point in its history. The gods themselves, it seemed, were so impressed by his way of life that they felt impelled to model themselves on his example. In imitation of Charles and Henrietta Maria—those earthly paragons—Jupiter had been learning how to lead his wife in the Milky Way, and had seen to it that the inscription *Carlomaria* was engraved on his bedroom floor. Jove's Ambassador explained that heaven was no longer the place it had been— it had become a cloister of Carthusians, a monastery of converted gods; ethereal nectar had now been purged of the narcotic weed. Edicts were being issued in the realms above remarkably like those which had recently emanated from the palace at Whitehall—directives for the restoring of decayed housekeeping, or prohibiting the repair of families to the metropolis. Everywhere a new moral tone prevailed; even Cupid was to go 'no more scandalously naked', and he had been told to make himself some breeches out of his mother's petticoats.

The anti-masque showed various deviations from this highly moral, almost Puritanical ideal. War, greedy pleasure, deformity, idleness were all personified, with on the one hand the gipsies living lazily in the 'cheap sunshine' and on the other those whose greedy ambition led them to despoil the earth of its riches:

> Climbing steep mountains for the sparkling stone,
> Piercing the centre for the shining ore,
> And the ocean's bosom to rake pearly sands,
> Crossing the torrid and the frozen zones
> Midst rocks and swallowing gulfs for gainful trade.

But at the end of the anti-masque such aberrations were banished one by one, and as each grotesque figure left the scene a star in the constellation above was extinguished and a light came on in the King's earthly Star Chamber below.

After the winter season was over, there were bills to pay—for two treble lutes, a fair sprig of egrets, white and yellow ribbon, aurora-coloured stockings, canvas, buckram, stiffening, buttons, silk and calico. But the King and Queen escaped to Newmarket, untroubled by the aftermath of their festivities. In the early summer the Court moved to Greenwich. Prince Charles, sometimes styled the Prince of Great Britain to remind everybody of the Stuart achievement in uniting the Kingdoms, was entertained on his fourth birthday in May with bear- and bull-baiting. Plans were being made for the summer progress which was to take the King and Queen over the route used by Charles on his way to Scotland the previous year, Henrietta having expressed a desire to visit some of the northern counties. It was possible for them to spend a more carefree summer than could some of the monarchs of Europe. The Protestant forces, rent since the death of Gustavus with faction and jealousy, were now facing a formidable Imperial force under the King of Hungary, who had joined the Cardinal Infante and his forces at Nördlingen. In the ensuing battle the Protestant forces were almost totally destroyed.

Richelieu was now tending towards an alliance with the Dutch to contain Spanish power in the Netherlands. He believed that the Protestant powers would have to be strengthened with French help if they were to resist the united strength of the Habsburgs. Abandoning the clear-cut fight between Protestant and Catholic, Richelieu was not afraid to regulate his actions by the light of national expediency. He could be as devious as the English King when it came to consolidating and expanding the position of France; unlike Charles he was willing and able to back up his diplomacy with a show of strength. At the risk of incurring the displeasure of Rome, he made Protestant alliances when it suited him, and began to play an increasingly active part in the disputes over vital territories along the Rhine. His perpetual dread of Spanish expansion was now augmented by the additional anxiety caused by Gaston, who had fled from France for the second time, to become a useful pawn in the Spanish game.

Charles, for his part, was willing to support a Catholic power in order to further the Protestant cause in the Palatinate. He still believed that he could exert pressure on the Spaniards by threatening to withdraw their valued privilege of landing supplies at Plymouth, transporting them across England before shipping them over to the Netherlands by the shortest and safest route. Provided he ran no risk of becoming involved in a dangerous war or of entering into a 'great and insupportable charge',

Charles was ready to equip a navy capable of helping the Spaniards counter the Dutch and of patrolling the French coast. Since he wished to achieve his aim without the aid of Parliament, that institution which he had recently described as a cunning and malicious Hydra, and the Spanish were unlikely to go beyond vague offers of financial help, another method of raising money had to be found. The idea of mastering the turbulent deep appealed strongly to the English King's imagination, and many of his subjects shared his belief that their country had a right to dominate this restless element. English pride had been hurt by the depredations of the Barbary corsairs and the Dunkirk privateers; there was much suspicion of the growing maritime strength of France which was enabling French ships to challenge the English in waters where 'anciently they durst not fish for gurnets without a licence'. For these reasons, there was at first surprisingly little opposition when writs were issued for the levy of Ship Money in the seaports for the purpose of defending the nation.

Fontenay had returned to France in May 1633 and it was not until July 1634, just before the King and Queen went on their progress, that the French King sent another Ambassador, the Marquis de Pougny. He had a private audience with the Queen at her special request and a few days later saw the King who had been 'scouring the country' round about Theobalds on horseback. Louis was suspicious of his brother-in-law's dealings with the Spanish, and disapproved of his sister's unconcealed sympathy for Gaston and the Queen Mother. Pougny, on the watch for slights, complained strongly to the Queen when he heard that he was to be presented at his public audience by a Scottish earl, but she soothed him, advising him to accept the situation as no offence was intended.

The King and Queen set off in mid-July with a large retinue which included Prince Charles's players, who had gained a good reputation since they first started performing in 1631 under the infant prince's patronage. They were set up with a large tent and a hundred pounds in expenses. Sir Thomas Roe, one of the most brilliant and much-travelled diplomats of the age, had the dubious honour of housing the Court at his house at Abethorpe. As one who had journeyed up the Amazon in search of gold, carried out embassies to the Mogul Emperor and the Shah of Persia, travelled to Turkey and Poland, and, as he put it himself, had also 'sweated and fried in both Indies, and frozen in the cold, and thawed in the middle climates', he felt that he deserved some royal recognition. As a reward for housing the whole contingent for five long days, he might well have expected the payment of arrears in his pension and recompense for pendants he had purchased for the King over three years previously for more than two thousand pounds. He was sure that the Queen was far too 'princely' to wear the jewellery he had bought for her if she knew it had never been paid for. But when he saw the King and Queen 'so cheerful and joyously disposed to gentle mirth', he felt quite unable to spoil their enjoyment by mentioning anything so mundane as the money that was owing to him.

After staying at Belvoir in Leicestershire, the King and Queen travelled north to Welbeck, which the Earl of Newcastle, sparing no expense, turned over to them for the duration of their visit. The King had been 'pleased to send my Lord word, that her Majesty the Queen was resolved to make a progress into northern parts, desiring him to prepare the like entertainment for her, as he had formerly done for him'. It was at the medieval castle of Bolsover, five miles away in Derbyshire, that the Earl entertained the King and Queen to a banquet and a masque-like show, paying out, it was thought, something between fourteen and fifteen thousand pounds. Ben Jonson had been commissioned to provide the text for this 'stupendious entertainment'. The decrepit poet, still smarting from his dismissal, had written the previous year a play called *A Tale of a Tub*, in which he had allowed himself the pleasure of making some satirical thrusts at the expense of Vitruvius Hoop, a rustic joiner. After certain passages had been struck out by the Lord Chamberlain at the request of Inigo Jones, it had been performed at Court by the Queen's players and 'not liked'. Far from the Royal Surveyor and the Lord Chamberlain's censuring hand, Jonson entertained the King and Queen after the banquet with a scene peopled by Iniquo Vitruvius, the surveyor, and his men—Quarrel the glazier, Fret the plasterer and others—all making music and measure with their sledge-hammers, and springing, leaping and capering on 'Holy-day' legs, much to the delight of the surveyor. He, in his ignorance, imagined that his 'musical, arithmetical, geometrical gamesters' were providing a high-class entertainment. Two Cupids, who expressed the Platonic love theme in poetic terms, were warned that rhyme was looked upon as a 'shrewd disease' at the King's Court, and that their versifying would gain them no credit 'here in the edge of Derbyshire (the region of ale)'. Jonson, however, finished on a more gracious note when he pictured the Fates spinning for the royal pair a thread of the whitest wool 'without brack or purl'. That they did not take offence is demonstrated by the fact that later in the year the King requested the City authorities to pay Jonson arrears of a salary that had been suspended when he failed to produce any work.

After leaving Welbeck, the King and Queen headed south, staying at Nottingham, Tutbury, Holdenby and Castle Ashby. At Tutbury two men were ordered by the High Constable 'to carry some part of his Majesty's carriage' and later Quarter Sessions records report that the 'pore petitioners' were still unpaid for their service. The royal contingent spent a day at Althorp, travelling over from Holdenby, and this time no opportune fit of the palsy could be used to protect the Spencer coffers. Household accounts show that over eight hundred pounds were paid out in one week. It was thought necessary to improve and enlarge the Great Chamber for the occasion; a new withdrawing chamber was built as well as a stone staircase, with casements to light the stair, new matting and gilt leather hangings, gilt chairs and stools for the parlour. Large numbers of workmen were busy wainscotting chambers, building a bower in the courtyard, covering and heating the ovens and setting up borrowed tables. Special kitchen ranges were installed, and it took one man seven nights and days to make racks for roasting the meat. Another spent four days and one night carrying water into the kitchen and the dog-kennel yard, and three days 'cleansing the courts'—he was paid five shillings and fourpence for his pains. Others were rewarded for bringing cakes from Shropshire, or for fetching borrowed plate from Holdenby, or for 'watching the tent at the end of the walks'. It took three women two days to pluck all the fowl, for the princely sum of one shilling, and others were kept busy gathering over a thousand eggs.

Sundry expenses included two pounds for the music of Daventry and 'ten yards of kersey for my lady', but the largest bills were for the banquet itself. The wine bill came to seventy-six pounds, there was another for over five hundred pounds of butter at fivepence a pound, as well as a hundred and twenty-five quarts of cream, '39 dozens of larks . . . 33 turkeys . . . 13 veals . . . 26 pigs . . . parsenippes and carrootes, cabbidges and herbes . . . hartichoakes and cowcumbers . . . 8 dozen lemons of the first sort, 8 dozen lemons of the 2nd sort . . . 2 great pikes . . . 23 couple of rabbits'. Although some of the neighbouring gentry helped to cut costs by contributing items such as chicken, duckling or quail, all the servants who brought food had to be tipped; six shillings a time was paid out to a man bringing partridges, as well as ten shillings to 'Dr Clayton's man for coming along with pheasants from Oxford'. Another was rewarded for bringing and carrying back eighteen spits, another for bringing lambs, Lady Anderson's man for bringing fruit, while Lord Brooke's keeper had to receive his 'fee for the stags'.

The Queen went to Oatlands after her return from the north and it was not until November that she returned to London with the King. It was a dry mild autumn, with the leaves still on the trees in December, and the river so low that barges could not pass upstream. Correr, the Venetian Ambassador, noticed, however, that the climate at the English Court was rather less mellow. There seemed to be a great deal of suspicion in high places, with much distrust of the French and what was considered their excessive craving for power. Charles was more sure than ever that an alliance with Spain was his best policy, and he told his sister

Elizabeth, the Princess Palatine, that the Spanish had promised to help him in the Palatinate and to respect her son's claims. Elizabeth, who had refused her brother's offer of asylum after her husband's death, had long ago learnt to treat Charles's manoeuvres with caution; she was unable to believe that the Spaniards would prove helpful now when they had shown so little sign of being so in the past.

In October Gaston returned to France and was greeted by Louis with a degree of affection surprising in view of all that had passed. The French hoped that this reconciliation would help Henrietta Maria to look more favourably on the French cause and to overcome her natural affection for her mother. Since she remained aloof from her husband's Spanish predilections, there seemed good reason to hope that she could be used to further Richelieu's policies. In Rome too she was viewed with hope and approval, and there was a growing conviction that since the young Queen had become so well established in her husband's affections, no opportunity should be missed of using her influence. It was thought that a representative should be sent to London to assess the position—to find out whether in his dealings with the Pope the King was motivated by a genuine sympathy for the Catholic cause or simply by his ever-lasting desire to help his sister in the Palatinate. Cardinal Barberini, the Pope's nephew and Secretary of State, was sure that it would also be easier for somebody actually in England to discover how far the Queen was a free agent or the tool of those who surrounded her.

As early as February 1634 a priest of the Chiesa Nuova, Gregorio Panzani, had been summoned by Barberini and told that he might be sent to England, but it was not until December 15 of that year that he arrived in London. He was met by Father Philip who presented him to the Queen the next day. The Pope, he told her, was impressed by the concessions she had already managed to acquire for the English Catholics. He hoped that she would 'show herself a parent to that neglected hand-ful of people, and use her interest to bring them to a good understanding among themselves, who of late had been unhappily divided'. Panzani also assured the Queen that his Holiness expected the Catholics to be 'exact and scrupulous in their civil allegiance to the King and govern-ment'.

Panzani had been warned that at first he would have to be extremely cautious. The English were always difficult to fathom and impossible to pin down. 'The sea which you passed to visit them,' Barberini wrote, 'is an emblem of their temper, and a direction how you ought to steer.' For the time being he must do no more than see, hear and observe.

It did not take Panzani long to sum up the position for himself. He soon realized that only a few men wielded any real power. Membership of the Council brought prestige but not necessarily great influence. Portland's disagreeable looks, rugged manners and blatant self-interest had earned him many enemies, but in spite of growing ill-health he was still uppermost in the King's favour. Holland, Carlisle, Arundel, Cottington, Coke, Windebank and Laud all had their importance but, as the Venetian Gussoni believed, they were in the main too frightened to offer any serious opposition to the Lord Treasurer. Panzani was of the opinion that they were all venal and could be bribed, perhaps with jewels intended for the Queen. He also thought that the Queen's ladies could be worked on to advantage. He was quick to add that such methods would have to be used with great care and must never be open to the wrong interpretation, as the English, with the irreproachable example of the King and Queen before them, 'took scandal at the slightest thing'.

During the first few weeks of Panzani's visit the Queen and her ladies were busy rehearsing their masque *The Temple of Love* which was first performed on St Valentine's Day and subsequently repeated. The text was by William Davenant, and Jones lavished particular care on the settings and costumes, adding prolific notes to almost every page of designs. The story was concerned with the quest of some fine Persian youths who had come in search of a shrine dedicated to the worship of a new kind of love. They encountered the magicians who warned them against the new doctrines which had originated in 'a dull northern isle they call Britain'. The theory that love must not court the person but the mind left them sceptical for, as one of them remarked:

Your spirit's a cold companion at midnight.

The Persians were not deterred, although the magicians tried to hinder them, tempting them away from the Temple with the figures of the anti-masque—who included a modern devil in the guise of a Puritan pamphleteer, 'a sworn enemy of poetry, music and all ingenious arts'.

It was appropriate, in view of the King's current obsession with the sea, that his wife should appear as Indamora, Queen of the island of Narsinga, on board a sea chariot decorated with shells, seaweed, coral and pearl, which came gliding into a calm and exotic lagoon edged with palm trees and strange vegetation. She had been informed by a Persian messenger that there were strangers on the island who would 'give your femaleships some cause to mourn' because, as he said:

. . . about them all
There's not one grain but what's Platonical.

In general the audience found it an evening of enchantment, altogether worthy in Salvetti's opinion of so great a Queen. The complete accord among the dancers was perhaps due to the fact that they had become by now a close circle of friends, many of them drawn from the Herbert, Villiers and Denbigh families. The death of the Duke of Buckingham had not led to an alienation of his relations, for the King had taken his children into the royal nursery, and Mary Villiers, now thirteen years old, had always been his particular favourite. Although she was still so young, plans had been made for her marriage with Charles, Lord Herbert, son of the Lord Chamberlain, the Earl of Pembroke. The Herberts were much favoured by the King and Queen who 'loved Wilton above all places and went there every summer', so the marriage seemed extremely suitable, although the bridegroom was little older than his bride. Van Dyck painted Mary before her wedding in the guise of Venus, attended by a Cupid in the shape of Lord Arran, the Marquis of Hamilton's son. In spite of her tender years she looked dignified and mature, a far cry from the days when her mother had written to Buckingham, reporting that 'our sweet Moll groweth dearer day by day, she lieth upon the floor and kicketh her heels over her head. I pray God that, as she grow older, she grow more modest.'

Mary Villiers was married on January 8, 1635 in the royal closet at Whitehall. Laud officiated and after the ceremony a banquet was served at the King's expense to 'the flower of the nobility'. The inter-marrying of the King's friends and relations helped to make the royal circle more compact, exclusive and insulated against the grimmer side of life. Both the King and the Queen were surrounded by young men and women in their teens and early twenties who formed a close-knit and isolated group. Mary Villiers, her cousins Lady Hamilton and Lady Elizabeth Feilding, her new sister-in-law, Sophia Herbert, Lady Carnarvon, were all members of the team of fourteen ladies who had danced so admirably in *The Temple of Love*. The little Lord Arran in Van Dyck's portrait of Mary Villiers was the fruit of a union between Buckingham's niece and James Hamilton, a childhood friend of the King's. Although the Marquis had at first taken a dislike to his thirteen-year-old wife and had retired to Scotland to continue his education and run his father's estates, the King had lured him back with the promise of a large pension and the Mastership of the Horse which had fallen vacant on the death of Buckingham. The King informed him, on the night of his return to London, that he would be expected to sleep with his wife, and refused to accept his excuse that he was tired after the journey and lacked clean linen. He was fitted out with a royal shirt, waistcoat and nightcap, and the Queen sent a posset drink to encourage him. After this unpropitious start the Hamiltons not only produced Lord Arran but three daughters as well, the eldest christened Henrietta Maria after her godmother, the Queen.

Those who surrounded the King and Queen were expected to live according to the strict code of morality laid down in the Court regulations. Whitehall was to resemble as closely as possible the ideal world projected in the royal masques, and the King did not scruple to take action when he felt that his courtiers failed to come up to the standards expected of them. 'Is it not fit for me to put on what countenance I please to a man that distastes me?' asked Lord Morley when he was called before the Star Chamber for bending his brow during a quarrel with Sir George Theobalds at the Banqueting House before the Templars' masque. The King's answer was most certainly in the negative. His dislike of 'fractions' made him threaten to close the Bowling Green in Spring Gardens where quarrels broke out every week and there was 'constant bibbing and drinking wine all day long under the trees'. He banished from the Court the Queen's favourite, Henry Jermyn, who had got Eleanor Villiers, Buckingham's niece, with child, and refused to have him back for several years.

The Queen often interceded on behalf of those in trouble, and it was thanks to her that the Bowling Alley was granted a reprieve, but she herself conducted her life with considerable moral probity. She had grown more beautiful and less waif-like with the years; maternity had brought a softening of the features and a serenity of mind. Her own graciousness spread out into her surroundings, in the rich gilding of the decorations at her palaces and in the simple elegance which her exquisite Gallic taste brought to English fashion. Her marriage provoked admiration among those who were privileged to watch the relationship grow and deepen with the years. It seemed really remarkable, as the Venetian Gussoni pointed out, that a genuine affection had grown up between two individuals of such different religions and nationalities. Neither seemed tempted to give the other any cause for jealousy, and their mutual belief in the Platonic ideal bridged the gap between their different ways of worship.

The civilized and tranquil atmosphere of the Court was sometimes misinterpreted by those who lived beyond the charmed circle. To his companions the King seemed sober and serious-minded, but to those who viewed him from a distance and according to different standards he could appear to be frivolity personified. For the humourless Malvolios of this world enjoyment is a sin, and religion a serious affair, for 'Christ wept oft but never laughed' according to Prynne, and life was 'no time of laughter, but of tears'. The golden lads with their 'long, false, curled hair and lovelocks', typified by Pembroke's five graceful, long-haired sons in Van Dyck's portrait of the Herbert family, were the epitome of decadence. To the old and the staid and the Puritanical members of society, long hair seemed to be 'an effeminate, unnatural amorous practice, an incitation of lust, an occasion of Sodomy'. Equally reprehensible was the current fashion for short hair in women, since a woman's long hair was given to her 'for a covering', and short styles were only suitable for lewd adulteresses and polled nuns. By encouraging and even setting the fashion for such practices, the King and his 'shorn-frizzled' Queen were opening the way for a decadence that would eventually destroy the established moral traditions of the country. In *Histrio-Mastix*, 'that voluminous invective', there were countless passages obliquely aimed at the royal way of life. Playhouses, which the King and Queen liked to frequent, were nothing but dens of lewdness, the devil's temples, stews of shame and Babylonish brothels, to mention but a few of Prynne's choice epithets. For the Queen, dancing was an image of harmony, but Prynne thought that it was likely to occasion 'dalliance, chambering, wantonness, whoredom and adultery'. Modern dancing in particular came in for criticism because it was 'for the most part mixed, both men and women dancing promiscuously together by selected couples' and accompanied by 'amorous gestures and gropings', quite unlike the simple, plain, unartificial measures of days gone by. The fact that David had danced before the Ark was no justification for the lascivious capers so popular at Court.

Both Prynne and the King were sincerely religious men and both in their different ways were intent on seeking the truth. But Prynne was incapable of appreciating the underlying gravity of the royal point of view, or of grasping the fact that music, poetry, images and icons can help to illuminate the truth and do not neccesarily prevent reason reaching out to the truth. The quarrel between the King and the Puritan sprang partly from a basic difference of opinion about the best way of seeking divine revelation, and Prynne, for striking out at so many of the King's sacred pastimes and, more seriously still, for covertly criticizing the chaste and admirable Queen, found himself sentenced to life imprisonment. He was expelled from Lincoln's Inn, both his ears were cut off and as he stood in the pillory he was nearly suffocated with smoke when the learned pages of *Histrio-Mastix* were burnt in front of him.

Meanwhile, life at Court continued unaffected by the Puritans' strictures. The marriage of Mary Villiers provided an excuse for prolonged festivities—not a day passed without dancing and comedies. When it was all over the Queen went to Newmarket. She had been hesitant about facing the rigours of an East Anglian spring, but her sense of duty prevailed, and before long she succumbed to the inevitable cold, being confined to bed for five days with a fever. The King came up from Hampton Court on hearing that she was ill, and when she had recovered they both went to inspect some ships which were being refitted, and seemed pleased with what they saw. All the same there was growing criticism of the 'tepidity' of the naval preparations; some said that they wished the fleet would sail with the promptitude which had been observed in the collection of the Ship Money.

At Whitsun the King and Queen moved to Greenwich and a few days later they took Prince Charles to see the Garter procession at Windsor, with three hundred gentlemen processing on splendid horses and everyone vying with each other in magnificence. Lord Cottington, in particular, was very rich in jewels and wore a feather in his cap in the Spanish fashion. The royal party returned to Greenwich the same evening and in June it was announced that the King would not go on his usual progress as the Queen was pregnant. Correr noted that the whole Court seemed extraordinarily pleased about it. At Oatlands the Queen and her ladies passed their time performing pastorals and comedies and enjoying 'other pleasant diversions'. As Prynne himself had pointed out in *Histrio-Mastix*, there were plenty of 'honest recreations' which even the virtuous were allowed to enjoy—the beauty of the English countryside, with its orchards, rivers, gardens, ponds and woods, as well as the comfort of friends, kindred, wives, children, and the pursuit of 'cheap harmless exercises' such as walking, riding, fishing, fowling, hawking and hunting. These were pastimes the King and Queen were as capable of appreciating as any Puritan. The Queen's parkland at Greenwich was this year furnished with rustic seats round many of the trees, perhaps as an encouragement to anyone who felt impelled to commune with wild— or comparatively wild—nature.

To add to her satisfaction, the Queen was able to watch the final stages in the building of her house at Greenwich, which was often referred to as the House of Delight. A plaque was fixed to the wall, recording the completion of the work, though there was still a great deal to be done in the privy garden and the tilt-yard. Van Dyck had returned to England and was busy during the summer months painting a picture of the two Princes and the Lady Mary, which the Queen intended to send to her sister Christine in Savoy. Although the King was not pleased with the result, as the Prince was wearing his infant's coats, Van Dyck brought out and emphasized in the children a latent nobility which would have been recognizable even if they had been dressed in rags, or brought up among the shepherds like Perdita in *The Winter's Tale*. In view of the almost unnatural serenity of the children in the picture it is refreshing to learn that its completion was delayed because the Lady Mary did not possess enough patience to sit for her portrait; but, in spite of the normal qualities, the nobility was there, 'inherent and natural'.

Van Dyck was also making sketches for two large portraits of the King in a rural setting, one on horseback, depicting the monarch as the archetypal Renaissance hero, wearing armour, and in complete mastery of the great dun horse he was riding. In the other Charles, on the edge of the same leafy woodland, was to be seen standing with the horse docile beside him, a courtly gentleman at peace with the world, at one with nature, and yet a little apart—that link between the natural and the divine which he and his Queen so sincerely believed him to be.

Chapter 12

LEADERSHIP CRISIS

THE SUMMER of 1635 was so dry that there was scarcely any grass on the upper grounds, hay was fetching five to six pounds a load, and it was hot enough to make a man mad. People around London were reported as being 'apt to hang themselves'. On the Continent it was likely to be a hot summer in more senses than one, for as Howell told Wentworth 'the fire betwixt France and Spain, which stood smoking a great while' had now broken out in flames. In January Louis had signed a treaty with the Dutch for the invasion and partition of the Spanish Netherlands, and on May 19 a French herald rode into Brussels and formally declared war. Louis, anxious to ensure English support or at least neutrality in the struggle that lay ahead, despatched an Ambassador extraordinary, the Marquis de Seneterre, to England, to help Pougny put the French point of view. Charles appointed Commissioners to deal with them, although he had little intention of coming to an agreement. He kept his Spanish negotiations secret and tried to arouse patriotic ardour with hints that the French were plotting to invade England. On June 6 the English fleet set sail under the Earl of Lindsey, and Pougny did all he could to extract from the Queen the secret of its destination. She questioned her husband on the subject, but he merely told her that his intention was to protect his coasts and the freedom of his subjects to ply their trade on the high seas.

Charles ordered Lindsey to exact from all passing ships an acknowledgment of the King's sovereignty, following the example of Queen Elizabeth who had told Henri IV that if he did not bow to her authority she would send his ships to the bottom of the sea. Not wishing to see the lilies of France being lowered before the cross of St George, Richelieu arranged for his ships to sail under a Dutch admiral who had no such scruples. Lindsey, bereft of an enemy to confront, could do little except ply pointlessly up and down the Channel with his ships, and apart from conveying some merchantmen into Dunkirk and persuading a few foreign ships to lower the flag he achieved nothing. He even failed to protect the English coast when Dutch ships pursued a Dunkirker into the port of Scarborough. Over sixty Dutchmen actually went ashore and at Blythe a Dutch captain landed with his men and pursued the pirates several miles inland.

The maintaining of a large fleet put the King in the position he least liked. The Attorney-General, William Noy, who had died the year before, managed before his death to relieve the King's financial difficulties 'by inventing', as the Venetian Secretary put it, 'various methods of extortion, though under the pretence of the breach of ancient and obsolete laws'. The King now decided to issue further writs for Ship Money, extending the tax to inland towns as well as the seaports, and pointing out that it was unfair for only a section to bear the cost of defending the country as a whole from invasion.

After the issue of the first writs, the money had been efficiently collected and used for the purpose for which it was intended, but the second writs immediately began to cause opposition. Since the King was not at war, his reasons for raising money were suspect, and there were fears that he was planning to institute a form of permanent taxation. Many people believed that before taking such a vital step he should certainly have called and consulted a Parliament, but this was precisely what he had wished to avoid; he had summed up the salient features of his current policies to Wentworth as 'the not continuing of the Parliament and the guard of the coast.'

There were invasion scares throughout the summer, and instructions were issued to the Council to arrange for the holding of musters and the enrolment of untrained men between the ages of sixteen and sixty. The beacons along the coast were made ready; on one occasion the sound of gunfire sent the Council hurrying down to Greenwich, although nothing more spectacular had taken place than a few salvoes from English vessels indignant because a Dunkirker had driven a Dutch ship into Dover harbour. But in spite of rumours of sea-fights and the controversial issue of the Ship Money, England was able to enjoy another summer of virtual peace. Many Council members could afford to take time off in spite of anxieties about affairs of state. Holland went to Tunbridge Wells to drink the waters; Lady Carlisle, who had recently been fully restored to favour, went with her sick husband to Petworth, and Laud spent his time inspecting building operations in Oxford and at St Paul's. The royal children stayed at Richmond and at the end of August the Queen went down there in a hurry on hearing that Prince Charles had fallen into a fever. The hot weather bred dangerous illnesses, and only a month earlier the mother of the maids had been carried away by an attack of the spotted fever.

The Earl of Portland had died in the spring and, when everyone began converging on London after their travels, the battle for the leadership began in earnest. The removal of the Treasurer had opened up new avenues of power for the Queen and her party in the Council. Laud was afraid that if any of her protégés were to succeed, Portland's inertia and inefficiency, characterized as 'lady Mora' in his correspondence with Wentworth, would be perpetuated. Laud and Wentworth, who corresponded prolifically during the latter's stay in Ireland, took 'Thorough' as their watchword, and in Laud's opinion the only man capable of carrying out an efficient policy was Wentworth himself. He was not too hopeful of success, being afraid that the King would succumb to Sir Francis Cottington's flatteries; it was noticeable that Cottington and Sir Richard Wynne, the Queen's Receiver-General, were 'marvellously inward' with one another. Altogether Laud was in a depressed state. 'This summer hath carried away many lusty young men,' he told Wentworth. 'And truly, my Lord, I begin to think I shall hardly live to see the end of this year. I have so many occasions of grief to see things so much out of the way, and see no help to alter anything.'

Throughout the summer Laud had opposed the King on the question of the soap monopoly. He believed that the power granted to the 'new soapers', to test all soap made by their rivals and to prohibit its sale if they thought fit, was bound to give rise to some abuses. There was still considerable controversy about the merits of the new soap and the old; Laud, with many others, pronounced the new soap 'vile'; he felt incredulous when two washerwomen were brought before the Court of Inquiry and the one using the official soap managed to prove somehow that hers washed whiter than the old. There were rumours that money for the new company had been raised by the Jesuits, and many of its members were thought to be Catholic friends of Portland's. The Treasurer's death had given encouragement to the independent manufacturers, and Laud took their part, feeling that it was better to entrust such a vital matter to experts rather than to a collection of gentlemen-amateurs. But when the matter was debated at Theobalds, Laud saw Windebank—whom he had originally raised from obscurity to his position as Secretary of State—now desert him along with other members of the Council; by October he had to admit that he was defeated. 'Never any man was so used on all sides as I was in that business,' he wrote; 'yet if the King may gain by it, and the public be satisfied, I am content to suffer. My way, I am sure, would have brought both ends together, and that is good in a pudding.'

By the end of November Laud was almost resigned to Cottington's appointment—metempsychosis was the more learned word he used. 'I have done my duty and the rest I shall leave to God, and will not give the King . . . cause to think my spleen is fuller than my judgment.' His attempt to have Wentworth recalled from Ireland had met with little success, and he knew that he could not compete when it came to wooing the ladies; in this department Cottington was sparing no effort or expense, and in October he invited the Queen and all her Court to dinner at his house at Hanworth.

Henrietta's child was due at the end of the year, but she was in excellent health and spirits. Plague had broken out in the Low Countries, but it was not until December that there were rumours of cases at Greenwich. Even then the outbreak was not serious enough to hamper the Christmas festivities. That autumn there were plays to watch by some Spanish players, and one evening the Queen went to Blackfriars to see *Arviragus and Felicia* by Ludovick Carliel, an employee of the Court, while the King spent the evening at Van Dyck's house nearby.

Towards the end of 1635 the young Elector Palatine arrived at Dover after a long and dangerous crossing. A badly-aimed shot from the welcoming salvo landed on the visitor's ship, killing five people and only just missing the Palatine himself. He was brought to London by the Earl of Arundel, and the Lord Chamberlain stood waiting for him at the palace gate at Whitehall. The King and Queen greeted him in the Queen's chamber 'in a private manner but most courteously', and he remained for a while talking to them in English. Elizabeth had sent her son over to England, hoping that with his boyish good looks and pleasing manner he would be able to plead his own cause more effectively than she could from a distance. Her brother's policy of applying diplomatic pressure here and there was driving Elizabeth to despair. She told the King that if he would not give her son, now that he had come of age, the 'means to defend what he has of his country and get the rest, but force him to sit still', then the world would think that England consented to the wrongs which were perpetuated in the Palatinate. Fortunately Charles took to his nephew, and all the great lords vied with each other to entertain him. The Ambassadors found they frequently had a chance to meet him as he chatted informally in the Queen's chamber. He visited Laud who described him as 'a proper gentleman' and treated him with great courtesy, showing him his library and seeing him home across the river.

On December 21, 1635, the King's birthday, the Queen's ladies presented the pastoral *Florimène* at the Banqueting House. Although the Palatine's English was better than everyone had expected, the ladies performed the play in French in his honour. The Queen went to Somerset House for her Christmas devotions, and then to St James's where on the Monday after Christmas she was delivered of a daughter, Elizabeth. It was a cold winter's day, with snow lying on the ground. The following Saturday the Princess was christened by Laud, and the Prince Palatine was a godfather. When the Queen was still in bed after her delivery a shipment of pictures arrived from Rome, sent over by Cardinal Barberini.

The King came hurrying across to watch as each canvas was removed from its wrappings. Panzani, noting the Queen's appreciation of an earlier present of artificial flowers and fruit, and a relic case containing the bone of a saint, had recommended that the quickest way of gaining her favour was to cultivate her love of the arts. All his conversations with the Queen were now devoted to this theme and he was determined to 'seduce the King himself with pictures, antiquities, images and other vanities brought from Rome'. He thought that it was worth robbing the Holy See of her most valuable ornaments if as a result he could add the King of England's name to the list of those who had submitted themselves to the Roman Church. The new consignment of pictures had been carefully chosen to include works by some of the King's favourite artists—Correggio, Veronese, Andrea del Sarto, and particularly Giulio Romano, whose vivid naturalism had influenced so many contemporary painters. In *The Winter's Tale* Shakespeare had named Giulio as the supposed creator of Hermione's statue, describing him 'as that rare Italian master . . . who (had he himself eternity, and could put breath into his work) would beguile nature of her custom, so perfectly is he her ape'.

The debt which Rubens owed to Giulio Romano and even more to Titian could be recognized at once in the canvases for the Banqueting Hall ceiling which were shipped from Antwerp in October 1635—in the brilliant *chiaroscuro*, the flying draperies and the fleshy, vigorous, foreshortened figures. During his strange career in art and diplomacy, Rubens had found unparalleled opportunities to steep himself in the work of the Italian masters, both in Italy and in Spain, where his diplomatic visits had given him the chance to study the magnificent royal collections.

Rubens did not himself come over to England to supervise the installations of the pictures; he had seen enough of courts, and probably of the paintings too, as they had been cluttering up his studio for some time, finished but unpaid for. He had worked without unduly consulting his patron, for he did not readily seek advice, and his opinions were 'like the laws of Medes and Persians which may not be altered'. All the same, when the paintings were installed, the 'cruel courteous painter' heard from his friends that the King was very well pleased both with the theme and with its execution. The interwoven images and symbols clearly expressed the Stuart achievement in uniting the crowns of England and Scotland and in bringing peace to the realm. The two rectangular panels depicted dramatic scenes that could have been taken from any of the moving shows staged on the floor below, with King James enthroned in heavily classical settings with cherubs or winged genii in the clouds above and figures of peace below, treading down the powers of war and rebellion. In the great central oval the artist seemed to open up the roof of the building, drawing the eye upwards into a luminous void in a vortex of spiralling figures, as the old King, one foot still touching the globe, is received up into the ethereal kingdom, his great work complete.

The installation of the Rubens canvases, the Queen's lying-in, and the growing incidence of the plague had precluded any possibility of a masque in the new year of 1636; all the same there was enough frivolity to make Correr complain that serious business was out of the question. A masque was, however, presented at the Middle Temple for the Elector, who sat under the canopy with his dashing brother Rupert who had come over to join him. The Queen, 'by putting off Majesty to put on a citizen's habit, sat on his right hand among her subjects', and she was accompanied by the usual collection of Hamiltons and Denbighs, similarly dressed. Afterwards the King took the Elector to Newmarket, where the young man was struck down by a fever and went into a state of acute depression, rare in one of his age, but perhaps not surprising in view of his uncle's indeterminate policies.

Soon after the King's return to London the whole Court was cast into gloom by the news that Charles Herbert, the Lord Chamberlain's son, had died of smallpox in Florence. The death of this promising sixteen-year-old left Mary Villiers a widow at the age of fourteen. The King felt great grief and sympathy for Mary, whom he loved as his own daughter, and for Pembroke, who was one of his closest friends. He refused to let the young widow go to her mother, for the Duchess had incurred the royal displeasure by marrying an Irishman who, it was rumoured, had recently gambled away two thousand pounds playing ninepins at Tunbridge Wells. To mark the general sorrow, various entertainments were cancelled; the Court had already resigned itself to a quiet Lent season because of a growing epidemic of the plague.

In the new year the King had still failed to fill the vacant post of Lord Treasurer, but Laud told Wentworth on January 23 that he was sure Charles would bestow the staff on Cottington when he returned from Newmarket. This result was confidently expected by the majority of people at Court; Cottington had been observed making every effort to win over the Queen, flattering her and pointing out the inconvenience she might suffer if Laud's parsimonious party should gain the ascendant. He also promised to support a French alliance in spite of the fact that now, as always, he was cultivating friendly ties with Spain. It was a surprise when, to quote Clarendon, 'on a sudden the staff was put into the hands of the Bishop of London, a man so unknown, that his name was scarce heard of in the kingdom'. Laud must have had his pontifical tongue in his cheek when he told a gentleman of the Queen's side that he 'meddled not with making treasurers', for Bishop Juxon was unmistakably one of his protégés, whom he had first introduced into the closet with the professed intention of having 'one that I might trust near his Majesty, if I grow weak or infirm'. Ignorant of politics, childless—a great advantage in Laud's opinion—Juxon's main claim to distinction was that he kept near his parish in Oxfordshire one of the best packs of hounds in the country. He was good-tempered, possessing 'as much command of himself as of his hounds', and he was unlikely to give offence willingly to anybody.

Some thought the appointment might set an alarming precedent; they foresaw the Church becoming a 'gulph ready to swallow all the great offices'. As Howell put it to Wentworth, 'it being now twice time out of mind since the white robe, and the white staff marched together; we begin to live here in the church triumphant'. Cottington received the news of his disappointment with equanimity, and it was thought that he would 'live longer and in better health than if he had had this great office conferred upon him'.

Cottington, in common with Windebank and other prominent men, had been incautious in his friendship with Panzani, which could have influenced the King to bestow the staff elsewhere. Charles was not insensitive to the murmurings of the anti-Catholics and had himself been careful to avoid too much association with the visitor from Rome. It was only to please his wife that he had agreed to the appointment of an agent who was to be sent to the Vatican on her behalf. The Queen selected a young and zealous Catholic, Sir William Hamilton, for the task, and at Nice he met George Con who was on his way to England to take over Panzani's mission. Hamilton carried messages from the Queen, and the King had instructed him to ensure that the English Catholics would continue to give him that loyalty 'which is due to us by the laws of God and man'.

In spite of the plague, plays—including Beaumont's *Knight of the Burning Pestle*—were performed at Court and there was some bear-baiting for the Elector's edification. Towards the end of February the royal children attended a masque especially written for the opening of Sir Francis Kynaston's Academy for young gentlemen in his house in Covent Garden. The King contributed a hundred pounds towards this venture, and Sir Francis had equipped his house with musical and mathematical instruments, books, manuscripts, paintings and statues, to provide an educational atmosphere suitable for nurturing the kind of man acceptable at the Court of King Charles. One day, after a shopping expedition, the King and Queen visited Bedlam, where they were 'madly entertained', and in early May the Queen accompanied the Elector to a theatrical performance at Blackfriars. By the middle of May 1636, however, all public appearances had been cancelled. Correr visited the Queen at Hampton Court and found her very anxious about the plague.

The weather had been fine and warm throughout April and showed no signs of changing. A rapid spread of the disease was forecast, people were beginning to panic and it was thought that the city would soon be deserted. No strangers were admitted at Court, and the Ambassadors were told that they would not be welcome if they had come direct from the infected areas. By mid-May there were cases in almost every London parish, the death toll was mounting, and Herbert issued orders for the closure of the theatres. The Queen's company, the King's Revels and Prince Charles's company were all affected, although a pass was issued to eighteen members of the King's company allowing them to accompany their patron on the summer progress.

One stranger who was admitted was Clement Radolti, an agent sent by the Emperor. His visit was awaited with interest by the King and the Elector, who hoped that he would be willing to discuss the perennial problem of the Palatinate. Although he had three audiences, he was equally vague each time, and refused to come to the point. On the final occasion the King could hardly contain his anger; the Elector said it was 'one of the usual tricks of the Austrians' and expressed himself in strong terms to Hamilton, Pembroke and Holland, all of whom, he believed, were sympathetic to his cause. The King went off to the country without seeing Radolti again, but the agent visited the Queen and made a speech in Latin lasting an hour and a half, which gave 'occasion for merriment at the Court and among the ladies for the rest of the day'.

On the Continent with the coming of summer the armies of the great powers began to go into action again. This year it was Spain who took the initiative; her troops crossed the border in Picardy on June 23 and the French army under the Comte de Soissons was unable to hold the invaders. For a while the road to Paris seemed open and plans were made for the defence of the city. Richelieu, although aware that the English King had no serious intention of making an alliance with France, gave a friendly welcome to the Earl of Leicester, who had apparently come to treat with him in some indeterminate way. The Cardinal did not object to talks, however insincere, provided he could keep England out of an active alliance with Spain.

In the summer of 1636 the English fleet sailed up and down the Channel as ineffectively as before, trying to assert itself in the face of an elusive if not an illusory opponent. It was this year under the command of Algernon Percy, Earl of Northumberland, whose sister Lady Carlisle was now strongly entrenched in the Queen's favour, and who was perpetually courted on account of her influence and personal charm. The Earl of Exeter paid her the compliment of saying that her perfections weighed down all other delights—even the approach of violets in the spring. She could feel well satisfied as she saw one brother established as

Lord High Admiral, and another, Henry Percy, advancing rapidly in the Queen's favour.

The Queen had the pleasure of learning that in June her agent had reached Rome. At his first audience Sir William Hamilton made an elegant speech in his mistress's name, ending with 'a modest representation of the Elector Palatine's case'. Urban answered the speech point by point 'with a great deal of good nature and sweetness of temper', though he felt obliged to say that the case of the Elector was very intricate, adding that the Roman see was not really in a position to sort out such difficulties. The arrival of Con in England caused some suspicion and disapproval but the well-bred Scotsman turned out to be so good-looking, tactful, and pleasant that he was soon accepted in royal circles. The King took to him at once, and his witty conversation soon earned him invitations to the tables of the nobility. After staying at Castle Ashby, Con was taken by the Marquis of Hamilton to Oxford where extensive preparations were in progress for a visit from the King and Queen. It had been announced that no undergraduate whose hair was longer than the tip of his ears would be allowed to take part in the festivities, for Laud, the Chancellor of the University, had no more love of long locks than Prynne.

On Monday, August 29 the King and Queen were welcomed a mile out of the city on the road from Woodstock, where they had been staying at the end of the summer progress. Laud was there to greet them, with the Vice-Chancellor and many members of the University in their scarlet gowns. The Queen was presented with a copy of Camden's *History of Queen Elizabeth* and a pair of gloves, there was a speech of welcome from the Vice-Chancellor, another outside St John's and yet another at Christ Church gate by William Strode, the University Orator and 'a most florid preacher'; he had written the play which was to be performed that evening, *The Floating Island*. Its theme was the calming of the passions and the quelling of rebellion, and, when order was restored under the rule of King Prudentius, the play ended with the usual compliments:

> Our scene which was but fiction now is true;
> No King so much Prudentius as you.

There was some ambitious scenery with a delicately-painted sky and the floating island itself rocking up and down on the billows, complete with church, houses, trees and hills. It was impressive for those not used to the glories of the royal masques to see a chair come gliding on to the stage 'without any visible help'. Prynne was suitably parodied, with a reference to a biting libel 'against some prosperous object which I hate', and to his long hair which, ironically enough, he had grown to cover his mutilated ears. The play was on the whole thought to be too 'grave' for the royal party who found it hard to understand; Lord Carnarvon, the

Lord Chamberlain's son-in-law, pronounced it the worst he had ever seen with the exception of one at Cambridge, although the 'togated crew' were apparently well satisfied with it, and thought that the undergraduates performed surprisingly well.

The next morning the King was taken to the Bodleian Library where a 'neat speech of welcome' was made by the Lord Chamberlain's son, William Herbert, who was an undergraduate at Exeter College. When word came that the Queen was ready, the King accompanied her to St John's where Laud was waiting for them at the foot of the library stairs, ready to show them his new building works—the Canterbury quadrangle with its castellated walls, graceful Italianate cloisters, its pillars in marble from a quarry discovered by Juxon when he was out hunting, and the busts of the King and Queen by Le Sueur. They went upstairs to the sound of 'a short, fine song' passing from the old library into the new —'built by myself,' Laud could not resist adding in his account of the proceedings. In the hall an enormous meal was served and the guests included many of the local gentry who had contributed venison and other food for the occasion. The King and Queen were delighted with the virtuosity of the chefs, who had embodied the concept of divine order in the form of baked meats cooked in the shape of archbishops, bishops and other dignitaries, all arranged in due degree.

After the guests had spent an hour in the withdrawing chamber, the windows of the hall were shuttered, candles were lit and the stage set for a play, *Love's Hospital* by George Wilde, one of Laud's chaplains, which was 'merry, and without offence and so gave a great deal of content'. In the evening, after a banquet, there was another play, *The Royal Slave* by William Cartwright, a student of Christ Church, who was later to gain a great reputation as a philosopher, playwright, poet and preacher. The settings were by Inigo Jones and the Queen was so delighted that she later asked to borrow the Persian costumes for a performance at Court. It was a memorable occasion, 'the day of St Felix (as the Chancellor observed) and all things went happy'. When *The Royal Slave* was published, many copies were sold as mementoes.

The next day the King and Queen were up early and were greeted in the Christ Church quadrangle by all the doctors. They both made a speech of thanks and Laud replied in the name of the University for 'their great and gracious patience and acceptance of our poor and mean entertainment'. The Queen spent that night at Henley and then went on in the direction of Winchester. Laud retired to Croydon. He felt weary after the 'expenseful' proceedings at Oxford, but there was no doubt that his life had taken a propitious turn. The appointment of Juxon had confirmed the belief, ominous for others but pleasing to himself, that the doors of power had opened for him both in Church and State. He wished to dominate the King's councils not so much for personal gain as to achieve his aims of furthering efficient government, upholding the concept of divine kingship and of guiding a King whose actions at times were irritatingly devoid of the divine. Already he could see the improvements which were taking place in every diocese as a result of his work—buildings were being cared for, the clergy working more conscientiously, and ceremony was being standardized. At Lambeth he himself had improved the chapel with the addition of a stained-glass window and a richly-gilded organ, with the added vanity of a window in the hall with the King's arms and his own appearing side by side. There were dissonant voices of course from such unenlightened people as Henry Burton who had written 'a peevish book about the Sabbath', containing an attack on banquets and profane plays at Oxford; statistics had also been produced to prove that during the 'scurrilous interlude' of the royal visit, the death toll from the plague had doubled—a sure sign of divine disapproval. There was distasteful evidence that the short-haired orderliness of the undergraduates had been only a veneer, for at a repeat performance of *Love's Hospital* a crowd of them broke into the hall and deprived outsiders of their places. But perhaps the most constant cross Laud had to bear was the eternal presence of the Queen. He was no lady-killer—'you know I have little conversation with women,' was how he himself put it to Wentworth. Although he had outwitted Cottington and Windebank, the Queen remained a tiresome barrier lying in the way of his complete domination of the King. He did what he could to oblige her but she was never content. 'I have satisfied the Queen about Lady Carew,' he told Wentworth, but he added, with all the weariness of the woman-hater, 'and so she must think of some other particular; and I doubt not but she will.'

After a pleasant summer the King and Queen went to Richmond to spend some time with their children. The King had been enclosing large areas of the forest there to keep out intruders, and alehouses in the vicinity had been suppressed because of their proximity to the Prince's palace. It was possible for the royal family to live for a while cut off from the world, savouring the kind of domestic happiness often denied to Kings. When the Italian sculptor Giovanni Bernini first saw Van Dyck's portrait of the King in three positions which was to help him fashion a bust of the man he had never seen, he mistook for melancholy the detached serenity which the painter knew how to capture so well; his reaction gave rise to the long-standing myth that the King was already tortured with a sense of impending doom. In fact, as he sat for Van Dyck, Charles was in all probability enjoying the ambience of the artistic world, for there was nothing he liked so well as to spend an evening at the studio at Blackfriars, escaping from those unpleasant problems connected with his political and religious enemies, which might have indeed made him melancholy had he devoted more time to considering them.

As for the Queen, she was too busy bearing children, seeking favours for those she liked and listening to eulogies to look too far into the future. All around her were people anxious to convince her that she was super-human, not to say divine. Her looks, her taste, her temperament, her singing voice all came in for praise. 'Never any earthly thing,' wrote the poet Townshend:

Sung so true, so sweet, so clear;
I was then in Heaven not here.

The foreign artists attracted to England had been beautifying her surroundings so that whichever place she chose to visit she could be sure to find a wealth of objects highly satisfying to the eye. At Greenwich she was re-organizing the pictures, and she had ordered frames and partitions to house new canvases, as well as 'tacklings to keep the sunshine from the windows'. The Bear Gallery at Whitehall and the Long Gallery at St James's were now filled with fine works by contemporary artists as well as older masters. Giulio Romano's equestrian portraits of Roman emperors in the Long Gallery were almost overshadowed by Van Dyck's painting of the King riding through a triumphal arch—the effect was so real that it seemed at first sight as if he were actually coming into the room on horse-back. In his bedchamber, the King had hung one of Van Dyck's earliest paintings of the Queen, dressed in grey satin trimmed with pink, her hand on a bunch of roses. They were watched over by idealized portraits of themselves and their outstandingly handsome children. There is little doubt that they were happy, and at that time had no reason to believe that their happiness would not last. For, as Clarendon later put it, the kingdom 'enjoyed the greatest calm, and the fullest measure of felicity, that any people in any age, for so long time together, have been blessed with; to the wonder and envy of all the other parts of christendom'.

Chapter 13

THE OTHER RELIGION

IN SEPTEMBER 1636 the Queen was told that a madman, brother to one of the Gentlemen of the Bedchamber, had broken loose and was declaring that he intended to marry her, having first killed the King. She was so upset by the news that her laces had to be cut 'to give her more breath', and it then became apparent that she was with child. Until the King arrived in person to prove that he was unharmed she refused to be reassured. He came quickly, for he was anxious about her health.

As autumn came on the plague showed no sign of abating. It had spread rapidly into the southern counties, and when the King went to Hampshire two servants were stricken in the house where he was staying. He moved on hastily, leaving his luggage behind. Villages around Windsor were affected and Londoners were restrained from coming within ten miles of Hampton Court or Oatlands. Barges were also forbidden to travel up-river with goods that might be infected. The playhouses were still closed and the Queen's players had been disbanded, although entertainment was provided by the King's men, who were granted an allowance of twenty pounds a week and ordered to stay near the Court.

After endless delays the Queen's Chapel at Somerset House was nearing completion, and in spite of the epidemic plans were going ahead for the dedication ceremony, perhaps in the hope that an aura of sanctity would act as a disinfectant. On December 10 the Queen arrived with all her Court to hear Mass. As soon as she was settled, curtains were drawn back, revealing a machine designed by the French sculptor François Dieussart. The sacrament, cleverly lit so that it appeared to be on fire, was at the centre of an oval-shaped, golden glory, representing heaven, with a dove hovering above seven layers of clouds where crowds of angels sat playing a variety of musical instruments. Two hundred lights and innumerable tapers gave an overwhelmingly ethereal impression. Afterwards the Mass was sung so melodiously that the Queen was moved to tears. Later in the day she attended vespers and heard Father Péronne preach a sermon on a text from the Psalms—'This is the Lord's doing, and it is marvellous in our eyes'.

There was a great crowd at the ceremony, and for three days the curious continued to flock into the chapel which was as gilded, ornate and sumptuous as Jones's church of St Paul in Covent Garden was rustic and unadorned in the Tuscan manner. The King finally ordered that the Chapel should be cleared and the doors closed so that he himself could make a visit. He sat looking at the spectacle for some time, and said that he had never seen anything more beautiful or more ingeniously designed. Not everybody agreed with him. Many people thought that the altar-piece was over-theatrical and extravagant, believing as they did that enlightenment should come from within and not from expensive visual aids and the glow of tapers and candles.

The Capuchins had not found Inigo Jones easy to work with; at times they suspected that he deliberately held up the work because he disapproved of its purpose. This was the kind of behaviour they expected in 'men of no religion'. Although Jones was the son of a Catholic and was often classed as one himself, the Capuchins labelled him *Puritanissimo*. Only gifts from the Queen and endless patience on the part of the Father Superior had prevented the whole project from ending in disaster.

After some hard frosts in December the plague began to die down, and the King and Queen felt that it was safe to travel down-river to view the work in progress at Greenwich. On the way they disembarked at the Capuchins' lodgings, and like many Englishmen the King was impressed by the friars and their frugal way of life—the bare cells, simple clothes and hard beds—as well as the 'scant ceremonies' which were austere enough to please any Puritan.

The visit caused a great deal of talk and speculation. At any other time it might have passed off without comment, but the presence in London of Con and of Panzani had put Protestants on the alert. Fears that the King might be veering towards the Roman Church had increased after reports that he had been seen bowing before the altar in the Queen's Chapel. A remark taken out of context—'I shall change the opinion I have hitherto held'—could be taken to indicate that he was on the verge of conversion. Seeing the crucifix Con had brought for the Queen, a beautiful piece encrusted with diamonds, he had asked, 'Is it possible, my dear heart, that the Pope has given you this?' All that in fact had changed was his belief that the priests of Rome were always ready to take away, but never to give.

Unlike many Englishmen, the papal representative quickly realized that there was little chance of the King embracing the Catholic faith. He spent hours discoursing with Charles, who enjoyed sophisticated doctrinal discussion at the supper table, but he never detected the slightest wavering from an orthodox Anglican viewpoint. Con found Laud equally staunch, although he too was under suspicion, particularly as he had once been offered a Cardinal's hat. It was evident to Con, if not to some of the more prejudiced Englishmen, that Laud distrusted Papists as much as he hated Puritans. The Queen, too, proved rather disappointing. Con found her charming, sincerely religious and apparently free from all temptations of the flesh, but he wished she would assert herself more in affairs of state and at least make some attempt to convert the King, as St Cicely had influenced her husband Valerian. She limited her activities to interceding on behalf of those who were already converted. When in 1634 she had asked Wentworth to ensure that some Capuchin friars, who were no more than 'poor harmless religious men', should be allowed to live without molestation, she assured him that she never asked a favour for those of the 'other religion', unless she judged it to be in accordance with the good of the state. She seemed unwilling to become embroiled when Walter Montagu returned to England at the instigation of Barberini. Montagu had been received into the Catholic Church by Father Philip in 1635 and the King had advised him to go into voluntary exile on the Continent. Barberini hoped that as one of the Queen's closest friends Montagu might be able to give Con valuable help, but since she refused to intercede for him, he went into the country to bide his time.

In February 1637 the plague seemed to be dying down and the theatres were allowed to open. Within a week they were closed again, Laud having pointed out that Lent was hardly the most suitable time to start operations. The Lord Chamberlain resented the interference, and remarked at a meeting of the Council that 'he hoped his Grace would not meddle in his place, no more than he did in his'. In any case an influx of Londoners returning to infected and unaired houses caused another virulent out-break of the disease, which gave a good enough excuse to close the play-houses. The Queen, however, insisted on returning to St James's for her lying-in. She had grown bored with her long exile at Hampton Court and said the facilities there were inadequate for an accouchement. On March 17 she gave birth to a daughter, Anne. The christening was a family affair, the Princess's own eldest brother and sister acting as godparents.

The death rate had continued to rise and it was thought that the Court would move back to the country as soon as the Queen was well enough. But she stayed on in London, determined to go to Greenwich in May. It was a dry spring with easterly winds and mist in the early mornings, and people feared that the epidemic would become worse than ever if the drought continued. By now it was apparent, too, that another disease was spreading through the Court, and one to which the ladies were particularly prone. Con, giving up all idea of converting the King, or of uniting the Catholic and Anglican Churches, had decided that he could do more for the faith simply by being agreeable, than polemics and the Pope com-bined. He himself was so personable, and it was so pleasant to be part of his circle, that those left outside soon began to feel jealous. On his arrival, Con had presented the Queen with rosaries of aloe wood, agate and buffalo horn, distributing others among the Catholic ladies at Court. The Queen's dwarf had looked on enviously, and when the presentation was over he called out, 'Madam, show the father that I also am a Catholic.' It was not surprising that there was criticism when the handsome young agent from Rome was seen frequenting the Court at all hours, talking to anybody he liked and even conversing with leading Protestants who seemed to seek out his company. It was scandalous the way Con's chapel had remained open throughout the theatre ban, providing a focus for large crowds of Catholics. The Queen herself had ostentatiously held a ceremonial service after the death of the Ambassador Pougny; more crowds were frequenting the Spanish Ambassador's chapel, and the priests themselves were going about openly and could be seen dining at the table of Catholic families. Even the cautious Péronne had now become positively confident and was canvassing for souls as shamelessly as everyone else. As the Capuchins went about their charitable business, visiting the sick and infirm, they found an increasing number of people ready to join their ranks. Some joined to satisfy a deep hankering for beautiful ornaments in churches, and others were converted after discovering that Catholic services were not full of devilish practices as they had been led to believe. Con found many allies among the ladies, and particularly relied on Mrs Endymion Porter, Buckingham's niece, who specialized in deathbed conversions. When her own father lay dying she hurried to his side and secured him for the Catholic faith before the arrival of her Protestant sister, Lady Newport.

Many people felt that Laud, known to some as 'the pope of England', ought to curb all this activity. The Archbishop would have liked to be as severe with the Catholics as he was with his Puritan critics, but his position was not secure enough for him to make a move in safety. It was true that his relationship with Cottington after the resolution of the power-struggle had been amicable, on the surface at least. He had gone out of his way to be magnanimous when he met Cottington in the quadrangle at St John's during the royal visit. Cottington appeared to bear no malice; he was doing well enough to be able to extend his house in the country, which now boasted one of the most up-to-date kitchens in England. All the same, Laud's letters to Wentworth were full of rueful comments on the current ascendancy of the Queen's party; he felt that the Court was peopled with crypto-Catholics, men like Endymion Porter who never went so far as to declare their faith, but who had all the same 'taken those beads into nearness'. It was as difficult for Laud as it was for the Puritans to tolerate the presence of Con who possessed all the charming qualities which he himself lacked. The two men treated each other with studied politeness, but there is no doubt that Laud's pleasure at sitting on the King's right hand was somewhat tempered by the knowledge that Con was installed on the Queen's left.

Early that summer, Con secured the reprieve and release of a Catholic priest under the death sentence, but there was no hope of a pardon for Protestants who had incurred the Archbishop's disapproval. Laud decided to make an example of libellers who had dared to criticise his policies, and Prynne, Bastwick and Burton were the scapegoats. They were brought before the Star Chamber on a charge of libel and condemned to lose their ears, pay fines of five thousand pounds apiece and face imprisonment for life. For two hours, as they stood in the pillory at Westminster, they talked to a vast crowd which had gathered to support and encourage them. Prynne's ears, or what remained of them, were removed, and Bastwick, himself skilled in medical matters, instructed the executioner to cut his off so closely that there was for him no danger of a second operation.

Before the King and Queen left on their summer progress there was a pleasant family occasion. The widowed Mary Villiers, still only fifteen years old, was married to James Stuart, Duke of Lennox, the King's cousin, in the chapel at Lambeth. Like his bride, Lennox had been brought up in the royal nursery and both of them were great favourites with the King. They were said to be deeply in love. The King and Queen were present with their children and the wedding dinner was held at York House, where it was said there were 'sixty cooks and but six lords'. The young couple had been granted more leave of absence than was usual among members of the Court, but as it turned out Lennox had to cut short his honeymoon and leave for Scotland on hearing news of his mother's death. The King was pleased with this development as he wanted a first-hand account from somebody he could trust of the troubles which had broken out across the border in recent weeks. Laud had for some time been planning to impose a service book in Scotland as part of his general scheme of unification, but when the liturgy was read in St Giles's Cathedral it was shouted down by a crowd of mainly female protesters who did not scruple to hurl bibles and stools at the Dean. The news of further riots was disturbing, but not serious enough to impede the King's visit to the New Forest for some hunting. On this occasion the Queen stayed behind at Oatlands as she was again with child. She spent a quiet summer, passing some time at Richmond with her five children who were all painted in a group by Van Dyck, including the infant Anne, a baby buxom enough to feature among the *putti* in a Rubens painting.

The final coup in the Catholic campaign came in the autumn when it was revealed that Lady Newport had now decided to go over to Rome. Lord Newport was enraged. He was one of the King's closest companions, a member of the team of fourteen masquers who had danced in *The Temple of Love*. He was afraid that his wife's defection might affect his position at Court, and he appealed to Laud for help. The Archbishop agreed that the time had come to suppress the upsurge of Catholic feeling before there were any more dangerous consequences. He spoke out strongly at the Council and most of its members were on his side, but the Queen, receiving a version of the proceedings from Con, decided for once to make full use of her power over the King and begged him not to be too harsh. The King hesitated, but eventually gave in to his wife, and the proclamation, when he finally issued it, was couched in such harmless terms that it turned out to be no more than a warning. Powerful voices in the Council had advocated an immediate closure of all Catholic chapels, but the Queen's was allowed to stay open even if some restrictions were placed on the Spanish Ambassador's. Laud protested about the Queen's interference, but the King answered mildly, suggesting that the Archbishop should approach her himself. 'You will find her very reasonable,' the King assured him.

Rationality was the last quality which Laud expected to find in this particular representative of the sex which had hurled bibles and abuse in response to the finely polished phrases of his beloved liturgy. He was quite overcome by the difficulties of his position. 'Indeed my Lord,' he wrote to Wentworth, 'I have a very hard task, and God, I beseech him, make me good corn, for I am between two great factions, very like corn between two millstones.'

The Queen had promised her husband that he would never regret his leniency. The Catholics, she assured him, would always remember what they owed him and would stand by him loyally in times of trouble. She did her best to soothe the Archbishop, who managed to bring himself to see her on December 12. 'We parted fair,' he wrote. She caused some criticism by marshalling all the recent converts for a Mass on Christmas Day in her chapel, but otherwise was as good as her word and saw to it that the Catholics did not cause her husband any more embarrassment. She warned Péronne to be more careful in future, and to make sure that the Capuchins' undoubted good works should be allowed to speak for themselves. From now on Con himself was more subdued. The English climate did not suit him, his health was suffering and he had lost his initial impetus. At the height of the crisis the King had been heard to say that if there were many more pervertings, to use Laud's word, the papal agent would soon find himself back in Rome. The stern reproof advocated by the Council had never been issued; all the same the Catholics had received a warning and they knew now that indiscretion could lose them all the concessions and lack of molestation which they had enjoyed in recent years. Walter Montagu and Sir Toby Matthew had both been named in connection with Lady Newport's conversion, and although guiltless in this case they were inordinately alarmed; Montagu kept to his chamber far longer than his current illness warranted, and Sir Toby was so distraught that everyone said he would never make a martyr.

For the time being there were other matters to take people's minds off religious controversy. The plague had died down at last; the playhouses were allowed to re-open, and a new masquing room with wooden cladding was being constructed, so that the smoke from innumerable candles, torches and lamps should not 'disluster' the gilding and spoil the Rubens paintings in the Banqueting House. Two masques were planned—the King's for Twelfth Night and the Queen's for Shrovetide.

When the audience assembled in the temporary building for the King's masque, the proscenium gave a foretaste of the propaganda which the work was to put across in unflinching terms. There were naked children riding on sea-horses, and the figure of Naval Victory with Right Government treading on the head of a serpent. For the noble and loyal audience gathered at Whitehall the reference was clear, for only that autumn most of the Court had travelled to Greenwich for the launching of the galleon, the *Sovereign of the Seas*, 'the goodliest ship that was ever built in Britain'. Although it was not until after the royal party had left that the tide was high enough for the ship to slip safely and majestically down into the river, nobody who had accompanied the King could fail to be impressed by this magnificent vessel which was a work of art as much as a warship. Many fine craftsmen had been employed in its construction, and throughout the year Inigo Jones had been carrying on an acrimonious correspondence with the Commissioners of the Admiralty concerning the impressment of two wood-carvers who had been working on the Queen's House at Greenwich. The ship was in itself a vindication of the Ship Money, and a symbol of naval power; in the King's masque, *Britannia Triumphans*, William Davenant emphasized the nautical element, and when the King as Britannocles appeared with his masquers, all in carnation-coloured costumes embroidered with silver, 'beautiful, rich and light for dancing', they had for a background the sea with haven and citadel; the sea nymph Galatea was seen singing and floating away on the waves, as well as a miniature fleet, which 'tacked about and with a prosperous gale entered the haven'.

The King and his courtly audience were naturally pleased with this device, which helped them to forget that the winds which blew outside the palace walls were not always too prosperous, that the great fleet under Northumberland had during its summer campaign done nothing more profitable than convoy the Elector Palatine and his brother back to Holland, and that government agents were finding it increasingly hard to keep up the flow of Ship Money payments.

For the last time a noble audience assembled to watch the optimistic celebration of the supremacy of monarchy. When all the festivities were over the King went away to Newmarket, but on his return the Queen noticed that he was 'much distressed in mind', a rather different figure from the triumphant Britannocles. The masques had in fact provided no more than a temporary escape from the problems which had come crowding in on him during the last months of 1637. On his return from Scotland four years before, the King had been greeted warmly all along the route, but since then he had done little to cultivate the general goodwill; it had been noted at Oxford that outside the colleges the welcome afforded to the King and Queen had been strangely lukewarm. The dissatisfaction caused by the Ship Money levies was only the most obvious of innumerable grievances, and many people were all too ready to criticize the King's mistaken piety, his petty rules, his muddled foreign policies, his Catholic wife. He himself was beginning to learn that the serpent under the heel of Right Government was a rather more slippery reptile than the dormant monster on Inigo Jones's proscenium arch. Secret presses were still publishing scurrilous literature; news-letters, printed abroad in Amsterdam or elsewhere, kept opposition groups well informed, and when works by Bastwick and others were burnt at Smithfield, title pages from their books were found pasted on walls in many parts of the city.

On February 28, 1638, at the Mercat Cross in Edinburgh, the National Covenant was read out, and for several days the Scots added their signatures—from noblemen down to the humblest citizens. Copies were then carried round to distant parts of Scotland so that everyone might have a chance to declare their sincere intention of defending their religion against all innovations—'as we shall answer to Jesus Christ in the great day and under pain of God's everlasting wrath'. When Charles read a copy of the document he was frankly angry—an emotion not often observed in this aesthetic and dignified King. Although it was said that an army of forty thousand men would be required to protect any minister brave enough to read from Laud's prayer-book, he was sure that by issuing strong statements in Whitehall he could reduce the tiresome Scots to order. If they were obstinate he would show them that he too was a Scot.

The Queen felt increasingly anxious about her husband's state of mind. He seemed melancholy and depressed and had ceased to enjoy himself; he had even given up playing tennis, a very bad sign. One evening she broached the subject of Scotland, begging him to avoid civil war with a policy of appeasement. He answered her with tenderness, telling her not to be alarmed, and assuring her that he could reduce his northern subjects to order whenever he felt inclined. But the thought of his personal danger continued to weigh on her mind.

It was a general belief that the Queen, perhaps under Con's influence, had begun to assert herself more, and during the winter months the foreign Ambassadors in London had found that it was often profitable to spend time on the Queen's side where many key people tended to gather. As it had been announced that in the near future Prince Charles was to be set up with his own household, there were also plenty of people hanging about the Court hopeful of promotion. The Queen's Secretary died suddenly in February and there was much speculation as to who would succeed him.

During the weeks before Easter, the Queen concentrated on her Lenten devotions, ordering fasts and frequent prayers to be offered up in her Chapel on behalf of the Queen of France who was thought to be pregnant after twenty-three barren years. Following the discovery of Anne's treasonable correspondence with Spain the previous year, there had been a reconciliation between husband and wife, and now the hope of an heir brought a more stable prospect to the French King, so long troubled by the uncertain loyalty of his brother Gaston. 'I pray God it may continue, and that it may be a Dauphin,' Henrietta Maria had written to Mamie. Louis, pleased with his sister's friendliness, gratified her in March by releasing her old friend de Jars from the Bastille, indicating at the same time that he was ready to give more than the usual vague promises concerning help in the Palatinate.

In Scotland, the Covenant was carried from place to place, thousands upon thousands signing, some in their own blood. Those who might have desisted tended to add their names out of fear. Meanwhile the King procrastinated, seeming unable to take action, until he finally consigned to the Marquis of Hamilton the unenviable task of persuading the Scots to see reason. Hamilton delayed his departure because his wife lay on the verge of death; she had already taken leave of her children so that they 'should not detract her thoughts from heaven'.

The Hamiltons had been leading figures at Court for years. The devout Marchioness had all the grace and good looks so lavishly bestowed on members of the Villiers family. She had succeeded in befriending the Queen even in the days when Buckingham's relations had not been welcomed by the French attendants. Her husband was just the good-mannered, handsome and cultured type of man that the King liked to have about him. His correspondence with his brother-in-law, Basil Feilding, the British Ambassador in Venice, was full of knowledgeable references to artistic matters, and he was more of a connoisseur than a diplomat, more of a listener than a leader. His ineffective expedition at the head of a contingent of volunteers bent on helping the Protestant cause on the Continent had demonstrated the point, but not to the King who placed in him the unshakeable confidence he reserved for his closest friends. Now Charles entrusted him with a mission that he neither wanted

but in the interest of economy few had been chosen. Familiar names appeared in the final list—Lennox, Hamilton, Seymour, Jermyn, Windebank. Nobody could accuse the royal family of encouraging new talent, and the completion of the Prince's household was the final proof for many who had planned a career at Court, that this was a world of shrinking opportunities, a narrowing circle from which they were excluded. The Earl of Newcastle, who had become the Prince's governor, was disappointed by what he considered to be the meanness of the new establishment. He had never imagined that he would be expected to share a table with anyone so beneath his dignity as the Prince's genial High Church tutor, Dr Duppa.

The Queen spent the summer quietly at Oatlands. She had written to Mamie, concerning the rumours of her sister-in-law's pregnancy, 'There will be work for Madame Péronne. I must let her rest.' In spite of this good intention, in July there were whispers that she too would be needing the international midwife. During the summer months Van Dyck finished three portraits of the Queen which, it was hoped, would encourage Bernini to carry out a companion piece for his much-admired bust of the King.

Not everybody was able to pass a peaceful summer that year. The King was often with his advisers, and Hamilton made three exhausting journeys to Scotland, finally offering concessions which arrived too late to appease the anger of the Scots against popery, foreign interference and episcopacy. There was an undignified exodus of Bishops from Scotland, all crossing the border in disarray, at least one of them in disguise. It was an unnerving summer for Laud whose particular brand of temperament did not help him to understand, even dimly, why his prayer-book should cause so much opposition. He could not tolerate criticism, and the ecclesiastical Court of High Commission was continually at work examining offenders such as Samuel Ward of Ipswich who had preached against a set form of prayer which to him brought a 'confining of the spirit'—he found it troublesome having to carry a manual wherever he went, and besides, 'a parrot might be taught to repeat forms without affectation'. All this was incomprehensible to Laud whose worst nightmare was finding himself about to take a wedding without a service book. The Archbishop was in such an over-sensitive state that when the King's fool, Archy, uttered some scandalous words about him, the Queen had to intercede to save the culprit from a session in the Star Chamber. Laud had finally succeeded in locking his old rival, Bishop Williams, in the Tower, but even in captivity the Bishop, described by Panzani as '*moderatissimo*', found ways of appeasing those who could be useful to him—he had always advocated a policy of concession rather than collision. 'He labours the Queen's side extremely,' Laud wrote.

The Court was full of rumours—Lennox had turned Catholic, Hamilton was treacherous, Cottington wanted a Parliament. 'I believe nothing in Court but what I see done,' Laud told Wentworth. The King was closeted first with one person, then with another; it was not surprising that no general policy emerged. He confided in nobody and kept bad news to himself. People outside the Court had the chance to know more through the outpourings of the illegal presses than those who were thought to be at the heart of affairs. Where complete mutual trust among the King's advisers might have helped to avert a crisis, suspicion and fear created their own kind of tension. The jealousy of petty men split the King's councils—Holland had coveted the post of Lord High Admiral and was extremely put out when the job once again went to Northumberland. He consulted his own cabinet of lady advisers, and retired to Kensington to take physic and to avoid hearing the official announcement —*per non vedere la crudeltà*, as Conway put it. The Queen found Holland's discomfiture rather amusing.

Northumberland, in fact, was not to be envied. He found the strain of shouldering high command at a time of great danger altogether too much. In May he was so seriously ill that it was doubtful whether he would ever live to take up his appointment. After Sir Theodore Mayerne had treated him, bleeding him four times and prescribing as many purges, he recovered, but it seems that during his illness he had time to take a long look at the general state of affairs. He knew that the King intended to call a meeting at Theobalds when the question of peace or war would be raised. Some, like Cottington and Windebank, were all for opening hostilities, but Northumberland confided in Wentworth that he was of a contrary opinion—who could be anything else when they knew that there were no more than a few hundred pounds in the exchequer? The King's magazines lacked arms and ammunition, there were no trained leaders available, and the people throughout England were 'generally discontented by reason of the multitude of projects daily imposed upon them'. The long years of peace had made men unaccustomed to the use of arms, and in the circumstances Northumberland felt it would be wise to treat with the Scots. 'God send us an end to this troublesome business,' he wrote, 'for to my apprehension, no foreign enemies could threaten so much danger to this kingdom, as doth now this beggarly nation.'

For the moment both sides played for time. Northumberland did not find himself despatched with inadequate forces to repulse an enemy; the mission on which he was sent in October was peaceable but strange. His orders were to supervise the landing at Rochester of Marie de Medici. 'You will easily decry her,' Sir Henry Vane told Pennington. The Dowager had not shrunk with the years and she would have been recognizable anywhere, even without the six coaches and seventy horses she was reputed to be bringing over with her.

At this time of crisis, the last thing the King would have asked for would have been the worry and expense of his mother-in-law. Many looked on her visit as an ill-omen, remembering her past history and how 'her restless spirit embroiled all where she came'. For years now the King had parried her many attempts to seek asylum in England, and when he heard this time that she had actually embarked he immediately sent orders that all the ports should be closed—there were even rumours that he had offered to pay her a large sum of money to stay away. The elements had done their best for him, whipping up contrary winds which gave him a short reprieve, but with his wife pleading in the background there was little he could do except set off to meet the unwelcome visitor, accompanied by Lennox and a number of other lords. The confrontation took place at Chelmsford and the King put up a show of cordiality, assuring his mother-in-law that she looked even better than in her portraits. They travelled up to London in the King's coach, Lennox sitting in the boot with his hat off—accompanied by a crowd of officers and gentlemen, the pensioners and the messengers, not to mention the six hundred or so retainers the Queen Mother had brought with her—'all of them in very great wants'. At Aldgate the Lord Mayor was waiting; speeches were made and the Queen Mother was presented with a gold cup. From Whitechapel to St James's the route was lined with armed men and the City companies.

In the courtyard at St James's the Queen waited with her children for the grandmother they had never seen. A chair had been brought out for Henrietta so that she could stay seated until the cortège arrived as her child was due in two months' time, and she had not been well. The day was wet and very windy—'Queen Mother weather,' the Thames watermen called it. All the same it was noted that the Queen looked more cheerful than she had done for some time. Her mother's plight had been a continual anxiety to her; often there had been rumours that the Dowager was ill or dying, and although the Cardinal Infante had 'caressed her for a while', he had eventually found her presence embarrassing and had sent her off to The Hague, where the Dutch made it clear that they would tolerate her for a short time only. In the summer Henrietta had made herself ill with anxiety and the King had come hurrying over to Oatlands to reassure her.

After thirteen years of separation the reunion of mother and daughter was bound to be an emotional moment. Henrietta went on her knees as her mother emerged from the coach, but Marie de Medici took her in her arms and kissed her repeatedly. Neither could speak, Henrietta's colour came and went, she wept and almost all the onlookers were in tears. The

Queen Mother finally turned to the five fine dark-eyed children, only one of whom, Elizabeth, had inherited her fair colouring, and greeted them with a great show of affection. As they all went up into the palace, Henrietta expressed her joy and excitement 'by the actions of her hands'— she was still very French, even after so many years in England. She had ordered improvements and renovations at St James's—far more than anybody could afford—to ensure the comfort of her mother and what Laud sourly described as 'the seditious practising train' that attended her. She visited her mother every day, but the lords and ladies who went to St James's to pay their respects were soon put off by the Dowager's haughty attitude. She was, as Giustinian put it, 'sparing of her courtesies', and when the Council arrived in a body to extend an official greeting, she remained seated and hardly said a word. Such behaviour was not altogether appreciated by the country which was entertaining her for a mere three thousand pounds a month.

It was hoped that Louis would be reconciled with his mother now that he had an heir, and that England would prove to be only a stepping-stone for the exorbitant visitor. The French Queen had given birth to a son that September—'the wonderfullest thing of this kind that any story can parallel, for this is the three-and-twentieth year since she was married,' as Howell put it, adding that as a result Gaston was likely to be 'more quiet hereafter'. But as the weeks went by, Louis showed no signs of softening his attitude and the English had to resign themselves to a prolonged spell of hospitality. Madame de Chevreuse was also still in England; it was easy to accuse the King of lavishing money on his wife's friends and relations to the detriment of Elizabeth and the Elector. Some point was lent to those accusations when it became known that the Elector, marching off with a small Dutch army to join the Swedes, had been surprised and cut off by Imperial forces. Charles Louis, always cautious, had managed to escape, but Prince Rupert, after characteristically dashing back into the fray, had been captured and was now a prisoner in Austria.

That Christmas, Whitehall was being prepared, not for a glittering entertainment, but for the Queen's confinement. Owing to her mother's presence at St James's she was for the first time unable to have her child there, and the atmosphere at Whitehall did not contribute to her peace of mind. The King was constantly involved in anxious discussions, and on January 15 Hamilton reported to the Privy Council the failure of his most recent mission to Scotland. In the deliberations which followed it was decided that the King should go to York in April to join a force of thirty thousand men which he optimistically planned to assemble in the north. It seemed that Britannocles must change his image, that love must give way to war. The King could no longer play the philosopher, standing relaxed and at ease on the edge of the forest. The time had come to assume his armour and ride away into battle.

The hero was willing enough, but he had few means at his disposal. Northumberland's strictures were now more valid than ever. There were no trained men, no arms, no commanders and, most important of all, no money. Laud believed that Juxon, left on his own, would have husbanded what resources there were, but as it was, he told Wentworth, he despaired utterly of any thrift. There were far too many keys to the coffer, and far too few loyal men in the provinces ready to contribute unstinted help in the form of men and arms—all in a cause for which they had remarkably little sympathy. It was not surprising that the Archbishop felt isolated and lonely, his power being wrested from him by a crowd of youthful courtiers, a disorderly rabble of Highlanders and a pregnant papist Queen. He was obsessed with the fear that Williams would 'come into play again' if the Scots were too successful, and he wondered uneasily if money was passing between the imprisoned Bishop and the Queen. With such matters on his mind, Laud was unable to direct his thoughts and energies towards his life's work. His energetic church reform stagnated, and there was little he could do by way of contributing towards the councils of war.

On January 20 the Queen gave birth to a daughter, Catherine, who lived only a few hours. It was a difficult delivery and at one time there were fears for the Queen's life. The King was distracted, moving from councils of war to his wife's bedroom. He was in the process of deciding who should command his armies. For his General-in-Chief he had chosen the Earl of Arundel, who, being as ignorant of war as he was knowledgeable about broken-nosed marbles, was likely to achieve as little as he had on an expensive diplomatic trip to the Habsburg court. The King intended to bestow the command of the cavalry on the staunchly Protestant Earl of Essex, who was one of the few men to have seen active service even on a minor scale. But Holland, soured by Northumberland's appointment the previous summer, had been working on the Queen, 'with shyness and serving of turns, and making means by others'. In her weak, unbalanced state following the birth of her child, she in her turn put pressure on the King, who at this time felt unable to deny her anything. When the news broke that Holland had been appointed, many people felt disturbed to think that the Queen could exert her influence in matters about which she knew even less than her husband.

In March the King left for the north. He took leave of the Queen tenderly and it became known that she was to be paid an exceptionally large dowry in the event of his death. He had also given orders for the Council to report to her every week. Northumberland, who had learnt something of the behaviour of the winds and waves during his recent

summer cruises, had been forced to stand by while the command of
the fleet was conferred on Hamilton—a man whose knowledge of boats
and the sea was virtually limited to the painted ships on Inigo Jones's
painted ocean. Northumberland's task was to ensure the safety of the
Queen.

The King's march was more like a royal progress than a military
expedition. It seemed that his supporters were more concerned with
plumes and ribbons than with muskets, and in camp he put great stress
on order and precedence, while paying rather less attention than he should
have done to military realities. At York, when he tried to impose his own
covenant on the great men who had gathered there with their own contingents, the Lords Saye, Warwick and Brooke refused to commit
themselves. Lord Saye was taken into custody but the King released
him; he responded by marching off with all his men, like any feudal
nobleman.

In April the Queen received letters from the King. He was in good
health and full of confidence, making plans for the defence of the border,
and putting all his trust in the fortresses at Carlisle and Berwick. He now
intended to march to Newcastle, where he hoped to gather his army—or
rather the untrained rabble that passed for one. The Queen was perhaps
under fewer illusions than her husband, and she was particularly aware
of the difficulty of acquiring essential arms without having the money to
pay for them. She had promised the King that he would never regret his
leniency towards the Catholics, and now she intended to give them a
chance of showing their gratitude. With Sir John Winter's help she wrote
a letter, copies of which were to be distributed under her own seal,
encouraging her fellow Catholics to contribute large sums 'freely and
cheerfully' to help the King's cause. She told Sir John that she was sure
they would be glad to have an opportunity of showing 'the persuasion
of their gratitudes', instead of endlessly soliciting benefits. A committee
of leading Catholics was formed for the purpose of organizing meetings
in London to set the campaign in motion. She put Con in charge of the
appeal, although he was in bad health and embittered because the red
hat the Queen had hoped to gain for him had never materialized.

The Queen sent several couriers hastening north to ask the King's
opinion but her campaign was well under way before there was any
possibility of a reply. She threw herself into the work, writing letters,
persuading the ladies at Court to fast and sacrifice some of their jewellery.
She was sure that nobody would feel able to refuse 'so just a request
from so great a lady'. The dangers which Catholics courted by contributing to her fund did not enter into her calculations. It apparently did
not occur to her that her well-intentioned activity could be misinterpreted,
and that in particular lengthy and secretive meetings of well-known

Catholics could seem sinister to suspicious Protestants. Her only thought was to help the King re-assert his divine authority, and she went ahead on her own initiative, never doubting for a moment that she was in the right.

Chapter 14

A PERPETUAL PARLIAMENT

HENRIETTA SPENT most of the summer of 1639 at Oatlands, waiting for news of a heroic military encounter between the English and the Scots. In June there were reports that the royal army had reached the border, but subsequently the Queen had a letter from her husband telling her that the Scots were ready to enter into negotiations. It seemed that Holland had advanced towards the enemy forgetting the elementary fact that foot soldiers tend to move more slowly than cavalry, and when he came unexpectedly within sight of the Scottish forces, his infantry was far behind. His troops were dispirited in the sultry lowland weather, and most of them were only too anxious to return to their quiet villages for the gathering-in of the harvest. The Scots on the other hand were bound together by a sense of religious mission, inspired by their preachers and by the sound of fiddle and bagpipe. Their forces were well deployed—with the help of a few cattle— to appear much larger than they actually were, and after a cursory assessment of the situation, Holland, who was unsure of himself and of the morale of his men, retreated as quickly as possible.

The King was hardly in a position to negotiate from strength, but he was optimistic of success and expressed the intention of going to Edinburgh for the opening of the Scottish Parliament. The Queen thought that in doing so he would be taking an unjustifiable risk and she wrote urging him strongly to change his mind. In the terms of the treaty signed at Berwick on June 18 he had been forced to agree that a Parliament and a General Assembly should be called, but he had only yielded on certain points in the hope of gaining time to build up his forces. Most people realized that the agreement was no more than a truce, 'the Covenanters being peremptory not to part with a hoof,' as Burnet put it.

To the Queen's relief Charles decided not to press on to Edinburgh and he travelled south at speed to be with her the sooner, spending only four days on the journey. Nobody had any heroic exploits to boast about. Hamilton's fleet had hardly acquitted itself better than the army. The Marquis sailed from Yarmouth to the Firth of Forth where he remained for some time in 'neighbourly residence', unable to make any impression on the fully-alerted population. The most notable feat had been a swift, efficient march north by the Earl of Essex to secure Berwick. The Earl, who had uncomplainingly taken second place to Holland, was discharged now without any mark of thanks. Instead of drawing together in the face of danger, the King's advisers became increasingly out of sympathy with each other, everybody blaming somebody else for the failure of the ignominious expedition.

Soon after the King's return, the Elector Palatine once more set foot in England and made an ill-timed appeal for help. Charles greeted him without enthusiasm, extending a warmer welcome to Carlo Rossetti, the new papal agent, a handsome and charming twenty-eight-year-old. Many lords gave Con presents on his departure, and the Queen insisted on providing him with a naval escort. He left England having failed to strengthen the Catholic organization in England, without a Cardinal's hat, his health broken by the anxieties of his mission and the vagaries of the English climate. He was frankly relieved that his three-year term was over, but he was not to enjoy the warmer climate of Rome for long—by the new year he was dead.

Although Con's main achievement had been to create a religious fashion among the ladies at Court, he had aroused antagonism in Protestant minds out of all proportion to the gains he had actually made. The English were apt to descry a Catholic *coup* round every corner at the best of times, and now they pointed to the presence of the Queen Mother and Madame de Chevreuse, to the appointment of Sir John Winter whose family had been associated with the Gunpowder plot, and the elevation of Péronne to the see of Angoulême. The worst possible interpretation was put on the Queen's artless attempt to raise money for the King's cause among the Catholics, and since many of the best officers in the royal army were papists, it was commonly believed that the time was not far off when the army would be taken over to enforce a universal obedience to Rome.

When Marie de Medici went down with a sharp fever, everyone hoped that as soon as she recovered the country would be relieved of 'this long and troublesome entertainment'. The French Ambassador, for his part, feared that the Dowager might well be persuaded by Henrietta to go back to her intriguing in Paris, especially now that her allowance had been cut by a thousand pounds a month. As the year went by, however, she still remained massively ensconced at St James's. The Cardinal Infante gave no sign that he would welcome back the expatriate Queen who made trouble wherever she went, and there was little chance that the French King would be ready to relieve Charles of his matronly burden. Relations between the two countries had deteriorated since the outbreak of the Scottish troubles, with Charles applying to Spain for arms and the French suspiciously active in Scotland.

In September a Spanish fleet laden with soldiers, who were to land at Portsmouth and march across to Dover, lay blockaded by Dutch ships in the Downs. Many English Catholics, too pro-Spanish for the Queen's liking, would have liked the British to chase the Dutch away, but the Protestants, easily convinced that a new armada had come to disembark troops in support of a Catholic plot, would have preferred the King to intervene on behalf of the Dutch. Charles, for his part, was determined not to commit himself to a naval battle, endangering the finely-carved prow of the *Sovereign of the Seas* with all her attendant vessels. To avoid the necessity for action, he retired to Windsor, where the days went by in a continual round of amusement with endless dancing which, the Venetian Ambassador reported, occupied 'the attention of this idle Court more than anything else'.

While the ships still lay off the coast, the Elector Palatine left Windsor. The English air had suited him and he would have stayed longer if he had not been intent on a plan to lead the troops of Saxe-Weimar to victory. He was soon tasting the air of a French prison, for Richelieu did not approve of his scheming and had him arrested, finding this the simplest way of keeping him out of trouble. The news of his nephew's fate reached the King soon after he heard that the Dutch had delivered a crippling blow to the Spanish fleet. Attacking decisively, the Dutch had driven many vessels ashore, capturing others and burning the rest, while the English fleet stood by, uncertainly neutral.

To deal with the increasingly difficult problems that faced him was beyond the King's capacity. No strong man had emerged to knit his Council together, and in September he recalled Wentworth from Ireland, greeting him with great affection, making him a member of the Council at once and before long creating him Earl of Strafford. This blunt, efficient Yorkshireman, with his rugged appearance and his marked disregard for people's sensitivities, was not an obvious candidate for the Queen's favour, all the more so in view of his long-standing friendship with Laud. Since Portland's death the Queen had in any case expended much energy in making sure that no one man should monopolize the King's counsels. She gravitated now towards old friends and in particular extended her favour to Hamilton who had finished cruising about in boats and was back assessing the shifting currents of court intrigue. To balance Strafford's power the Queen and Hamilton lent their support to Sir Henry Vane, a courtier who had risen with the help of money wisely laid out in early days, starting with the purchase of a place in the Household for five thousand pounds. Backing up this initial investment with a strong and consistent support for the King's policies, Vane had worked his way up steadily throughout the peaceful era until he became Comptroller of the Household. Strafford regarded Vane as a timeserver and was opposed to the removal of Coke, the Secretary of State, who was now nearly eighty years old. This, as Clarendon later expressed it, 'put the Queen to the exercise of her full power to perfect her work', and it was thanks to 'the dark contrivance of the Marquis of Hamilton, and by the open and visible power of the Queen' that Strafford faced his difficult task with a Council which included several members he would certainly not have chosen for himself. It was said that the appointment of the Earl of Lanark, Hamilton's brother, as Secretary of State for Scotland, and of the arrogant, unpopular Finch as Lord Keeper came about largely as a result of the Queen's recommendation; those who were excluded at this time were naturally ready to join the ranks of her enemies at a later date.

It was decided in the autumn that rehearsals should begin for a masque in which both the King and Queen would take part. It was reported that they both spent as much time perfecting the dances as they had in happier times. Although the King had many more important affairs to attend to, the effort expended on a mere entertainment was justifiable in so far as the masque was the King's principal means, other than the bald language of edict and proclamation, of countering the opposition's well-organized propaganda machine.

The title of the masque, *Salmacida Spolia*, revealed in advance that the evening's entertainment would contain a topical message, for the fountain of Salmacis was situated in border country pillaged by barbarians who were eventually tamed after drinking its waters. The design on the proscenium arch reiterated the theme of the Rubens paintings on the Banqueting House ceiling and showed kingship triumphing over rebellion, establishing peace where before there had been discord. The good and reasonable virtues were personified in an army of winged children, including one riding a furious lion which had been tamed with reins and a bit. Perhaps most significant of all, in view of what was to come, was the inclusion of a military-looking woman who represented Resolution.

The King and Queen had at least resisted the temptation to present two masques and *Salmacida Spolia* was to act as a vehicle for both of them. This year it was intended that the Queen Mother would preside, with her grandchildren, although Rossetti reported that she fell ill with a feverish cold and was unable to attend. Windebank's nephew, Robert Read, was told that the performance went very well although 'the disorder was never so great as at any'. In other masques, chaos had featured in all the texts, but had played a subservient role, being quickly overcome by the forces of order, but in *Salmacida* the contemporary situation was mirrored in the opening scene which depicted a stormy scene, grotesque and ugly, with bent trees.

The storm gave way, as the King unshakeably believed it would in

Charles I in robes of State

Henrietta Maria in 1640

Designs by Inigo Jones:
(*Above left*) For *Britannia Triumphans*. A Haven
(*Below left*) For *Salmacida Spolia*. Upper stage scenery.
(*Bottom left*) *The Triumph of Peace*. Costumes for the Sons of Peace. (*Bottom right*) *Salmacida Spolia*. Costume for Henrietta Maria as the Amazon Queen

Marie de Medici arrives at St. James's Palace and is greeted by Henrietta Maria and her children

Somerset House

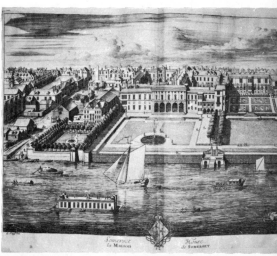

The Trial of Strafford. The Queen is seated in the box to the left of the throne

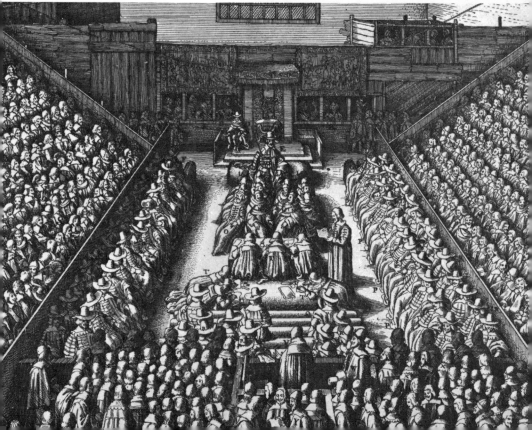

Henrietta Maria greeted outside the castle at Heemstede on her way to Amsterdam in 1642

Royalist troops on the beach at Scheveningen at the time of the Queen's departure for England in January 1643

real life, to a landscape of peace, with cornfields and pleasant trees, a country where the harvest could be safely gathered in without the disruption of war. Out of the sky came Concord in a chariot, who enquired, once she had touched down:

Why should I hasten hither, since the good
I bring to men is slowly understood?

Since she had come, however, she hastened off with her companion, the Genius of Britain, to instruct the 'beloved people' in the value of the peaceful life they enjoyed, and to incite them to indulge in the honest pleasures and recreations peculiar to the nation.

The anti-masques took up much of the playing time, but when they were over and all the grotesques had vanished, a song was sung in honour of the Queen Mother, an echo of the eulogy Henrietta had delivered in the role of Iris years before at the Paris Court. Significantly the words recalled the influence Marie de Medici had wielded over her husband:

Your beauty kept his valour's flame alive,
Your Tuscan wisdom taught it how to thrive.

The separate appearances of the King and Queen seemed to stress the new part Henrietta had begun to play, perhaps following her mother's example. It was Charles who was revealed in a passive tableau as Philogenes, the lover of his people, a patient, philosophical ruler. He sat on a throne decorated with palm trees, with rebels bound beneath his feet. He and his masquers were dressed in watchet-blue, a colour symbolizing all those divine and ethereal qualities—wisdom, reason, patience—which would help him outlast the storms raised by 'the people's giddy fury'. The Queen by contrast appeared on a multi-coloured cloud in an aura of dazzling light, drifting softly down without the usual accompaniment of music—the wooden pulleys having been carefully greased with lard and soap to prevent any creaking. If Philogenes was ready to sit passively waiting for everything to come right, it was left to his Queen to descend from the heavens and inspire him to take resolute action. Henrietta and all her ladies were dressed as Amazons in habits of carnation—the colour often reserved for the heroic warrior—with plumed helms and antique swords; and the song which greeted her arrival explained that the valiant would 'take from her their fire'.

The masque ended on the usual note of optimism. A crowd of deities hovered above a fine city where people, horses and coaches were seen in the distance moving over a bridge. It was Inigo Jones's last stroke of virtuosity, and the audience left the hall with the image of harmony and civilization superimposed on the dark chaos of the opening scene. The newcomer Rossetti felt quite overwhelmed by the whole occasion. All the principal personalities at Court had taken part, the Howards and the Herberts, the Feildings and the Lennoxes, Lords Russell and Lanark— 'a company of worse faces did I never see . . . not one new woman among them,' Northumberland commented sourly, perhaps because neither of his sisters was taking part. Rossetti thought the costumes were *super-bissimi* and found every detail delectable—the frequent change in the dances, the sound of various instruments, the variety of scenery which included six or seven machines at least. The festivities began after midnight and went on until the early hours, but for most people as they went out into the 'overcast morning' the impression of magnificence, order and peace can only have been short-lived. Life in the real world, for the King's supporters, was beginning to look like one long anti-masque, and there was little hope of harmony dropping from the clouds. All the money raised the previous year had been dissipated in a pointless expedition, and the truce with the Scots was unlikely to last. Unrest across the border was matched by a growing lack of co-operation at home. Many of the rules imposed by the King in a sincere bid to make his vision of the ordered realm a reality had caused offence, usually among the most vocal sections of the community. The King and Laud had genuinely set out to impose justice on rich and poor alike; if, for example, a young woman accused of adultery in a country village was forced to stand in a white sheet in front of the congregation in church, it seemed only right that a noble lady should suffer the same fate if she indulged in an adulterous liaison. Rich men offending against the building regulations had to expect to be heavily fined just as much as a member of the 'poorer sort' putting up a hovel illegally against the walls of a church, but this did not mean that there was not a great deal of resentment among the men of quality who regarded any prosecution as 'an insolent triumph upon their degree and dignity'. In the same way the sums levied by the Ship Money tax did not fall heavily on any individual. At Sudbury in Suffolk, for example, the tax worked out at roughly a shilling a head which was hardly exorbitant; when the Sheriff of Northampton ordered the churchwardens and overseers in the parishes to prepare a fair copy of the last taxes so that he could raise money to prepare a ship of '600 tun furnished fit for the seas' at a cost of six thousand pounds, he could expect opposition not because his county was too far from the sea to appreciate the need for coastal defence, or because the levies were likely to cause financial hardship. What people feared was the encroachment of royal authority, a fear that had been exacerbated by the judgment in a test case which had established the legality of the Ship Money levies, all the more so as one of the judges had unflinchingly stated that 'rex is lex'. The King's machinery for enforcing his edicts was altogether inadequate and he relied largely on those very property owners who were now preparing to resist his policies. Some, like Lord Saye and Sele, openly defied the King in the hope that a clash would provide the chance to debate the rights and wrongs of the tax itself. In some counties there were so many refusers that the prisons would have been overflowing if they had all been brought to justice, and it was easy enough to defy overworked government agents sent to take away cattle by way of a penalty—it was not beyond the bounds of human ingenuity to mix up the herds so that a puzzled official was unable to identify his quarry.

The King had determined to subdue the Scots by force, but to do so he needed money. There was talk early in the new year of calling a Parliament; this could only cause apprehension among those who were nearest to the King. Rossetti found the prospect distinctly unnerving, especially as reports began coming in from all parts of the country that it would be very strong against the Catholics and against his agency in particular.

Strafford, by contrast, was full of confidence. He had managed the Irish Parliament with great skill and did not doubt his ability to master the English equivalent. In early March he left London for Ireland in the Queen's coach which she had lent him for the first stage of his journey. It was a sign of the Queen's dawning favour for a man she had at first mistrusted and opposed. Gradually, in the months following the Pacification of Berwick, her attitude had been changing. A year before she had begged the King to make concessions and to avoid a course that might lead to war. Now all her energies were directed towards stiffening her husband's resolve. She disapproved of the agreement made at Berwick, feeling that the King had behaved in a way unworthy of a great monarch. All around her, in the decorations she had herself commissioned in the houses where she lived, she saw the image of the rose and the lily intertwined—the rose for peace and the lily for war. The coins that had been thrown down from the roof of Notre-Dame at her wedding, Simon de Vouet's ceiling at Oatlands and many other artistic works, celebrated in their imagery of lily and rose the marriage of Charles and Henrietta Maria, a mating of the warlike Henri's daughter and the son of the peacemaker James. Financial circumstances and his own natural inclinations had led Charles to cultivate his pacific tendencies, and now it was the daughter of Henri le Grand who was to keep the flame of valour alive in her peace-loving husband. For nearly a decade the Queen had imbued the young men around her with the ideal of chaste and courtly love. The masque served as a warning that she had changed her own image and would now set a new fashion of gallantry and military ardour. Young men were encouraged to wear swords and to sport the boots and spurs which ten years before had been banned from the palace by special edict.

Lent passed quietly for the Queen, and the King was cheerful, often playing cards late into the night. In the counties there was a fever of electioneering activity, and in April the new Members came crowding up to London for the opening of the session. Proceedings followed a predictable and familiar pattern. Realizing how urgent was the King's need, the opposition had made up its mind that not a farthing would be contributed for the expenses of war until Charles had redressed all grievances. Pitched against the government were experienced Members of great ability who had been schooled in the fiery sessions of the twenties, and the young men in whom the King put his trust were no match for parliamentarians of the calibre of Pym or Hampden. His older advisers tended to be good administrators and poor debaters. Strafford, the only man who could have controlled the Parliament, lay sick at Lichfield, and the King wrote begging him to take care of his health and to avoid travelling until he was better. By the time he was able to push on to London the situation was already out of hand, and it was unlikely that he would be able to repeat his success in Ireland where he had persuaded the Parliament to contribute four subsidies. Charles had offered to abandon the Ship Money tax in return for substantial grants, but Pym was determined to drive a harder bargain. Many more grievances would have to be redressed before the King would be allotted any subsidies at all. At a meeting of the Council, Vane gave a depressing account of the temper of the House and suggested that a dissolution was the only safe policy. Strafford, arriving late, counselled caution, but Vane had already swayed members and a decision was taken to dissolve the short-lived Parliament.

'There could not a greater damp have seized upon the spirits of the whole nation than this dissolution caused,' wrote Clarendon. In early May rioting broke out; apprentices and sailors marched on central London, attracted to the south bank by the sound of a drum. Although Laud had faded as a force in the King's Council, his known hatred of Parliament made him the obvious scapegoat. His palace at Lambeth was besieged by an angry crowd which hammered on his doors, calling in vain for the episcopal body it would have enjoyed pulling to pieces. Laud had by this time taken refuge at Whitehall, and the mob went on to demonstrate outside the palace, calling for the Archbishop and the Catholic Queen. Rossetti's house was also threatened and he sought sanctuary with Marie de Medici at St James's Palace, which was heavily guarded.

On a window in the King's antechamber at Whitehall somebody had scratched the words, 'God save the King. God confound the Queen with all her offspring. God grant the Palatine to reign in this realm.' The King shattered the pane with his own hand, but he could do little to stop the 'cheap senseless libels' aimed at Bishops and Catholics which were appearing on walls and gateposts all over the capital. He hurried his wife out of London, fearing for her health—she had been two months pregnant when she entrusted her royal person to Inigo Jones's cloud machine. She spent the summer at Oatlands, while the King did what he could to raise funds for an army to be used against the Scots. Strafford was convinced that the 'barbarians' could be brought into line, not by drinking the waters of Salmacis, but by a short and decisive campaign. At a Council meeting he reminded the King that a well-trained Irish army was at his disposal—'an army in Ireland you may employ here to reduce this kingdom' were the words which Vane, accurately or inaccurately, jotted down in his notes.

Remembering the difficulties she had experienced the previous year, the Queen was apprehensive about her accouchement, but on July 8, 1640, she gave birth with surprising ease to a healthy son, Henry, Duke of Gloucester, who was often known in later years as Henry of Oatlands. A fortnight later Laud travelled down from London for the christening, and one day the Queen invited Rossetti, who had taken a house in Surrey for the summer, to see her son, which pleased him very much. The King, as always, was delighted by the arrival of another 'prop of empire', and he rewarded the Queen by sanctioning the release of some Catholic priests from prison.

In mid-August news came that the Scots had crossed the border in large numbers. The King immediately announced that he would go north to rally the English forces. In the Council meeting that followed, Holland asked pertinently, 'Whether the King shall have money when he shall be there?' The King answered with his usual optimism that he would have funds enough to last for a long while, all the more so if he attended the campaign in person, for, as the Lord Keeper put it, 'the subject will not be in so good temper as under the King'.

Northumberland had been given command of the army, but as always when faced with a daunting task he fell conveniently sick. It was Strafford, racked with gout and the stone, who travelled north a week after the King to take control of the situation. Before he had time to organize the royal forces, the Scots had crossed the Tweed and pushed on to the Tyne which they forded at Newburn, putting the English 'to the most shameful and confounding flight that ever was heard of'. The King's letters to the Queen reflected his waning optimism, and his gradual realization that he would have to come to terms with the enemy. The armistice concluded at Ripon left him under an obligation to pay a large sum to the Scots as long as they remained in England, and to raise even more money to be rid of them. His hopes had faded of extracting payment from the Spanish in return for convoying supplies across the Channel, and the Queen had met with little encouragement when she wrote to Rome requesting a loan in recognition of the services she had rendered the Catholic cause in England. Money contributed by officers of the Court had quickly vanished, leaving nothing in reserve. Once again it seemed that the only way of raising funds was to call a Parliament.

Strafford, though unafraid, was under no illusions about the ordeal that lay ahead. Even Barberini, far away in Rome, realized the seriousness of the situation and prophesied that it would be a long time before this Parliament would be dissolved. He even feared that it might become a *parlamento perpetuo*. The Queen viewed developments with increasing alarm. When Montagu pestered her to back his candidacy for the Cardinalate she hinted that she had more important things to think about than the red biretta. Rumours reached her at Oatlands that a remonstrance was being prepared for presentation to the King on his return, and she knew that many complaints would be directed against the Catholics. Already chapels had been damaged and altar rails, images and stained-glass windows smashed. It was easy for Pym to work up a whispering campaign about the dangers of Catholic infiltration, for, as Davenant had put it in *Salmacida Spolia*:

Murmur's a sickness epidemical:
'Tis catching and infects weak common ears.

Now it was time for the Catholics to regret their open visits to the Queen's chapel, their blatant entertainment of priests, and the conversion of those few 'weak uninformed ladies'.

The King returned from the north to be greeted by 'a kind of ovation . . . being conducted through the streets of London with a most splendid cavalcade'. For the opening of the parliamentary session, however, all pageantry was missing and Charles went privately by barge to the Parliament stairs. His opening speech was direct and fearless and he stammered far less than usual. All the same he made little impact on the hostile assembly. Pym lost no time in mounting his attack. He knew that he was in a strong position but still feared the power of Strafford. The Earl, whose health had not improved, had only just managed to drive himself on in time to arrive for the opening. He was as experienced as the opposition leaders in parliamentary tactics, and it was only a matter of time before he would begin to rally the King's supporters and perhaps set the Lords and Commons at variance. Giving him no chance to counter-attack, the Commons quickly reversed all the King's policies, declaring Ship Money illegal, forbidding monopolists to take their seats, ordering all priests to quit the country. A committee was formed to inquire into recusancy. Williams was released from the Tower and rode along streets lined with cheering crowds to take his place in the Lords. Prynne, Bastwick and Burton returned from their far-flung places of confinement to the acclamations of the populace.

While the 'terrible reformers' were at their work, the King and Queen suffered a personal blow. Death took from them early in December their youngest daughter, a delightful three-year-old, the fine baby in Van Dyck's picture of the children. For a while it seemed as if their whole secure world was disintegrating around them as almost all those they most liked and trusted were snatched away. Each day another familiar face was missing. Laud was in custody; his Church policies, his so-called trouble-making in Scotland, the canons drawn up by Convocation the previous spring, were all enough in the opinion of the opposition to justify such a move. Strafford was confined in the house of the Gentleman of the Black Rod while evidence was collected—'ripping up the course of his life' as Clarendon put it—to prove him guilty on a charge of high treason. Windebank, knowing that the recusancy committee had proof of sixty-four orders issued under his hand for the release of priests, forestalled trouble by escaping to France, carrying a letter of recommendation from the Queen to her brother in which she said that his only crime lay in his fidelity to the King. Lord Keeper Finch, threatened with impeachment after a brave defence of the Ship Money, also took refuge on the other side of the Channel. Van Dyck had left for the Continent in the autumn; it was no climate for portrait painters, and he went off in search of patrons who could afford to subsidize the grandiose work he had for a long time hankered to carry out.

There were rumours in the new year that the leading Catholics at Court—Montagu, Digby, Winter, Matthew—would all be forced to leave. The Queen warned Rossetti that she did not know how long it would be safe for him to remain in England. One evening his house was raided by three Justices at the head of a hundred men. Officially they were searching for arms, but Rossetti suspected that they hoped to find incriminating correspondence. He treated them with the courteous charm which had made him so popular at Court, and they went away without further trouble. Marie de Medici, accused—in some degree justly—of influencing her daughter, was another whose presence offended the Commons. Her allowance had been cut and she was living frugally 'as a private person'. She had sold her horses, coach and plate, and was left with only twenty retainers, but there was nothing she could do to mitigate the unpopular fact that she was a Catholic.

One last hope of raising money remained to the King if he was able to exploit the value of his children. Plans to marry Mary to a Spanish Prince had come to nothing, but the Prince of Orange, understanding the financial situation as clearly as the English Parliament, now intimated that he was ready to pay a large sum only on condition that it would purchase the eldest daughter. Henrietta would have preferred to reserve Mary for one of the crowned heads of Europe, but now she accepted the prospect of a Dutch match, realizing that at this time money mattered more than royal blood.

Early in the new year of 1641 there were rumours that the nine-year-old Princess would soon be betrothed. There was much speculation about the price the King would put on his daughter and it was believed that she might fetch as much as a hundred thousand pounds. The fear that the King would at least temporarily solve his financial problems in this way made Pym drive his supporters on, allowing no relaxation of effort. At Court, too, during the festive season, there was great activity. Energy which any other year might have been used up in rehearsals and dancing was now directed into different channels. The King was making concessions wherever he could, reassuring the moderates and drawing support away from the extremists. The Queen had written again to Rome, pressing for a loan and pointing out that it was largely thanks to his leniency towards the Catholics that the King was in such a difficult position.

Although the forces in the north were riddled with discontent as pay fell into arrears and all available money went to indemnify the invaders, most of the officers were loyal and eager to prove themselves in the King's cause. Northumberland's brother, Henry Percy, had schemes for reorganizing the northern army to ensure that it could be relied on in an emergency. The military men in the south were equally dedicated to the royal cause, and the dashing young soldiers who now haunted the Court, swaggering about the palace with swords much in evidence, could not wait for the moment when they would rally in defence of the Queen who was their inspiration. In taverns and private houses and in rooms at the palace, ambitious but embryonic schemes were adumbrated. Men who were more at ease on the dance floor than the battlefield saw themselves marching on the Tower and releasing Strafford, or defending Portsmouth for the King until outside help could be brought in, perhaps from France. That the Queen supported the conspirators was unwise but not surprising. The previous May she had experienced her first taste of real danger when the mob moved from Lambeth to Whitehall, and the ever-growing hatred of Catholics was enough to warn her that even greater hazards might lie ahead. It would perhaps have been foolish not to ensure in some way the safety of her family, but the real folly lay in putting her trust in what Essex was to describe as 'the new Juntillio', a group led by the poets Suckling and Davenant, George Goring, Jermyn, 'and such youths (unsworn counsellors)' as one contemporary called them. Rumours of their indiscreet conferences were bound to reach Pym before plans had materialized, and the dangers of betrayal were great.

In an attempt to co-ordinate army supporters in the north and south, the King charged Jermyn with the task of working out possible plans with Henry Percy in case military action should prove necessary. The Queen would have preferred her Master of the Horse and trusted confidant to play a less dangerous role, but she submitted to the King's wishes. Her entire life was now dedicated to the task of extricating her husband from his troubles. She was doing all she could to hasten the arrival of the French Ambassador, believing that his presence might discourage Parliament in its campaign against the Catholics and its defiance of the marriage treaty.

The more the Queen made her influence felt the more she played into Pym's hands. The opposition leaders knew that in standing against the King they were on dangerous ground, for the reigning monarch was the symbol of unity and order, and many people still believed that he was touched with the divine. To criticize the King could be seen as a kind of blasphemy, but no such inhibitions troubled the critics of an imported Catholic Queen. In the past Buckingham had been singled out as the butt of all blame, now the Queen could be used conveniently as a scapegoat, her actions twisted and magnified. Although most Catholics—and some of the King's best officers—had been diplomatically removed from the Army, it was still possible to point to the money raised by the Queen through the Catholic collection as a sinister preliminary to a new 'powder plot'. The fact that, in January, the King interceded for a Catholic priest who was under sentence of death added yet another indication that the Queen, urged on by her mother who had spent a lifetime meddling in power politics, would continue to use her influence until she had persuaded her husband to dispense with lawful government.

In an attempt to still the increasing clamour and to protect Montagu and Digby, who had been brought before the House to answer charges concerning the Catholic contributions, the Queen sent a humble message to the Commons on February 5, 1641, insisting that all her actions had been motivated by a desire to remove misunderstandings between the King and his people. She claimed that, far from dissuading the King to avoid holding a Parliament, she had actually urged him to call one. As for her appeal to the Catholics, 'she was moved thereto merely out of her dear and tender affection to the King'. If what she had done was illegal, she pleaded ignorance of the law and promised to be more cautious in the future, asking Parliament to overlook mistakes made in the past.

The Queen's promise, that she would check 'the great resort' of people to her chapel and send the papal agent home, helped to lower the political temperature, which was precisely what Pym feared most. He knew that he would never feel confident until Strafford's case was settled. The trial opened on March 22 in Westminster Hall which was crowded with spectators. Even larger crowds had gathered outside to watch the arrival by river of the dread traitor whose wicked cruelty and tyrannous policies had been enshrined in the articles of accusation which had been printed and distributed in the capital. Strafford's appearance was in fact something of a disappointment. He had driven himself too hard for too long; years of ill-health had culminated in a spell in the Tower and now he looked shrunken, stooping and old before his time.

A curtained box had been prepared for the royal party 'at a very convenient distance for hearing', and throughout the weeks of the trial the Queen attended every session with all her ladies 'like so many Sempronias', taking notes throughout the day and discussing the proceedings at night. She watched with growing admiration the man she had at one time so gravely misjudged, listening as he answered his accusers calmly and incisively, confident in the knowledge that he could deal with all the charges levelled against him. Never, she wrote, had she heard any man speak 'so audibly and clearly with so little gaping'. Pym saw his case against 'the wicked earl' disintegrate as the days went by. Article after article was demolished, and soon it seemed that the whole case rested on whether or not Strafford had intended to bring over the Irish army with the intention of subduing England by force. Although Hamilton and others insisted that Strafford had meant Scotland when he referred to 'this kingdom', Vane still maintained that the Earl had England in mind when he spoke at the Council meeting.

It was clear that the testimony of one man resting on a few equivocal words was not enough to bring the accused to justice. Summing up his defence on April 13, Strafford listed all the false evidence, and the charges for which no convincing proof had been produced. His only crime, he maintained, was that he had worked too hard for the King's prerogative. This word had become a term of abuse, but Strafford set out to re-instate it. He was well versed in music—once the Queen had admired one of his compositions, expressing amazement that anybody English could have produced anything so spirited—and he used a musical image to press home his point:

> As on the lute if anything be too high or too low wound up, you have lost the harmony, so here the excess of prerogative is oppression, of a pretended liberty in the subject disorder and anarchy.

It seemed that Strafford had outwitted his accusers and could now hope to go free, taking his place once again in the King's counsels, playing off Commons against Lords and working to re-establish the sovereignty of the King. He had at his disposal the controversial Irish army and the English forces which remained restlessly at York, eager for payment and action. Money would now be forthcoming as the Dutch marriage settlement had been completed, and at the end of April the fifteen-year-old Prince arrived for the wedding ceremony.

William of Nassau entered the city in an atmosphere of rising tension.

Alarmed by the possible reinstatement of the man who could so easily in his turn accuse his enemies of treasonable dealings with the Covenanters, Pym had deliberately set about arousing popular unrest in the capital. The Prince went straight to Whitehall where he was met on the staircase by Charles and James. It was noted that neither the Queen nor the Lady Mary allowed William to kiss them, as they would have done had he been the member of a royal family. Although the Elector Palatine was in England having been released from prison in France, he did not appear—he had always understood that Mary was his destined bride, and he felt aggrieved that she had been offered to the highest bidder. He made matters worse by appealing to Parliament for the aid he had never succeeded in extracting from the King—not the most tactful gesture for a would-be son-in-law.

The celebration of the marriage had to wait until the end of Holy Week, which gave the bride and groom a short time to get to know each other. The Prince was pleased with his pretty nine-year-old bride; he soon detected signs in himself that he was deeply in love and hoped that she reciprocated, even though her mother had taught her to look down on a mere Dutchman. When the marriage took place on May 2 they were already beginning to feel more at ease with one another. The Queen watched the simple Protestant service from a recess in the chapel and in the afternoon joined William and Mary and all her other children for a stroll in the park. In the evening she supervised the undressing ceremony and put her daughter to bed. The King and Queen, who had been joined by a large crowd of courtiers, waited while the Prince of Wales fetched his brother-in-law. The King drew back the curtains of the bed and allowed William to kiss his bride; there was some amusement when the Queen's dwarf produced a pair of shears to cut the Princess's nightdress which had been sewn up as a precaution.

The wedding provided a short distraction at a time of great anxiety. Even before Strafford's triumphant summing-up, Pym had resolved to introduce a bill of attainder which would state baldly the necessity of putting Strafford to death in the interest of state security. Meanwhile Pym set to work, inciting the London mob and spreading rumours of mutiny, of an escape plot by Strafford, of an attempt to seize the Tower, of an outbreak of civil strife. It was said that the King of France stood ready across the Channel with military aid for his brother-in-law. May was the traditional time for the apprentices to gather in the streets, and the floating population of London—the casual labourers, the masterless men, the unemployed, the disenfranchised, the vagabonds—needed little encouragement to flock to Westminster. They beat on the door of the Parliament House, demanding Strafford's blood. The King, refusing to be intimidated, announced that he did not consider Strafford guilty according to the law of the land, but the Lords were frightened into passing the Bill at its third reading. It was Strafford who recognized the great danger that now threatened the monarchy. He saw that if the sentence was carried out when the King had refused to sign the Bill, his authority would be undermined for ever. He wrote the King a letter, touching but firm:

> To say, Sir, that there hath not been strife in me, were to make me less man than God knows my infirmities make me, and to call a destruction upon myself and my young children will find no easy consent from flesh and blood. To set your Majesty's conscience at liberty, I do most humbly beseech your Majesty (for preventing evils which may happen by your refusal) to pass this bill.

The next day Pym revealed details of the Army Plot, betrayed several weeks before by Goring, who had grown impatient because his plan had not been implemented. The plotters—Percy, Suckling, Davenant, Jermyn —fled the country. The crowds at Westminster grew larger, noisier and more violent, driven on now by fears of a Catholic coup. When the Bill of Attainder was taken from the Lords to Whitehall for the King's signature, the mob crowded round the palace, its clamour clouding the King's judgment as he struggled with his conscience and sought legal and spiritual advice in his terrible dilemma. Although Strafford had begged him to sign the Bill, he could not lightly go against his conscience, nor could he jeopardize the safety of the Queen.

The royal children were in comparative safety at St James's but Whitehall was more difficult to defend. The King had ordered that guards should be put on all the staircases, but he knew that at any moment the rabble might break into the scattered interconnected buildings by one of the many entrances, overpowering the small force he had at his command. On Saturday, May 7, the royal pair contemplated flight, but the French Ambassador and others dissuaded them and pacified the crowd with assurances that rumours of a French invasion were false. Over the weekend the clamour continued to mount, and there were threats that the crowd would storm the palace and take the Queen to the Tower if the King did not sign. Henrietta was now pictured as the arch-plotter, and libels were circulated, accusing her of too great an intimacy with the tall, engaging but chastely faithful Jermyn.

On Monday afternoon a representative from Parliament, guarded only by two men, came to fetch the Bill, and the King signed away his friend's life with tears in his eyes. The representative went to the window and told the crowd to disperse as the King had promised to do all they asked. The next day Charles sent his son to the Lords with a letter begging for a reprieve. He promised that if his request were granted he would be more 'cheerful' in granting their just grievances. But although he had chosen as his messenger 'him . . . that of all your house is the most dear to me', the appeal was in vain. Two days later, Strafford went to the scaffold. As he passed Laud's window in the Tower, the Archbishop fell into a dead faint, overcome with grief. Rossetti said that the scene at the palace was indescribable. Many were on their knees, fearing that their last hour had nearly come, making their confession, or disconnectedly saying prayers. The Queen, believing like many others that Strafford's death would be the signal for a Catholic massacre, was in a state of great affliction. Father Philip felt unable to talk to her but Rossetti said what he could, telling her that he knew the Pope would be shocked to hear of the troubles she was passing through. She said, weeping, that this gave her little comfort; she was preoccupied with her sorrow at Strafford's fate, and her fears for her Catholic friends. She begged Rossetti to escape from the palace at once by a secret route.

Strafford faced his last ordeal with calm courage, professing his loyalty to the King and his 'affection to the peace and welfare of the kingdom'. He then submitted his neck 'with most Christian magnanimity to the stroke of the axe, which took his head from him at one blow'.

Chapter 15

THE UNTUNED LUTE

AT THE end of May Prince William returned to Holland. He would have liked to take his bride with him, so that she could learn to know Dutch ways and undergo a Protestant education, but the Queen persuaded him that Mary was as yet too young and too delicate to face a change of air and diet. Once the bridegroom had gone, the King began to extend his favour openly to the Elector Palatine, taking him everywhere and showing a revived interest in the Protestant cause. He worked harder than ever to achieve an alliance with the moderates in England and Scotland, and did what he could to pacify his opponents by dismissing Cottington and admitting Lord Saye and Sele to the Council.

The crowds had been allowed to disperse, but Pym still had to walk warily even though he had rid himself of the greatest threat to his power. There were many people who in retrospect regretted the events of the spring and felt disturbed when they remembered the forces that had been unleashed at the time of Strafford's trial. They had looked for a redress of grievances and the removal of a few powerful men, but not for the abolition of kingly power. A more radical overturning of the established order of things opened up a frightening abyss. Strafford had summed it up in his image of the untuned lute, and Shakespeare had issued the same warning in *Troilus and Cressida*:

> Take but degree away, untune that string,
> And hark! what discord follows;

If the King's authority was shaken, the pattern could be repeated all over the country, as nobleman and gentleman, sheriff and justice all found their positions threatened, with a consequent breakdown of law and order. Men feared an oppressive ruler but they dreaded even more the 'rudeness and rankness' that led to chaos, the influence of 'odious incendiaries' and that spirit of 'division and contradiction' which if unchecked could undermine the whole settled system, encouraging Levellers and all kinds of extremists. Where the root-and-branch Puritans advocated a total abolition of the episcopacy, many more moderate men held back, believing that a break-up of the Church hierarchy would open the way for any crack-brained preacher who thought he could unravel for himself the secrets of the Almighty.

Already the smooth conduct of affairs had been affected by the disappearance of men who had been virtually running the country for the last ten years. The administration was suffering particularly from the loss of Windebank who had kept the Secretary's office going with a faithful and overworked staff of friends and relations. The King did his best to pacify the 'grand contrivers' by filling the vacancies with moderate men from the opposition ranks. When he found an excuse to dismiss Pembroke —'having been long incensed by the passionate, indiscreet, and insolent carriage of the Earl'—he sent a gentleman usher to fetch the Chamberlain's staff and bestowed it on the Earl of Essex, 'who, without any hesitation, took it'.

The King, feeling that the time had come to extend to Scotland his policy of moderation, had made up his mind to travel north for the opening of the Scottish Parliament. The Queen viewed the prospect of his absence with apprehension. Although there had been a lull in Pym's campaign, the committee set up to investigate the Army Plot was still in existence, and it remained a psychological weapon which Pym did not scruple to use whenever his own cause was in danger. It was reported that opposition Members were searching through old records to find out if there were precedents for bringing a Queen to trial. On June 25 a letter was read in the House, allegedly written from Father Philip to Montagu in Paris, appealing for immediate help from France. A warrant was then issued for Philip's arrest. In July the Queen at last persuaded Rossetti to leave England, and the Queen Mother was also making plans for departure—the only thing that was keeping her in England was the sad fact that she had nowhere to go.

At first the Queen made plans to travel with Charles as far as Holdenby, but gradually it became known that she intended to leave England with the double intention of going to Spa for the sake of her health and of delivering her daughter to the Dutch. The news was greeted with disapproval in parliamentary circles where opinion prevailed that whenever the Queen was busy she was up to no good. An approach was made to the King, who promised to point out to his wife that it would be ignominious for her to take her daughter at a time when the right ceremonial could not be observed—especially as the Prince of Orange was 'in birth and other prerogatives . . . so inferior to this august house'. The Commons refused to believe that the Queen was going for the sake of her health, guessing, rightly, that she intended to take the Crown jewels with her to raise money for her husband's cause. Her medical adviser, the venerable, white-bearded Sir Theodore Mayerne, was called to the House to answer questions about her physical state. He spoke cautiously, hinting that her illness was primarily psychological and that her greatest need was for a change of scene and the chance to 'have her mind quieted out of reach of employments that may disturb her'. Parliament remained unconvinced that a visit to Spa was necessary, and sent a message ensuring that everything would be done to promote her peace of mind provided she cancelled her arrangements for going abroad. At the same time steps were taken to ensure that the jewels could not be smuggled out of the country. The Queen wrote a formal note thanking both Houses for their good care, adding somewhat sharply, 'I hope I shall see the effect of it'. To the Prince of Orange she wrote that it caused her 'no small grief' to be unable to bring over her daughter as she had planned.

There were many people who felt that in any case it would be unwise for both the King and Queen to be out of the capital at the same time. Bishop Williams was among those who believed that the King should stay close to Whitehall, and he advised him to 'keep near to the Parliament; all the work is within those walls; do what you can to win them man by man'. Ignoring this counsel, the King went ahead with his plans to leave for Scotland and was busy up to the last moment, bestowing baronetcies —at a price—and doing his best to build up a store of money and gratitude. The Queen went to Oatlands with the children, and Charles instructed her to work closely with Edward Nicholas, one of the few men he could trust. Nicholas was also knowledgeable about the everyday workings of government, having served as a clerk to the Council and in several other administrative capacities.

While she was at Oatlands the Queen wrote to her sister the Duchess of Savoy describing the almost unbelievable change in her fortunes. She was bereft of many of her friends and retainers, and was forced to sit by and watch the persecution of her fellow Catholics. Pondering her own plight she was almost relieved to think that Mary had not married a crowned head of state, for she was beginning to realize that kingdoms do not necessarily bring happiness. On August 20 she had the melancholy task of accompanying her mother on the first stage of her journey to the coast, but she went back to Oatlands at once to rejoin her children and carry on the important work the King had delegated to her. It was her task to implement the policy advocated by Williams of winning over Parliament 'man by man'. Although many people distrusted his wife's judgment, Charles believed that with her charm and energy she was the person most likely to keep alive the loyalty of the young peers in particular, who increasingly resented the presumptuous attitude of the Commons. It was also hoped that the royal party could be strengthened with the support of moderate men, who, by their very nature, were likely to be less diligent than the extremists and less vocal than the agitators. Many potential supporters had vanished away at the first sign of good weather, saying that they had family affairs to attend to, or that they wished to escape from the latest outbreak of the plague. The Queen, to counter this exodus, began writing to key men in the counties, urging them to round up their friends; 'for many others,' she told Nicholas, 'I have spoken myself to them already.'

As his regal parliamentary manager worked hard in the south, the King dealt benignly with his old enemies in Edinburgh and ignored many of those who had previously supported him, including Montrose who was shut up in the Castle asking in vain for a trial. The Queen was much reassured by reports that the King had been well received; 'the people,' she told Nicholas, 'have showed great joy to see the King, and such that they say was never seen before; pray God it may continue.' This news, so encouraging for the Queen, made Pym for his part redouble his efforts to build up a strong majority in Parliament. There were reports that Essex, Warwick, Newport and others had been engaged in long conferences, sometimes at the house of Northumberland who had transferred his loyalties to the opposition. Both Nicholas and the Queen begged the King to return in time for the opening session to counter Pym's machinations. It seemed that a Grand Remonstrance was being prepared, setting out all the wrongs and mistakes of the reign, and it was certain that the rabble, having proved such an effective weapon, would be roused again with rumours of popish plots and foreign intervention.

The Queen was told that at a banquet held at Holland's house, the view had been expressed that if the King should make any rash move the Queen would be seized with all her children. Precautions were taken to ensure that she did not make any attempt to fly the country, taking her children—those valuable hostages—with her. The loyal Newcastle had been removed from his post as the Prince of Wales's governor, and the Marquis of Hertford, a brother-in-law of the Earl of Essex, had been appointed in his place. Dr Duppa had also been removed; the genial don was considered too Laudian for comfort. Pym pointed out to the House that the Prince was at Oatlands, and moved that he should be returned to his governor, pointing out that 'though her Majesty was a loving Mother, yet there were such about her as were not friends to prince or state'. The message was brought to her by Holland, her former favourite. Although she did not wish to part with her children, she let them go, not daring, on her own initiative, to defy the Parliament. The Prince went back to his governor, who had been recalled unwillingly from the Latin and Greek studies which were his passion. He had instructions never to leave the Prince alone for a moment 'under pain of forfeiting his head for any mischance that may ensue from such neglect'.

Pym was anxious to hurry through a bill excluding the Bishops from the Lords, since they provided a solid royalist vote. As the opening of the autumn session came nearer, the Queen intensified her campaign to ensure that the King's supporters returned to the capital in good time. Nicholas had tried to communicate with Carnarvon at his house outside London, but the Earl was away from home and the message was returned to the Queen who burnt it at once. 'It should be very necessary that you should enquire where he is, and write to him,' she told Nicholas, 'and send to my Lord Cottington for his proxies, for I hear he had two, and his own; and send to my Lord Southampton and Dunsmore to send their proxies, till they come themselves; they are in Warwickshire.'

Soon after the opening of the session there was disturbing news from Scotland. It seemed that the King had condoned a plot as dangerous and as ill-digested as the scheme betrayed by Goring. Continuing to trust in the audacious young officers as an insurance against trouble, the King had ignored secret meetings and clandestine comings-and-goings which had preceded the premature revelation of a plot, labelled 'the Incident', to kidnap Hamilton in the King's bedroom. Whatever the truth about the King's connivance might turn out to be, the trust he had built up among the moderates seemed to dissolve overnight, and the Incident, like its counterpart in England, became a powerful propaganda weapon in the hands of the opposition.

In Ireland, the Catholics, fearing that the establishment of a Puritan regime in England would lead to religious repression, now rose against the Protestant settlers, and soon there were reports of barbarous massacres. Before long the Queen was being publicly condemned for inciting the rebels. Father Philip was called before the Commons for questioning, and although he knew nothing of the Irish rebellion, he did not relish the thought of having to answer pertinent questions about the Queen's appeals to the Pope for aid. He refused to swear on the Protestant bible and was committed to the Tower.

At last the Queen heard that her husband was on his way home. 'The King commanded me to tell this to my Lord of Essex,' she informed Nicholas, 'but you may do it, for those lordships are too great princes now to receive any direction from me.' Nicholas urged the King to make a public entry into London and to greet his people with a smiling countenance. He was met at Theobalds on November 24 by the Queen and his children. When they entered London the streets were decorated and lined with friendly crowds. After a banquet at the Guildhall the royal party went to Whitehall by torchlight; hearing as they went the 'great acclamations and joy of the giddy people', it was hard to imagine that they had any enemies.

The Grand Remonstrance had been passed after a stormy session that went on late into the night, but the King took courage from the fact that voting was a hundred and fifty-nine to a hundred and forty-eight. The

Queen had done her work well, but it was evident that a close struggle lay ahead. Pym was anxious to bring matters to a crisis before the King could exhort his supporters to leave their estates and journey up to the troubled capital in winter weather. He knew that in the fullness of time the King would be able to rally more than enough loyal Members to cover the narrow margin of eleven votes. In the Lords the Earl of Bristol and his fine fair-haired son Lord Digby were whipping up support and in particular were hoping to attract the younger peers to the royalist side. The King himself was working hard to capture the support of the City. He had made an initial blunder in retiring to Hampton Court, for it was feared that his absence from the capital during the festive season would badly affect trade. When a delegation of mayor and aldermen went down to visit him, 'beseeching him to dismiss from his thoughts the memory of certain offences which he had received in the past', he took the opportunity of saying that he regarded London as 'the chief limb of his crown, and that upon which his greatness rested'. He promised to return to Whitehall the following Monday, and, in the presence of the Queen, he knighted all the aldermen for good measure.

While the King struggled to increase his popularity with a show of mild and balanced behaviour, Pym harnessed the presses and kept the mob in reserve. He encouraged the printers to propagate libels inflaming public opinion. One of many widely-circulated sheets was the *Copy of a Letter Found in the Privy Lodgings at Whitehall*, published with the intention of awakening the fear that some Royalists, like the writer of the letter who urged the King to do 'something extraordinary', were plotting to overthrow the Parliament. When the King took the sting out of the Grand Remonstrance by ignoring it completely, Pym had the text published and distributed as a detailed reminder of all the King's tyrannous acts.

Charles was determined at all costs to avoid a repetition of the days of terror preceding Strafford's death. To counteract the Bill passed in Parliament which took the responsibility for naval and army appointments out of his hands, the King removed the lieutenant of the Tower and substituted Colonel Lunsford, a typical swaggering and hot-headed Royalist. He replaced the London trained bands commanded by Essex with a force recruited in the neighbourhood of Westminster, composed mainly of friends and dependants of the Court. All the same, the crowds around Whitehall grew larger and more angry every day, and cries of 'No Bishops' mingled with shouts of 'Down with Lunsford'.

Almost two years before, in the Queen's dancing barn, as the Puritans disparagingly labelled it, the figure of Concord in *Salmacida Spolia* had remarked prophetically: 'They will miss me when I am gone.'

Knowing that many of his subjects did indeed look back with nostalgia to the more settled days of the past, the King made it clear that his only aim was to re-establish an ordered way of life. Moderate Church of England men, worried by chaotic services and unqualified preachers, were reassured by his insistence that the Book of Common Prayer should be read in all churches, and by his firm announcement that he had no intention of re-modelling the system on Scottish lines. 'I am constant,' he wrote, 'for the doctrine and discipline of the Church of England, as it was established by Queen Elizabeth and my father, and resolve, (by the grace of God) to live and die in the maintenance of it.' The King's apparently sincere desire to help the Protestant settlers in Ireland convinced many waverers that neither he nor his Queen had encouraged the Catholics to rebel, and the fact that he had allowed the armies in England and Ireland to be disbanded seemed to suggest that he had never contemplated a military *coup*.

Pym's popularity started to wane as the King's increased. Now men began to wonder whether the parliamentary leaders refused to treat with the King because they feared the consequences for themselves of any peaceful settlement. Strafford had referred to the King as his sacred Majesty, and there were many people now who saw Pym's actions as a kind of profanity. Realizing that the tide was flowing against him, Pym whipped up the discontented poor of London who were easily persuaded to blame the King for the slump in trade, the rising prices and the scarcity of coal. In the new year there were strong rumours that the Queen would be impeached, and that proceedings would be initiated before all the royal supporters had arrived from the country. The King's position in the Lords had already been threatened by the impeachment of a number of Bishops, and he recognized the need for immediate action. On January 3 the Attorney-General accused Pym, Haselrig, Holles, Hampden and Strode of high treason. The move would have been more effective had the King been able to send the accused to the Tower, which was already sheltering two Archbishops—Laud and Williams, newly appointed to York—as well as eleven other mitred heads. But the House refused to deliver up any of its Members.

In spite of all his concessions and protestations of peaceful intent, the suspicion remained that the King had always intended to resort to force when the moment came. The fact that officers from the disbanded army at York had been gravitating to Whitehall heightened the belief that there would soon be bloodshed, and the night of January 3 passed in an atmosphere of tension. The King sent a message to the royalist Lord Mayor, Sir Richard Gurney, ordering that no trained bands were to be on guard at the Commons. The next morning the House met as usual and denounced the King's actions. When news of its defiance was brought to the King at Whitehall, he took leave of the Queen with his usual tenderness, telling her that he would return within an hour, master of his enemies. As he went down the steps of the palace he called out to his loyal subjects and guards to follow him, then stepped into the first coach he saw—it did not belong to him—and set off on the short journey to Westminster with a contingent of armed men whom he left at the door, entering the Chamber accompanied only by the Elector Palatine.

The Queen saw him go and remained waiting for news, convinced that at last, with this bold step, her husband would silence his enemies. With the ringleaders safely in prison, the King's moderate supporters would no longer be afraid to stand up for the royal cause. When Lady Carlisle entered the room, the Queen was unable to resist telling her to rejoice, for at this moment the King had made himself master of the state. Lady Carlisle, whose brother was in the enemy camp, and who had been in her element during the previous months, gleaning information for both sides, now quickly sent a message of warning to Pym.

When the King returned to the palace he was not the triumphant hero the Queen had expected to see. He had left the Commons in an angry passion, finding, as he put it himself, that the birds had flown. His plan of arresting the five Members had failed. The Queen was full of remorse, blaming her own indiscretion for the fiasco. He did not reproach her, either then or later, and she always remembered his forbearance with gratitude. His immediate need was to do everything possible to salvage his plans. He issued commands to the heralds to use every possible means to arrest the men; he addressed the City Council with assurances that he had no intention of changing the religion of the realm or of depriving Parliament of its ancient privileges. All his protestations were treated as if they were nothing more than empty phrases. As he drove back from the Guildhall hostile crowds greeted him with cries of 'Privilege' and demands for the liberty of Parliament.

The King mounted guns at the Tower, but he was helpless now in the face of rising hostility in the City. The Queen told the Dutch Ambassador, Heenvliet, that the rebellion had begun. Parliament was now meeting in the Guildhall for safety. The trained bands were under parliamentary control. When the French Ambassador offered to mediate, the King refused to treat with him. Like Lady Carlisle he had for months been playing a double game, and it is probable that his message of warning had reached the five Members even before Lady Carlisle's, allowing them to slip away by river in good time. The Venetian Ambassador was urged to intervene, but he refused to meddle in 'a difficult affair where success was unlikely'.

With the City in arms, Pym and his companions still at liberty and royal supporters too frightened to show themselves, the King and Queen took the decision to move out of London to Hampton Court. On the evening of Monday, January 10 with only a few of their closest friends and their three eldest children, they left Whitehall, travelling through grim crowds of close-cropped apprentices. No preparations had been made at Hampton Court and King, Queen, Princes and Princess all spent the night in one bed.

After a few days at Hampton Court the King took his family to the greater security of the castle at Windsor. The King made no attempt to comply with requests that he should return to London, although reassuring remarks had been made about the Commons' care for his safety. He had by now made up his mind that he would not return to the capital unless he was backed by a force strong enough to subdue the rebels. He sent Newcastle on a journey north to take possession of the valuable store of arms and ammunition at Hull, and messages were despatched in the hope of securing Portsmouth.

The Queen told Johan Heenvliet, the Dutch Ambassador, all her troubles—how she was accused, falsely, of influencing the King and giving him bad counsel, of encouraging the Irish rebels whose atrocities she detested as much as everybody else. She told him that she would never persuade the King to oppose his Parliament, provided he was allowed to enjoy his due rights and possessions, and was not reduced to the level of the Duke of Venice—a fear that was to haunt all Stuart monarchs throughout the century.

Many of the King's supporters, finding life in London too dangerous, had gone away to the country, leaving a thin House with a comfortable majority for Pym's party. Digby quietly removed himself to Holland; early in February a letter addressed by him to the Queen was opened and found to contain a request for a cipher, as well as a promise that he would soon be back to serve the cause, provided the King would 'betake himself to a safe place, where he may avow and protect his servants from rage and violence'. Parliament issued a stern warning that the Queen was not to correspond with this 'bold and envenomed' man. It was voted in the Commons that the Queen should have no priests about her and that she should take an oath 'not to meddle in any matter of state'. Although reassuring messages came from the Commons it still seemed certain that an impeachment was intended, since it was believed that she was no greater than a subject and could therefore be punished like anybody else.

The Queen had come to realize that while her safety was threatened the King would never be able to display the resolution which was needed to restore his position. She knew now that as long as she remained in England he would be forced to make concession after concession, even if it meant endangering all his most loyal friends and servants. Reluctantly, she had reached the conclusion that she would have to leave him at this time of crisis, thus ridding the opposition of the lever they would not hesitate to use until they had rid the King of all his power. Mayerne told the Dutch Ambassador that it was essential on medical grounds for the Queen to leave England at once. Reduced to a state where they felt they could trust nobody, the King and Queen were carrying out almost all business themselves, working without a break and hardly finding time to sleep. The Queen afterwards told her sister that it was a wonder she did not go mad. The agonizing decision concerning her departure for Holland was taken without consultation and there was consternation at Court among those who did not fully understand the reasons which lay behind it.

Heenvliet was asked to send a plea that the Prince of Orange should request the Lady Mary's immediate departure. On February 7 the King despatched a message to Parliament announcing his plan. The Queen's enemies let her go as willingly as they had been reluctant for her to leave the previous summer, because, or so Giustinian thought, they were of the opinion that without her they would be able to direct the King's will with complete freedom. At Windsor hasty preparations were being made in an atmosphere of gloom. The Princess was pleased enough at the prospect of a new life, but her brothers were grieved to lose her and to be parted from their mother. Ships had to be found to convey the bride to Holland, and arrangements made for pilots, pennants, barge and ketch, meals on board and the shipment of six coaches and a hundred and twenty horses, not to mention all their fodder.

The royal party spent a few nights at Greenwich on the way to Dover. The House of Delight was now virtually complete, with its re-organized picture gallery, and the Queen's cabinet decorated by Jacob Jordaens. Henrietta had no time to enjoy the beauties of the house which had been her own especial care. She was busy collecting up her own jewels and her husband's with as many of the crown jewels as possible. Most of those who were with her hoped that at the last moment she would change her mind and stay in England, but her thoughts were all on the future and the work she intended to carry out for her husband.

The King and Queen parted at Dover, where they had first met sixteen years before. They talked together quietly, with frequent embraces, and the Queen made her husband promise that he would not surrender to his enemies or make a bad settlement while she was away. It was a long time before they could bring themselves to make the final break; at the end neither of them could restrain their tears, and most of those around them were weeping. When the King parted from his daughter he expressed the fear that he would never see her again.

The Queen embarked in the *Lion* with her small train. All her closest friends were with her—Mary Villiers, Duchess of Richmond, Father Philip, two of her favourite Capuchins, and the dwarf Hudson. As they sailed away they could see the lonely figure of the King riding along the shore, waving his hat and looking for a last glimpse of his beloved Queen who stood on deck watching the land recede.

Chapter 16

RESOLUTION

⁑

THE WEATHER worsened as the Queen's small flotilla reached the other side of the Channel accompanied by fifteen ships sent out by the Prince of Orange. At the entrance to the harbour of Helvoetsluys one of the baggage ships went to the bottom, taking with it the Queen's chapel plate and all the Duchess of Richmond's luggage.

Young William was waiting to escort his bride to Rotterdam by water, but all the English felt they had seen enough of the sea and it was decided that they should go to the palace at Honselaersdyck before continuing their journey to The Hague. When the procession set off across the flat February landscape, many people gathered along the route, in spite of stormy weather, to catch a glimpse of the bride. Elizabeth of Bohemia had come out to greet her niece and sister-in-law with a selection of daughters including the future Electress Sophia who was much the same age as Mary. The two Queens travelled in the same coach, sitting opposite William and Mary, and they were soon deep in conversation. Sophia, a high-spirited and irrepressible child, was much impressed by her poised and superior-looking cousin, but she was disappointed by the Queen, who had appeared so beautiful in the Van Dyck portraits and now turned out to be a small misshapen woman with long lean arms and teeth that stuck out like guns from a fort. However, Sophia had to admit, after a more careful examination, that the Queen had beautiful eyes, a well-shaped nose and a beautiful complexion. 'She did me the honour,' Sophia wrote in her memoirs, 'to say that she thought me rather like Mlle her daughter. So pleased was I, that from that time forwards I considered her quite handsome.'

The royal party was given a modest reception at The Hague; a few fireworks were let off and there was a salute of cannon—nothing which would not normally have greeted the Prince of Orange on his return from the country. Comfortable lodgings had been prepared for the Queen in the Prince's new palace, and after two days Mary was fetched formally by her husband and father-in-law and led away to her own apartments where she was to begin her education in the Dutch language and customs. Owing to the precipitate departure from England, no details concerning the Princess's dowry or the maintenance of her household had yet been decided, but the Queen did what she could to ensure that arrangements were made fitting for a royal princess. It was soon evident that the Prince of Orange had come by a rather more expensive daughter-in-law than he had originally bargained for. Many changes had to be made to give her the kind of life she was used to, and there were all kinds of unforeseeable expenses.

Henrietta Maria found that the Dutch had little respect for royalty and were quite ignorant when it came to protocol and ceremony. Prince Frederick Henry, William's father, treated her courteously, but he was in bad health and full of complaints. His wife, Amalia van Solms, who had been so eager to acquire a royal princess for her son, developed an instant dislike for her daughter-in-law, who displayed an inbred sense of majesty which the Dutch mistook for haughtiness. The Queen, for her part, found it hard to like the solid Dutch burghers who remained sitting in her presence with their hats on.

The Elector Palatine had warned his mother about the Queen's forceful nature, and the Dutch were soon to find out that their visitor had not come for a spell of passive asylum. As soon as the formal welcome was over she set to work energetically on her task of organizing the shipment of money and supplies, which would enable her husband to put into practice the strong policy she had mapped out for him. She planned to raise money on the jewels and she also set about writing to sympathetic heads of state, starting with the King of Denmark, begging for help. Meanwhile she waited impatiently for news of her husband's progress and was disappointed to hear that he had gone no further than Newmarket when she had expected him to be already at York. 'Delays have never been to your advantage,' she reminded him. Rumours that he had decided after all to return to London caused her great perturbation; 'you have learnt to your cost,' she wrote, 'that want of perseverance in your designs has ruined you.' For the first time she threatened to go into a convent if he weakened and played into the hands of his enemies. 'If it be so, adieu,' she wrote. To her relief the next letter confirmed his intention of pushing on to York, but this could not remove the fear that he would not be resolute enough to succeed. The doubt was now in her mind that it was not fear for her safety which had made him irresolute but rather an innate weakness of character, a tendency to be taken in, and an inability to keep to a few clearly defined aims. Growing increasingly frustrated because of the distance which separated them, she wrote to him without ceasing, poring over the cipher they had exchanged at parting. 'Do not lose time,' she instructed him. 'Do not break your resolution . . . Hull must absolutely be had . . . It is necessary to have a seaport . . . Put in nothing which is not in cipher . . . Take care of your pocket and not let our cipher be stolen . . . I should also wish you to send for Essex and Holland to come and serve you; if they refuse, take away their places and keep them vacant, unless you come to some contest; else restore them as they were, provided they serve you.'

She was endlessly at her desk, writing and translating into cipher and deciphering her husband's letters until her eyes ached and she was too weary to go on. Her own letters spontaneously recorded her joy and affection, her disappointment and despair. If at times the tone was shrewish, she was prepared to risk the King's displeasure, for, as Kent put it in *King Lear*, 'To plainness honour's bound, when majesty stoops to folly.'

It was at any rate a relief to know that the King had received a good welcome on his arrival at York and that loyal supporters had come to join him in large numbers. The results of her own work in Holland were so far disappointing; the Dutch merchants were chary of offering large sums of money for the crown jewels, believing that the Queen had removed them from England without authority. She had been forced to pledge all her small pieces, many of which had been given her by the King as tokens of his affection, and the dealers, knowing her urgent need for money, were able to make her accept only half their value. 'You may judge . . . how they keep their foot on our throat,' she told the King.

By the spring there were rumours that the Queen intended to spend the summer at Breda, probably with the intention of escaping to France in case of trouble, for the Earl of Holland had already suavely suggested to the Dutch that they should return her to England now that she had safely delivered her daughter to Prince William. The Dutch would have liked to see her go, and at the Prince's Court many people believed that once she was away Princess Mary would settle more quickly and many expensive innovations could be dropped.

In May 1642, Henrietta visited Amsterdam with all the Orange family. Although the Hollanders were proudly independent and disapproved of the royalist pretensions of the House of Orange, the town extended an elaborate welcome to the visitors. They were met by a fine barge and conveyed into the city 'by divers living swans', and there were triumphs on the water and pageants in the streets. On her return to The Hague, the Queen was greeted with bad news. Her husband had sent their son James and the Elector Palatine on a friendly visit to Sir John Hotham who was in charge of the important ammunition store at Hull. While their party was still being entertained inside the town, the King had arrived outside with a party of men, but Hotham closed the gates against him, coming out on to the walls to tell the sovereign that he would not be allowed to enter.

The Queen was incredulous. She did not believe that Charles had endangered his son's life so carelessly and had lost the magazine into the bargain. 'I have wished myself in the place of James in Hull,' she told him; 'I would have flung the rascal over the walls or he should have done the same thing to me,' she added. Her husband's reluctance to make the first belligerent move was incomprehensible to her. In her opinion it was an act of war on the part of the parliamentarians to put an unsympathetic governor in the town in the first place. 'You see what you have got by not following your first resolutions, when you declared those of the Parliament traitors,' she lectured him. Surely he ought to know by now that 'to begin, and then stop' always led to disaster? She had reached a crisis of despair, realizing that he was back at his old game of giving in on every occasion. She reminded him that she had left England so that her safety should no longer be a factor dominating his decisions, but now that she had made this great sacrifice he was as irresolute as ever. 'My journey is rendered ridiculous by what you do,' she told him, adding that she might just as well be with him in York for all the good her absence had done. 'My whole hope lies only in your firmness and constancy, and when I hear anything to the contrary, I am mad,' she wrote. There were rumours that he was prepared to give his consent to the Militia Bill, which would put the control of such armed forces as there were into parliamentary hands. She found this *insupportable*. If he set his seal to the Bill, that would be the finish, she would be forced to enter a convent, or at least, 'some place where I can pray for you'. She warned Mamie that she might well have to take refuge with the Carmelites in Paris. 'I assure you it is the one thing I can think about with pleasure,' she wrote.

In late May the Prince of Orange left to join his army for the summer. The Queen and her daughter followed a few days later and reviewed the Prince's experienced and well-armed troops. After this short break she set to work to acquire the arms the King needed even more urgently since he had failed to gain the magazine at Hull. He had written to her, listing the ammunition needed to equip the thousands of volunteers who had joined him at York. She managed to buy all that he had ordered with the help of money raised on her jewels, adding on her own initiative a thousand muskets, pikes and swords. Goring was despatched to Antwerp to see whether he could raise money on some of the larger pieces of jewellery.

The arms were loaded on to a small ship which was convoyed by a royal vessel, the *Lion*, but within a few days the whole consignment was back in the Dutch port having encountered a violent storm. The Queen decided to delay a second departure as she had in the meanwhile received news that the fleet had declared for Parliament under the Earl of Warwick. To make things worse the Amsterdam authorities were now objecting to the shipment of arms. The Prince of Orange received a succession of letters and messengers from the Queen—he might well have found a bombardment from the enemy rather easier to handle. The Queen even brought herself to part with Lord Digby, who like many other young exiles had gravitated to her side. He went off to the Prince's army, and Frederick Henry gave him a sympathetic hearing, although he was not over-enamoured of the young man's character—he found him too 'violent'. Jermyn, who was rapidly becoming the Queen's right-hand man, explained to Heenvliet the desperate situation she was now in, and the kindly Dutchman did what he could to help dispose of the jewels and raise a loan from the East India Company. The Prince lent his name to some of the Queen's requests for money, but was not forthcoming when it was a question of contributing himself. The arrival of his daughter-in-law had already run him into a great deal of unlooked-for expense, and in any case he was more inclined 'to gather than to scatter'.

Although both sides were reluctant to fire the first shot, civil war in England now seemed inevitable. 'I can send you little news out of England that is good,' Elizabeth of Bohemia told Sir Thomas Roe. 'All goes apace to a breach.' If it came to a conflict, Elizabeth above all hoped that none of her sons would become involved with the King's cause, for she still relied on Parliament to supply her with an annual grant. The Elector had now left England, believing that he had been 'sorely catched in' when the King had tried to take Hull by a ruse; but Rupert and Maurice had been helping the Queen and were making plans to join the King in the near future, although their mother had done her best to find them harmless posts in Venice and other remote places. Prince Rupert had already made his name as a cavalry officer on the Continent and he had just the kind of experience that most of the King's supporters lacked. He was tall, pleasant-looking and full of energy, but the Queen warned her husband that he was still very young and strong-willed and, in her opinion, not yet ready for too much responsibility.

When the two Princes set sail in July 1642, Henrietta decided to send her ammunition ship over with them in convoy. Rupert took with him all the money she had left, including what remained in her privy purse. As she told the King, she was now without a single *sou*. She wrote to France requesting aid, and plagued Frederick Henry for passports which would enable her to send over the experienced officers her husband so badly needed. 'We are not yet at the end of the English demands,' Constantine Huygens wrote wearily to the Prince in August, complaining also of the sterility of life at The Hague in the summer season—there was scarcely enough news to make it worth the Prince's while opening a letter. Most people had by now left the city, but the Queen had abandoned her plan of going to Breda. At The Hague they would have been glad to see her go, since everyone was growing tired of her obsessive preoccupation with cannon, engineers, officers, pistols, carbines and barrels of powder.

In England there were still many people who deplored the idea of civil war. Sir Benjamin Rudyerd expressed a common feeling when he said in the House, 'Blood is a crying sin; it pollutes a land.' Even so, spasmodic fighting had broken out in many parts of the country even before the King raised his standard at Nottingham on August 22. The Queen, too, disliked the thought of war, but she believed that a short, decisive campaign would be preferable to a dishonourable settlement. Elizabeth of Bohemia, hearing the Queen discourse with her attendants, gained the impression that they wanted everything to be done by force. In London the parliamentary leaders viewed the Queen's activities with suspicion, and at the end of August they sent over a representative, Walter Strickland, with a letter of credence to the States. Heenvliet noticed that Henrietta looked extremely troubled when he broke this news to her. She wrote at once to the Prince, pointing out that there was already a lawful Ambassador at The Hague. The Venetian Ambassador reported that Strickland had come to point out to their High Mightinesses that the English Parliament would order Lord Warwick to treat Dutch ships with hostility if the States continued to allow the Queen to ship arms to the King. Henrietta told her husband that she was not afraid of their threats; all her thoughts now were on the possibility of being re-united with her family.

At the beginning of September she was ready to leave. The weather seemed settled and she wrote to the King asking where she should land. But as the month wore on she became increasingly anxious. Parliamentary ships were intercepting letters from the King and for days on end she was without news. Rumours that even now he might have come to an agreement with his enemies caused the Queen a great deal of disquiet. On September 6 Parliament issued a declaration stating that it would not disband its forces until the King delivered up all delinquents, who would be fined to help pay off parliamentary debts. The Queen was not slow to apprehend that the vague term 'delinquent' could be stretched to cover not only the King's closest friends, but anyone who had not openly declared for Parliament. She was fearful that he would succumb to parliamentary blandishments and risk betraying all his friends. 'You are lost if ever you abandon your servants,' she told him, ' . . . if you do you will never find them again.' She reminded him that as long as he had right on his side he need never fear the outcome. 'Justice is a good army,' she wrote, 'always take care that we have her on our side.'

The weather in Holland turned very cold in late September. 'I do not wish to stay in this country,' she told the King, but her journey to England met with delay after delay. Mary was unhappy; she believed that she was being spied on, and told her mother-in-law so, 'clearly expressing her contempt, hatred and dissatisfaction'. Her *gouvernante*, Lady Roxburgh, was removed and replaced by Lady Stanhope, who had married Heenvliet the previous year. Mary made no secret of the fact that she was displeased and even at the age of ten she was capable of expressing her dissatisfaction in a very effective manner. As the weeks went by the Queen became increasingly anxious about the rest of the family—Henry and Elizabeth, now virtually held hostage in London, and the two older Princes who were bound to become involved in hostilities. To complete the mournful picture, Marie de Medici had died in penury that year at Cologne.

The affection between the King and the Queen was deep, but separation and the difficulties they were both facing at times put a strain on their relationship. 'Her sympathy with me in affliction will make her virtues shine with greater lustre as stars in the darkest nights,' the King had written after the Queen's departure, but some of her letters struck a chill—there are limits to the amount of female interference a man can stand. When she heard that he was dissatisfied with the amount of money and arms she had managed to send, she defended herself hotly, refusing to accept blame. 'If everyone had done their duty as I have,' she remarked somewhat acidly, 'you would not be reduced to the condition you are now in.'

To remove any further cause for misunderstanding, the King sent his trusted cousin Richmond to explain that Parliament's declaration had proved advantageous for the royalist cause because it had driven many waverers to come out openly in the King's support, realizing as they now did that they would have much to lose if Parliament gained the ascendant. And if the King had hesitated, appearing to give the Declaration a sympathetic reception, this was only because he wished to gain time. When the young Duke delivered his message, the Queen was completely reassured, and she felt ashamed now of her harsh words, admitting that in her anxiety she had at times allowed herself to be carried away. 'It is the affection I have for you, which makes me do it, and my care for your honour,' she told the King. She admitted that she had never felt so cheerful since she first reached The Hague, and it was a happy time, too, for Mary Villiers, who now planned to return to England with her husband.

The Queen's delight was short-lived, for soon The Hague was full of rumours about an engagement between parliamentary and royalist forces. 'As for battle,' she told the King, 'there is not a day in the week when you do not lose one.' There were people who talked of having actually seen and touched Prince Rupert's dead body. More reliable news came through gradually of an encounter at Edgehill in Warwickshire, and the Queen was soon to learn that her husband and sons were safe. It seemed that

Prince Rupert had acquitted himself brilliantly, even though his over-impetuousness had left the infantry dangerously exposed. Hearing that nothing now lay between the royalist troops and the capital, the Queen began to hope that she might soon set out for England. 'This country,' she told Charles, 'is too trying to the patience of persons who, like me, scarcely have any;' and she added a few days later, 'I need the air of England, or at least that in which you are, to cure me of a very severe cold I have got.' In December she reported that she had such a bad headache that she could hardly see, but her hopes of a change of air receded when York fell to Sir John Hotham's son. She busied herself raising troops that might help Newcastle recapture the city, putting them in charge of George Goring who had quitted his command at Portsmouth when the fleet fell into parliamentary hands. New Year came and she was still in Holland, but there was little more that she could do for the King. She herself was penniless. 'Adieu my dear heart,' she wrote at the end of the year, 'I am going to take my supper, and as it has cost money I must not let it be spoiled.'

The King had been unable to press on to London but he was soon well settled at Oxford, and his troops, headed by those young and debonair gentlemen who were attracted to the King's cause, had met with success in several areas. Although Leeds had fallen to parliamentary forces under Fairfax, Newcastle had regained York, and in January the Queen began once again to make plans for her departure. She managed to gather together several shiploads of arms, some professional soldiers and money raised from loans, all of which was to be convoyed across to England by a Dutch fleet under Admiral van Tromp. The weather was fair and she embarked at Schevelingen with every prospect of a smooth crossing.

Soon after her small fleet had set sail the wind slackened, giving the ships no chance to get away from the coast which was notoriously treacherous. Next, the wind began to rise and by midnight had turned into a tempest with violent gusts that ducked the sails into the sea. The ships were driven to and fro on the Dogger Sands, and for nine days and nights the Queen's ladies were strapped in their bunks, unable to sleep, fearing death at every minute and, when they were not being seasick, making their last confessions, which the Queen found interesting. She comforted them all, saying that a Queen would never submit to death by drowning, and her remarkable courage prevented the spread of panic.

At last the ship turned back towards the Dutch coast, and a welcoming salvo from guns on the shore told those who had been waiting anxiously at The Hague that the Queen was safe. The Prince and Princess of Orange with the Elector and his mother took a coach and drove to the coast; in their relief they ran down the sand, wading out into the breakers to greet the Queen, who came ashore, not without some 'dangerous welterings', in a fishing boat. Although warned that the auguries could not have been worse, she immediately began to make plans for a second departure. Her other ships returned gradually; two had reached Newcastle, but the rest came limping back without masts, sails or tackle. While these were repaired the Queen spent her time profitably acquiring some more ammunition and converting a loan from the King of Denmark into coin.

The Hollanders now found an excuse to detain two of the Queen's ships, while vessels of the parliamentary fleet stood off the mouth of the Maas threatening to impede their departure. She sent a message through the English Ambassador at The Hague complaining of this 'injustice and affront'. The ships were released, the parliamentary vessels were ordered to stand off, and at last, accompanied by the Dutch fleet, almost exactly a year after leaving England, she sailed off on a calm sea, heading for Newcastle. When they were almost within sight of the coast the wind veered, forcing the ships to drop anchor in Bridlington Bay. Two hours later a contingent of royalist cavalry appeared on the shore and the Queen disembarked, to be greeted by the troops and a large crowd of local gentry and country people who had brought provisions which the Queen graciously accepted. Lodgings were found for her in a thatched cottage on the quay and the next day more contingents of the army arrived. The Earl of Newcastle came to see her while she was at dinner and he told her that she had been led to Bridlington by God's providence, for she was now only thirty miles from York. The Earl's army had recently emerged from a successful encounter with the enemy at Stamford Bridge; his men were tired and it would have been difficult to undertake the task of convoying the Queen and her retinue in safety all the way from Newcastle.

When the meal was over the Queen reviewed the troops and that night went to bed in the house on the quay. She was awakened next morning at about four o'clock by the sound of gunfire. Some Parliament ships had sighted the Queen's vessels lying in the bay, and with an ammunition ship standing only a short way from the cottage where she was staying it was necessary for her to leave at once and without ceremony. Accompanied by her ladies and her lap-dog she ran through the streets of the town with the cannon balls whistling around her, and took shelter in a ditch—'like those at Newmarket,' she told the King. As they sat there, the balls continued to pass overhead, sometimes showering them with dust. 'You may easily believe that I loved not such music,' wrote the Queen. A sergeant was killed only twenty paces away and there were other casualties. For two hours the firing continued and it was feared that the enemy might attempt a landing; had that happened, the Queen told her husband, she would herself have acted the captain, although admittedly rather too small for the part. Finally Admiral Van Tromp sent a message to the parliamentary ships saying that if they did not desist he would 'fire on them as enemies'. In the Queen's opinion he could have saved a great deal of trouble if he had said so earlier; 'he excuses himself,' she told the King, 'on account of a fog which he says there was'. As the tide went out the ships were forced to retreat out of range. The ammunition was hastily unloaded in case of another attack and stored in a local church while the Queen moved her lodgings to a house further away from the quay. She invited the local people to join her for worship since their own church was being used as an ammunition store, and many were surprised to find that only a few of her train were Catholic, having imagined that they would all be papist—'so willing are some to deceive and others to be deceived'.

Before Van Tromp sailed back to Holland, the Queen gave him letters to the Prince of Orange thanking him for his help and hospitality, and to Elizabeth describing the 'incivility' of the Parliament ships. She also wrote to the King, giving him an exact description of the bombardment while the facts were still fresh in her mind. When she had finished writing, she told him, she intended to have something to eat 'having taken nothing to-day but three eggs, and slept very little'.

The Queen spent nine days at Bridlington awaiting the arrival of the baggage wagons. It had been decided that half Newcastle's forces should be left to guard the ammunition and that the rest should accompany her on her journey. She spent the night of March 5 in the Manor House at Burton Fleming with the army encamped nearby. Everybody knew that great vigilance was necessary, for it was believed that the Parliamentarians hoped to capture her on her way to York. Sir John Hotham had offered to open up his wine cellars for her at Hull, and Fairfax wrote offering her an escort. She treated these suggestions with the same caution as a message from Parliament which assured her that, if she cared to 'reparty' to London, she would find herself royally and lovingly entertained.

Although York was deeply divided, like many other towns and cities throughout the country, the Mayor felt able to commit himself to the extent of spending a hundred and fifty pounds on the Queen's entertainment, with additional tips to her confectioner for setting out the banquets, to her own cooks and scullery staff who helped out and to the men who carried in the special hangings. In the Corporation minutes no mention was made of her stay—a wise precaution at this time when the military situation was fluid and towns were apt to change hands rapidly several times in succession. The Queen could feel optimistic about the situation in the north, for the Earl of Derby had taken Lancaster, Preston and Blackburn; Sir John Hotham's loyalty was wavering in Hull and Sir Hugh Cholmley, the parliamentary Governor of Scarborough, gave up his fortress to the Royalists after travelling to York for the purpose of kissing the Queen's hand. It seemed that the Queen's stay in the town would be short since Newcastle would be able to take his armies towards Oxford now that the north seemed virtually subdued.

It was a fine warm spring and the Queen was comfortably accommodated at the house of Sir Arthur Ingram. Soon she was as busy as ever, receiving visits from the local gentry, conferring with Newcastle and other leaders, including Montrose who explained to her the need for organizing the loyalists in Scotland while there was still time. She felt inclined to trust this fine-looking, grey-eyed man who coupled an adventurous spirit with an ability to write poetry, but her husband could not quite forget that at the outset Montrose had supported the Covenanters. Charles preferred to take the more cautious advice of his old friend Hamilton who also visited the Queen at York, advocating the avoidance of 'an over-hasty rupture'. When Montrose wrote to her on his return to Scotland, telling her that the King's affairs there were in a serious state, and blaming her for not following his advice, she assured him that she had always disregarded reports that he had formed treacherous associations. Her trust in him was not built 'upon so slippery a foundation as mere rumour', but in the last resort she always followed the commands of the King.

Elizabeth of Bohemia had written that she hoped Henrietta would go to England as 'an angel and mediatrix of peace', but there was nothing noticeably angelic about this Amazon Queen with her cannon, pistols, saddles and suits of armour. Rumours were circulating in London that she had come at the head of an army of papists carrying a standard emblazoned with the Pope's arms. The Parliament men feared her resolution more than all the arms and ammunition she had brought with her, for they believed she was the only person who could keep the King from vacillating. When Hampden tried to conduct secret negotiations with her, she appeared for a while to favour the idea of a truce, but it soon became clear that she, like her husband, was only playing for time. She continued to work with an energy that put many of the men around her to shame, and she was often up early, writing and deciphering letters. She wrote frequently to France, although affairs in that country were in an uncertain state after the death of her brother Louis. She was also in touch with the Danish King. There had been a suggestion that the Danes might provide naval support in return for a base on the Orkneys, but the Queen wisely advocated caution so that the Scots should not 'avail themselves of this opportunity to take offence'.

Since the Parliamentarians were strong in the Midlands, communications between the royalist forces in the north and south were often difficult and inevitably there were misunderstandings. At times the King was critical of Newcastle's policies and extended his disapproval to the Queen. 'You are not the only one who has been chid,' she told Newcastle ruefully. She for her part was always fearful that the King would weaken and she sometimes wrote vehemently, urging him never to agree to the disbandment of his army until the perpetual Parliament had been dissolved. There were times when her optimism about the King's position in the north was tempered by the realities of the situation. 'Let us not mind our passions and let us reflect that for a small offence we may ruin all,' she wrote to Newcastle when she found royalist supporters quarrelling among themselves. There was an air of amateurishness, sometimes even of indolence among the royalist commanders. When the Queen granted Newcastle eight days' leave of absence to visit his dying wife, he stayed away so long that she began to consider seriously the possibility of leaving York without him. The Earl had proved an excellent governor for the heir to the throne, teaching the Prince to 'ride leaping horses and such as would overthrow others', but as a general he had his limitations. Lady Cornwallis described how he often lay in bed until eleven o'clock in the morning and sometimes until midday; he would then visit the Queen, 'and so the work was done'. According to this same observant lady it was General King, the experienced soldier much recommended by the Queen, who did all the work. Henrietta herself confided in the King that at times she found Newcastle 'fantastic and inconstant' although she remained on good terms with him. She was coming more and more to the conclusion that firmness and unity among the Royalists were essential if a quick victory were to be won. No amount of arms or ammunition could take the place of diligence and resolution. At best the royalist forces were dashing and courageous, at worst they were indecisive, inefficient and lazy. 'This army is called the Queen's army,' Henrietta wrote, 'but I have little power over it, and I assure you that if I had, all would go on better than it does.'

The Parliament showed its respect for the Queen's abilities and 'ardent French temper' by carrying out at last its long-standing threat of an impeachment. On May 23 Archbishop Laud who still lay, almost forgotten, in the Tower, recorded the fact in his diary. 'This day,' he wrote, 'the Queen was voted a traitor in the Commons House.' Her treason lay in her support for the papistical religion, and in her alleged influence over the King; she had induced him to make war against the State, procuring foreign assistance for this end. Writing to Hamilton at the end of May, she asked him to pass on news to her friends—'if any dare own themselves such after the House of Commons hath declared me traitor'. One of her brother's last acts before his death was to complain strongly about the treatment being meted out to his sister and her priests, who had been unceremoniously shipped home down the river, with their debts unpaid and their chapel in ruins after a raid by parliamentary troops.

The Queen's stay at York lasted far longer than she had originally hoped, as royalist fortunes fluctuated. Prince Rupert, who had been clearing a way for her journey south with spectacular success at Birmingham and Lichfield, had been recalled to Oxford to support the King after the fall of Reading. The army commanders at York were reluctant to release much-needed forces to escort the Queen, and Newcastle begged her to stay at least until Leeds was taken. When Wakefield fell to Fairfax in May the consequent loss of arms and men made Newcastle even less inclined to deplete his army. In early June, determined to set out without further delay, the Queen wrote to Newcastle, requesting him to call a council of war at Pontefract so that her reasons for wishing to join the King could be carefully explained and any misunderstanding cleared up.

The northern commanders were continually pressing the Queen to let them make use of the arms she had brought over for the King's use. She had parted with five hundred saddles soon after her arrival, justifying her action by pointing out to the King that they would have been particularly bulky to transport half-way across England. She dispensed some of the ammunition and pistols after the Earl of Derby came into York, bringing the news that he would have to disband his forces for lack of money and arms. Everywhere the Royalists were crying out for supplies, and the fall of Wakefield had shown everybody how easily men and equipment collected after so much sacrifice of time and money could be squandered in a moment of negligence. The capture of Leeds, the Queen believed, could have been achieved if the more cautious officers had listened to George Goring's plan for a decisive and daring assault. She admitted that she herself would have liked to witness the fall of the town before she set off—'I am so enraged to go away without having beaten those rascals,' she wrote.

Henrietta Maria believed that speed and secrecy would be her surest escort, but she did not journey unprotected, for when she set out she travelled with two thousand foot, twelve companies of cavalry and two hundred dragoons as well as six pieces of cannon. She put the faithful Jermyn in command of her forces, and described herself to the King as 'her she-majesty, and extremely diligent generalissima, with one hundred and fifty waggons of baggage to govern in case of battle'. While she was at Newark she heard that Tamworth had fallen to the enemy, and the unstable military situation made it difficult for her to plan her route with certainty. She pressed on to Stamford and Ashby-de-la-Zouch where she could rely on the loyal Colonel Hastings; 'I pray be careful to let me hear from you what the rebels do,' she had written in a letter to the Colonel on June 1.

When the Queen left Newark on July 3 it was already high summer. She rode at the head of her army, like a small-sized general, and in the heat of the day the whole contingent rested and she ate her meal under the trees with her men. She told the King that she mingled on friendly terms with her soldiers and was beginning to feel like the great Alexander. It was possible for her to see for a while the more romantic side of war, but she remained fully aware of its less chivalrous aspects, and it upset her to think that she had gained a reputation for favouring 'violent measures'. She recognized all too clearly that the England she travelled through now was not the peaceful countryside she had seen when she accompanied the King on his summer progresses. The champaign country which had provided Inigo Jones with the image of perfect harmony now often lay untended, the rural workers away serving King or Parliament, the gardens and orchards plundered by hungry troops and the horses commandeered for use in the armies. Many fine estates had been sequestered to provide funds for one side or the other, with towns and villages, and even families, divided in their loyalties. The Venetian Ambassador in London noticed the horror on the faces of Londoners when they saw the sick and wounded brought in from the siege of Reading; 'people here,' he wrote, 'are quite unaccustomed to the horrible aspects of war, especially civil war.'

Already, the Queen had been closely affected by the death of friends. The Earl of Northampton, who had entertained her at Castle Ashby in happier times had fallen at the battle of Hopton Heath. His son, the new Earl, wrote, 'Casualties in this world will happen, and in such a cause who would not have ventured both life and fortune?'; and yet it seemed a sad and unnecessary death. One of the Queen's closest associates, the Countess of Denbigh, had lost her husband after he had been fatally wounded at the battle of Birmingham, 'with many hurts on the head and the body with swords and poleaxes'. The Countess had celebrated their last wedding anniversary alone with the Duke of Hamilton's daughter, Lady Susanna, drinking her husband's health and eating three cherry pies. Now there would be no more celebration, and the fact that her son Basil had joined the rebels was an added desolation. 'I beg of you my first-born to give me the comfort which you owe me now, which is to leave those that murdered your dear father, for what can it be called but so,' she wrote on hearing of her husband's death. The Queen showed great kindness and sympathy for her widowed friend and sent her money, without which, Lady Denbigh wrote, 'I should not know what I should have done, I was in so great want'.

If the Queen urged the King to take resolute action it was only because she wished to ensure that the tragedy and disruption of war did not lengthen out into an extended conflict. Her one thought was to reach the King so that when she was near him she could stiffen his resolve. From Ashby she pressed on to Croxall, Walsall and King's Norton.

Almost all the way along her route the records remain silent about her stay. Entries in the otherwise meticulously kept minute-books of the Stratford-on-Avon Corporation were short and spasmodic during that troubled summer and no mention was made of the royal visitor who spent the night at New Place with Shakespeare's daughter, Susanna Hall. The Chamberlain's accounts do show, however, that a total of twenty-eight pounds, two shillings and elevenpence was paid out for her entertainment. The bellringers received two shillings for their welcoming peals, footmen, oarsmen and porters all had their fee, and payment was made for bread, geese, beans and beer, three hens, eight chickens, as well as four quail at a shilling each, while the most expensive item was a present of cakes for the Queen costing all of five pounds.

Prince Rupert came to Stratford to greet the Queen, which was ironical in view of the fact that the previous October the town had seen an influx of wounded Parliament men after Edgehill—'the Kinton battell' —and there had been disbursements for shrouds and dressings and payments to carriers who had transported the disabled to Warwick and Evesham. The Prince, who had repeatedly advised the King to strengthen the defences of Reading, may well have been responsible for ensuring the Queen's safety with fortifications which were brought from Warwick at a cost of three pounds.

The Queen did not stay long in the town associated with the playwright who had so often pointed out the horrors of civil disorder and of times such as the present when the sea-walled garden of England could become a whole land of weeds:

Her fruit-trees all unpruned, her hedges ruined,
Her knots disordered, and her wholesome herbs
Swarming with caterpillars.

Intent as always on reaching her husband so that she could help him to restore order to his country, she left Stratford and took the road for Kineton. On July 13, at the foot of Edgehill, she was re-united with the King and her two sons who had grown out of all recognition during her absence.

Chapter 17

THE POLLUTED LAND

～～～～

WHEN THE Queen entered Oxford, bells were ringing and enthusiastic crowds turned out to greet her. She lodged at Merton in apartments conveniently vacated by the Warden, a Parliament man, and after all the vicissitudes of the previous months she was able to enjoy the cloistered peace of the College and worship undisturbed in its chapel. The King could come to her privately from his lodgings at Christ Church, and the many royalist families who had moved into the town could often see the Queen with her husband and her spaniels out walking in the shady college gardens and quadrangles. Although fortifications had been thrown up outside the town and the cavalry clattered away most evenings to carry out midnight raids on the enemy, there was a carefree atmosphere as if the war were already over, and for many there was a temporary renewal of the kind of life they had lost as they paraded through the town in their fashionable clothes.

In London a different atmosphere prevailed. A succession of parliamentary reverses had lowered morale and there were rumours of a rising in Kent. Prince Rupert's marauding cavalry had curtailed supplies bound for the capital and already there were serious shortages. A growing peace party contemplated nothing less than capitulation, and in early August the fall of Bristol added to the general gloom. At Westminster men dissipated valuable energy apportioning blame for the scandalous fact that the Queen had travelled from York to Oxford through areas dominated by Parliament, without once sighting a Roundhead. Hampden had died that June from a bullet wound in the shoulder, sustained when Rupert's cavalry fell on parliamentary forces in Chalgrove Field. The most admirable and likeable among the parliamentary leaders, Hampden, had proved particularly astute when it came to smoothing out difficulties that arose between the irascible Essex and the men at Westminster, none of whom possessed the charisma of the King, the magnetism of Prince Rupert or the charm of the Queen. Pym, though an able politician, was small, plump and uninspiring—hardly the man to breathe fire into an all but defeated party. While the King melted down college plate at the mint set up in New Inn Hall at Oxford, creating coins to pay his troops, the rebels waited with empty pockets while measures for raising money were discussed in the Parliament House—measures as unpopular and illegal as anything the King had forced on his subjects in the Ship Money days.

With divisions in the rebel ranks, sickness rife among the troops encamped along the steamy Thames valley and a serious lack of funds threatening their cause, the Parliamentarians, or so many Royalists believed, had little fight left in them. The Queen was among those who believed that the time had come for a determined attack on the capital, but as always there were others who recommended a more cautious course, advocating a preliminary assault on Gloucester to open up the way for additional forces from Wales. After several days of argument, the King marched off to Gloucester, and the Queen communicated her disapproval to Lord Newcastle to whom Jermyn had given the key to the royal code. 'The King is gone himself in person to Gloucester,' she wrote, 'which gives no small dissatisfaction to everybody here, and with reason too, to see him take such sudden counsels; and all those who have advised him themselves disavow it.' She found that during her absence men who were often ambitious and pushing had worked their way into his counsels; 'the fault is partly yours,' she told her husband, 'for if a person speaks to you boldly, you refuse nothing.'

The news from the north was good. Gainsborough and Lincoln had fallen to royal forces, and he was still advancing in spite of Oliver Cromwell's attempts to contain him. The Queen felt a vicarious pleasure when she heard of the successes of Newcastle's 'whitecoats'—the army with which she had been so closely associated. 'I think you will easily imagine my joy in your prosperity,' she wrote, adding that she disagreed with the King's advice that he should push on into East Anglia. 'The truth is,' she added, 'that they envy your army.'

While the Royalists wasted precious time discussing the merits of an assault on Gloucester, the Parliamentarians staged a remarkable recovery. Pym took the lead in backing Essex against those who had wished to appoint Waller in his place. The resistance put up by the young Governor of Gloucester inspired the parliamentary forces with new courage and put heart into the City of London. The trained bands which had been bracing themselves to defend their own city now joined Essex as he marched out of London reinforced by five new regiments of foot, and a thousand horse. The Queen feared at first that he was heading for Oxford, which was now denuded of all the troops who had left with the King. 'It is not ill done in a person who is expecting a siege to be able to write,' she told Newcastle; 'but at this time, so it is that I must coax you, in order that if the King do not come to help us, you may do it.' A few days later she felt more reassured, since Essex had not advanced any further in her direction; it was now generally believed that the rally of parliamentary forces on Hounslow Heath was nothing more than a demonstration of strength, and she told Prince Rupert who had offered to come to her aid that she hoped that she would not be in need of him.

At the end of August the King and Rupert paid a brief visit to Oxford. They were accompanied by Montrose who had travelled down from Scotland to warn the King that the Covenanters were arming themselves with a view to helping the English rebels. The King still refused to listen to him or to sanction a royalist counter-move in Scotland. His thoughts were all directed towards the acceleration of a truce in Ireland so that troops could be released to help the cause. While the King was at Oxford it became known that Essex had set out, presumably to go to the relief of Gloucester. Wilmot was sent to intercept him, and Prince Rupert made an attack near Stow-on-the-Wold, but was unable to halt his advance. Essex arrived within sight of his goal on September 5, and before long the King abandoned the siege, hoping that he would be able to intercept Essex on the return journey to London. The Parliamentarians arrived at Newbury to find that Prince Rupert was there before them, and an inconclusive battle was fought. 'It is just as at Edgehill—both sides say they have the victory,' wrote Elizabeth of Bohemia. Casualties were heavy, and there had been much loss of life with very little gain. Among the dead was the Earl of Carnarvon, one of the elegant young men in Van Dyck's portrait of the Pembroke family, who had often been a member of the King's team of masqued dancers.

At Oxford spirits were low. 'I am so weary not of being beaten, but of having heard it spoken of,' wrote the Queen. The failure to take the strategic town of Gloucester was a bitter disappointment, and the fact that Essex had returned to London not unscathed but certainly un-defeated was a bitter blow to royalist pride. As autumn came on, a dampness settled on the colleges and sickness began to spread through the overcrowded lodgings of the royalist gentry. The King's habitual optimism at times deserted him; he was easily affected, especially now that the war had lengthened out into what promised to be a protracted struggle, by the bloodshed caused by Englishmen making war among themselves. After the battle at Newbury he wrote to the mayor asking him to bring in from towns and villages round about the sick and wounded for, he wrote, 'though they be rebels, and deserve the punishment of traitors, yet out of our tender compassion upon them as being our subjects, our will and pleasure is, that you carefully provide for their recovery'.

The French Ambassador, Harcourt, who visited Oxford ostensibly to mediate a peace, was not impressed by the atmosphere. Before long he was confirmed in the opinion, which he shared with other diplomats, that the wisest policy was to deal exclusively with the Parliamentarians, who controlled the capital, and the navy and, in consequence, almost all the trade of the country. The King was evidently finding it hard to prevent quarrels and jealousies breaking out among his supporters at Oxford, and it was even more difficult for him to co-ordinate all his far-flung generals; these now included the indomitable Archbishop Williams who was holding Conway Castle for the Crown—much to the annoyance of the local general, Sir Arthur Capel, who greatly resented the intrusion of this martial prelate. It seemed to Harcourt that the King and Queen were surrounded by pro-Spanish hangers-on, and there was also an element of hard-swearing professional soldiers who had seen service in the Spanish Netherlands and whose presence effected an inevitable coarsening in the courtly way of life. Those who had gained an ascendancy in the King's counsels during the Queen's absence, viewed with suspicion her attempts to re-establish her own position as her husband's principal adviser and confidant. Considerable dissatisfaction grew up in some quarters when George Digby became Secretary of State after the death of Lord Falkland, and Edward Hyde was one of those who felt that his position was threatened by the return of the Queen. Even Prince Rupert was now unable to guarantee that the King would follow his advice and support his plans. There were differences of opinion too when some Royalists advocated the reinstatement of Lord Holland and others who had defected from the Parliament side. The Queen felt unable to trust her former favourite, and opposed his resumption of his old post as Groom of the Stole. Her belief was that the best appointments should be bestowed on those who had proved loyal throughout the troubles and who did not suddenly put in an appearance when the fortunes of the opposite side began to wane.

In spite of the jealousy which the Queen's presence engendered, life at Oxford was not altogether unpleasant. She had many of her old friends around her, including the widowed Lady Denbigh and the self-effacing Jermyn whom the King had created a baron in recognition of his success in bringing her safely across England. The poet William Davenant had reappeared, although William Cartwright whose play *The Royal Slave* had so greatly pleased the Queen at Oxford in 1636 was one of the few fatalities caused by a mild version of the plague which raged in Oxford that autumn. During the summer months the Court had been entertained with some open-air performances of pastoral plays, and during the winter there was some dancing and games of tennis. The artist William Dobson had found a clientele able to pay for his vigorous portraits and he was working on a symbolic presentation of the current strife in France, showing the horrors of civil war and the blessings of peace.

In London, by contrast, austerity prevailed. All forms of entertainment were associated with the devil; the playhouses were closed, and fasting and prayer were the order of the day. The works of art which had graced the rooms at Somerset House had been removed, for the furniture and effects of a papist Queen were as redolent of hell as tapers and images of the saints. When Pym died that December his remains were lowered under the floor of Westminster Abbey which by now was denuded of most of its ornaments.

The festivities at Oxford at least helped to distract the thoughts of Royalists from the more disturbing elements in their situation. The news from Scotland was not encouraging, for Hamilton had been unable to prevent the Scots entering the war. When he came south to explain his failure he was promptly arrested, and Charles now belatedly listened to the councils of Montrose. A truce had been concluded in Ireland, releasing confederate troops which the King hoped to ship to England, thus laying himself open to the accusation that he intended to subdue England with the help of wild Irish papists. Characteristically, Charles treated with warm friendliness the men who had been fighting against him for two years, and extended a cool reception to Lord Inchiquin who had been unswervingly loyal throughout the rebellion.

After the death of Pym the King declared that the Parliament in London was no longer free and summoned Members to a session at Oxford. He hoped to attract a reasonably large assembly drawn from royalist Members and Parliament supporters who were out of sympathy with the course of events in Scotland and who disapproved of the general hardship caused by the war. In January 1644 the weather turned cold and there were heavy snowfalls which curtailed the activities of the armies, and prevented some of the hoped-for Members reaching Oxford for the opening of Parliament. The Scots, who had hoped to capture Newcastle, were held up by the snow and the deep mud which followed the thaw; finally they were halted by the necessity of besieging the city. In late March the bells of Oxford pealed out and bonfires blazed to celebrate one of Prince Rupert's most dashing and brilliant victories—the relief of Newark.

In February there were rumours in London that the fortifications at Oxford were being strengthened to make the city 'safer for the Queen'. Her reunion with the King had produced a predictable result and she wrote to her sister Christine on February 9 announcing that she was *grosse*. She confessed that she did not know where she would be able to go for safety, since in this country which had been free from wars for so long there were no strongholds. In April reports were circulating of a miscarriage brought on by a fall; the Queen spent some days in bed and no serious harm resulted although there were rumours in London that she was dead—'as they would like,' wrote the Venetian Ambassador. She sent to London for some necessities for her lying-in, but the Parliament men 'made no small difficulty about allowing them to go'.

Her own condition and the state of the King's armies made the Queen long for peace, but, she told Newcastle, 'I believe they are so haughty at London that they will make no propositions'. She wanted to know whether a cessation would be advantageous for the northern forces; 'the truth is, that the King's army here needs it'. She congratulated the Earl on holding the town of Newcastle, adding that she was glad he had not as yet been reduced to eating rats. Everything depended on keeping the Scots at bay, so she very much hoped that they would not have a chance of tasting Yorkshire oatcakes. 'Sir Thomas Fairfax is marching towards you to join the Scotch' she told him. 'Therefore lose no time, and do not allow yourself to trifle, for if the Scotch pass the river Tees, I fear that there will be no more remedy. All is lost.' When Newcastle showed signs of anger at this unsolicited advice, she reminded him that, as she had told him at York, she only scolded her friends, and never those she cared nothing for. 'With this I end, hoping that this letter will reach you, when you have beaten the Scotch and are in so good humour, that you will find nothing disagreeable.'

As soon as the weather improved and the Scots began to push southwards, Newcastle found little time to be offended. He was threatened from the north and by troops from the Eastern Association. Prince Rupert, who had been busy training recruits and keeping the route open for troops from Ireland, abandoned everything on receiving an urgent call for help from Newcastle and went at once to the relief of York. The King would have liked his nephew at Oxford which was also threatened, but the Prince though gifted with superhuman energy was incapable of being in two places at once. Enemy forces were closing in round the town and it was thought that it would soon be under siege. The King feared for his Queen's safety; it was unlikely that the enemy would show her any mercy if the town was taken and she were to be captured. The damp cold winter had done nothing to improve her health, and although she should by now have recovered from the troubles of early pregnancy, she was suffering new and alarming pains and felt full of dread about the future.

Easter week had nearly come, but there was no time to waste, and on the Thursday in Holy Week, April 17, the Queen left Oxford in a coach with her husband and sons, guarded by an escort of cavalry. At Abingdon she watched Charles and the two boys ride back in the direction of Oxford. According to one report, she fell into a merciful swoon as they went out of sight, and by the time she recovered her coach had already travelled ten leagues. She was suffering from excruciating pains which were intensified by every jolt of the carriage. Although at one time there had been some thought that she might take the waters at Bath, her stay in the town was short, and the Chamberlain's accounts mention only one item—'paid for candles for the Queen's coming to town 0-6-8d'. Her 'rhume' was worse than ever and she was in fact feeling extremely ill, but she pressed on with her usual intrepidity, changing her plan of travelling to Bristol and instead heading south-west for Exeter. She wrote to the King from Bridgwater, but she was too tired to expatiate at length on state affairs as she had done until then. It was Jermyn who took over the rest of the correspondence for her. The bells were rung at Axbridge as she passed through, and on May 3 she arrived at Exeter.

There were many reports of the Queen's illness; one said that she had miscarried, others that she was suffering from a palsy, a paralysed arm, a consumptive cough or hysteria. She had written to Mayerne asking him to come to her, but he was reluctant to make the hazardous journey to Exeter and he sent his advice in writing. There were rumours that a safe-conduct requested from Oxford for a midwife with a coach and six horses had been refused by the Parliamentarians, who placed little trust in any 'she-Oxonians', but Anne, now Queen Regent of France, solved the problem by despatching the perennial Madame Péronne.

In June Henrietta was still awaiting her child although she believed that by now she was well over the nine months. She told the King that her pains were so severe that it was impossible for anyone who had not experienced them to know what they were like. She was beginning to feel that she would soon be in another world. 'If it be so, the will of God be done,' she wrote. Alarmed by his wife's description of her state, the King sent a terse note to London. 'Mayerne, if you love me, go to my wife,' he pleaded. On receiving this *cri du cœur*, the eminent physician, now in his seventies, set off for Exeter, taking with him Sir Matthew Lister to give a second opinion.

The delayed birth gave time for Madame Péronne to arrive from France with a complete *layette*. The Prince of Orange sent a present of linen, but this was intercepted by Parliament ships. The Queen grew more apprehensive with every day that passed. She told Mayerne that she was afraid she might go mad, to which he replied, somewhat harshly, 'Madam, you already are.' As always he believed that her symptoms were to some extent hysterical, but he was shocked by her state and believed that it would be at least three weeks before she would be out of danger. On June 16 she was brought to bed of a daughter, 'a lovely princess' according to the French agent de Sabran, who saw the child when she was eight days old. The Queen had hoped that the pains which she had first felt before leaving Oxford would die down after her confinement, and it was disappointing to find that they were as bad as ever. She was so weak that she could hardly move, her body felt heavy and at times she had such a constriction in the area of her heart that she believed she might suffocate. She told the King that it seemed as if she had been poisoned.

Although one arm was still without feeling, and the sight of one eye was affected, the Queen was already making plans to leave Exeter. The armies of the Earl of Essex were now threatening the town and the sound of cannon fire revived all her old fears of capture. She knew that once she was in the hands of her enemies they would make the King agree to unfavourable terms in order to secure her release. She warned her husband that she would soon be leaving England, ill though she was. 'I shall show you by this last action,' she wrote, 'that nothing is so much in my thoughts as what concerns your preservation, and that my own life is of very little consequence compared with that; for as your affairs stand, they would be in danger, if you come to help me, and I know that your affection would make you risk everything for that.'

The Marquis de Sabran visited the sick Queen in the hope of persuading her that she would be unwise to leave England; he advised her to apply to Essex for a safe conduct to Bath where she could take the waters. But the Queen did not trust Essex, and Essex did not trust the Queen—he believed that she had invented her illness in an attempt to hold off the siege. He was ready to escort her to Bath, and he would then be happy to take her to London, where she would receive what he considered to be some very suitable treatment. Leaving her infant daughter in the care of Lady Dalkeith, the Queen set off in disguise, accompanied by her medical adviser, Sir John Wintour, Father Philip and one of her ladies. They joined up outside the town with Jermyn, the dwarf Hudson and one of her lap dogs, and the whole party hid for two days in a small hut until it was considered safe to continue the journey. A later report described how the Queen heard enemy troops pass by discussing the reward of fifty thousand crowns which had been put on her head.

When the Queen reached Falmouth she wrote to her husband, telling him little about her adventures or the intense pain she had suffered as she was carried in a litter all the long miles through Devon and Cornwall. 'I am giving you the strongest proof of love that I can provide,' she told the King. 'I am hazarding my life.' She had decided to send back the company that had escorted her and used some of the little energy that remained to her to request favours for some of her officers.

Mayerne, seeing the Queen before she left Exeter, prophesied that she had not long to live. A Cornishman who caught sight of her at Falmouth described her as 'the woefullest spectacle my eyes yet ever beheld on'. Still she allowed herself no rest; as soon as arrangements could be made she boarded one of the Dutch vessels which lay at anchor in the estuary and set off for France. She had not been long at sea, however, before her fleet was sighted by vessels under the command of Warwick who had been supporting an attempt to raise the siege of Lyme. The Dutch captain put on all the sail he could, but the parliamentary ships stayed within range and 'bestowed a hundred cannon shot' on the Queen's vessels. Fortunately their fire was none too accurate, and there was only one direct hit. The Queen with her ladies went down into the hold for safety; she showed her usual courage, and told the captain that if there was any danger of capture he was to ignite the powder on board and blow his ship up, although afterwards she regretted having given such selfish orders. While the battle was in progress she lay motionless and silent—a pattern of behaviour which was not followed by the rest of the ladies on board.

When they were almost within sight of Jersey, the Queen's vessels drew away out of range, and when some French ships appeared the rebels gave up the chase. Once the danger was passed, the Queen was helped up on deck. The Parliament ships were pointed out to her and she showed her anger by grinding her teeth—about the only movement she was capable of making at this particular moment. Safety seemed to be almost within sight, but the Queen still had to face her customary battle with the forces of nature. Her suffering was prolonged when a violent storm blew up, scattering the ships, and making the Queen's attendants so sick that they were unable to minister to her. One of the Capuchins, who had spent many years at sea, was able to wait on the Queen, doing the work usually divided among twenty people, and comforting her in her extremity, for several times she seemed to be on the point of death. Even when the coast of Brittany came into sight there were further difficulties; the Queen's ship was mistaken for a pirate vessel, but the fishermen who came out to investigate finally accepted that the unexpected visitor was indeed a daughter of France. They rowed her to the rocky shore and she scrambled up a precipitous path to the top of the cliff. It was July 16— just a year had passed since her happy reunion with her husband at the foot of Edgehill.

The Queen despatched Jermyn with letters for the Queen Regent and her chief adviser Cardinal Mazarin. The next morning the local gentry arrived in large numbers to pay their respects to her at the grey stone cottage where she had spent the night. They were shocked to see this woman who had left France as a vivacious and healthy girl. Nine pregnancies, years of anxiety and now several months of severe illness had aged her so much that she was hardly recognizable. Soon she was journeying again, in the scorching summer weather. She was still in great pain and at times she was held up by strong attacks of fever associated with a breast abscess. The Queen Regent had sent two of the best physicians from Paris to attend her, and when she had been on the road for twelve days, she wrote to the King telling him that she was waiting to hear whether or not the waters of Bourbon would be considered efficacious for her condition. Jermyn had not yet returned from Paris and she had not the strength to write at length without his help, but she told the King that she had been received in France with great affection by everybody 'from the greatest to the least'. At Amboise, Jermyn rejoined her and she went on to Tours where on August 18 she was entertained in the Archbishop's palace. It had been decided that the waters might help to reduce the swelling in her body and limbs, and she reached Bourbon on August 25. She was so weak that she could not walk without an attendant holding her on each side, but she was given an enthusiastic welcome here as everywhere else. 'If my lords of London saw it, I think it would make them uneasy,' she told the King. The Jesuits presented her with a paper of verses, expressing the hope that Bourbon would provide her with an effective cure. Her reply was characteristic. 'This is well done, but do still more,' she said, hinting at her husband's need for financial aid. The parliamentary commentators, hearing the story, suggested that she had need of waters from a very different source—the waters of repentance which would cleanse away her popery.

Bourbon was a fashionable watering-place but the Queen was able to find peace there, and after the abscess in her breast had been lanced and she had taken a fortnight's course of the waters there was some improvement in her health. The swelling subsided, although she still suffered from numbness and a rash resembling measles which covered her whole body. She told the King that she had given up hope of ever seeing him again, but, she wrote, 'God is pleased to preserve me still in this world, to serve you, as I hope'. Although the waters at Bourbon were mainly taken internally, the Queen was treated with one bath a week; John Evelyn, who visited the town when the Queen was there, noted in his diary that some of the springs welled up 'in the midst of the streets . . . some of them excessive hot, but nothing so neatly walled and adorned as ours in Somersetshire'. She would have been happier if her improvement had been more marked and if the pain she felt had not prevented her from attending to business. She did all she could to disguise her suffering in order to prevent her enemies gloating over her misfortunes, but it was difficult for her to appear cheerful when she was separated from her husband and her children. 'I think I shall never have my health till I see you again,' she wrote.

The Queen Regent had sent her sister-in-law money to pay for immediate expenses and promised that a pension of thirty thousand livres a month would be forthcoming. She also despatched Madame de Motteville, one of the royal ladies-in-waiting, to help care for her. The Queen was able to unburden her heart to this sympathetic companion, going over the events of the last years. She recalled the more dramatic incidents, when she had tried to help Strafford during the time of his trial, meeting parliamentary leaders secretly at night, lighting her own way down a secret stair by the light of a torch, or later in the same year when she had organized the servants at Oatlands, arming them with primitive weapons after hearing that an attempt would be made to frighten her into flight. To dwell on the past gave the Queen some respite from her continual anxiety about her family, and particularly her concern for her infant daughter whom she had abandoned to 'the fury of those tigers'. Days went by without any letters coming from the King, and it was impossible for her to know with any certainty how the royal cause was faring. She knew that soon after her departure the King had left Oxford and spent some time campaigning in Worcestershire. Undaunted by the royalist defeat at Marston Moor and the loss of York, he had marched westwards, taking his eldest son with him, and reached Exeter just under a fortnight after the Queen left England. He had been told that his youngest child was the prettiest of them all, and when he saw her he found that she resembled her mother so strikingly that he had her christened Henrietta at a service in Exeter Cathedral. After the ceremony he pushed on to the small fishing port of Fowey where Essex had withdrawn with his army.

In late September the doctors decreed that the Queen had taken the waters for long enough and was unlikely to gain further benefit. Her favourite brother Gaston came to fetch her; he was middle-aged now and although with his dark hair, blue eyes and small moustache he was still handsome, he bore the marks of a life of frustration spent endlessly supporting the unsuccessful *coups* of his brother's enemies. His perennial hope of succeeding to the throne had finally disappeared with the birth of his nephew Louis, and he himself had been singularly unsuccessful in his attempts to produce a son; his first wife, Mademoiselle de Montpensier, had borne him one daughter, and his second wife, the Princess of Lorraine, showed no signs of bringing forth anything but girls. She was a strange woman, clever and faithful but neurotic, refusing to leave the house for months on end and living on crusts of bread which she kept in her pocket.

Brother and sister set off for Paris and at Nevers they were greeted with news of a royal victory in Cornwall. For the first time, in her eagerness to speak to the messenger from England, the Queen found herself walking a few steps unaided. Soon, however, she suffered a relapse and it was three weeks before she was fit to continue her journey. An abscess appeared in her arm accompanied by a high fever, and the doctors put her on a course of asses' milk—'a strong cordial for a Queen,' commented the parliamentary propaganda machine. The delay put an end to plans for meeting her sister Christine, but she wrote instead, telling her that affairs in England looked so favourable that there were hopes of a speedy return.

The Queen explained to her sister that she had good reason to feel content in France since she had received such kind treatment from the Queen Regent and Cardinal Mazarin and from everybody else right down to the common people. All the way along the route to Paris, crowds ran after her coach, hoping for a glimpse of the Queen who had once been so spirited and loquacious but who was now silent and frequently in tears. After spending two nights at Fontainebleau, the scene of so many carefree childhood visits, the Queen proceeded with a guard of six archers and ten Switzers. She was met ten miles out of Paris by Gaston's eldest daughter, Anne-Marie, Mademoiselle de Montpensier, a tall, bony and rather arrogant blonde, who remarked, with all the superiority of the seventeen-year-old, that her aunt had taken too much trouble to hide the ravages of time—and with remarkably little effect.

Accompanied by trumpeters and city dignitaries, her coach drawn by horses caparisoned in gold-embroidered velvet, the Queen entered the outskirts of Paris. Her sister-in-law was waiting for her near the Croix de Montrouge, and after the Duc d'Anjou, Henrietta's small nephew, had made a speech of welcome, the two Queens descended from their coaches and embraced each other. The English Queen looked shrunken, half-paralysed, her mouth, always large, appearing out of all proportion in her thin and pallid face; Anne of Austria by contrast was extremely fit for she had grown robust and strong on her favourite diet of cutlets and sausages. The French Queen's luxuriant chestnut-coloured hair was as fine as ever, and her looks had improved so much since she had left off wearing rouge, as befitted a widow, that many of the ladies at Court had followed her example.

After their meeting the two Queens continued their journey in the same coach, followed by many others carrying the Princesses of the Blood and members of the nobility, with the Queen Regent's bodyguard on the right side and the young King's on the left. The glittering procession passed through the Faubourg Saint-Jacques, the Rue Saint-Denis and La Ferronnerie. Every street was richly decorated with hangings. On her arrival at the Louvre, although she was hardly strong enough to undergo such formalities, Henrietta was treated to a succession of visits, from the Governor of the City, the *Prévôt des Marchands* and a red-robed deputation from the Paris Parlement. The Queen Regent also brought the six-year-old Louis to see his aunt, having carefully worked out where *Sa Majesté Britannique* should meet him, so that exact protocol could be observed. Three armchairs had been set out for them, and after this formal interview, the Queen went with her relations just as far as the door of the ante-chamber and no further.

In the palace where she was born Henrietta now met with all the respect and ceremony she had known as a child. Her sister-in-law treated her with unfailing kindness, never allowing anyone to forget that although she had no money she was still a Queen.

Chapter 18

AN ACTIVE INSTRUMENT

LIFE IN Paris soon fell into the same pattern as the months of exile in Holland. Although she was never fully to recover her health, Henrietta was well enough now to work actively for her husband's cause, and she found herself once again becoming importunate, swallowing all pride and begging for help. She often dictated her letters and gave Jermyn the task of translating them into cipher to avoid the headaches which assailed her whenever she spent too long at her desk; all the same she allowed herself no respite as she explored every possible field where help might be forthcoming—often with a disappointing lack of results.

Although the Queen Regent had resolved to avoid her husband's mistake of falling under the influence of one man, her innate laziness quickly led her to hand over entirely to Cardinal Mazarin the tiresome business of government. In November 1644 she informed her council that she intended Mazarin to lodge in her palace, 'his indisposition rendering him unfit without great danger to his health to pass through a Long Garden so often as she hath cause to consult him about important affairs of state'. Henrietta soon found that she could expect sympathy from her sister-in-law but little more, and promises of help from the smooth Mazarin tended not to materialize. The Cardinal, like Richelieu before him, was happy to see the civil war lengthen out, since it kept England away from the game of power politics on the Continent. 'I have not found the means of engaging France as forwardly in your interest as I had expected,' the Queen confessed to the King on December 18. When Péronne made an oration attempting to persuade Catholics to give money for the royalist cause, and describing in pathetic terms the plight of the Princess in whose veins ran the blood of Saint-Louis, he only succeeded in raising a sum 'fitter to buy hangings for a chamber than prosecute a war'.

Before long the Queen began sounding out the ground in Rome, but her dealings were signalized by mutual distrust. The Pope seemed chary of providing her with money that would in all probability be squandered on ill-planned military operations, while the Queen viewed with suspicion all papal interference in Ireland; she feared the Pope might encourage the confederates to break free from their allegiance to the English crown. Sir Kenelm Digby, who was in Rome on a royalist mission, was too unpredictable to command respect; at the Vatican they found him uncertain in his Catholicism and mercurial in his diplomacy—they even thought he was a little mad.

It was unlikely that the Queen would let the Prince of Orange escape her attention now that she was back on the Continent and she despatched her Anglican chaplain, Dr Goffe, to treat with him. Goffe had instructions to approach the Duke of Lorraine in the hope of persuading him to provide troops for the royalist cause. The Queen's plan was that the long-suffering Stadholder should provide ships to transport Lorraine's troops in return for the rather doubtful pleasure of bestowing his daughter on the fourteen-year-old Prince Charles. Frederick Henry was sceptical, however, about the prospects of gaining help from Lorraine, and his doubts were justified when the Duke went off to serve his old master, Spain. In any case he had learnt his lesson; the price of marriage with proud and penniless members of the Stuart family tended to be high, and he felt disinclined to become involved in another long drawn-out attempt to provide his son's in-laws with cannon and other paraphernalia of war. Although a number of letters passed to and fro on the subject of the marriage, any hope that the Prince might help to transport troops seemed to come to an end when the Dutch sent shipping to help the Danes in their war against Sweden. Frederick Henry was forced in any case to be more careful than ever now in his dealings with the Estates of Holland, and it was unlikely that any ships carrying royalist troops would find a haven at Amsterdam.

As she laboured to translate vague promises into terms of solid help, the Queen suffered endless anxieties about her husband and children, and the old dread came back when she heard that peace talks between Royalists and Parliamentarians were to be held at Uxbridge. She fell once more into the school-magisterial style, rebuking her husband for his weakness, as she had done so many times before. She urged him never to abandon those who had served him, 'as well the Bishops as the poor Catholics'. She was shocked to hear that he had referred to the assembly in the capital as 'the English Parliament', not realizing that he had been overruled by his Council. He reassured her in a letter, telling her that if peace could be achieved it would only be on terms that would enable her to return to England in safety, and which would ensure the dissolution of the perpetual Parliament and show his faithfulness to the Bishops and all his friends. He probably did not need his wife's encouragement but she never failed to give it, reminding him forcibly that he should not quit the sword that God had placed in his hand until he was truly a King again.

In February the negotiations at Uxbridge came to an end with nothing achieved, and the armies marched on. The King's cause was still strong in the west, although in the north it had not recovered after the defeat at Marston Moor. Newcastle interpreted this disaster as the death of the King's hopes. Having seen his own soldiers in their homespun coats fight it out to the death, he could face no more. He took refuge across the Channel and the Queen wrote to him, assuring him of the continuance of her esteem, 'not being so unjust as to forget past services upon a present misfortune'.

The King warned his wife that during the summer campaign he might not have time for letter-writing. He had to go to the relief of Chester before dealing with the Scots who were advancing south. 'I must go to see if I can beat them,' he wrote, adding, 'If I may be assured of thy health, I shall cheerfully proceed in this summer's work.' He had no plan of campaign; 'I shall resolve according to occasion' was how he put it to the Queen. Some of his supporters favoured a march westwards, but Prince Rupert's advice was to draw enemy forces away from Oxford into the Midlands and, after councils of war had produced nothing but a crop of quarrels, the King finally marched off to Leicester. On May 31 he wrote giving Henrietta an account of the taking of the town, with quantities of arms and ammunition, and expressed his intention of hastening back to Oxford which was threatened by Cromwell's troops now lying across the river at Islip. Prince Rupert would have preferred to push on northwards, hoping to draw Cromwell after him, but he was overruled by Digby and Ashburnham who favoured the return to Oxford. The battle of Naseby, fought against the Prince's better judgment, turned out to be the most decisive encounter of the war—and it was not won by the Royalists. The King lost all his guns and most of his baggage, including the trunk containing all his correspondence which Digby had failed to secure in the confusion.

No help could now be given to Montrose who had been winning a succession of spectacular victories in Scotland. The King gathered up the troops that remained to him and took Huntingdon before moving across to the relief of Hereford. As long as he was on the move he could bring himself to believe that all was not lost, but his depleted forces were no match for Cromwell's New Model Army which after preliminary difficulties had been moulded into an efficient striking force. Swift-moving cavalry, adept at harrying the enemy, had always been the Royalists' strongest weapon, but without infantry it could do little except carry on its own inconclusive guerrilla warfare. Prince Rupert, now the King's most experienced commander, had been accused of treachery after the fall of Bristol, and the King was soon to be bereft of his counsels; Digby withdrew diplomatically to the Isle of Man, having managed to lose his own cabinet of correspondence after a minor engagement at Sherburne in

Yorkshire, just as he had lost the King's. To lose one might be regarded as a misfortune, but to lose two looked remarkably like carelessness.

The two trunkloads of correspondence were published in London and *The King's Cabinet Opened* provided valuable evidence that the Queen had been 'an active instrument in contriving and fomenting the long and bloody civil war in England'. *Lord George Digby's Cabinet Opened* contained equally incriminating material, and the Parliamentarians did not fail to make use of it.

News of the King's setbacks and misfortunes came through to the Queen gradually, often from parliamentary sources. She had moved to Saint-Germain for the summer months; the knowledge that her husband needed her help more than ever increased her frustration at a time when most of the people who mattered were out of the capital and she was herself cut off from the diplomatic world that meant so much to her. Had she been in Paris she might have arranged an informal meeting with the Papal Nuncio, Giovanni Rinuccini, who spent most of the summer in France waiting for transport to take him to Ireland. The Queen was anxious to build up a strong force of Confederate Catholics and Anglo-Irish, believing that the King in the last resort might have to seek a retreat in Ireland, which would at least be preferable to falling into the hands of the English or Scottish rebels. She became increasingly irritated by the unreasonableness of the Irish, and found it hard to understand why they could not unite in the cause; as far as she was concerned it was all an affair of state and not of religion, and the King therefore should not have any scruples about making use of Catholic aid. 'If I were a Protestant, I would write a great deal more on this subject,' she told the King.

Mutual distrust between the Queen and Rinuccini made it difficult to arrange a meeting at Saint-Germain. The Pope, ironically, was dissatisfied with Henrietta's brand of Catholicism and was disappointed by her insistence that her husband should maintain a position of absolute sovereignty in Ireland; it seemed that during her stay in England she had become too thoroughly indoctrinated with the royal philosophy. The Queen, on the other hand, distrusted Rinuccini's motives, suspecting that as he had not sought the King's permission to visit Ireland he was intent on setting up an independent Catholic state. She had at first expressed her approval of a scheme to levy ten thousand Catholics under Colonel Fitzwilliams, but later regretted having given it her support as more and more demands were made on the King to promise complete religious freedom to the Catholics in exchange for any form of help.

All that the Pope was prepared to give the Queen at this stage was a contribution of seven thousand pounds, but Jermyn noted that France and other European powers showed signs of becoming more co-operative after the defeat of the royalist forces at Naseby—what Ludlow described as 'the deciding battle'. This, he had to admit, was because they were 'willinger to interest themselves to prevent our ruin than to make us very happy'. There were still 'some little remote hopes' that the Duke of Lorraine might provide a force, although Jermyn warned Digby that these 'ought not to be built upon'. He was himself in favour of a plan to enlist Spanish prisoners still in French hands; they were in the main experienced soldiers, well-officered 'and of the nation fittest to discipline the Roundheads, as being more nationally than others engaged against their opinions'. Jermyn would have liked to provide a thousand or so 'strangers' to help garrison Exeter, Dartmouth and Barnstaple, and he thought he would have no difficulty in finding the men; the one drawback lay in the fact that he had no means of raising the three months' pay in advance which they demanded as a condition of their service. The Queen had managed to collect and pay for out of her own funds a shipload of arms, powder, match and other lethal properties, cutting down her own expenses so that she could devote as much as possible to the cause. She wrote to her husband in September suggesting that she should live in a convent for the time being to save money, so that she could send him more ammunition and also redeem her jewels which were in danger of being sold.

During the summer months the Queen was under some pressure to publish details of the proposed marriage between the Prince of Wales and the Prince of Orange's daughter, but she herself was less than sanguine about the whole matter, having met with nothing but *froideur* on Frederick Henry's part. She told her husband frankly that she found the Prince condescending in his attitude, seeing himself as a powerful monarch and Charles as a prince *en misère*. There was no joy, in her opinion, in having to demand the Dutch princess on their knees, and in any case it seemed that Frederick Henry was not prepared to give his daughter more than the rather meagre sum of forty thousand jacobus. It was time to explore other possibilities; the King himself had contemplated the idea of a Portuguese princess, Catherine of Braganza, who was likely to provide a useful dowry if nothing else, and the Queen suggested Gaston's daughter Anne-Marie who was at least *extra ordinairement riche*.

Just before Naseby the King had written to Nicholas that 'if we peripatetics get no more mischances than you Oxfordians are like to have this summer, we may all expect probably a merry winter'. The reality was far from the King's cheerful prophecy; he himself remained at Oxford with parliamentary troops massing all round him and his own forces—what he had left of them—beginning to desert as the money ran out. The capture of Plymouth put an end to further hopes of sending supplies from France. Despairingly the King authorized his wife to promise complete freedom for the English Catholics in return for a loan, but the Pope insisted that all his terms should be met, and these went much further than freedom of conscience. In a last attempt to save the situation the King offered to go to London in person, but he met with a blank refusal, much to the relief of the Queen, who did not think much more of the idea than her enemies.

As parliamentary forces moved deeper into the west country, the Queen grew increasingly anxious about the Prince of Wales who had become separated from his father, remaining with the royal forces in Cornwall. Her aim was to bring him over to France as soon as possible, but Edward Hyde, who had been appointed the Prince's Governor after the failure of the negotiations at Uxbridge, had opposed Henrietta ever since Oxford days. He now used his position to ensure that she did not dominate her son as she had ruled her husband. When Cornwall became too dangerous, the Prince moved to the Scilly Islands, much to the disapproval of the Queen who had been told that there was no guarantee supplies would be able to reach St Mary's, or that the islands could be adequately defended. 'I shall not sleep in quiet until I shall hear that the Prince of Wales be removed from thence,' she wrote. She reminded Hyde that she had 'strained' to send shipping and money for the move to Jersey, but although she insisted that she was carrying out the King's requests, Hyde and the other counsellors were reluctant to take orders from the Queen.

The Royalists' last hope seemed for a while to lie with Montrose, but even as the Queen celebrated his successes with a special Te Deum, the Marquis was suffering a reverse which would put an end to the Royalist dream of receiving salvation from the north. Mazarin, anxious to reduce the strength of the Parliamentarians, was happy to foment differences between the more radical elements and the Scottish Covenanters, and when he sent Montreuil on a mission to Scotland, he gave the envoy orders to treat, not with Montrose as the Queen had hoped, but with the Covenanters.

Although Exeter surrendered to the enemy on April 13, 1646, and Prince Charles was forced to make his way to Jersey later in the month, the King refused to give way to despair. He still had hopes of making capital out of the differences that had appeared on the parliamentary side between the more rigid Presbyterians and the free-thinkers who contemplated a more far-reaching change in the system than some Parliamentarians had originally visualized. There were many people who had supported Pym in the belief that they were defending the ancient privileges of Parliament. They were anxious to curb kingly prerogative and did not feel averse to dispensing with bishops, but they were alarmed at the unleashing of uncontrollable democratic forces that threatened the position of the gentry and undermined the whole hier-archical system. 'For news,' Howell wrote in February 1646, 'the world is here turned upside down and it hath been long agoing so.' The King hoped that the more reactionary elements would come to realize that he was the only unifying figure who could hold the system together.

Meanwhile Parliament waited complacently for Oxford to surrender and the distinguished person of the King to fall into their hands. Gradually, even he began to give up hope. There was little chance of escape, aid from Ireland was not forthcoming, the Queen was helpless, and the Scots had come as far south as Newark. Charles wrote to Prince Rupert on April 10 from Oxford, telling him not to underestimate 'the eminent danger to my person in respect of the numbers and placing of the rebel forces between this and where I am to go'. By the end of the month, however, he had left Oxford, slipping out of the town disguised as a valet, and for days there was speculation about his whereabouts; some thought he was in hiding in London, others that he was on his way to Ireland or to Scotland, even that he had escaped to France. Then on May 5 he entered the Scottish camp and placed himself in the hands of the Covenanters. Shortly afterwards Oxford surrendered, delivering into parliamentary hands a rich haul of prisoners, including James, Duke of York, the Duke of Richmond, the King's gentle and faithful cousin, as well as Prince Rupert and Prince Maurice.

Princess Henrietta had fallen into enemy hands after the surrender of Exeter, and the Prince of Wales was now the only member of the family at liberty. 'Send for him to wait upon thee with all speed; for his preserva-tion is the greatest hope for my safety,' the King wrote from Newcastle where he had been taken by the Scots. 'And for my sake, let the world see that the queen seeks not to alter his conscience,' he added. The Queen wrote to her son, sending him money, as well as a portrait of his rich cousin, Anne-Marie; but she warned him of the dangers that surrounded him, despatching Jermyn to appeal to the Prince's Council. It was all to no avail. The King also wrote to Charles, telling him to obey his mother in everything except religion, and in July parental insistence prevailed. Charles arrived in Paris almost alone and the Queen Regent greeted him formally, offering him a seat 'on an equality' with Louis. She also granted him a pension, but some people doubted whether he would ever obtain it, if his mother's experiences were anything to go by.

With the help of Montreuil the King and Queen were able to corres-pond. Henrietta continued the campaign she had started earlier in the year to persuade her husband that he would do well to embrace the Covenant; it would surely be a small step to move from one form of Protestantism to another. She felt it was not worth sacrificing a kingdom and all that he loved for the sake of a few bishops. The King found his wife's attitude distressing, all the more so as his captors subjected him to daily sessions in the hope of converting him to Presbyterianism. 'I never knew what it was to be barbarously baited before,' he told the Queen. He explained to her that the only comfort he had lay in her love and a clear conscience.

Now that the King was in custody, he authorized the Queen to manage his business and she worked for him as hard and as conscientiously as ever. Painstakingly she went over the details of the terms Parliament wished him to accept, berating him sometimes for his weakness, sometimes for his obstinacy, which to him seemed ironical. 'I am blamed both for granting too much, and yet not yielding enough,' he wrote, adding, 'It must be a strange unluckiness for a man to be guilty in both kinds upon one occasion.' She would gladly have gone to Ireland in person on his behalf, but he resisted the idea, fearing for her safety. Although she had suffered a bad relapse in the spring of 1645 and was sometimes troubled with drowsiness, migraine headaches and numbness, her strength had gradually returned, as the Parliamentarians knew to their cost. 'She is the same woman she was, and is resolved to her power to manage the business for the continuance of the wars here.' Even though there was little to alleviate her cares and anxiety, Madame de Motteville noticed that her vivacity could not always be contained, and even in the middle of a sad or serious conversation she would often throw in an amusing remark. The King, sending messages to Jermyn and others expressing gratitude for all they had achieved on his behalf, added that she must make his acknowledgments 'to the Queen of England (for none else can do it), it being her love that maintains my life, her kindness that upholds my courage, which makes me eternally hers'.

In all the anxieties of that summer, the Queen at least knew the joy of being reunited with two of her children—the eldest who had always been her favourite, and the youngest. Princess Henriette-Anne and her governess, Lady Dalkeith, had been given a safe conduct after the fall of Exeter, with such plate, money and goods as she possessed; 'fit and convenient carriage' had been provided, at reasonable rates, but it had seemed unlikely that she would ever be able to leave England. In August, however, the Queen received a message to say that the Princess had arrived in France with Lady Dalkeith. Disguised in old and patched clothes, the pair had looked so convincingly impoverished that the English authorities had let them go, glad to think that they would prove a burden to the French rather than to themselves. The Queen sent carriages to meet them, and hugged and kissed the child she had hardly known and never expected to see again.

As the year 1646 wore on the Queen, like the King's captors, came to accept the fact that he would never change his religion. 'With what patience,' he asked her, 'wouldst thou give ear to him who should persuade thee for worldly respects, to leave the Communion of the Roman Church for any other?' Alexander Henderson, who had worked on the King daily, could in the end only admire his constancy and deep devotion to his faith. No threats or blandishments would ever make him betray the Church without which, he believed, his throne was meaningless. He was prepared to make other concessions; he would recognize the perpetual Parliament, he would give over the control of the militia, but he would not part with a single Bishop. The Queen would have been happy to sacrifice the ecclesiastics, but once he had surrendered the military power, she told him, 'you can no longer refuse them anything, not even my life, if they demand it from you'. The King reasoned with her, explaining that the militia was not like the great standing army that a French monarch might have at his command. It troubled him when she accused him of ruining by his 'rigidness' all that was dear to him, and it was an infinite relief to him when he knew that she had at last accepted his scruples. When she expressed the fear, once again, that he might be 'cozened' by his enemies, as he had been over the perpetual Parliament, he replied:

> Indeed, with grief I must acknowledge the instance, nor can I promise not to do the like again, when I shall (as I then did) suffer myself to sin against my conscience; for the truth is, I was surprised with it instantly after I made that base sinful concession, for which, and also that great injustice in taking away the Bishops' votes in Parliament though I have been most justly punished.

In Paris as the festive season came on and the French Court gave itself over to balls and entertainments, the English Queen's last hopes of her husband's salvation began to grow dim. There had always been a chance that he might have escaped from Newcastle and joined her in France, but early in the New Year she heard that the Scots, accepting the fact that the King would never sign the Covenant, had handed him over to the English before withdrawing across the border. Now he had been taken under guard to Holdenby House. In early February Henrietta visited the Queen Regent and, weeping bitterly, expressed her despair. There was no longer anything to work for; all the ports were closed, there was no means of sending help, all messages were intercepted, and there seemed little chance of arousing sympathy among the other crowned heads of Europe even though her husband's cause, she believed, was 'the cause of every king in christendom'. The Queen Regent was sympathetic; she had resigned herself to housing the exiled Court and could now see that she would in all probability be providing hospitality for some time. All the same she had no wish to do anything that might offend the Parliamentarians who were capable of causing great trouble for French shipping in the Channel.

Henrietta's father, Henri IV, might have thought that Paris was worth a Mass, but she had to accept the fact that her husband did not consider the whole of England, Scotland and Ireland worth a Mass or a Covenant. She had often complained in the past that he was irresolute, but now his determination to be true to his conscience and to his friends had put him beyond help.

Unable to communicate with her husband or to send him assistance, the Queen directed her energies to the cause of finding her son a rich wife who might save the whole family from penury. The Prince of Wales was arousing much admiration in Paris. He had grown very tall, he had dark eyes and luxuriant hair, and his disposition was easy and cheerful. Even the haughty Anne-Marie had to admit that he was good-looking, and his height was an added attraction for a girl who tended to tower above most of the men at Court. She had, however, set her sights higher than a penniless Prince, and she pictured herself on the throne beside the Habsburg Emperor whose wife had recently died. Henrietta Maria assured the heiress that her son was overcome with love, but when she searched her niece's face for a reciprocal affection, she found only a look of coldness and superiority. The Prince's education, never intellectually strenuous even in times of peace, had been interrupted by the comings and goings of war, and his elementary French proved inadequate when it came to conversing with the astringent Anne-Marie. She treated him with condescension and let him hand her into her coach, lie decorously and decoratively at her feet as she sat watching a comedy, or hold the flaming torch while she made up her face at the mirror. When Prince Rupert came to Paris—he had been appointed general of all the exiled English— he helped Prince Charles by acting as an interpreter, and Henrietta did what she could by lending her niece the few jewels she still possessed to wear at the smartest ball of the season. Anne-Marie was positively covered in precious stones, and her head-dress, which may have proved to everybody not only that she was rich, but also that she had more money than taste, consisted of a vast bouquet of flowers strewn liberally with enormous pearls and diamonds.

Some of the Queen's jewels had been redeemed with the help of a shipment of tin mined in Cornwall before the final defeat of the Royalists, but she had given so much of her money away to help the King that she was now reduced to living a life devoid of any luxury. She had little left over for the many Royalists who gravitated in increasing numbers to her Court. Father Cyprien recorded that she let her mind dwell increasingly on devotional subjects as she learned the lesson that honours, wealth, pleasure and grandeur are evanescent and valueless. Many of her retainers were less able to take a philosophical view of their exile and there was an atmosphere of unhappiness at the parsimonious Court which sometimes erupted in violent quarrels. When Montrose visited the Louvre he was shocked by the general air of discontent and futility. 'I am weary of this place,' Lady Denbigh wrote to her son, 'the air is not good, and to be deprived of your company and the rest of my children is very troublesome to me.' Jermyn threw himself into the social life of Paris, where he was extremely popular; he began to delegate the transcribing and deciphering of the Queen's letters to Abraham Cowley. Madame de Motteville described him as 'a rather worthy man, of a gentle mind which seemed very narrow and more fitted for petty things than great ones'. There were rumours, all unsubstantiated, that he had become the Queen's lover, and Lady Denbigh complained to her son that there were people in the exiled Court who were writing 'untruths' about the Queen in letters to England.

Other old friends reappeared in Paris. The Queen Regent allowed the personable de Jars, in spite of his past record as a trouble-maker, to frequent the English Court. Davenant was there, and the Queen used him in an attempt to make the King change his mind about the Covenant. The poet visited the King at Newcastle, but his mission ended quickly when he was tactless enough to intimate that the Church was not the most important institution in the world. The obese Endymion Porter also carried messages for the Queen, 'his fat guts, peppered with popery, hindering his speed in riding post'—to quote a parliamentary report.

That summer, for a short while, hope revived in the exiled Court as encouraging rumours came across the Channel. It seemed that London was in a turmoil as the rift widened between Independents and Presbyterians. There were reports that a contingent of cavalry had arrived to take the King from Holdenby, after arresting the Commissioners of Parliament who were guarding him. Some said that Fairfax had defected and was marching on London with the King at the head of his forces. It had become evident that Parliament intended to disband the army without making adequate arrangements for settling arrears of pay or for granting the religious toleration which many of the soldiers believed they had been fighting for. At Newmarket the army refused to disband and the King was secured to prevent him reaching an agreement with the Presbyterians. Once he was in army hands the King was less closely guarded; his chaplains had access to him, and he was able to communicate with the Queen. He was taken to Hampton Court where he was allowed to play tennis, enjoy some hunting and even see his children, James, Elizabeth and Henry, who were in the care of the Earl of Northumberland close by at Syon House.

The Independents submitted a document to the King entitled Heads of the Proposals, which was radical in approach although at least

calculated to restore the King to his throne. The Queen despatched a
messenger, Sir John Berkeley, begging her husband to accept the terms
which were offered to him. Stephen Goffe was among the many who urged
him to accept the army's terms, beseeching him not to insist 'too nicely
upon terms in the present exigency of his affairs'. But the King believed
that the offers were made simply 'to cajole him to his ruin'. He pre-
varicated, still hoping to play one side off against the other. The extremists
were soon weary of Cromwell's indeterminate negotiations with the King,
and rumours that he was to be kept a closer prisoner made Charles take
the step of escaping from Hampton Court on November 10. As usual his
plans were ill-considered and muddled, and his decision to throw himself
on the mercy of Colonel Hammond, the Governor of Carisbrooke,
proved disastrous. He found himself a prisoner in the castle, this time
under close guard, and although he made several attempts to escape he
was quickly recaptured each time.

In the new year the Queen found that once again all communication
with the King had been cut. She did not give in, of course, and wrote to
him regularly in cipher, but her messages were intercepted, and she
received no word from the King. It was a gloomy winter in Paris. Both
Louis and his brother had undergone bouts of serious illness, and there
was growing opposition to the Queen Regent's regime as she allowed
herself to drift increasingly into a life of pleasure, leaving Mazarin to
control the country and fill all the key posts with his own candidates.
Some of the unrest was a legacy of Richelieu's policy of creating a strong
centralized government, but there was also much jealousy of those in
power, and a great deal of discontent caused by unpopular taxes. Encouraged by the success of the English Parliament in overturning the
establishment, the bourgeoisie of Paris rioted in January 1648.

The Queen was naturally anxious about her husband, and disappointed
that once again he had refused to accept terms that might have saved him.
Not surprisingly, all sides now suspected the King's motives. Parliament
passed a Vote of No Addresses to the King, and before dividing up to
quell uprisings in Wales and elsewhere; the army held a prayer meeting
at Windsor for a renewal of faith in the word of the Lord, the righteous-
ness of the cause and the determination to bring Charles Stuart, 'that
man of blood', to justice for the misery he had brought upon the country.

The Prince of Wales too was dispirited. After the glitter and excitement
of his first months in Paris, he had begun to find life trying under his
mother's surveillance. His main pleasure lay in playing with his youngest
sister whom he had nicknamed Minette. He longed for action and
resented the fact that Henrietta would not allow him to plan a military
expedition to help his father. Gradually, however, the outlook brightened
as the news came through of a threatened mutiny in the navy as well as

Henry Jermyn 1st Earl of St Albans

Photograph Courtauld Institute of Art

William Cavendish, 1st Duke of Newcastle

Photograph A. C. Cooper

The Death of Charles I

The Banqueting House, Palace of Whitehall, c.1640

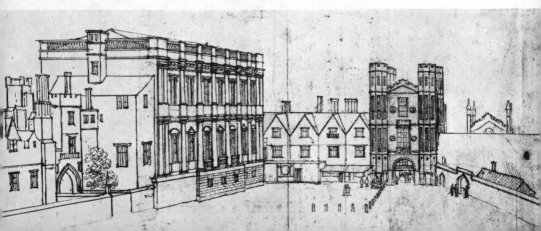

The three children of Charles I, James, Elizabeth and Henry, in 1647

Henriette-Anne (Minette) with Henry, Duke of Gloucester

Henrietta Maria as a widow

uprisings in Essex, Kent and Wales. The Queen, cautiously optimistic, despatched Sir William Fleming to Amsterdam to pawn the last of her jewels, and sent Prince Charles to Calais in case he should be needed in a hurry. When the King entered into a secret agreement with the Scots it became evident that the Queen would be required to resume her old task of collecting arms and ammunition. He had promised to accept the introduction of Presbyterianism for three years with the proviso that the form of the established religion should be discussed at the end of that term. 'Let no reports of any personal threatening against me stagger your constancy,' he told his supporters. Many members of the Scottish nobility were prepared to help him, but he was warned that the clergy would not be satisfied with his offers; unless he were prepared to make more concessions, he could not look for assistance from the Covenanters. He remained as uncompromising as ever. 'I desire you do not expect it from me,' he wrote. 'I am still resolved rather to suffer than to wrong my conscience or honour.' Since this was the case, the well-trained army already in existence was not available, and Hamilton was appointed general of those who had entered into the Engagement with the King. Soon he and his fellow 'Engagers' were looking to the Queen to send arms and ammunition—'whereof we are absolutely unprovided,' they wrote. They also believed that their cause would be much helped if the Prince of Wales were to cross over to Scotland, and they sent Sir William Fleming in April to assess the Queen's reaction to such a proposition. The Prince himself was anxious enough to leave the stagnant Court at Saint-Germain, and the Queen told her closest friends that she intended to let him go. On July 9 he sailed from Calais for Helvoetsluys where he was met by his brother James who had just escaped from England.

The Queen devoted her usual energy to the task of raising arms, but she met with nothing but delays and lack of co-operation. A spirit of lethargy settled on her impoverished Court; Jermyn had lost much of his enthusiasm and he was even accused of devoting some of the Queen's income to his own use. The English community was more poverty-stricken than ever, and there had been some unpleasant scenes before the Prince's departure when some of the officers of his Household demanded arrears of pay, declaring that they refused to go with him unless they were satisfied. In an attempt to alleviate her grief and perhaps also to save money, the Queen went into retreat at the Carmelite convent. Madame de Motteville visited her there on July 14 and found her alone in a small room writing letters which she said were of great importance. She confessed that she had grave apprehensions about the expedition which the Prince was about to undertake, and for which she had sacrificed everything; to prove her point she showed her visitors a small drinking cup which she said was the only piece of gold now left to her. Her plight aroused in Madame de Motteville a feeling of great compassion, and caused her to reflect on the misfortunes of Kings and Queens.

On July 17 Charles sailed from Brill, his expedition much augmented by at least ten ships from the parliamentary navy brought over by Vice-Admiral Batten. In Scotland Hamilton was forced to set off across the border before he was ready, owing to the premature outbreak of various uprisings in England. Only a small number of his raw and undisciplined troops knew how to handle a musket, he had no artillery—not a single field-piece—little ammunition and no horses to transport what he had. It was an exceptionally wet August all over the Continent which made the march heavy going. Cromwell's forces, hurrying north after a successful campaign in Wales, encountered the Scottish Engagers at Preston, and had little difficulty in inflicting a decisive defeat. By the beginning of September Charles was back in harbour with many of his sailors in a mutinous frame of mind for the usual reason—lack of pay.

After the battle of Preston the King, purged at last of all optimism, wrote a letter to his son which read like a final message. 'We know not but this may be the last time we may speak to you or the world publicly,' he wrote. He advised his son to 'prefer the way of peace' and to pardon rather than to punish. A King, he could now see, should never 'affect more greatness and prerogative than what is really and intrinsically for the good of our subjects (not satisfaction of favourites)'. The English nation was now under 'some infatuation', but he still believed that the orthodox religion, as it had been established in the kingdom since the Reformation, would prevail over the new revelations and the fanatic humours. 'The Commissioners are gone,' he wrote; 'the corn is now in the ground; we expect the harvest.' Not long afterwards he was moved to Hurst Castle and the army entered London, where Colonel Pride carried out his famous purge of the Commons, reducing it to little more than fifty Members—the merest 'rump'. This obedient body passed an ordinance appointing a large court of one hundred and thirty-five Commissioners to try the King.

In Paris the Queen waited at the Louvre for news. In the gilded and finely-furnished rooms she was alone with her retainers. The Queen Regent had left Paris secretly for Saint-Germain with her sons, and her troops under Condé were blockading the city. Trouble had flared up in France that summer, with the Paris Parlement demanding its rights, many provincial assemblies siding with them and forcing Mazarin to make concessions. All through the autumn the streets of Paris had been plastered with defamatory placards and libels; the Queen Regent had promised tax reforms and other changes, but these were promptly revoked when the Treaty of Westphalia released troops under Condé who put himself at the Queen Regent's disposal.

With the French royal family out of Paris and affairs in such an unsettled state, nobody felt inclined to supply the English Queen on credit. She had no money to buy food or fuel, but she stayed on at the Louvre, believing that news from London would come to her more quickly if she remained in Paris. When Cardinal de Retz visited her, he found her with Henriette-Anne, who was in bed. She explained that she was keeping her small daughter company; there was not a single stick of wood for firing in the whole palace, and bed seemed the warmest place for the little girl on this bitter January day. The Cardinal, shocked by the spectacle, promised that Madame d'Angleterre would not be forced to stay in bed again for lack of a log. He painted a vivid picture of the Queen's plight to the Paris Parlement, which immediately voted her a grant of forty thousand livres. It also issued a passport for her son James who had been on his way to join her when the troubles broke out.

The Queen knew that her husband was now on trial, accused of violating the law, of seizing more than the limited power which was his by right, and of waging 'unnatural, cruel and bloody wars'. Having seen Strafford go to the block despite the brilliance of his defence and the inadequacy of the charges against him, she could only cling to the hope that in the last resort the Commissioners would recoil from the final responsibility of spilling the sacred blood of the King. He was beyond all help now, alone before his accusers, but in a last pathetic bid to be with him, she wrote to the Speakers of both Houses of Parliament, sending the letters through de Grignan, the French Ambassador in England. 'I have specified nothing to the Parliaments,' she told the Ambassador, 'but to give me the liberty to go see the King my lord.'

The days went by and no answer came, for after a debate the Commons had decided that the letters should be put aside unopened. Believing that messengers from England were unable to enter the city, the Queen attempted to escape with Minette, but she was stopped in the Tuileries gardens. A few days later Madame de Motteville found her in a state of agitation after hearing rumours that the King had been taken to the scaffold but had been saved at the last moment by onlookers who refused to let their King suffer such a fate. On February 8, still having received no official news, the Queen despatched a messenger who made his way through the forces of the Fronde which were guarding the city and through Condé's besieging army, with orders to go to Saint-Germain in case news had been received there concerning the King's fate.

At lunch-time Father Cyprien was told that he was not to leave the Queen after grace was said as his services might be needed. There was some desultory conversation on trivial matters, and the Queen remained uneasy, wondering why her messenger had not returned. Jermyn said that he might have come sooner if the news had been good. The Queen then suspected that Jermyn already knew the truth and pressed him to tell her. He found the task intolerable, but after much hesitation he broke it to her at last that her husband was dead.

The Queen stood as if turned to marble, deaf to anything her distracted attendants tried to say to her, and utterly motionless. Some of those around her were weeping, others stood silent. Night came on and she remained in her shocked state; they began to fear for her reason. It was the Duchesse de Vendôme, the wife of her illegitimate brother and one of her closest friends, who finally broke the spell as she knelt and kissed the Queen's hand. It was then that Henrietta Maria broke down and broke into passionate weeping.

Chapter 19

THE KING MY SON

TWO DAYS after hearing the news of Charles's execution Henrietta Maria summoned Madame de Motteville to the palace, charging her to go to Saint-Germain. She was to ask the Queen Regent to recognize Prince Charles as the new King of England, and to grant to James, who had arrived in Paris a few days previously, the respect which had until recently been extended to his elder brother. Madame de Motteville was also to warn the French Queen of the danger of aggravating her subjects unless she had the power to quell them. With strange clarity the widowed Queen, 'enlightened by adversity', diagnosed the reasons for her husband's tragedy, and prophesied similar disasters for the Queen Regent if she failed to learn from the mistakes of others.

The Queen now longed to leave the empty glitter of the palace, and she soon sought out the peace and comfort of the Carmelite convent, as she had done on the eve of her marriage. In his last letter to the Prince of Wales, the King had spoken of those inward refreshments which enabled him to remain immune to all the malice of his enemies. 'We have learnt to own ourself by retiring into ourself, and therefore can the better digest what befall us,' he had written with Stoic simplicity. Although husband and wife had worshipped in different ways both had been sincerely borne up by their spiritual nourishment, and Henrietta knew that as she gave herself over to prayer and submitted to the discipline of the religious community, she would gradually come to accept the inscrutable ways of God.

Father Philip, who had helped Henrietta through so many crises in her life, was now dead, and it was the gentle Father Cyprien who went to her at last at the convent in the Faubourg Saint-Jacques and told her that all her children needed her counsel and help. She accepted his advice and emerged into the world outside. Wearing a black dress of the kind she was to affect to the end of her life, simple in style with a white collar and cuffs, she might almost have been mistaken for a Catholic nun—or for a Puritan. The critical Anne-Marie was of the opinion that her aunt did not look as sorrowful as she might have done, considering that the King had died such a terrible death and had treated her so *divinement bien* during his lifetime. All the same, she allowed that this apparent serenity could be attributed to the power of the spirit which God grants to people at times such as these.

For the Queen and for all Royalists in England and on the Continent, the death of the King was not an end but a beginning. Cromwell had said, 'We will cut off the King's head with the Crown upon it,' and had taken steps to ensure that after the execution no successor was named. Though some of the regicides had signed the death-warrant under pressure, many believed that their action was prompted by the will of God, and they felt that they were taking the first step towards the establishment of the kingdom of heaven on earth. Convinced of the wickedness of the King, and more particularly of his wife, they were surprised by the reaction of horror aroused in England and all over Europe. The King's courage in the face of death, his re-affirmation of the principles he stood for, his refusal to buy his own safety at the cost of his conscience, added a Christ-like aura to the majestic dignity he had so carefully cultivated throughout his life. Imprisoned, bereft of all ceremony, attended by only a few servants, Charles could have echoed the words of *Richard II*:

> I live with bread like you, feel want,
> Taste grief, need friends: subjected thus,
> How can you say to me I am a King?

And yet there was something about him even at the last that was unmistakably kingly—even divine. As he walked through the Spring Gardens into the Palace of Whitehall and across the hall which had been the setting for so many of his dramatic appearances, he put on his finest performance, an apotheosis of kingship more complete than anything Rubens had conveyed to canvas on the ceiling above. 'I go from a corruptible to an incorruptible crown,' he said as on the scaffold he removed his cloak and the Order of the Garter, that symbol of the almost mystical chivalry he had tried to establish at his Court.

On the day of the King's death copies were on sale in London of the *Eikon Basilike, The Portraiture of His Sacred Majesty in his Solitude and Sufferings*. The frontispiece showed the King kneeling, like Christ in the garden of Gethsemane, spurning the earthly crown beneath his feet, clasping in his hands the crown of thorns, his eyes turned upwards to the heavenly crown above. The book became a best-seller and ran into many editions, in spite of attempts to suppress it, as the concept of the martyr King quickly gained currency. For people who faced living in a world bereft of those symbols and images which had helped them to an understanding of the divine truth, the *Eikon Basilike* provided an iconographical satisfaction, nurturing an occult feeling that could grow gradually in worth sacrificing thirty thousand pounds a year for the unproductive satisfaction of refusing to speak to one's daughter-in-law. Just when everybody thought that the Queen Mother was about to show her disapproval by retiring to France, the Abbé Montagu visited Anne's father on a mission of reconciliation. Hyde expressed surprise, but there was little doubt that he appreciated the reasons which lay behind the visit.

As Christmas drew nearer there were festivities on a scale which the royal family, and the nation as a whole, had been deprived of for years. After a succession of late nights Mary fell ill, and the doctors were not sure at first whether she was suffering from smallpox or measles and the purples together. For five days they bled her unceasingly, but her mother was kept well away from her side for fear that she might attempt a death-bed conversion. On Christmas Eve Mary died, thus putting a sudden end to everybody's enjoyment.

Smallpox was rife at the Court and the Queen Mother now began to prepare for her departure; she had no wish to risk losing a third child within the space of a few months. Before she left she formally received her daughter-in-law, and her bedchamber was crowded with people who had come to view the reconciliation scene. She agreed to be godmother to the child, and spoke graciously to Hyde. When she set off, the King took his leave of her at Portsmouth, but she was soon back in England again. Typically, the sea which had been calm at first, quickly became tempestuous and her ship ran aground; no sooner had they all re-embarked than Minette went down with a suspected attack of measles. Her illness caused a great deal of alarm, and it was said that when her fiancé in France heard the news he nearly died of anxiety. The whole party landed at Portsmouth again, a town which Father Cyprien found extremely dull—he amused himself, however, conversing with the 'Huguenot' minister, believing that he made some progress in showing him the folly of his ways. After submitting to the usual letting of blood, the Princess succumbed to a 'looseness' which eventually carried away her fever.

On the way home, at Pontoise, Montagu entertained Henrietta Maria and her daughter in apartments he had fitted up superbly for the occasion. While the Queen was still being shown round the rooms of the Abbey with their beautiful pictures, porcelain and jewellery, the sound of trumpets and kettle-drums announced the arrival of the French royal family. Monsieur seemed overjoyed to see his betrothed again and they sat up talking late into the night as he listened with 'extreme attention and rapturous delight' to her account of the visit to England. He appeared to feel great jealousy at the presence of the Duke of Buckingham who had come over with the royal party, and the Duke was told that he must go back to England immediately. Negotiations were entered into at once to

secret, until the time came when they could take up arms for the new
King. Montrose, who was said to have swooned away when he heard the
news of his master's death, wrote in the final lines of a poem on the
subject:

I'll sing thine obsequies with trumpet sounds,
And write thine epitaph in blood and wounds.

King Charles II spent the summer trying to raise funds. It seemed
certain that he would go to Ireland where Ormonde's campaign had met
with considerable success, bringing much of the country into Royalist or
Old Irish hands. The Queen did her best to redeem three rubies which
were in pawn to raise money for arms. 'We have a fleet at sea of twenty
ships under the command of my nephew,' she told Christine. When
Charles arrived in Paris she was able to report to her sister that the visit
had passed off successfully. 'I am sure you will not be displeased when I
tell you,' she wrote, 'that the King my son gets on with me as amicably
as could possibly be.' All the same she now had to face the fact that
Charles had a mind of his own. The question of whether he went to
Ireland or accepted terms offered to him by the Scottish Commissioners
who had visited him at The Hague was his decision and not hers. It was
something of a shock to find that although his father had charged him to
obey her in everything, he was now more ready to listen to the advice of
his Council than to take orders from her. In spite of this he remained her
favourite. Charles was not a man to precipitate quarrels; he tended to
leave the room when his mother showed signs of being difficult. James,
on the other hand, was inflexible when he believed himself to be in the
right and never swerved to avoid a collision. Yet in spite of all differences
of temperament, the royal children felt that close bond which sometimes
especially unites the members of a one-parent family. In Holland Mary,
too, felt the link deeply, and she devoted much of her energy and resources
supporting her brother's cause, often arousing the disapproval of the
Dutch in so doing.

Although it was evident that her sons were breaking away from parental
control, the Queen Mother had not yet surrendered her right to indulge
in some match-making, and she sent Jermyn to Mademoiselle de Montpensier with an offer on Charles's behalf. The unromantic Anne-Marie
suggested that a match would not be feasible unless the English King
were prepared to change his religion. This, Jermyn pointed out, was
quite out of the question. Any slender hopes the King might entertain of
regaining his kingdom would vanish for ever if there was the slightest
suggestion that he might enter the Catholic faith. Of the two brothers *La
Montpensier* in any case preferred the younger. She was attracted by
James's handsome features and fair complexion, and he was at least

prepared to converse with her, unlike Charles who invariably went silent whenever she was in the vicinity. The fact that Charles was now a King carried some weight, but his penniless condition was hardly a recommendation. Anne-Marie pictured herself languishing at home in one of the several houses she owned while her husband was away endlessly fighting in Ireland or Scotland with the help of her fortune. All the same she had to face the fact that she had not as yet received any other offers of marriage in spite of her confident belief that half the world was in love with her. '*Voilà votre galant qui vient,*' the Queen Regent had remarked when a courier brought news that King Charles had arrived in France, It was noted that Anne-Marie rose early on the day he was due in Paris, and even put her hair in curlers, something she rarely bothered to do. She was impressed by the improvement in his appearance brought about by greater maturity and responsibility, but she soon became disillusioned when he relapsed into silence, except when he discussed with his cousin Louis such *bagatelles* as hounds and hunting. She disapproved even more strongly when he spurned the delicate ortolans which had been prepared for his supper, and threw himself, to use her expression, at a shoulder of mutton. When they were left alone together after the meal she swore that it was a full quarter of an hour before he uttered a word. He dutifully answered her questions, but quite failed to treat her to any *douceurs*. When she accompanied him a little way out of the town to say goodnight in the middle of a romantic forest, he simply told her that Jermyn would speak to her about his intentions. Meanwhile, he was her *très obéissant serviteur*. She replied that she was his *très obéissante servante*. Jermyn paid her some compliments, the King saluted her and went away.

On September 19 Charles left for Jersey, taking James and most of his retainers. Although Anne-Marie went down to Saint-Germain when she heard that he was about to leave, she never received any of the *douceurs* she secretly hoped for.

After the departure of her sons, the Queen spent the winter quietly, entering the convent for Christmas. There, where there was no pretence or dissimulation, she felt capable of praying more effectively for those she loved, including her sister Christine, to whom she now wrote more regularly and in deeply affectionate terms. The brothers, far away from any vestigial relics of parental control, passed the winter pleasantly in the Channel Islands, but the arrival in Ireland of Cromwell—'the archrebel' as Elizabeth of Bohemia called him—and the defeat of Ormonde near Dublin after Christmas put an end to their plans. Prince Rupert's ships, having been ignominiously blockaded in Kinsale Harbour, escaped to Portugal, and those that remained after a storm off the Spanish coast made for the West Indies. Charles had to look elsewhere for a chance to re-establish himself, and as important decisions were called for,

Nicholas wrote advising him to form a full Council of 'able, grave and experienced persons of unblemished integrity'. In Jersey he was surrounded by callous and often unreliable younger men, including the Duke of Buckingham, who had none of his father's charm and ability and was more than a little inclined to dissipation. His more sober advisers, most of whom were still on the Continent, would have liked him to lie low in the Netherlands until conditions seemed more propitious, but he himself felt inclined to explore all possibilities, and he agreed to meet the Scottish Commissioners at Breda. On the way he encountered his mother at Beauvais and they were together for three or four days. Henrietta wrote to Christine as soon as she returned to Paris, saying that she was unable to prophesy the outcome of his meeting with the Scots. She told Mademoiselle that the King still professed his love for her.

Elizabeth of Bohemia felt uneasy about Charles's future. 'For God's sake,' she wrote to Montrose, 'leave not the King so long as he is at Breda; for without question there is nothing that will be omitted to ruin you and your friends.' Montrose, ignoring Elizabeth's advice, went off to Orkney when the talks were only just beginning. Charles held out for nearly two months before he came to an agreement with the Scots in which he undertook to enforce the laws against the Catholics and to establish Presbyterianism in both England and Scotland. Not long afterwards he left for Edinburgh. The Queen Mother spent the next two months anxiously waiting for news. Charles was not a good correspondent at the best of times and he seldom favoured her with letters. Most of the rumours which reached Paris were far from encouraging. He was now firmly in the hands of the Covenanters, and was likely to risk being handed over to the English if he did not give way to demands which his father had resisted to the end of his life. It seemed unlikely that the pleasure-loving Charles would readily ally himself with what Elizabeth described as the godly kirk, but he was also unlikely to risk going to the scaffold like his father, the Duke of Hamilton and more recently, Montrose, who had received too late the King's message telling him to lay down his arms. Charles was quite capable of playing a part when it suited him; he made himself pleasant and amenable and awaited better times. In November the Queen Mother was able to impart to Christine the more encouraging news that all Scotland had apparently united under her son's banner after the severe defeat inflicted on the Covenanters by Cromwell at Dunbar. She had been told that he was shortly to be crowned at Scone.

James, left behind with his mother in Paris, envied his elder brother's success and wished that he too could immerse himself in action. Much against Henrietta's wishes he left for Brussels early in October with the intention of joining the duc de Lorraine. He had been misled into thinking that he would find money deposited there for him by his brother, but when he arrived in the city there was nothing. His mother was afraid that he would be tempted to join the Spanish army and risk offending the Queen Regent and Mazarin. She told the Cardinal that she had 'small influence' over her son. James next made plans to visit his sister Mary who was expecting her first child; he had actually set out for The Hague when news came that his brother-in-law, the Prince of Orange, was dead. Even before this shock Mary's health had given cause for concern and it seemed unlikely that she would be safely delivered. 'My poor niece is the most afflicted creature that ever I saw and is changed as she is nothing but skin and bone,' wrote Elizabeth of Bohemia. Nevertheless, a week after her husband's death, on her own birthday, Mary brought forth a somewhat sickly son, the new William of Orange.

There was another death in the family that autumn. When Charles landed in Scotland, the two younger royal children, Elizabeth and Henry, had been taken for safety to Carisbrooke after spending some happy and healthy months at Penshurst. Elizabeth had always been delicate; born on a December day when snow lay thick on the ground, she had often been termed the Winter Princess, and her frail fair looks encouraged the epithet. It was said that she had never recovered from the shock of seeing her father on the eve of his execution. After only a week in the dismal castle she caught cold and was unable to withstand the high fever that followed. She died with her head resting on a bible which lay open at the text, 'Come unto me all ye that travail'.

Henrietta was beginning to think that God had sent her all these anxieties and sorrows to show her that she must retire completely from the world. Had it not been for her duty towards Minette she would have entered a convent long before, but she was looking now for a compromise solution. Although she had no money—her allowance from the Queen Regent, though generous in the circumstances, she described as 'little for a poor *demoiselle* like me'—she was yet determined to found a religious house which would provide for her own spiritual needs. St Francis de Sales had established earlier in the century a religious order designed to accommodate ladies of gentle birth who were unable to withstand the discipline of the more austere foundations. Although there was already one house in Paris, Henrietta planned to open another at Chaillot in a small and dilapidated château once owned by the Marquis de Bassompierre. The house was only a short drive out of Paris down the Cours de la Reine, but it was peaceful and secluded, with its own garden and pleasant views over the countryside. To the ex-Queen of England it must have seemed unpretentious and shabby enough, although the nuns were suspicious of its faded luxury and at first refused to sleep anywhere except the attic. Undeterred by legal difficulties caused by Bassompierre's heirs and creditors, Henrietta had given herself to her old task of raising money, this time for more peaceful purposes. A large sum was contributed by an anonymous donor, and the Queen Regent herself lent her name to the appeal. Henrietta Maria, as the 'reputative' foundress, gave it the dignity of a royal foundation. The front of the house was reserved for her use, and the rooms, which she furnished herself, were always available, so that she could go there whenever she pleased to pray and catch up on her correspondence. She always retired to Chaillot for religious festivals, and sometimes stayed for three months at a time, submitting herself to the same discipline as the dozen or so nuns who lived there with the Mother Superior, even talking to her visitors through a grille.

If life proved hard for Henrietta Maria during 1650 the Queen Regent too faced many difficulties. The old quarrel had broken out fiercely between the Crown and the Princes of the Blood, Gaston having been persuaded to throw in his lot once again with the opposition. Mazarin had been forced to take flight across the border and the Queen Regent was herself for a while virtually a prisoner at the Palais Royal. Pent up and bereft of her favourite, she was beginning to resent the presence of her sister-in-law and more particularly of the Protestants in her train who openly attended their own services at the Louvre. The Queen Regent was inclined to believe that her troubles had been inflicted on her as a punishment for allowing heretical practices to be carried on in her palace. This was a more comfortable theory than the idea that God might think fit to judge her unfavourably on account of her illicit relationship with the Cardinal. Henrietta, who had spent much of her life provoking criticism for her protection of the Catholics, now faced opprobrium for tolerating the Protestants who had served her so faithfully. Knowing that she depended on her sister-in-law for charity, she felt bound to comply with a demand that the Anglican chaplain, Dr Cosin, should be dismissed from her service. She arranged for her Anglican retainers to worship at the house of the British Ambassador, and the Queen Regent was pacified.

For a while the new year brought an improvement in Royalist fortunes. In Scotland Charles appeared to be making good progress, reconciling hostile elements and raising an army to resist the parliamentary threat to the country. As early as April there were rumours that he was ready to advance into England, but it was not until the end of August that definite news came of his progress south. 'The King they say advances towards London apace, Worcester and Coventry are declared for him,' Elizabeth of Bohemia told her son. 'It is thought Gloucester will follow, there is great distraction in London.' Royalists greeted the news of the King's spectacular march with delight, almost with incredulity. But in September there were disturbing rumours that Charles had been defeated at

Worcester. 'I cannot go to Chaillot today,' Henrietta Maria wrote to the Mother Superior, 'for I have found here more business than I expected, not having yet been to the Palais Royal, on account of the bad news from England, which nevertheless I hope is not quite so unfortunate as it is represented. My uneasiness renders me unfit for anything, until I receive the news which will arrive to-night. Pray to God for the King, my son, and believe me, mother, your very good friend.'

Henrietta Maria tried to convince herself that it was in fact Cromwell who had suffered the defeat, but as everybody began to treat her with increasing sympathy she at length came to accept the truth. It seemed that Charles had acquitted himself well and with great courage, and the disaster that had undoubtedly happened could be attributed to the bad luck which, as Mademoiselle noted, had a habit of haunting all his ventures. For weeks the Queen Mother did not know whether her son was alive or dead, and at any moment she expected to hear that he had fallen into the hands of his enemies. Each day a succession of visitors came to condole with her, but their efforts only helped to augment her agony. Then, after six weeks, she was told that Charles had landed in France. With James, who had returned to Paris in the spring, she set out to meet him, and they were re-united at Rouen. On their return to the capital they were greeted with expressions of joy. Henrietta Maria was so relieved to have her son back safely that she went down to Chaillot far less frequently than usual, and then only to take physic. It was reported that she was 'constantly wonderful merry'.

Charles, however, at times seemed to be brooding over the terrible scenes he had witnessed, when so many of his friends had lost their lives and his army had been annihilated. The British Ambassador noticed how silent he had become, whether he was with his mother or in other company. The Queen Mother warned Mademoiselle, when she first came to see him after his return, that she might find his looks a little strange, because in order to escape detection during his escape he had cut his hair short and grown a beard. Mademoiselle thought that this new style suited him and altogether believed that the ordeal he had been through had brought about an improvement in his character. Unaccountably he seemed able to speak French more fluently as a result of his stay in Scotland. After a while he overcame his melancholy and became his old debonair self, amusing people with flippant descriptions of his spell hiding in an oak tree, or the times when he had ridden with a young lady, Jane Lane, à croupe behind him, both of them disguised as country people. It was really a relief to be back in Paris, where everybody was so charming and amusing, after his long spell among the psalm-singing and over-serious Scots. He asked Anne-Marie when there would be dancing in Paris, so that he could enjoy it again, and hear the sound of violins which the Presbyterians regarded as instruments of the devil. 'The King my son is incorrigible,' the Queen Mother told Mademoiselle. 'He loves you more than ever—I have scolded him about it.' To please him, Anne-Marie had dancing every evening at her house which soon became a focus for all the young and fashionable world. She found Charles more forthcoming than he had ever been; at times he seemed so animated, so infatuated, that he quite lost his English accent. And yet he still did not declare his love. Not that she minded, she told the Queen Mother. She had no intention of marrying anybody, she was quite happy as she was, and if there ever were any question of matrimony she might well ally herself with the King of France, even if he was eleven years her junior.

The house of Stuart needed Mademoiselle's millions more than ever. In Paris all reserves of money had gone, and during the months after Charles's return the English royal family watched the country which had given them hospitality move rapidly towards the kind of misery and destruction which they had lived through on the other side of the Channel. Mazarin returned to France with a small army and joined the French Court at Poitiers. The Paris Parlement sided with Gaston and the Princes, and the Duc de Lorraine put his army at their disposal. Turenne, however, lent his brilliant generalship to the royal cause. Life in Paris became harsh and dangerous. Henrietta Maria told Christine that it looked as though God had singled out the family for suffering—Bourbons and Stuarts alike. Nobody dared venture outside the gates of Paris where they would be a prey to soldiers or robbers, or to the unfortunate peasants whose lives had been ruined by the outbreak of civil strife. It was becoming dangerous to venture as far as Chaillot; the soldiers did not respect anyone, and Henrietta had been forced to return to the Louvre on more than one occasion.

Charles and James, without money and without an occupation, were rapidly becoming demoralized. Charles easily relapsed into idleness, and his mother had to make excuses for him when he failed to thank Christine for a pair of gloves she had sent him. He would have written himself, Henrietta Maria explained, if his French had been more fluent or he could have dictated to a secretary. The energetic James, on the other hand, found inactivity unbearable; ignoring all opposition he went off to lend his services to Turenne, having with some difficulty raised enough money for his equipage. Charles's only contribution was an attempt at mediation through the duc de Lorraine. His mother warned him against interfering, but he ignored her advice, immediately realizing his folly when he found himself trapped as Lorraine's camp was surrounded by Turenne's forces. Both sides suspected his motives, and even before his return to Paris rumours had been spread that he was instrumental in making Lorraine surrender and accept the hard terms offered by Turenne.

Feeling ran so high that neither he nor his mother dared to leave the palace until one wet night in August they managed to make their way surreptitiously to the safety of Saint-Germain.

The Queen Regent had been ill for some time, and it was not surprising that she was in poor spirits after the ordeal of the previous months which had brought slaughter to the streets of Paris and mob violence culminating in the burning of the Hôtel de Ville. The French royal family had split into factions and, in the final bitter battle outside the walls of the city, Mademoiselle turned the guns of the Bastille on the royalist troops in the pay of her cousin the King whom she had at one time talked of marrying. When Henrietta Maria attempted to offer the Queen Regent some advice based on her own experience of civil war, she was asked whether she wished to be Queen of France as well as England. She replied rather acidly that as she was nothing, she thought she would at least try and help her sister-in-law to remain something.

By the autumn the outlook for the French King improved considerably. When Henrietta Maria wrote to Christine she was able to report that peace was in sight. Louis entered the capital before the month was out to cries of *vive le roi*, and Gaston hastily withdrew—he had once again backed the losing side. In February Mazarin was able to return after a spell in voluntary exile, and the country settled down to an era of greater stability. The wars of the Fronde had brought much unnecessary suffering to many people, particularly the poor, but they had not raised the deeper constitutional issues or the anti-monarchical feeling which had come to the fore in England. Once the power struggle was resolved, it was easier for the young King and his mother to carry on much as before.

Early in 1653 there was another cause for rejoicing. The death of Elizabeth at Carisbrooke had aroused considerable sympathy in England, and the Parliamentarians had decided that they would like to rid themselves of further responsibility for Henry, Duke of Gloucester, who was sent abroad to his sister Mary. The Queen Mother knew that the rebels would not wish him to come under her influence, but this did not prevent her putting pressure on Mary with the object of bringing the thirteen-year-old to Paris. Mary soon grew fond of her brother, feeling that she had more in common with the handsome vivacious Henry than she had with her own delicate and precocious son, but she let him go at last. In Paris, Henry, who was perhaps the most attractive of all Henrietta's good-looking children, caused a great deal of approval and brought a stream of curious visitors to the palace. So many people came to see the *petit cavalier* that the Queen Mother could not find time for anything else—even to write to her sister.

At first the arrival of her youngest son brought Henrietta great happiness. He had come accompanied by his tutor, Richard Lovell, and he continued his education at the palace, walking through the streets of Paris to attend lessons in riding and fencing, and attending Protestant services with the English Ambassador. After a while, however, Henrietta began to complain that he was consorting with companions below his station, and she arranged for him to be sent to Pontoise where her confessor, Montagu, had recently been appointed Abbot. Father Philip, who had always encouraged her in her religious life, had never propelled her into the dangerous path of the proselyte. Walter Montagu was different. His influence was as close as his predecessor's but far less beneficial; he had all the single-mindedness of the convert and the fanaticism of a man who had practised his religion in a minority group under some persecution.

The French relations were naturally pleased to see Henry ensconced at Pontoise, but the move caused alarm in the English family. Elizabeth of Bohemia found Mary in 'much trouble for her dear brother the Duke of Gloucester'; although she herself believed that her nephew possessed enough 'good resolution' to resist all blandishments, she admitted that it was hard to be sure with one of his tender years. James wrote to his mother rebuking her for taking the Duke away from his Protestant companions, and Charles, who had left Paris for Cologne, despatched Ormonde who journeyed to Paris with the object of discovering the true situation.

Henry found himself surrounded by priests and subjected to continuous propaganda. He was, however, so uncooperative in his dealings with Montagu that the Abbé was relieved when he went away to visit his mother in Paris. Henrietta Maria immediately dismissed Lovell and sent her son back to Pontoise, but before he went Henry visited Dr Cosin and asked for some good Protestant arguments to help him resist Montagu's insidious casuistry. Each evening his young English servant Griffen recited as much as he could remember of Cosin's refutation of popery. 'By this post I have had very good news of the Duke of Gloucester's constancy in his religion,' Elizabeth wrote to her son on December 3, 1654, 'and of my Lord of Ormonde's handsome carriage in that business.'

Ormonde had taken a firm line, removing Henry from Pontoise at once and taking him to Paris. After an emotional scene in which the Queen Mother ordered her son to enter the Jesuit College at Clermont, and he staunchly refused to do so, he was treated to another session with Montagu which left him even more obstinately Anglican then ever. Later Montagu delivered a message from his mother telling him that he would never be allowed to look on her face again. He intercepted her as she drove to Chaillot, going down on his knees to ask her blessing, but she turned away and refused to speak to him. When he returned to the palace, he found that his bed had been stripped, his horses turned away and orders given that no food was to be prepared for him. He tried to see Minette, but she began to scream at the very thought of confronting such a heretic. It was the Earl of Ormonde, faithful and resourceful, who pawned his Garter insignia to provide funds for the Duke's journey to Cologne.

The Queen Mother had deprived herself of the company of her much-admired youngest son, she had alienated the King and told James that she never wished to see him again. Ormonde, the fine virtuous man who had supported her husband's cause in Ireland through so many long and difficult years, was also now her enemy as were many Protestants who had stood by her throughout her exile. Minette, the only child left to her, began to pine for her lively brother, and it was a sad life for a child, thrown into the company of a melancholy and unbalanced mother in apartments permanently draped in black.

Even at times of greatest sorrow Madame de Motteville had noticed that Henrietta's natural gaiety had broken through, but now it seemed that she had become totally dispirited. She had almost given up all hope of a restoration, and she argued that Henry might have found in the Catholic hierarchy the pomp and financial security which now looked like being permanently denied to all other members of the family. Although she had pleased her sister-in-law by sending the Duke to Pontoise, relations with the country which harboured her had become uneasy since the conclusion of the civil wars in France. She had been deeply disturbed when 'mock ambassadors', as Elizabeth of Bohemia styled them, had first come over from the English Parliament; and when Louis sent an agent to London she felt that this was tantamount to a recognition of the rebel government—'the last death-blow which I never expected to receive from France,' she told Christine. Nothing since the death of the King her *seigneur* had affected her so much as this. The French had good reason to seek an agreement with the unlawful but established government, for an alliance could only bring trading advantages as well as added strength in the struggle with Spain. All the same, Henrietta Maria found it hard to accept such a surrender to expediency. 'These reasons of state are terrible,' she wrote.

It had been feared that to pacify *cet abominable Cromwell* the French would insist that James left the country, but even though a treaty was concluded with the Protectorate in 1655 he was allowed to continue his promising military career. Charles offered his services to the Dutch who were at war with England largely as a result of conflicting mercantile interests, but his overtures were repulsed—the Dutch had no desire to become involved in a deeper dispute with the English republicans. He was forced to stay at Cologne awaiting his opportunity. Cromwell was facing up to discontent in the army, criticism in Parliament, and radicalism among the Levellers. There was talk of a royalist rising, but the

King's supporters found it hard to agree, the more influential members of the Sealed Knot, the Royalist underground movement, counselling caution and the more reckless action group advising the King to strike at once. Charles vacillated, failing to give his support fully to one side or the other, and when the uprising took place in March 1655 it proved to be totally ineffective.

In February 1656 Mary extracted from the King a promise that she could visit her mother in Paris as a reward for lending him money to send an agent to Spain. The widowed Princess was met by her younger brother between Péronne and Cambrai, and later the whole French Court came out of Paris to greet her, accompanying her to the Palais Royal where she was reunited with her mother. It was twelve years since they had last seen each other in Holland and then Mary had still been a child; now she had become a beautiful woman with all the Stuart good looks—the luxuriant hair and lustrous eyes characteristic of her family. Her visit provided a welcome excuse for the outbreak of festivities, and at a ball given by the King's younger brother Philippe, Louis himself opened the proceedings with Minette. Summer came on and Mary showed no sign of returning to her humdrum existence in Holland. Mademoiselle, who had been in exile in the country ever since her tactless intervention in the wars of the Fronde, met the Queen Mother and her elder daughter at Chilly, where she showed them the great rooms, cabinets and gallery of that magnificent château. It made a pleasant interlude in a boring existence which was punctuated only by endless quarrels with her father. The Queen Mother had persuaded her daughter to wear black for the occasion, but Mary had brightened up the outfit with a pearl necklace, bracelets and rings studded with large diamonds and some pendant ear-rings—'the most beautiful in the world' in Mademoiselle's opinion. Henrietta Maria felt bound to apologize for her daughter's magnificence. 'She has jewels and money and is not afraid to spend it,' she told Anne-Marie. 'I tell her that she ought to be *ménagère*; after all, I once had as much as she has and even more, and she can see the state I am in.' Inevitably, Charles's name was mentioned and Mary remarked that her brother had often talked of his cousin with much *amitié*. The Queen Mother could not resist saying that if only Mademoiselle had married the King she would not be slighted by all her French relations as she was now.

In September James was called away from Paris by the King who was in Brussels, planning to join the Spaniards in their campaign against France. James left unwillingly. In the French army he had always felt happy and fulfilled; in addition, during the summer months he had come to know Anne Hyde, the daughter of Charles's chief adviser and one of Mary's ladies-in-waiting. He naturally viewed with repugnance the thought of joining the Spaniards in their campaign against Turenne, and the French were reluctant to let him go, knowing that he would take with him some of the well-trained Irish and English troops under his command. Although James had little love for the country he was now obliged to fight for, he was a professional soldier at heart and he lent to his new masters the skill he had learnt from their enemies.

In the autumn Mary reluctantly went back to The Hague. Once again Henrietta Maria was left alone with Minette in the large rooms at the Palais Royal. It was a very severe winter in Paris, but when the spring came she began to go house-hunting, searching for a place of retreat not too far from Paris. Mazarin had been persuaded to approach the Protectorate for some help towards the Queen Mother's expenses, but he received the chilling reply that as the Queen had never been crowned she could not expect any assistance. It was her kindly sister-in-law Anne who saw to it that her pension was increased so that she could afford to buy a small château in the peaceful village of Colombes, a few miles out of the capital. She furnished the house simply, in exquisite taste, and she was able to find there the peace she needed so badly after the years of stress. All the same, her health deteriorated and she paid several visits to Bourbon to take the waters. She played little part now in affairs, although she still hoped to make a good marriage for Minette, if possible with her nephew Louis, although the young King took little interest in his waif-like cousin and in general found girls distinctly boring.

In the summer of 1658 there was a half-hearted rising in England which led to the execution of several Royalists. Their leader, John Mordaunt, had escaped conviction when one of the judges who could have given the casting vote left the room feeling ill—as a result, in the opinion of Mordaunt's pious wife, of the prayers she had been offering up unceasingly on his behalf. The death of Cromwell in September brought less promise of a reversal in their fortunes than the Royalists might have expected. All the French Court visited the Queen Mother to congratulate her on the demise of the monster, and Mazarin referred to the late Lord Protector as *cette vipère*. Henrietta herself felt strangely unmoved by the news. 'In truth, I thought you would hear with joy of the death of that wretch,' she told Madame de Motteville; 'yet, whether it be because my heart is so wrapped up in melancholy as to be incapable of receiving any, or that I do not as yet perceive any good advantages likely to accrue to us from it, I will confess to you, that I have not felt myself any very great rejoicing, my greatest being to witness that of my friends.' Her pessimism was justified, for Cromwell's son Richard took over as smoothly as any legitimate King, and Hyde confessed that Charles's position had never seemed more hopeless.

The battle of the Dunes in June 1658 gave the French an undeniable advantage over the Spanish who now hastened to bring to an end their long and debilitating conflict. The Queen Mother's two sons had acquitted themselves well; wherever James went he heard cries of *viva el duque de Yorke*, and he himself reported that Henry had behaved 'as bravely as any of his ancestors had ever done'. Charles, hoping that some advantage might be gained through the reconciliation of the two warring powers, travelled incognito to Fuenterabia in the Pyrenees where the negotiations were taking place. His mother started to work for him again, writing the letters which he himself found it so hard to compose, and she began rallying the Royalists on the Continent, including her old friend Newcastle, who had spent his time in exile establishing a riding school at Antwerp and compiling a book on the subject of dressage. Not that Henrietta Maria felt hopeful about the possibility of re-establishing her son on the English throne. She was beginning to feel that the day she had longed for, when her son would return in triumph to London, was one that she would never live to see. She had been disappointed, too, in her hope that Minette might one day become Queen of France, for the peace negotiations at Fuenterrabia had brought the prospect of a Spanish match for Louis. Mazarin gave Charles no help; now it seemed that he would be forced, for lack of money, to sit by while one power group or another took over in the confusion that had resulted from Richard Cromwell's inability to control the disparate elements once held together by his father's strong personality.

Badly slighted at Fuenterrabia, Charles travelled back through France, calling in on his mother at Colombes on his way. As he entered the house he embraced one of the ladies-in-waiting, mistaking her for the sister he had not seen for six years. For a few days, in the peace of the secluded château, mother and son were able to go over all that had passed and discuss their plans for the future. Charles had brought with him nobody except a personal servant, and without the advisers who so much resented the Queen's influence they were able to talk frankly and without constraint. Not that there was much to give them hope in those discussions, and the pleasant interlude came to an end after a few days when a message was received from Mazarin insisting that Charles must leave France immediately.

The Christmas of 1659 was perhaps the darkest that the unhappy Queen had ever spent. The future stretched ahead in a prospect of endless penury and humiliation. She had even become estranged from Christine, having taken offence when there was talk of a possible match between Louis and one of the Savoy daughters. She was on bad terms too with Elizabeth of Bohemia, whose daughter Louise had turned Catholic, choosing tactlessly to take up residence at Chaillot.

In England, Richard Cromwell was proving himself unequal to the task of governing the country which had dispensed with its King. His father had bequeathed him a fine army but had failed to formulate a constitutional basis for his dynasty. After the first euphoria when idealists of the calibre of the poet Milton had exulted as they saw England cast 'far from her the rags of her whole vices', many people had begun to long for the old disciplines. Others found that poverty can be as painful in a republic as it is in a monarchy—perhaps even more so. In the early days of 1660, as the country was once again threatened with chaos and bloodshed, the people of England began to see the King as the only possible unifying force. 'At last the good God has looked on us in his goodness,' Henrietta Maria wrote '. . . having changed the hearts of a people in an instant, who from the greatest hate have turned to the greatest possible friendship and submission.' To Elizabeth of Bohemia the events of the new year seemed almost unbelievable. 'I confess it is a great miracle to see so sudden a change,' she wrote.

In the dark days at the end of the year it would have been hard for the Queen Mother to imagine that by June 4, 1660 she would be writing to her sister, with whom she had become reconciled, 'At last my son has departed, and I believe that yesterday he set foot in England.' The Almighty had brought about without bloodshed the resolution which her husband had always expected. Peace and justice returned to the land as if on a cloud, resolving the conflict and banishing rebellion as neatly and as splendidly as the final scene of a Davenant masque. The hand of God, the Queen Mother told her son, was 'perceptibly traced therein', but she added, with a touch of her usual humanity, 'I will finish my sermon for fear of wearying you.'

Henrietta Maria felt some anxiety on the day Charles set sail from Schevelingen, that treacherous shore where she herself had once so nearly foundered. But when the express came bringing news of the King's landing in England, her last fears vanished. Charles was met on the shore at Dover by General Monck who had marched down from Scotland at the new year, giving confidence to those who felt that in monarchy lay the only answer to anarchy. As the General knelt in the sand, the King admitted him into the Order of the Garter—that select band which had symbolized for Charles I all that was noble and chivalrous. As the young King entered London a week later the people turned out to give him a tumultuous welcome. 'I stood in the Strand and beheld it and blessed God,' wrote John Evelyn.

Chapter 20

THE PEACEFUL MOTHER

IN PARIS there was great rejoicing at the restoration of the English crown. Henrietta Maria told her sister that she hardly had a 'poor minute' to herself on account of all the congratulatory visits she received and the business she had to attend to. 'If you are torn to pieces in England with kindness I have my share of it also in France,' she told Charles. 'I am going this instant to Chaillot to hear the Te Deum sung, and from thence to Paris, to have bonfires lighted.' Soon her correspondence was almost as voluminous as it had been in the old days, and she was growing importunate again, which worried her. 'My conscience is troubled about writing to you so often, but at this beginning, one must often be troublesome in writing,' she explained to Charles; 'so many people come to beg me to recommend them to you, whom I cannot refuse, being old servants, and that is the cause of it.' Crowds of Royalists, threadbare, impoverished, ageing, now arrived at Colombes, begging her to intercede with the King. She found it hard to refuse them, knowing what they had suffered as a result of their fidelity in the family cause, especially as many of them looked old and tired, like the Earl of Bristol, whom Elizabeth of Bohemia found 'much changed, his face ... like a withered apple'. The Queen Mother herself could now look forward to receiving her jointure once again, duly voted by Parliament, but, she wrote to Charles, 'as to what concerns my own affairs ... I will say nothing of them'.

August saw the arrival in Paris of the French King's bride, Maria Theresa of Spain. The state entry, Henrietta Maria told her son, was very fine, although somewhat spoiled by quarrels about precedence. Mademoiselle in particular made so much trouble when Minette was allowed to precede her that 'at length the Queen was very angry with her, and told her nobody but a mad woman would act as she did'. For years Mademoiselle had been in a position to treat the Queen of England and her daughter with condescension. The restoration to his throne of the man she had once loftily spurned, the marriage of her nephew with 'a bastard of Spain'—all this had been enough to disconcert her. Worse was to come, for now that Minette's brother had regained his throne, definite

offers were made for a match that would make the English Princess
Madame, while Gaston's daughter remained a spinsterly Mademoiselle.
Now Minette's good Catholic education with the nuns at Chaillot was
bearing fruit, and Father Cyprien was constrained to publish his *Exercices
d'une Âme Royale* in three volumes—a record of the instruction he had
given the royal child, to prove how well grounded she was in the Catholic
faith. Both Minette and her mother were delighted at the prospect of a
match with the King's younger brother, Philippe, who became Duc
d'Orléans on the death of Gaston. He was handsome enough in an
effeminate way, but he showed a disconcerting tendency, much encouraged at Court, to enjoy dressing up in women's clothes. Nobody
wished him to grow up in a war-like frame of mind and so be a continual
menace to his brother, as Gaston had been.

The Queen Mother found in her daughter's forthcoming marriage an
excellent excuse for going to England so that she could obtain her son's
consent. She already had two other good reasons for making a descent on
that kingdom. Not without a sense of shock, she had heard that Anne
Hyde was with child by the Duke of York who had firmly announced that
he would honour the promise of marriage he had made to lure her into
his bed. She also wished to do some match-making on Charles's behalf,
for, as she put it to Christine, 'I think that until he has married his
kingdom, he will scarcely think of marriage himself'. On October 28 she
told her sister that she planned to leave for England the next day 'in
order to marry off the King my son, and to try and unmarry the other'.
With Minette she took the quickest route from Calais but even so the
crossing lasted two days as the sea was so calm that it looked like glass.
The Duke of York, who had assumed his command as Lord High
Admiral, brought the whole fleet to meet them. Father Cyprien was
impressed by the innumerable masts which made the whole assemblage
look like a large wood. When the guns began to thunder, 'each ship firing
in its turn and order, one after another, they kept up a noise marvellously
loud and delightful', as the reverend Father put it.

The Queen and her daughter spent their first night in the castle at
Dover. James had laid on a fine feast and was thoughtful enough to
provide sturgeon as he had heard that the Capuchins were fasting. Later
the King arrived to greet his mother, and his declaration that he would
grant religious toleration in the kingdom was put to the test when he
dined with her for the first time. His chaplain having said grace in the
Anglican manner, Father Cyprien unashamedly made the sign of the
cross, saying as he did so, *benedic Domine nos, et haec tua dona quae de tua
largitate summus sumpturi, per Christum Dominum nostrum.* This, Father
Cyprien rather naïvely noted, caused some astonishment among the
Puritans, Independents and Quakers 'of whom the town of Dover is full'.

Their astonishment was even greater when he said Mass the following day in a large room with all the doors open, watched by a curious gathering. In his optimism he believed that many admired the devotion of the Catholics, although others, he had to admit, 'were inflamed with rage from a blind and highly criminal aversion which they bear to the Romish church'.

In view of such proceedings it was perhaps hardly surprising that Henrietta received an unenthusiastic reception when she arrived in London. Pepys counted only three bonfires, 'whereby' he wrote in his diary, 'I guess that (as I believed before) her coming doth please very few'. All the same the river was crowded with craft as she made her way to the Whitehall stairs, and Pepys, who hired a sculler for sixpence, found the water so crowded that he could not catch so much as a glimpse of her. Somerset House, dilapidated now and denuded of furniture, was not at present in a fit state to accommodate a Queen, and apartments had been made ready for her at Whitehall. A large crowd of courtiers was waiting to greet her and there were still some familiar faces.

The moment had come which the Queen Mother had lived for and at one time had given up hopes of seeing, when she would be reunited with all her family in London. But, as Father Cyprien put it, 'these earthly joys are generally mingled with bitterness', and it seemed, the Queen told Christine, that God did not wish her happiness to be whole and entire. James's unsuitable marriage hung like a cloud over the family reunion, and more distressing still was the sad fact that the Queen Mother would never have a chance now to be reconciled with her youngest son. Although Henry had written to her in the spring of 1660 expressing a wish to visit Paris, she had suspected that he would never come. 'I am afraid' she wrote, 'that in order to avenge yourself because I would not let you come when you wanted to, you may go back to England without seeing me—if you do I will never forgive you.' In June she expressed the fear that since his brother's restoration he had become such a *grand seigneur* that he would despise poor people like herself; all the same she assured him that however weighed down she was herself with tiresome visits, she would never forget him. In September he fell ill with smallpox; in Burnet's opinion all the 'mirth and entertainment' to which he was unaccustomed, had heated his blood and made him less able to withstand the disease. Mary, who had come over from The Hague, had found her pleasure at returning to the country she had left as a child quite spoilt by her annoyance at the behaviour of her maid-of-honour, and by the death of the handsome and high-spirited youth who had always been her favourite.

It was an ordeal for Henrietta Maria to return to the palace where she had spent so many happy years and where many of the walls were bare, the Van Dycks sold for a few pounds and the Giulio Romanos for a little more—all to help Cromwell solve his financial problems. Realizing that she was now so close to the exact spot where her husband had met his death, she broke down and wept. Within a few days, however, she had recovered enough to take part in the ceremonies which had been arranged for her. On November 19 Monck entertained the royal family with a dinner followed by a play at the Cockpit. They travelled in a silver coach preceded by a bodyguard of five hundred men, and Minette provoked much admiration as she was seen at the window, her head encircled with a crown of golden roses. The King caused some offence to the English musicians at the entertainment by inviting the 'French musique to play', but it had to be admitted that the imported variety was superior; it was not so long before that all public performances in England had been frowned upon and the tradition had only been kept alive by private people playing instruments at home for their own enjoyment.

When the Queen Mother dined in public with her son, Pepys saw to it that his wife secured a good place behind her chair. He himself described the Queen as 'a very little plain old woman'. Even Minette did not quite come up to expectation; Pepys disapproved of her hair which was 'frized short up to her ears', and altogether he thought that his own wife, standing near with two or three black patches on her face, was handsomer than either of the royal ladies. Others were more impressed with Minette, and crowds of people flocked to the palace to see her. It was easier to forgive somebody for being a Catholic when they were young and beautiful, and the good impression she had made was increased when she told Parliament in a message of thanks for the money she had been granted, that she possessed a truly English heart. For the first time in her life she was able to enjoy the sensation of having plenty of money, which the Duke of Buckingham, who fell in love with her, was very ready to help her spend at the gaming-table.

The Queen Mother's attitude to her son's 'base marriage' was at first so uncompromising that it seemed as if she might cut short her visit and go home in disgust. Elizabeth, however, was sceptical when she heard that her sister-in-law intended to be back in France by the new year, and on November 27 Pepys wrote that the departure had been postponed— 'which doth like me well'. The Queen Mother took Minette to Tunbridge Wells, and told Mazarin in December that she would not leave England until she had finished some business relating to her Household. The Cardinal was anxious that she should make her peace with Hyde who had become the most powerful figure in the new government. Mazarin had been responsible for the Dowager's upkeep for long enough already and he failed to see the wisdom of alienating the man who might relieve him of a long-standing and troublesome financial burden. It was hardly

complete the marriage settlement, and a special dispensation was sought from the Pope since the couple were so closely related. This arrived on March 9, the day of Mazarin's death. The marriage was celebrated in the Queen's Chapel at the Palais Royal, privately as it was the season of Lent, and the Princess was also still in mourning for her brother and sister. Monsieur then removed the bride to his apartments at the Tuileries. The parting between mother and daughter was touching; Father Cyprien reported that it 'made some weep, melted the hearts of others and pained all'. The Princess begged Father Cyprien not to abandon her, and this gave him an excuse to visit the young wife frequently, pointing out to her on every possible occasion the necessity for humility and constant prayer.

The Queen Mother went back to Colombes, to the quiet house and Minette's empty room. Louis and all his court returned to Fontainebleau and soon the Duc and Duchesse d'Orléans followed, joining in the open-air fêtes, the summer excursions, the bathing parties. The King's ash-blonde wife, quiet, virtuous and at the best of times a little cold, was expecting a child and could not join in the festivity, but Minette suffered from no restrictions. Away from the watchful eye of her mother for the first time, reacting against her sad childhood and no longer called on to play the part of the poor relation, she began to blossom; her eyes sparkled, the fresh air touched up her flawless complexion and her lively grace of movement made up for the fact that she was rather thin and that her spine, like her mother's, was a little crooked. Louis forgot altogether that once he had remonstrated when Philippe had told him he would marry Minette; he had inquired then whether his brother really wished to wed the bones of the Holy Innocents. As a married woman she had all the attraction of the unattainable, and her mischievous animation compared favourably with the dull propriety of his Spanish wife. The King put her in charge of all the outdoor entertainments; they danced together, and took part in a ballet. The weather was very hot and they went down to the river every day, returning on horseback with crowds of ladies all in magnificent dresses, the horses decorated with a mass of plumes.

When Minette went to visit her mother at Colombes, Father Cyprien gave her a quiet talking-to, reminding her of all that he had taught her over the years. But after three days she returned to Fontainebleau, the King coming part of the way to meet her. At first Minette's success in high society afforded her mother nothing but pleasure, but she became anxious after some ladies who had come from Fontainebleau dropped a few hints. 'If you have much noise where you are, I have here much silence,' she wrote to Madame de Motteville who was at Court. 'You have with you another little edition of myself, who is, I assure you, very much your friend. Continue to be hers. I have said enough.' But the affair had gone too far even for an old family friend to be able to help. Queen Anne wrote complaining of Minette's behaviour, and Maria Theresa became understandably upset at her husband's infatuation, which was undesirable in view of the fact that she was carrying what everyone hoped would turn out to be the Dauphin. Monsieur, after at first condoning the relationship, had by now become extremely jealous. The Queen Mother, convinced that her daughter's amusements were foolish rather than immoral, went down to Fontainebleau in an attempt to smooth out the troubles, which were in any case much eased when Louis went away on a visit to Brittany. On his return he ignored Minette and began to look with a covetous eye at one of her maids-of-honour, Mademoiselle de la Vallière. In November his Queen, dutifully, and with some difficulty, presented him with an heir.

Minette was not so attractive now as she had been in the magic months of summer. She became pregnant and soon lost her youthful bloom. She was brought back to Paris on a litter, coughing incessantly and taking opium to help her sleep. This did not prevent her holding her Court every day at nine o'clock, when a number of witty friends made a point of going to see her. They included the Comte de Guiche who was said to be quite infatuated and who further aroused the jealousy of Monsieur. The fact that her child, when it arrived, turned out to be a girl, was not at all helpful. Monsieur was patently disappointed, and it was rumoured that when Madame was told the sex of the child she had laboured to produce, she suggested to her attendants that they should throw it into the Seine.

The Queen Mother did what she could to reconcile the young couple. She had always been on affectionate terms with her two nephews and continued to find her son-in-law congenial in spite of his peculiarities. But she was naturally upset by her daughter's behaviour, and it was distressing that all her three surviving children had failed so signally to absorb the chaste ideals their parents had always advocated. Henrietta herself, in spite of all the rumours concerning her own association with the fat and gouty Jermyn, had never looked on another man besides her husband; she had often aroused admiration in the male sex, but never, it seems, lust. Now she felt out of sympathy with the fashionable younger set at the French Court with its scepticism and shameless indulgence of the passions, and accepted thankfully a pressing invitation from Charles to return to England. She was in any case eager to meet the Portuguese Princess, Catherine of Braganza, whom her son had recently, and prudently, married.

Leaving France late in July 1662 Henrietta Maria spent the rest of the summer happily, at peace with her son and on good terms with his wife. 'The Queen, my daughter-in-law, is the best creature in the world,' she told Christine. She herself was courted by crowds of people who had

found out that this mellow, witty and lively woman was not the formidable religious fanatic they had been led to expect. By now Somerset House
and Greenwich were again fit for habitation, and although many of the
treasures were still missing, she was able to restore something of the
splendour of the past. She was allowed a well-dressed and numerous train
of gentlemen, and a dozen liveried watermen to convey her when she
travelled by water. In December Henrietta Maria told Christine, 'We are
very occupied with *ballets*, and the King presses me to see them.' The
political situation, she assured her sister, seemed very stable, and apart
from a rumoured assassination attempt there were very few worries.
Although Thomas Hobbes had for a while tutored the King in exile,
Charles failed to assimilate the cynical philosophy that man, being
naturally bestial, must be curbed by an absolute power bearing the
sword. By nature he was a conciliator and did not share his brother's
inability to hide his feelings in the interests of expediency. In the declaration which he had signed at Breda in 1660 he had undertaken to ensure a
general amnesty and he was true to his word, extending his mercy even to
some of those who had signed his father's death warrant. His own personality and charm had done more than political theories to assist his
establishment on the throne. 'Though he be my nephew,' Elizabeth of
Bohemia had written just before he left for England, 'I must say this
truth of him that he is extreme civil.'

Charles's Court, though lascivious and extravagant, was less cut off
from the rest of the world than his father's, and he had a deeper understanding of the beliefs and fears which motivated his subjects' actions.
Following Monck's advice he had ordered that the remnants of the Rump
Parliament should readmit those excluded by Pride's Purge, prior to the
establishment of the free Parliament which Henrietta had so often urged
her husband to regard as the first priority. He was ready to enter into an
unformulated social contract with his people that recognized the rights of
the property-owner and laid less stress on the divine and absolute power
of the King.

There were many, like John Evelyn, who viewed with disapproval the
excesses tolerated at Court, but the inevitable reaction against the austerity
of the Interregnum was not limited to royal circles, and except among the
'Fanatiques' the feeling for luxury, indulgence and enjoyment was
general—at least among those who could afford it. The King flaunted his
mistresses, but kept his Catholic leanings to himself, knowing that his
subjects were better able to accept adultery than popery. His own love of
music was reflected in the large-scale creation of theatrical and church
orchestras—he himself employed twenty-two violinists. But it was not
only the King who appreciated the sound of music which was to be heard
everywhere, in churches and taverns and in the country on a Sunday.

The maypoles had been set up again as soon as the news came of the King's restoration. Many organs, destroyed in an excess of zeal, had been replaced, and the King set a fashion by introducing a full orchestra into his chapel; he always kept time with his foot and liked any tune provided it had a good rhythm.

The King's perennial fear of having to face all the discomforts of exile made him constantly careful to take note of his subjects' predilections and to avoid giving the kind of offence that might have tempted them to dispense with him. The Queen Mother told some young people who visited her at Somerset House that if she had once understood the English as she did now, she would never have been forced to leave the palace they were sitting in at that moment. During her first visit after the Restoration she had supported two meetings of influential Catholics when the question of toleration had been discussed, but she became increasingly aware that she was more likely to be allowed her chapel and her Capuchins if she kept well away from politics and made it clear that she had no intention of interfering in her son's affairs. She naturally disapproved of the Act of Uniformity which in theory granted little independence either to Presbyterians or Catholics, but she did not openly lend its opponents her support, realizing that unless the temperature were raised as a result of Catholics calling attention to themselves, there was a good chance that the Act would not be too strenuously implemented. Her ability to be pleasant and amusing, her determination to meddle in nothing, and her insistence to her priestly entourage that services in her beloved chapel must be carried on discreetly ensured that now she did not attract the attention which her less circumspect actions had provoked in the past.

The Queen Mother's aim was to live 'with the least offence imaginable to any sort of man'. She gave much of her income to charitable works and devoted some to improving and extending Somerset House—'The Peaceful Mother on mild Thames does build' as a contemporary verse expressed it. Inigo Jones, after being besieged at Basing House and carried away in a blanket without his clothes by the Parliamentarians, had worked for the Earl of Pembroke at Wilton before his death in 1652. The Queen Mother was able to implement a design that he had drawn for a gallery with rusticated arches on the ground floor, and she took a personal interest in the work, keeping a careful eye on the cost.

Henrietta Maria always retained a great affection for her husband's country and in France defended it strongly against all criticism. During her first summer in England she had been struck by the beauty of the Thames valley at Windsor, and in her enthusiasm she had seized a fork and joined in with the haymakers. Now, nearly forty years later, she had to admit that the rigours of the English winter and the dampness of the atmosphere were affecting her health. The mists that rose from the river and penetrated the rooms at Somerset House caused chronic catarrh. She made few complaints but the Capuchins and those who were close to her knew that she suffered. Her anxiety about her daughter-in-law was a contributory factor, for Catherine showed little sign of producing an heir even though every time she kept to her room with a sore throat there were hopeful rumours that she was with child. The Queen Mother had been impressed by Catherine's piety—though she had to admit that the monks she had brought with her were inclined to chant in a very peculiar manner—but religious fervour was a poor substitute for fertility. In 1663 Catherine fell ill, talking in her delirium of the children she had hoped to have—children who would resemble the husband she persisted in loving despite his infidelity and his open acceptance of the handsome child borne to him by Lucy Walter.

The summer of 1664 was very hot and by the autumn the plague had begun to take its toll. On Christmas Eve, libels appeared threatening 'the extirpation of popery' in the Queen Mother's chapel. The guards were doubled, and she stayed on in England obstinately, determined to prove wrong those who had said that she would never survive the weather or the political climate. Her son now told her that her chapel could remain open if she returned to France, and she felt that the time had come to escape the English winter. She advised the Capuchins left behind to give no cause for complaint to Protestants or Puritans, and to be if anything even more cautious than they had been during her stay. 'As God had endowed her with a shrewd and ready understanding and great fluency of speech,' wrote Father Cyprien, 'she made us immediately a fine address in which she declared that her journey, with the grace of God, would not last long.'

The outbreak of the plague which had precipitated the Queen Mother's departure soon turned into a major epidemic, and it became evident that she would not be able to return to England as soon as she had expected. She wrote to the Capuchins suggesting that her chapel should be closed, but they pleaded that their services were more than ever needed at this sad time. While they ministered to the sick, two of them dying of the disease, the Queen Mother spent a quiet summer at Colombes. The drier atmosphere and a course of the waters at Bourbon did little to improve her health. She was suffering from fainting fits, insomnia and other troubles, but Father Cyprien noted that she disguised the sharpness of her pain whenever possible, maintaining her serenity and 'a majestic cheerfulness'.

Henrietta Maria had returned to find her daughter unhappier than ever. Minette had recently given birth to a dead child; she did not look well— she no longer had that delicate natural colouring which Madame de Motteville had described as 'a mixture of rose and jasmine'. At the end of

1666 she lost her two-year-old son, but she tried to forget her own intense sorrow by watching at the bedside of the French Queen Mother who was dying painfully of cancer. Monsieur became as jealous as ever if she so much as looked at another man, while she was expected to accept without complaint the presence in her house of her husband's depraved male companions.

The course of the Queen Mother's life never ran smooth for long, and her sorrows were intensified when she learnt that France and England were at war. She warned Louis, who had always been fond of her, and treated her as his own mother, that she would not be able to pray for his cause, but it has to be admitted that without her prayers Louis achieved rather more than the son for whom she interceded so fervently with the Almighty. Louis at least allowed her the satisfaction of taking part in the peace negotiations; Henry Jermyn, now Earl of St Albans, somewhat elderly though he was for such a task, was despatched to England to open talks. For a few months she welcomed envoys and Ambassadors at Colombes while negotiations were in progress. Louis felt that the aunt he had always respected was an obvious intermediary, but in England, Hyde made objections to the intervention of his old enemy. The King was persuaded that as long as his mother remained in France his people would suspect him of partiality towards this Catholic country. He tried to persuade her to return to England, and when she refused his next move was to cut down her allowance. As always the money granted to him by Parliament had proved inadequate, and his own extravagance, and in particular his indulgent behaviour towards his mistresses, made it difficult for him to balance his budget. It was tantalizing for him to think that his mother, who had now been out of the country for over two years, was drawing sixty thousand pounds of good English money. He knew that she lived a simple life, that she was unlikely to use such a sum in a year, and was certainly donating the surplus to Catholic causes. It was Jermyn's task, once again, to break the unpleasant news, and Henrietta reacted vigorously; she had no intention of submitting to this 'unlooked for' blow. She had arranged her budget to meet her expenditure and any retrenchment would take her back to the old struggles of her penniless years. 'I feel assured that when you have reflected, you will change your opinion,' she told Charles.

The Queen Mother's health continued to deteriorate; she had to be carried into Chaillot from her coach in a chair and she was often in bed. During the summer of 1668 she had for company at Colombes her grand-daughter Anne, a fat and rather greedy child who had been sent over to be treated by a French eye specialist. Monsieur and Madame were always kind to her, and she stayed with them sometimes at Saint-Cloud. Minette had undergone two miscarriages in recent months, and she had to suffer the perpetual presence of the Chevalier de Lorraine, a good-looking young man who was the main object of her husband's affection—Philippe's second wife was to describe him as 'one of Lucifer's subjects'.

In April 1669, when the usual purging, bleeding and asses' milk had done nothing to improve the Queen Mother's recurrent fever and chronic insomnia, Monsieur and Madame ordered a team of leading Paris physicians to examine her. She gave them a careful description of her symptoms and they assured her that her illness although painful and distressing was not likely to prove fatal. They were unable to suggest any further remedies although three grains of opium at night to help her sleep were recommended. She had always been reluctant to take any sedatives, especially as Mayerne had once warned her against them, but the Paris physicians assured her that there was no danger involved.

After the consultation the Queen supped at her normal time and 'amused herself agreeably after her repast, laughing as if nothing ailed her'. As night came on she grew a little feverish, but at about ten o'clock she asked that her curtains should be drawn. In the quiet bedroom with its grey damask curtains and furnishings fringed with silver and gold and her only portrait of the King, her husband, on the wall, she found it impossible to sleep. She called her own physician and told him that after all she would take the grains prescribed by the eminent practitioners. She swallowed them down, mixed in the yolk of an egg. Soon after she had taken the draught, her doctor, who had stayed with her, noticed that she had fallen into an unusually deep slumber, and her pulse rate also changed. Becoming alarmed, he tried to rouse her and called for help, but all attempts to revive her failed, and between three and four in the morning she died.

A messenger was sent at once to Saint-Germain to break the news to the King and Queen, to Monsieur and Madame. They all broke down and wept when they heard what had happened. Charles and James, who were informed when they were on a hunting expedition in the New Forest, seemed less stricken. They had seen little of their mother over the last years, and she had become something of an embarrassment—both financial and otherwise.

Henrietta Maria had always hoped that she would die at Chaillot and it is certain that she would have liked time to prepare herself for death. She had given instructions that her heart should be buried at the convent she had founded, while her remains would be interred at Saint-Denis, as befitted a daughter of France. The pomp of her lying-in-state, which lasted for six weeks, contrasted strangely with the simplicity of the last years of her life. Her coffin lay under a black velvet dais, a golden crown resting on the pall, and the body was guarded night and day while her stricken almoner and chaplain celebrated Masses. The mausoleum was a magnificent affair, complete with marble pillars, sculptured fleurs de lys, and four white figures *au naturel* representing the four virtues. This 'pompous machine' was lined with silver cloth and illuminated by a fine crystal chandelier. The nave of the church was covered in black velvet up to the vaults of the roof.

On the day of the funeral, when the congregation was settled, Madame was fetched; four hundred mourners dressed in grey and carrying lighted torches formed up on either side of the nave. The procession, headed by heralds, went slowly up towards the altar where Madame knelt to kiss her mother's ring and La Grande Mademoiselle, Anne-Marie, did the same. When Henrietta Maria's coffin was laid to rest in the vault near her father, the herald ordered the Earl of St Albans to bring the Queen's flag and crown, and the captain of the guard broke his baton and threw it into the vault.

A few weeks later at Madame's request, Jacques Bossuet delivered a funeral oration at a service held in the chapel at Chaillot. All the fashionable world of Paris went down the tree-lined avenue, now decorated with black flags, which had become so familiar to Henrietta Maria. The chapel was packed to the doors, and the elderly priest, in a simple robe, delivered his celebrated address. In the flowery language of which he was a master, he went over the life of the great Queen—the daughter, wife, and mother of kings. He told his audience that few other lives had ever revealed such extremes of happiness and misery, of power and humiliation, of riches and poverty. It seemed that the purpose of her life had been to help God show the world the worthlessness of its pomp and grandeur.

There had been occasions, during the last summer of her life, when Henrietta had sat on the terrace at Chaillot with Madame de Motteville, talking about the past, going over the events of her life and tracing in them the imperceptible hand of God. She had told her friend that if only in childhood she had been taught a little history, she might have made fewer mistakes. Looking back over the years it was easy to understand how her own follies had made her in the eyes of many Englishmen the prime cause of the bitter struggle which had disrupted the peaceful English way of life. 'She was our particular enemy,' wrote Ludlow in his memoirs when he recorded her death. As a young bride she had been thoughtless and selfish, making little effort to understand the country where she was to make her home. She had believed, when troubles came, too much in the power of the sword, too little in the possibility of a settlement based on an assessment of the real issues involved. Only in later years had she realized the value of detachment, letting others complete the work—and then too late to cancel out completely the image of the domineering woman.

Tracing in the pattern of her life, as simply and sincerely as any Puritan, the providential hand of the Almighty, the Queen had seen how

man must learn through suffering. She had watched her husband fall out
with the propertied classes, and the struggle which had resulted had in
her eyes been a battle for power rather than the religious conflict others
believed it to be. The resolution had come in the re-establishment of the
monarchical principle, and the realization of the need for a central figure
whose dynastic right was irrefutable. The chaste happiness of her married
life and the fine legitimate children she had produced gave to the English
scene for a while the stability which was always missing in monarchies
where the King's bastards provided a focus for the disaffected and those
out of favour with the established regime.

The Queen Mother's life had spanned the best part of a century. She
had outlived all her family and most of her children; Gaston, Christine,
Anne of Austria and Elizabeth of Bohemia all were dead. A few of her
servants who had remained loyal to her for several decades still survived;
Henry Jermyn, Earl of St Albans, returned to England and lived on
into old age, always the faithful administrator, never the powerful adviser.
It was as well, perhaps, that Henrietta Maria herself did not survive to
witness the agonizing death of Minette, or the ousting of her son James
from the throne of England by her grandchildren William and Mary. The
doctors who prescribed a sleeping draught which, to use Mademoiselle's
words, was 'so successful that she never woke again', had, after all, done
her a good turn, releasing her from the continual pain which she had
borne without complaint, accelerating her departure from a material
world as evanescent as any of Inigo Jones's settings, and hastening her
reunion with the King, her *seigneur*.

Bibliography

An alphabetical list of sources referred to in the notes on page 265–279.

ALBION, GORDON: *Charles I and the Court of Rome* (1935).
ASHLEY, MAURICE: *Charles II, the Man and the Statesman* (1971).
AYLMER, G. E.: *The King's Servants : The Civil Service of Charles I* (1961).
BAILLON, LE COMTE DE: *Henriette-Marie de France* (1877).
BASCHET, ARMAND: *Le Roi chez la Reine* (1866).
BASSOMPIERRE, MARÉCHAL DE: *Mémoires* (1850).
BATTIFOL, LOUIS: *Le Louvre sous Henri IV et Louis XIII* (1930).
BAZIN, M.: *Histoire de France sous Louis XIII*, vol. II (1846).
BENTIVOGLIO, CARDINAL: *Letters* (1753).
BENTLEY, G. E.: *The Jacobean and Caroline Stage*, 7 vols. (1941–68).
BIB. NAT.: Bibliothèque Nationale, Fonds français.
BIRCH, THOMAS: *The Court and Times of Charles I*, 2 vols. (1849).
BODLEIAN: Bodleian Library, Carte Mss, Tanner Mss, Clarendon State Papers.
BONE, QUENTIN: *Henrietta Maria, Queen of the Cavaliers* (1973).
BOSSUET, J. B.: *Oraisons Funèbres du Cardinal* (1816).
BRIENNE, COMTE DE: *Mémoires* (1950).
BM: British Museum, Additional Mss, Harleian Mss.
BURNET, GILBERT: *The Memoirs of James and William, Dukes of Hamilton* (1677).
CABALA: *Cabala*, vol. V, (1691).
CHARLES I: *Charles I in 1646* (1856). See also under Petrie.
CHETTLE, G. H.: *The Queen's House Greenwich* (1937).
CLARENDON, EARL OF: *The History of the Rebellion*, 7 vols. (1849).
COUSIN, VICTOR: *Madame de Chevreuse* (1856).
CRUMP, LUCY: *Nursery Life 300 Years ago* (1929).
CSPD: *Calendar of State Papers Domestic.*
CSPV: *Calendar of State Papers Venetian.*
DAUNCY, JOHN: Henrietta Maria (1660).
DAVIES, GODFREY: *The Early Stuarts, 1603–1660* (1959).
DENBIGH, CECILIA COUNTESS OF: *Royalist Father and Roundhead Son* (1915).
D'EWES, SIR SYMONDS: *Autobiography*, ed. J. A. Halliwell (1845).
D'ISRAELI, J.: *Commentaries on the Life and Reign of Charles I*, 5 vols. (1828).
DODD, CHARLES: *Church History of England*, vol. V (1843).
EG: *Letters of Queen Henrietta Maria*, ed. Mary Anne Everett Green (1857).
ELIZABETH, QUEEN OF BOHEMIA: *Letters*, ed. L. M. Baker (1953).
ELLIS, HENRY: Original Letters, Series I and II, vols. iii and ii (1825, 1827).
ERLANGER, PHILIPPE: *La Vie Quotidienne sous Henri IV* (1958).
—*L'étrange Mort de Henri IV* (1957).

ESTOILE, PIERRE DE L': *Mémoires-Journaux*, vol. X (1889).

EVELYN, JOHN: *Diary and Correspondence*, ed. William Bray (1870).

FAYETTE, MADAME DE LA: *Memoirs of the Court of France*, ed. J. Shelmerdine (1888).

FERRERO: *Lettres de Henriette-Marie de France à sa Sœur Christine*, ed. H. Ferrero (1881).

FINETT, SIR JOHN: *Finetti Philoxenus* (1656).

FORSTER, JOHN: *Sir John Eliot*, 2 vols. (1865).

GARDINER, S. R.: *History of England*, 10 vols. (1884), (G. in notes).

GIBB, M. A.: *Buckingham* (1935).

HACKET, JOHN: *Scrinia Reserata*, 2 vols. (1693).

HARDWICKE, PHILIP EARL OF: *Miscellaneous State Papers*, 2 vols. (1778).

HASWELL, JOCK: *James II, Soldier and Sailor* (1971).

HÉROARD, JEAN: *Journal of 1601–28*, ed. E. Soulié and E. de Barthélémy, 2 vols. (1868).

HM: *The Life and Death of that Matchless Mirror of Magnanimity Henrietta Maria* (1669).

—*Memories of the Life and Death of Henrietta Maria* (1671).

—*Life and Death of Henrietta Maria de Bourbon* (1685).

—*See also* Baillon, Bone, Dauncey, EG, Ferrero, Oman, Strickland.

HEXTER, J. H.: *The Reign of King Pym* (1961).

HEYLYN, P.: *Cyprianus Anglicus or the Life of William Laud* (1671).

HIBBERT, CHRISTOPHER: *Charles I* (1968).

HILL, CHRISTOPHER: *Society and Puritanism in Pre-Revolutionary England* (1964).

—*The World turned Upside Down: Radical Ideas during the English Revolution* (1972).

HMC: Historical Manuscripts Commission, Report XI, i (Salvetti Manuscripts), Buccleugh, III, Cowper, II, Egmont, I, Hastings, II, Portland, I.

HOWELL, JAMES: *Familiar Letters*, 3 vols. (1903).

HUTCHINSON, LUCY: *Memoirs of the Life of Colonel Hutchinson* (1908).

HUXLEY, GERVAS: *Endymion Porter* (1959).

JAMES II: *Memoirs of his Campaigns as Duke of York*, trans. E. Lytton Sells (1962).

KENYON, J. P.: *The Stuarts: a Study in English Kingship* (1958).

LACROIX, P.: *Ballets et Mascarades de Cour* (1868).

LAUD, WILLIAM: *Works*, ed. W. Scott and J. Bliss, 7 vols. (1847–60).

LUDLOW, EDMUND: *Memoirs with a collection of original papers* (1771). *Memoirs* ed. C. H. Firth, 2 vols. (1894).

MAGNE, ÉMILE: *La Vie Quotidienne au Temps de Louis XIII* (1964).

MAGURN, R. S. ed.: *The Letters of Peter Paul Rubens* (1955).

MASQUES:

ADAMS, J. C.: *The Dramatic Records of Sir Henry Herbert* (1917).

BENTLEY, G. E.: *The Jacobean and Caroline Stage*, 7 vols. (1941–68).

CHAMBERS, EDMUND: *The Elizabethan Stage*, vol. I (1923).

NICOLL, ALLARDYCE: *Stuart Masques and the Renaissance Stage* (1937).

ORGEL, STEPHEN: *The Jonsonian Masque* (1965).

—*Inigo Jones: the Theatre of the Stuart Court* (with Roy Strong), (1973).

REYHER, P.: *Les Masques anglais* (1909).

SIMPSON, P., AND BELL, C. F.: 'Designs by Inigo Jones for Masques and Plays at Court', *Walpole Society*, XII (1923–4).

STEELE, MARY: *Plays and Masques at Court* (1926).

WELSFORD, ENID: *The Court Masque* (1927).

MAUROIS, ANDRÉ: *Trois Portraits de Femmes* (1967).

MERCURE, FRANÇOIS, LE: ed. J. and E. Richter (1611–44).

MILLAR, OLIVER: *The Age of Charles I*, catalogue of an exhibition at the Tate Gallery (1972).

—*The Tudor, Stuart and Earlier Georgian Pictures in the Collection of her Majesty the Queen* (1963), (*Queen's Catalogue* in notes).

—*The Whitehall Ceiling* (1958).

MONTPENSIER, MLLE DE: *Mémoires*, 4 vols. (1891).

MOTTEVILLE, MADAME DE: *Mémoires sur Anne d'Autriche et sa Cour*, 4 vols. (1886).

NEWCASTLE, MARGARET DUCHESS OF: *The Life of William Cavendish, Duke of Newcastle*, ed. C. H. Firth (1886).

OGLANDER, SIR JOHN: Memoirs, ed. W. H. Long (1888).

OMAN, CAROLA: *Henrietta Maria* (1936).

PALME, P.: *The Triumph of Peace* (1957).

PANZANI, GREGORIO: *Memoirs*, trans. Joseph Berrington (1813).

PATMORE, K. A.: *The Court of Louis XIII* (1909).

PEACHAM, HENRY: *The Compleat Gentleman* (1634).

PENNINGTON, D. H.: *Seventeenth Century Europe* (1970).

PEPYS, SAMUEL: *Diary*, ed. R. Latham and W. Matthews, 4 vols. (1970–4).

PERÉFIXE, H. DE: *Histoire du Roy Henri le Grand* (1679).

PERRENS, F. T.: *Les mariages espagnols sous le règne de Henri IV et la régence de Marie de Médicis 1602–15* (1869).

PERRINCHIEF, R.: *The Life and Death of King Charles I* (1693).

PETRIE, SIR CHARLES: *The Letters, Speeches and Proclamations of Charles I* (1968).

PHILIPS, AMBROSE: *The Life of John Williams* (1700).

PONTCHARTRAIN, PHILIPPE: *Mémoires de France sous la Régence de Marie de Médicis*, 2 vols. (1720).

POWELL, S. CHILTON: *Puritan Village* (1963).

PRINSTERER, GROEN VAN: *Archives ou Correspondance, inédite de la Maison d'Orange-Nassau* Series II, vols. iii and iv (1859).

PRUNIÈRES, HENRY: *Le Ballet de Cour en France* (1913).

PRYNNE, WILLIAM: *Histrio-Mastix* (1633).

PRO: Public Record Office, Phillips Transcripts, Rossetti Papers, Queen's Establishment Books etc.

RICHELIEU, CARDINAL: *Lettres, instructions diplomatiques et papiers d'état*, ed. M. L. Avenal, 8 vols. (1853–77).

—*Mémoires*, 10 vols. (1821).

ROUS, JOHN: *Diary*, ed. Mary Anne Everett Green (1856).

RUSHWORTH, JOHN: *Historical Collections*, vol. I (1659).

SECRET WRITING: *Secret Writing in the Public Records*, ed. Sheila R. Richards, (1974).

SPALDING, RUTH: *The Improbable Puritan; a Life of Bulstrode Whitelocke* (1975).

STONE, LAWRENCE: *The Crisis of the Aristocracy, 1558–1641* (1965).

STRAFFORD, EARL OF: *Letters and Despatches*, ed. William Knowler, 2 vols. (1739).

STRICKLAND, AGNES: *Lives of the Queens of England, Henrietta Maria*, vol. VIII (1845).

STRONG, ROY: *Charles I on Horseback* (1972).

—*The King's Arcadia* (with John Harris and Stephen Orgel), a catalogue of the Inigo Jones quatercentenary exhibition (1973).

—*Inigo Jones : the Theatre of the Stuart Court* (with Stephen Orgel) (1973).

SULLY, MAXIMILIEN DE BETHUNE: *Mémoires et sages economies d'estat* (1851).

SUMMERSON, JOHN: *Architecture in Britain 1530–1830* (1955).

TAPIÉ, VICTOR-L: *France in the Age of Louis XIII and Richelieu*, trans. D. McN. Lockie (1974).

TILLIÈRES, LE COMTE DE: *Mémoires*, ed. M. C. Hippeau (1863).

TOWNSHEND, DOROTHEA: *Life and Letters of Mr. Endymion Porter* (1897).

TREVOR-ROPER, H. R.: *Archbishop Laud* (1940).

V and A: Victoria and Albert Museum, Foster Mss.

WEDGWOOD, C. V.: *Strafford* (1935).

—*The Great Rebellion*, 2 vols. (1955, 1958). Wedgwood I and II in notes.

WHITELOCKE, BULSTRODE: *Memorials of the English Affairs*, 4 vols. (1853).

WILLEY, BASIL: *The Seventeenth Century Background* (1934).

WILLSON, D. H.: *James VI and I* (1956).

WITTKOWER, RUDOLF: *Palladio and English Palladianism* (1974).

WOTTON, SIR HENRY: *The Life and Death of George Villiers, Duke of Buckingham* (1642).

YONGE, WALTER: *Diary*, ed. George Roberts (1848).

ZAGORIN, PEREZ: *The Court and the Country* (1969).

$\mathcal{N}otes$

Chapter 1: DAUGHTER OF FRANCE

Page

1–2 *The birth of Henriette*: Louise, Bourgeois, 'Les Six Couches de la Reine' in *Archives Curieuses de l'Histoire de France*, 2nd series, vol. II, 215–17; Héroard, I, 413–14; L'Estoile, II, 63.

The Louvre and Fontainebleau: Henry Peacham, *The Compleat Gentleman*, (1643), 233; Magne, 50–2; Lord Russell of Liverpool, *Henry of Navarre*, (1969), 150.

2 *The font*: *Mercure françois*, I, 36.

3–5 *Charlotte de Montmorency*: Bassompierre, 56, 67–8.

6 *The Queen's coronation*: L'Estoile, X, 216.

7–8 *The assassination of Henri IV*: Bassompierre, 71; Erlanger, *L'étrange mort*, 265; Héroard, II, 430; L'Estoile, X, 218–19; Sully, 382–4.

9 *Coronation of Louis*: Bazin, I, 72–3; Patmore, 287–9.

10–12 *Life at Saint-Germain*: Bentivoglio, 70–1; Crump, 35, 239; Erlanger, *La Vie Quotidienne*, 197 et seq; Héroard, I, 54, 69; HM (1671), 3–4; Magne, 150.

The King's and Marie de Medici's instructions to Madame de Montglat: Bib. Nat. 13669, ff. 82–4, 3815, f. 67.

13 *Illness and death of the Duc d'Orléans*: *Mercure françois*, II, 184–5, 290.

Chapter 2: A ROYAL EDUCATION

15 *Madame dresses à l'éspagnole*: Bib. Nat. 3798, f.35.

Celebrations in Paris: Bazin, I, 154–5; Perrens, 19.

15–16 *The christening*: Héroard, III, 141.

Louis on tour, his return to Paris and his majority: Bazin, I, 154–6; Baschet 85; Bib. Nat. 3815. f. 17; Héroard, III, 147, 159; *Mercure françois* III, 397 et seq.

16–17 *The States-General*: Bazin, I, 101, 190–1; Tapié, 73.

17 *The copy-book*: Bib. Nat. 3815, f. 16.

18–19 *Le Triomphe de Minerve*: Lacroix, II, 63 et seq; *Mercure françois*, IV, 7–16; Perrens 521; Prunières, 114–15, 149 et seq, 177.

19 *Preparations for the wedding*: Bib. Nat. 9747, ff. 139–44.

19–20 *The journey south*: Baschet, 104–7; HM (1671), 4; Perrens, 537 et seq.

20–1 *The court at Bordeaux*: Baschet, 196–8; Héroard, II, 186; Perrens, 544–52.

21 *The return to Paris*: Baschet, 210–14; Héroard, II, 187, *Mercure françois*, V, 19, 63.

Page

Anne of Austria : Bib. Nat. 76, f. 145; Motteville, I, 8–9.

21   The Concini : Pontchartrain, II, 306–7.

The King's convulsive fit : Bassompierre, 121; Héroard, II, 19.

21–2   La Délivrance de Renaud : Prunières, 115–19, 138, 153–7, 176, 187.

22   The assassination of d'Ancre : Bentivoglio, 59; Magne, 39 et seq; Pont-chartrain, II, 312–13.

The Queen Regent exiled : Baillon, 10; Bentivoglio, 59 et seq.

Chapter 3: FAMILY CONFLICT

23   Letters from Elisabeth : Bib. Nat. 3815, ff. 11, 14, 19, 37.

24   De Soissons : Bib. Nat. 3815, f. 14; Richelieu, Mémoires, I, 188.

Savoy's comment : Perrens, 431.

24–5   Louis and the Queen : Héroard, II, 230.

25–6   Tancrède and Psyché : Baschet, 282; Lacroix, II, 161 et seq, 201 et seq; Prunières, 121–2, 155–7, 187, 210n, 229.

26   Marie de Medici writes from Blois : Bib. Nat. 3816.

The meeting at Tours : Bassompierre, 129; Bentivoglio, 157.

27   'I cannot be good' : EG, 4.

Condé and de Soissons : Bazin, I, 361–2.

28   'What is the Dauphin doing?' : Bentivoglio, 144.

Schomberg and Bassompierre : Bazin, I, 399.

Letters from Saint-Foy and Montauban : Bib. Nat. 3818, ff. 1, 4.

29   Queen Anne's miscarriage : Bassompierre, 193–4.

Chapter 4: MADAME HENRIETTE

30   Le Grand Ballet de la Reyne : Lacroix, II, 347–54.

Henriette's singing voice : HM (1671), 6.

30–1   Prince Charles's visit to Paris : Lord Herbert of Cherbury, Autobiography, 238–42; Petrie, 8–9; Wotton, 8.

31   'The braveliest received' : Townshend, 48.

31–2   Charles and Buckingham in Madrid : Dodd, V, 140–2; Hibbert, 57; Petrie, 11.

32   Henriette's remark : HM (1669), 15.

De la Rochefoucauld's warning : HM (1671), 7.

33   The 'maladie espagnole' : PRO Phillips, 31/4/4, f. 25.

The monkish ambassador : PRO Phillips, 31/4/5, ff. 2–5, 18, 19; Tillières, 52–6.

De Tillières' despatches : PRO Phillips 31/4/5, ff. 9–21.

34–5   Kensington in Paris : Cabala, V, 287–90; Hackett, I, 209; HM (1669), 21–3 (1671), 9–10; La Porte, 295; PRO Phillips, 31/4/5, f. 76.

35   De Soissons : Cabala, V, 288, 291; HM (1671), 8; Howell, I, 252.

The Spanish Ambassador : Cabala, V, 289.

36   The indissoluble knot : PRO Phillips, 31/4/5, f. 87.

The Valtelline : Bassompierre, 238–9; Bazin, II, 9.

36–7   James's légèreté and timidité : PRO Phillips, 31/4/1, ff. 13, 43.

37   Friction between Charles and his father : ibid, ff. 4–8, 11, 28–30, 67.

The obnoxious petition : Dodd, V, 132, 151; Rushworth, I, 146.

38   De Tillières too 'jesuited' : CSPD 1623–5, 292.

Page

D'*Effiat leaves for London* : PRO Phillips, 31/4/1, ff. 279, 292.

The Ambassadors confer daily with the Queen Mother : Denbigh, 28.

39–40   *Negotiations, autumn 1624* : Albion, 55–7; Brienne, 31; Hardwicke, I, 524–5, 538–41; Richelieu, *Mémoires*, II, 297–302.

40   '*The King of Spain would march*' : BM Harleian 1581, ff. 31–2.

41   *Letters to and from Pope Urban and Prince Charles* : Brienne, 31; Dodd, V, 158n; EG 4–7; PRO Phillips, 31/4/1, ff. 383–7.

Orders to bring over Madame : CSPD 1623–5, 369.

Chapter 5: THE LITTLE BRIDE

42   *The marriage articles and the écrit secret* : Dodd, V, Appendix LXII; Hardwicke, I, 540, 546 et seq; Howell, *Louis XIII*, 62 et seq.

French Ambassadors in London and Cambridge : CSPD 1623–5, 389, 400, 401, 411–12.

43   *The incident at Westminster Abbey* : Brienne, 32; Philips, 138–9.

Release of the Catholics : Brienne, 33; Dodd, V, Appendix LXII; CSPD 1623–5; 417.

44   *Mansfeld and his troops* : CSPD 1623–5, 401, 411, 417; PRO Phillips, 31/4/2, f. 404.

Buckingham—his party and the interview : Brienne, 32–3; CSPD 1623–5, 417.

Financial problems : ibid, 401, 411.

Carlisle's complaints : Hardwicke, I, 551–5.

45   *Henriette's letter to the Pope* : EG 9–10.

De Soissons ordered to meet Buckingham : PRO Phillips, 31/4/4, f. 346.

Illness and death of James I : CSPD 1623–5, 507; Hardwicke, I, 564; Howell, I, 245; PRO Phillips, 31/4/4, ff. 334, 344, 349, 358.

Louis advises restraint in sorrow : ibid, f. 375.

46–7   *The engagement ceremony* : Battifol, 218–25; Bib. Nat. 23600.

47–9   *The wedding* : ibid; CSPD 1623–5, 507; Howell, I, 256; HM (1671), 11.

49–50   *Buckingham in Paris* : Bassompierre, 240; Hardwicke, I, 571–2; HMC XI, i, 19; Magurn, 123; Palme, 79; Wotton, 96.

50   *The insupportable delay* : Petrie, 39.

Henriette's trousseau : Bib. Nat. n.a. 6, 23600, ff. 190 et seq.

50–2   *Her journey to the coast* : Bodleian, Tanner Mss 74.40 (Sir Toby Matthew); Brienne, 37; *Mercure François*, XI, 367–8; Motteville, I, 16; Richelieu, *Mémoires*, V, Appendix 275–83 (Marie de Medici's letter).

52   *Her arrival in England* : HM (1669), 28 (1671), 11 : Magurn, 112.

First meeting with Charles : Ellis, I, iii, 197–8; HM (1669), 28–30.

53   *The scene in the coach* : Richelieu, *Mémoires*, V, 142; Tillières, 90.

Canterbury : Ellis, I, iii, 198; Huxley, 127–8.

First impressions of Henrietta : Ellis, I, iii, 197–9; Howell, I, 271–2.

53–4   *Journey up the river and first night at Somerset House* : HM (1669), 30–2; (1671) 13; Richelieu, *Mémoires*, V, 142–3, Tillières, 92.

Chapter 6: QUEEN OF ENGLAND

55   *The first days in London* : Brienne, 39; CSPD 1625–6, 48; Ellis, I, iii, 201, 204; HMC XI, i, 22.

Page
56   *The opening of Parliament :* Brienne, 39; Ellis, I, iii, 202; Forster, I, 223, 226.
        The Queen's religious practices : Brienne, 38; Ellis, I, iii, 201, 206; HMC XI, i, 25.
57   *Charles and James :* Hutchinson, 67; Maurois, 99.
        The new order at Court : HMC XI, i, 6–7.
        Buckingham : Aylmer, 165, 258, 270, 345; Brienne, 39; Howell, I, 253; HMC XI, i, 3; Whitelocke, I, 1.
        The Queen's train : CSPD 1625–6, 48.
58   *The King's debts :* Forster, I, 421.
        His innate sweetness : ibid, 220.
        The Pool of Bethesda : ibid, 224.
58–9   *The plague :* Bentley, II, 655–6; Ellis, I, iii, 205, 208, 210.
59   *Incident at Hampton Court :* Tillières, 94.
        The Queen's bad temper : Ellis, I, iii, 206.
60   *The French Ambassadors leave :* Brienne, 41–2; HMC XI, i, 28.
        The adjournment : G.V., 377; Hackett, II, 13.
        '*The coals of contention*' : G.V., 339.
        Pardons for Jesuits : Philips, 163–4.
60–1   *Montague :* G.V. 400 et seq; Forster, I, 252–8, 338–9, 341, 385–6, 426.
61–3   *The session at Oxford :* ibid, 347–8, 373–80.
62   *Bérulle and Buckingham :* G.V., 422–3.
63   *The dissolution :* Howell, I, 272–3.
63–4   *The forced loan :* Rushworth, I, 192–3.
64–5   *Titchfield :* HMC XI, i, 38; Tillières, 100–3.
65   *The fleet :* Denbigh, 41; HMC XI, i, 15, 20, 32, 33, 36.
66   *The jewels :* CSPD 1625–6, 123, 125.
        Disarming of the recusants : Rushworth, I, 194–5.
        Blainville : HMC, XI, i, 27.
        Buckingham's visit to Holland : Denbigh, 48; HMC XI, i, 34.
67   *Marital differences :* Ludlow, III, 305–7; Petrie, 40.
        Williams dismissed : CSPD 1625–6, 249; Hackett, II, 18.
        Buckingham's projected visit to France : Cabala, V, 233.
68   *The plague :* John Taylor *Works* (1630), 61.
68–9   *The coronation :* Finett, 169; Laud, III, 181; Philips, II, 67.

Chapter 7: PETITE RÉPUBLIQUE PARTICULIÈRE

70   *Queen Henrietta Maria's men :* Bentley, I, 218–19.
        The argument at the opening of Parliament : Finett, 171–2; HMC Rutland, I, 476; Abbé M. Houssaye 'L'ambassade de M. de Blainville à la cour de Charles I^ier^', *Revue des questions historiques*, XXIII (1878), 176–204; Tillières, 118–19.
        The 'ill-faced Parliament' : CSPD 1625–6, 252.
70–1   *Cadiz :* Charles Dalton, *Sir Edward Cecil, Viscount Wimbledon* (1885), II, 83–241.
71   *The fleet returns :* CSPD 1625–6, 184.
        Finch's speech : Rushworth, I, 204.
72   *Quarrel and reconciliation :* CSPV XIX, 329, 392; Tillières, 122.

Page

The pastoral: CSPD 1625–6, 273; Jane, Lady Cornwallis, *Private Correspondence* (1842), 138; Strong and Orgel, I, 24–5, 383–8.

73   *Blainville and the troubles at Durham House:* Catholic Record Society, VI, Miscellanea, V, A, 'Relation of a brawl', 93–5.

74   *The threatened impeachment:* Aylmer, 126; Forster, I, 500–1, 514, 535, 553–6; Gibbs, 231 et seq; Whitelocke, 7–9.

75   *The storm on June 13:* Birch, I, 113–14; Forster, I, 577.

    'A Parliament, a Parliament': Birch, I, 130.

76   *The fast day:* Yonge, 94.

    'An argument of dangerous times': Birch, I, 124–6.

76–7   *The Queen's illness and troubles in the Household:* Tillières, 134–8; Richelieu, *Mémoires*, VI, 230–1.

77–8   *Carleton's instructions:* Ludlow, III, 305–9.

78   *The incident at Tyburn:* Birch, I, 121, 132; Petrie, 44.

    The Ambassadors: Finett, 182–4.

78–9   *The great scene:* Bib. Nat. 16139, f. 217; Birch, I, 134–8; Denbigh, 50; Tillières, 144–5; Howell, I, 277; HM (1671) 14–17; Petrie, 45; Richelieu *Mémoires*, VI, 233.

80   *'Une petite république':* Bib. Nat. 16139, f. 217.

    Henrietta's letter to her mother: Baillon, 350.

Chapter 8: THE GREAT DELINQUENT

81   *The defeat of the Danes:* Birch, I, 148.

81–2   *Bassompierre in England:* Bassompierre, 252–5; Bib. Nat. 3692, 16139, ff. 220–4; Birch, I, 151–2, 157, 162.

82   *The Lord Mayor's show:* HMC Buccleugh, III, 310.

82–3   *The Duke's entertainment:* Birch, I, 166, 169, 180; Yonge, 98.

84   *Bassompierre's departure:* Bassompierre, 257; CSPV 1626–8 32; Finett, 190–1.

    The Queen's luteplayer: Birch, I, 183, 186, 189, 190; CSPV XX, 97; HMC XI, i, 104, 107.

84–5   *The Queen's masque:* CSPD 1627–8, 88, 89; CSPV XX, 107; HMC XI, i, 103.

85   *The Duke's masque:* Birch, I, 226; CSPD 1627–8, 239; HMC XI, i, 118.

85–6   *The Duke's expedition:* Birch, I, 247; CSPD 1627–8, 222, 228–9.

86   *Henrietta Maria visits Wellingborough:* Birch, I, 244; CSPD 1627–8, 242, 266, 276, 283; CSPV XX, 297; Early Spencer Papers at Althorp, Box 3; HMC XI, i, 122; Oman, 55n.

86–7   *The Île de Rhé:* Birch, I, 256–9; CSPV XX, 497; HMC XI, i, 126, 130–2.

87   *The Queen offers condolences:* Baillon, 351; HMC XI, i, 124.

88   *The Buckingham christening:* Birch, I, 324.

    The new session: G.VII, 230–5; HMC XI, i, 141–2; Oglander, 37.

89   *The summer progress and the Queen's lack of funds:* CSPD 1627–8, 242, 266, 276, 283.

89–90   *Assassination of the Duke:* CSPV XXI, 260; Ellis, I, iii, 256; Oglander, 42–5; Wotton, 23–5.

Chapter 9: A New Order

Page

91   *Buckingham's funeral*: Birch, I, 399; CSPV XXI, 297, 337.
     Rochelle: Bib. Nat. 3816, ff. 16, 45; Birch, I, 424.
     Negotiations leading to peace of Susa: Birch, II, 13–14; CSPV XXI, 293–4, 310, 426; G.VII, 77–8; HMC, XI, i, 165.

92   *The Queen's pregnancy*: Birch, I, 417; CSPV XXI, 565, 593, 600.

93   *The lawless Puritan*: title of a pamphlet by Prynne, written as 'a confutation of an appendix concerning bowing at the name of Jesus'.

94   *Weston and the Parliament of 1629*: Birch, II, 11–12; Clarendon, I, 84–96; G.VII, 77–8; Rushworth, I, 655, 662.

95–6   *The Queen's premature delivery*: Baillon, 352–3; Birch, I, 355–6 (wrongly dated); II, 14; CSPV XXII, 68–70; EG 13–14; d'Ewes, II, 411–12.

97   *Relationship between the King and the Queen*: G.VII, 106–7; CSPV XXII, 136.

98   *The Queen pregnant again*: Bib. Nat. 3816, ff. 35, 40; CSPD 1629–31, 158; EG 14–16.

98–9   *Arrival of French and Spanish Ambassadors, and the Capuchins*: Birch, II, 35, 63–4, 65–6; CSPV XXII, 291, 298, 303, 308–9; Millar, *The Whitehall Ceiling*, 1; Rous, 49–50.

100   *The birth of Prince Charles*: Albion, 107; CSPD 1629–31, 268–9; CSPV XXII, 315, 344–5, 370, 388; EG, 16–17; Heylyn, 197–8; Rous 52–3.

102   *Orders to curb irregularities*: CSPD 1629–31, 478.

103   *The Queen's costume*: Strong *The King's Arcadia*, 168–9.

103–4   *Chlorydia*: see Bibliography, Masques; Ben Jonson, *Works*, ed. C. H. Herford and P. and E. Simpson, VII, 747 et seq; X, 681–96.

Chapter 10: The Triumph of Peace

105   '*A people rich and happy*': Magurn, 320.
     Drought and famine, 1630–1: CSPD 1629–31, 500; Powell, 40.

105–6   *Laud and Williams*: Hackett, II, 86; Philips, 204–6.

106   *De Jars and the theft of correspondence*: G.VII, 186–7.

107   *French influence*: EG, 17, 19; Strong *The King's Arcadia*, 152–3.
     The birth of Mary: Birch, II, 140; BM Harleian, 7000, f. 445.

108   *The quarrel between Jones and Jonson*: D. J. Gordon, 'Poet and Architect: the Intellectual Setting of the Quarrel between Ben Jonson and Inigo Jones', *Journal of the Warburg and Courtauld Institutes*, XII (1949), 153–78.
     Jones's method: Wittkower, 51–64; Ben Jonson, *Works*, ed. C. H. Herford and P. and E. Simpson, III, 78.

109–10   *Albion's Triumph and Tempe Restored* (1632): see Bibliography, Masques; Aurelian Townshend *Poems and Masks*, ed. E. K. Chambers (1912), 55–78, 91–4; CSPD 1631–3, 270.

110   *Proclamation for leaving London*: Birch, II, 192.

110–11   *Foundation stone laid in the Queen's chapel*: ibid, 176, 308–9; BM Harleian, 7000, f. 336; Ellis, II, iii, 271.

112   *Orders for regulating the Queen's court*: *A Collection of Ordinances and Regulations for the Government of the Royal Household*; CSPD 1631–3, 347.

Page

112-13 *The Shepherd's Paradise:* Birch, II, 176, 214, 216; CSPV XXIII, 63;
Ellis, II, iii, 270; Strong and Orgel, I, 63; II, 505 et seq;
Histrio-Mastix: BM Harleian 7000, f. 350, 464; CSPD 1631-3, 524;
Ellis, II, iii, 280-1; Heylyn, 250.

113 *The King's smallpox:* Birch, II, 202-3; BM Harleian Mss, 7000, f. 344;
Ellis, II, iii, 274; Whitelocke, I, 49.

113-14 *The Queen's letters intercepted:* CSPD, 1633-4, 3, 11, 16; G.VII, 217-19.
A 'mourning turtle': HMC Cowper, II, 10, 16.

114 *Laud becomes Archbishop:* Clarendon, I, 156-62; Heylyn, 250; Laud, III,
219; Philips, 170.
The birth of James: EG 22-3; Strafford, I, 141.

115 *'Never was there a private family':* HMC Cowper, II, 25.
The Book of Sports: Heylyn, 241; Laud, IV, 133; Powell, 68, 72;
A. F. Scott, *Every One a Witness* (1974), 59, 177.

116 *The soap monopoly:* Birch, II, 229-30; Strafford, I, 141.

116-17 *The Triumph of Peace (1634):* see Bibliography, Masques; *Dramatic
Works and Poems of James Shirley,* ed. A. Dyce (1833), vol. VI, 257-85;
Strafford, I, 207; Whitelocke, I, 53-61.

Chapter 11: THE TEMPLE OF LOVE

118-19 *Cœlum Britannicum (1634):* see Bibliography, Masques; *The Poems of
Thomas Carew,* ed. Rhodes Dunlap (1949), 151-85, 273-83; Strafford, I,
177, 207; Willa McClung Evans, *Henry Lawes, Musician and Friend of
Poets* (1941).

119 *'A great and insupportable charge':* G.VII, 352.

120 *The cunning Hydra:* Petrie, 95.
The French shipping challenge: CSPD 1634-5, 338.
The arrival of Pougny: CSPV XXIII, 247-9.

120-1 *The northern progress:* Bentley, I, 49-50; CSPD 1634-5, 26-7, 73-5, 149,
167, 213.

121 *Love's Welcome at Bolsover:* Ben Jonson, *Works,* ed. C. H. Herford and
P. and E. Simpson, II, 333-4, VII, 806-14, X, 709-10; Newcastle, 90-2.
Tutbury: Staffordshire RO, Q/SR T 1635, f. 23.

122 *Althorp:* Spencer Papers, Household Accounts, 1634; J. N. Simpkinson
The Washingtons (1860), appendix.

123 *Panzani:* Albion, 149; Panzani, 132-4, 157, 173.

124 *The Temple of Love (1635):* see Bibliography, Masques; CSPD 1634-5,
482, 510; CSPV XXIII, 334; Strafford, I, 360; William Davenant *Works*
I, 281-316.

125 *The wedding of Lady Mary Villiers:* Laud, III, 222; Millar, *The Age of
Charles I,* 71; Strafford, I, 359.
The Hamiltons: Birch, I, 417; Denbigh, 78, 139-41; HMC XI, i, 91.

126 *Lord Morley and Sir George Theobalds:* CSPD 1633-5, 455.
Jermyn and Eleanor Villiers: ibid, 50; Strafford, I, 175.
Quarrels in Spring Gardens: ibid, 261-2.
The Platonic ideal: Howell, II, 31.

126-7 *Histrio-Mastix:* 186-203, 293-4; BM Harleian Mss 7000, f. 350.

127 *The summer of 1635:* CSPV XXIII, 323, 334, 346, 399; Laud, III, 223;
Strafford, I, 423, 427.

Page
128   *Honest recreations :* Prynne, *Histrio-Mastix*, 965–6.
      Greenwich : PRO AO1 63/2427, E 351/3269; Summerson, 119–20.

Chapter 12: LEADERSHIP CRISIS

130   *The hot summer :* Strafford, I, 429.
131   *'The not continuing of the Parliament' :* Petrie, 96.
      Invasion scares, summer visits : CSPV XXIII, 404, 445; G.VII, 382.
131–2 *Leadership crisis :* Laud, VII, 174, 175, 203, 207, 209–10; Strafford, I, 463.
132   *Soap new and old :* Laud, VII, 140, 175, 206.
133   *Ludovick Carliel :* PRO 438/11, 14.
      The Elector Palatine : Laud, VII, 206; Strafford, I, 489–90.
      Florimène : see Bibliography, Masques; Adams, 41, 55; Orgel, 'Florimène and the Anti-Masques,' *Drama* IV (1972); CSPV XXIII 499.
      Birth of Elizabeth : HM (1671), 23; Laud, III, 225.
133–4 *The new pictures :* Panzani, 194–5, 251.
      Giulio Romano : William Shakespeare, *Winter's Tale*, V, ii. 110.
134–5 *Rubens ceiling :* Magurn, 402; Millar *The Whitehall Ceiling*, 5–23; Palme, 77–80, 230–62; Willson, 447.
135   *The King and the Palatine at Newmarket :* CSPV XXIII, 514–15.
135–6 *The appointment of Juxon :* Clarendon, I, 175–60; CSPV XXIII, 527, 531, 540; Laud, III, 215–16, 226; Strafford, I, 522; Trevor-Roper, 130–1; Whitelocke, 69.
136   *Hamilton's mission :* Albion, 156–8; Panzani, 233, 252.
      Visit to Bedlam : Birch, II, 244.
137   *The plague :* CSPV XXIII, 560, 568, 570.
      Spanish invasion, Leicester's mission : G.VIII, 161–3; Tapié, 352.
      Lady Carlisle : CSPD 1634–5, 108.
138   *Con arrives :* Albion, 159–61.
139–40 *The visit to Oxford (1636) :* Bentley, III, 134–41; V, 1189–95, 1259–64; VII, 103; Birch, II, 266; CSPD 1636–7, 113, 114; Laud, V, 148–56; VII, 278.
140   *Stained glass at Lambeth :* CSPD 1635, 57, 487.
      Laud and the Queen : Laud, VII, 248, 276.
      Richmond : CSPD 1634–5, 19.
141   *'Never any earthly thing' :* Aurelian Townshend, 'On Hearing her Majesty Sing', *Poems and Masques*, 13.
      'the fullest measure of felicity' : Clarendon, I, 130.

Chapter 13: THE OTHER RELIGION

142   *The madman :* Birch, II, 250; CSPV XXIV, 77.
      The plague : CSPD 1636–7, 105, 228; CSPV XXIV, 44–5, 53.
142–3 *The dedication of the Queen's chapel :* Birch, II, 311–14; Isaac Disraeli, *Commentaries on the Life and Reign of Charles I* (1851), I, 215–18; Summerson, 128–9; Wittkower, 70.
143   *Visit to the Capuchins :* CSPV XXIV, 120–1.
      The crucifix : ibid, 70.

Page
144 *Con and the Queen*: BM Add. Mss, 15389, ff. 196–7; EG 32.
'*Poor harmless religious men*': Wentworth Woodhouse Muniments, Strafford Letters, Sheffield Public Libraries, 40–3.
Montagu: Albion, 204; Strafford, I, 373, 505.
Birth of Anne: CSPV XXIV, 174, 188; Strafford, II, 57, 73.
Outbreak of the plague: CSPV XXIV, 135, 177; Strafford, II, 56, 75.
145 *The dwarf and the rosaries*: EG 31. A nurse was paid £25.00 quarterly for keeping the dwarfs—PRO 438/11, 14.
Cottington's kitchen: Strafford, II, 118.
'*Those beads*': Laud, VII, 210.
146 *Bastwick, Burton and Prynne*: Laud, II, 228; Strafford, II, 85; Trevor-Roper, 317.
The Lennox wedding: Denbigh, 71; Wedgwood, I, 178.
146–7 *Lady Newport's conversion*: CSPV XXIV, 319; Laud, III, 229, VII, 379–80; Strafford, II, 128.
148 *The temporary masquing house*: J. P. Feil 'Dramatic references from the Scudamore Papers', *Shakespeare Survey* XI (1956), 111.
The Sovereign of the Seas: Chettle, 33; CSPV XXIV, 282; Strafford, II, 118.
Britannia Triumphans (1638): see Bibliography, Masques; William Davenant, *Works*, II, 245–301.
149 *The Covenant*: G.VIII, 329–333.
The Queen's anxiety: CSPV XXIV, 395.
150 *The French Queen's pregnancy*: EG 23.
150–1 *The Hamiltons*: Rosalind Marshall *Duchess Anne* (1974), 15–16.
151 *Madame de Chevreuse*: CSPV XXIV, 404, 407–8.
Sir John Winter: Wedgwood, I, 52, 210.
152 *The Prince's household*: Strafford, II, 148, 154, 166.
The narrowing circle: CSPV XXIV, 459; Kenyon, 73; Stone, 502, 743.
Three portraits: Millar, *Queen's Catalogue*, 97.
Laud and Williams: Albion, 413; Laud, VII, 373, 421, 481, 511; Strafford, II, 154.
Samuel Ward: CSPD 1634–5, 417–18.
153 *Holland and Northumberland*: CSPD 1638–9, 506, 607, 622; Laud, VII, 441–2; Strafford, II, 168.
153–5 *The arrival of Marie de Medici*: CSPV XXIV, 471; Denbigh, 148 et seq. (contemporary description by Percy Church); Laud, III, 231; VII, 496; P. de la Serre, *Histoire de l'entrée de la reine mère dans la grande bretagne* (1639).
155 *Birth of the Dauphin*: Howell, II, 63.
156 *The keys to the coffer*: Laud, VII, 511.
The birth of Catherine: CSPV XXIV, 495, 497.
157 *The King in York*: CSPV XXIV, 525, 533.
157–8 *The Catholic collection*: Denbigh, 165–6; EG, 24–6; HM (1671), 24–5, 27–30; *A Copy of the Letter sent by the Queen's Majesty concerning the Collection of the Recusants' Money for the Scottish Warre, April 17, 1639*.

Chapter 14: A PERPETUAL PARLIAMENT

159 *The English army in Scotland*: Clarendon, I, 209–10.

Page
        The treaty : Burnet, 140–3; CSPV XXIV, 548, 550, 561.
160   *Death of Con :* PRO Rossetti, 31/9/18, f. 102.
        The 'long and troublesome entertainment' : CSPV XXIV, 571–2.
161   *The Spanish and Dutch fleets :* Whitelocke, 91.
161–2   *Sir Henry Vane :* Aylmer, 85, 354; Clarendon, I, 222.
162–4   *Salmacida Spolia :* see Bibliography, Masques; PRO Rossetti, 31/9/18,
        f. 76; C. V. Wedgwood, 'The Last Masque', *Truth and Opinion.*
164   *Ship Money :* Powell, 49 (Sudbury); Early Spencer Papers, II (Notting-
        ham).
165   *Rossetti's apprehension :* PRO Rossetti, 31/9/18, f. 76.
        Strafford and the Queen's coach : Wedgwood, *Strafford,* 235.
        The lily and the rose : Millar, *The Age of Charles I,* 56.
166   *Strafford at Lichfield :* Petrie, 105.
        The dissolution : Clarendon, I, 245–6.
        The Council meeting : Trevor-Roper, 286.
        Troubles in London and the message on the window pane : Albion, 339;
        Wedgwood, I, 349–50.
        'Cheap senseless libels' : Clarendon, I, 252.
167   *Birth of Henry, Duke of Gloucester :* HM (1671) 24; Laud, III, 236; PRO
        Rossetti, 31/9/18, ff. 281, 300.
        The Council Meeting : Hardwicke, II, 147–51.
        Newburn : Clarendon, I, 255.
168   *'Parlamento perpetuo' :* Albion, 340n.
        The red biretta : ibid, 327–8.
        King's return, the opening of Parliament : Clarendon, I, 296; Evelyn, 10.
169   *The 'terrible reformers' :* Clarendon, I, 296.
        The flight of Windebank : PRO Rossetti, 31/9/19, f. 219.
        The Queen warns Rossetti—his house raided : PRO Rossetti, 31/9/19,
        f. 235; Albion, 341.
169–70 *Negotiations for a marriage :* Prinsterer, II, iv, 353.
170   *The Queen writes to Rome for a loan :* CSPV XXV, 52.
        The Army Plot : HMC Egmont, I, 134; Motteville, I, 197–8.
        *A Message sent from the Queen's Majesty to the House of Commons by Mr
        Comptroller February 5 1641 :* HM (1671) 27–31.
171–2   *The trial of Strafford :* ibid, 32–3; Spalding, 74; Prinsterer, II, iii, 454,
        462; Wedgwood, *Strafford,* 292–330.
172–3   *Prince William and the wedding :* Prinsterer, II, ii, 434, 455–6, 462; PRO
        Rossetti, 31/9/20, f. 79.
173   *The rabble :* Hill, *The World turned Upside Down,* 33.
174–5   *The week-end before Strafford's death :* PRO Rossetti, 31/9/20, ff. 193–5.
175   *The execution :* Clarendon, I, 454; Heylyn, 451.

Chapter 15: THE UNTUNED LUTE

176   *'Take but degree away' :* Troilus and Cressida, I, iii, 109.
        Spirit of division : Clarendon, I, 355; Spalding, 78.
177   *Pembroke and Exeter :* Clarendon, I, 460–1.
        The letter to Montagu : A Copy of a Letter of Father Philip . . . lamentably
        complaining of the Times, 1641.

Page

The Queen to visit Holdenby or Spa : CSPV, XXV, 184, 186, 189; EG, 39–41; Prinsterer, II, iii, 483–7.

178 'Win the Parliament' : Philips, 271–2; EG, 44–5; Evelyn, 752.

179 The Prince, Hertford and Newcastle : Clarendon, II, 243–5; CSPV XXV, 241; EG, 289; Newcastle, 120; Motteville, I, 203.

180 The Incident : CSPV XXV, 231–2; Hardwicke, II, 299–303.
The King's return : EG 46; Evelyn, 28, 793.

181 Delegation of Mayor and Aldermen : CSPV XXV, 261.

182 'I am constant . . . for the Church' : Petrie, 364.
'Your sacred Majesty : Wedgwood, Strafford, 327.

183 The five Members : CSPV XXV, 276–80; HMC Montagu, 139–41; Ludlow, I, 25–6; Zagorin, 276 et seq.
The French Ambassador intervenes : CSPV XXV, 283.

184 The move to Hampton Court : Prinsterer, II, iii, 502.
Digby's letter : CSPV XXV, 297; EG 47–8.

185 Plans for departure : CSPV XXV, 296; CSPD 1641–3, 282–4.

185–6 The parting : Birch, II, 349; CSPV XXVI, 1, 5, 26, 31, 45; HM (1671), 28–32; Motteville, I, 208.

Chapter 16: RESOLUTION

187 The ship founders : CSPD 1641–3, 293; CSPV XXVI, 13.
Sophia's impression of the Queen : Electress of Hanover, Memoirs (1888), 13.

188 The first weeks in Holland : CSPV XXVI, 21; Ellis, II, iii, 293–5.

188–9 Letters to the King : EG 52–62; 64–5 (jewels); 70, 79 (Hull).

189 'To plainness honour's bound' : King Lear, I, i, 150–1.
Breda and Amsterdam : CSPV XXVI, 28, 59, 64; News from Holland of the Entertainment of the Queen's Most Excellent Majesty, 1642.

190–1 The Prince of Orange, Digby etc : CSPV XXVI, 32, 94; Prinsterer, II, iv, 37.

191 Elizabeth of Bohemia's views : CSPD 1641–3, 329–30; Elizabeth, 152–3.
Prince Rupert : CSPV XXVI, 41; EG, 86, 97–8.

192 'Blood is a crying sin' : A Worthy Speech spoken in the House of Commons by Sir Benjamin Rudyerd July 9, 1642.
Huygens and Heenvliet : Prinsterer, II, iv, 38, 46, 60.
Strickland's visit : CSPV XXVI, 145, 147; EG, 103.

193 Mary's lack of co-operation : CSPV XXVI, 159, 169.
'Her sympathy with me' : HM (Dauncey), 72.
Rumours of battles, Edgehill : EG, 128, 147, 153.

194 Arms and ammunition : CSPD 1641–3, 390; The Queen's Resolution Discovered; Strange and Terrible News from the Queen in Holland 1642.

194–6 The Queen's return to England : A True Relation of the Majestie's returne out of Holland 1643; EG, 161–6; Elizabeth, 153; Ferrero, 63 (the thatched cottage); Prinsterer, II, iv, HM (1671) 34 et seq; Motteville, I, 211.

196 Offers of help from Hotham, Fairfax and Parliament : EG, 169–71; HMC Portland, I, 99; University of Hull, the Brynmoor Jones Library, DDHO/1/22.
The night at Burton Fleming : 'The Queene's Majesty did lie at noth [sic]

Page

Burton with her army the 5 of March 1642'. Burton Fleming parish register, Humberside County RO, PR931.

The Queen at York: Bodleian, Tanner Mss LXII, 608; York City Archives, C23, f. 71.

197   *Montrose at York:* Burnet, 212; EG, 217.

Hamilton: Burnet, 212, 215–16; CSPV XXVI, 259, 262, 266; EG, 186–7.

Rumours of a popish army: BM, Add. Mss, 27, 962 K, April 10, 1643, Salvetti news-letter.

Possible peace negotiations: Hexter, 71–2.

Denmark and the Orkneys: Baillon, 181; EG, 209.

The Queen's letters from York: ibid, 173–219.

198   *The Earl of Newcastle:* ibid, 188–90; Newcastle, 120; University of Hull, Brynmor Jones Library, DDHO/1/12. I am indebted to Mr N. Higson for providing this reference as well as that on page 196, which varies slightly from the version printed in HMC Portland, I, 99.

The threatened impeachment: Laud, III, 251.

199–201 *The journey to Oxford:* CSPV XXVI, 269; EG 219–23; HM (1671), 36–7; HMC Hastings, II, 102–3; de Motteville, I, 111.

200   *English horror of war:* CSPV XXVI, 269.

Death of the Earls of Northampton and Denbigh: The Battaile on Hopton Heath: a Letter from Lord Compton, 1643; Denbigh, 190–3.

201   *The Queen's stay at Stratford:* Shakespeare Centre, Stratford-on-Avon, *Book of the Corporation of Stratford-on-Avon* vol. C, 1628–37, 'Money disbursed and paid when the Queene Majesty laye in the town', *Chamberlain's Accounts, 1622–47.*

The land of weeds: Richard II, II, iv, 44–7.

Chapter 17: THE POLLUTED LAND

202   *The Queen at Oxford:* Oman, 150–2.

203   *Letters to the Earl of Newcastle:* EG, 225–6.

Royalist successes and the parliamentarian recovery: Hexter, 128–9, 149.

204   *The Queen's letter to Prince Rupert:* V. and A. Forster, 253.

Gloucester and Newbury: EG, 227–8; Elizabeth, 161; Wedgwood, II, 243–55.

The King's 'tender compassion': Petrie, 409.

205   *Archbishop Williams:* B. Dew Roberts, *Mitre and Musket* (1938), 191–258.

206   *The truce in Ireland:* Petrie, 135–6.

The death of Pym: Hexter, 4.

The Queen's pregnancy: CSPD XXVII, 75, 90, 92; Ferrero, 62.

207   *The parting at Abingdon:* EG, 239; Oman, 157.

208   *The Queen's stay at Bath:* EG, 240, a letter to the King, presumably by the light of candles provided, information from Bath City Council Records.

The bells at Axbridge: F. A. Knight, *The Heart of Mendip* (1915).

208–9 *The Queen at Exeter:* CSPV XXVII, 11, 121; EG, 242–9; HMC Report on the Records of the City of Exeter.

209   *The journey to Falmouth:* EG, 249–50; Ellis, III, iv, 303.

209–10 *The crossing to France:* Birch, II, 360; Prinsterer, II, iv, 106–7.

210   *Arrival in France:* BM Add. Mss, 12184, ff. 11, 315.

Page

211–12   *The Queen goes to Bourbon :* Birch, II, 359; EG, 252–6; Evelyn, 51, 53; Motteville, I, 187 et seq.

212   *Her stay at Nevers :* EG, 259–60; Ferrero, 64–5.

213   *The entry into Paris :* Bib. Nat., 9747, ff. 175; Montpensier, I, 98–100.

Chapter 18: AN ACTIVE INSTRUMENT

215   *Queen Anne and Mazarin :* Add. Mss., 12, 184, f. 334.
     Péronne's appeal : EG, 294–5.

216   *Sir Kenelm Digby :* Bone, 191; Wedgwood, II, 521–2.
     Marriage plans : Prinsterer, II, iv, 107–10, 132–5, 137.
     Peace moves at Uxbridge : EG, 276–8; Evelyn, 795–7.

217   *Letter to the Earl of Newcastle :* EG, 261.
     The King's letter : The King's Cabinet Opened, 14.
     Naseby and the capture of the cabinets : Ludlow, I, 122–3.
     Montrose : Prinsterer, IV, iv, 141–2.

218   *The situation in Ireland :* Bone, 188–94, 221–6; John Curry *The Civil War in Ireland* (1786), II, 1–12; *The Embassy in Ireland of Monsignor G. B. Rinuccini* (1873).
     'If I were a Protestant' : Secret Writing, 129.

219   *Jermyn's plans to raise forces :* ibid, 123.
     The marriage plans : ibid, 124, 125, 127.
     The peripatetics : Evelyn, 801–2.

220   *Anxiety concerning the Prince of Wales :* BM Harleian Mss, 6988, f. 205; EG, 314–22.

221   *'The world is here turned upside down' :* Howell, III, 5.

222–3   *The King's letters from Newcastle : Charles I in 1646,* 19, 22, 45, 55, 74, 79, 81.
     The Prince of Wales arrives in Paris : CSPV XXVII, 270, 275.

222   *The escape of Henriette-Anne : A True Copy of the Articles agreed on at the Surrender of Exeter 1646 ;* CSPV XXVII, 276; Birch, II, 409–10.
     The Queen's migraine headache : Secret Writings, 131.
     Her vivacity : Motteville, I, 223.

224   *Mademoiselle and the Prince of Wales :* Montpensier, I, 136–45.
     The Falmouth tin : Lord George Digby's Cabinet Opened, 21.
     Prince Rupert in Paris : CSPV XXVII, 293, 296.

225   *Jermyn :* Motteville, I, 283.
     Endymion Porter : EG, 306–7.
     The King taken from Holdenby : Burnet, 314–15; CSPV XXVII, 321.
     The Heads of the Proposals : Ludlow, I, 179.

226   *Winter at the French court and the illness of the French princes :* Montpensier, I, 137–8; Motteville, I, 302–3, 312–15, 363, 393–7.

227   *'Let no reports' and 'I am still resolved' :* Burnet, 337.
     Lack of ammunition : ibid, 344.
     The Queen in the Carmelite convent : Motteville, II, 104–5.

228   *Hamilton's expedition :* Burnet, 354–66; Davies, 155.
     The King's letter to the Prince of Wales : Petrie, 239–41.
     The Rump Parliament : David Underdown, *Pride's Purge : Politics in the Puritan Revolution* (1971).
     Defamatory propaganda in France : Motteville, II, 270.

Page
229   *Henrietta in penury at the Louvre :* Motteville, II, 300–1, 343–4; Cardinal
         de Retz, *Memoirs* (1723), 142.
         The trial of the King : Roger Lockyer ed, *The Trial of Charles I* (1959);
         Petrie, 241–61.
         The letters to the Speakers : EG, 347–50. The letters came to light in 1683
         when they were opened by the clerk of the Parliament who found them
         still sealed among other papers in a desk in the Parliament office.
229–30   *News of the King's death :* Birch, II, 381–2; Motteville, II, 352–4.

Chapter: 19 THE KING MY SON

231   *'Inward refreshments' :* Petrie, 295.
         The Queen's message to Anne of Austria : Motteville, II, 353.
         Her widow's weeds : Oman, 204–5.
231–2   *Montpensier's comment :* Montpensier, I, 210.
232   *'I live with bread like you' :* Richard II, III, ii, 175–7.
         The Eikon Basilike : Strong, *Charles I on Horseback*, 29–30.
         Montrose's reaction : EG, 358.
233   *Charles and James :* Ashley, 32; Ferrero, 70, 74; Montpensier, I, 211.
233–4   *Marriage proposals with Mademoiselle :* Montpensier, I, 217–20; 233–5.
234   *Christmas with the Carmelites :* Ferrero, 79.
         Cromwell, the arch-rebel : Elizabeth, 167.
235   *The 2nd Duke of Buckingham :* Denbigh, 251–2.
         Nicholas's advice concerning the Council : Evelyn, 822.
         Charles and his mother meet at Beauvais : Ferrero, 81, Montpensier, I, 319.
         Negotiations at Breda : Elizabeth, 167; Burnet, 522 et seq.
         Charles II in Scotland : Ashley, 36–43; Elizabeth, 177, 180; Ferrero, 92–3.
         James Duke of York goes to Brussels : EG, 368; Haswell, 52–3.
236   *His financial difficulties :* Evelyn, 826.
         Death of Prince of Orange, and birth of William : Stephen Baxter *William
         III* (1966), 1–9; Elizabeth, 179; Ferrero, 93–4; Nesca A. Robb, *William
         of Orange*, I (1962), 52–6.
         The death of Elizabeth : Ferrero, 89–90.
236–7   *Chaillot :* EG, 369, 372; Oman, 215–17.
         Troubles in France, Mazarin's flight : Perrero, 99–100; Pennington, 277–8.
238   *The battle of Worcester :* EG, 372–3; Elizabeth, 184, 186; Richard Ollard
         The Escape of Charles II (1966); Montpensier, I, 319.
         Charles returns : ibid, 320.
         Talk of a match between Mademoiselle and Louis XIV : ibid, 315, 335, 338.
239   *Henrietta makes excuses for Charles :* Ferrero, 97.
         Charles mediates with the Duc de Lorraine : ibid, 98, 100; Haswell, 77–81.
240–2   *Prince Henry of Gloucester in France :* Elizabeth, 222, 224; Ferrero, 104–5.
242   *Mock ambassadors :* Ferrero, 107–13.
         'Cet abominable Cromwell' : Ferrero, 112.
         The risings in 1655 : Ashley, 75; Doreen Cripps *Elizabeth of the Sealed
         Knot* (1975), 47–8.
243   *The Princess of Orange in Paris :* James II, 219.
         The meeting at Chilly : Montpensier, II, 436–7.
244   *Colombes :* Oman, 339–44, detailed description from an inventory, PRO,
         SPD Fr 78/128.

Page

The trial of John Mordaunt : The Private Diarie of Elizabeth, Viscountess Mordaunt (1856), 16–17.

Death of Cromwell : EG, 388–9; Elizabeth, 278.

245   The royal brothers' military prowess : EG, 386–7; Elizabeth, 276; James II, 266.

Charles at Colombes : Oman, 263.

Louise of the Palatinate at Chaillot : Elizabeth, 266 et seq.

246   The restoration : EG, 397–400; Elizabeth, 303–6; Evelyn, 233; Ferrero, 119–21.

Chapter 20: THE PEACEFUL MOTHER

247   Celebrations in Paris : EG, 398–9; Ferrero, 122.

The Earl of Bristol : Elizabeth, 284.

The Queen Mother's jointure : EG, 399; Elizabeth, 316–17.

Louis enters Paris with his bride : EG, 403–4.

248   Offer of marriage for Minette : Birch, II, 415.

248–51 Henrietta's visit to London : ibid. 420; EG, 406–7; Elizabeth, 329–33; Ferrero, 124; Ludlow, II, 327; Pepys, I, 260, 279, 281–2, 299, 302, 303, 322–3.

249   Henry, Duke of Gloucester : two letters from Henrietta Maria to her son 'le duc de glosester' April 22, June 17, 1660, expressing the hope that she would see him before his departure to England, prove that she hoped for a reconciliation. The letters are in the possession of Mr T. Cottrell-Dormer at Rousham Park.

251   Minette falls ill : Elizabeth, 338; C. Saint-André, Henriette d'Angleterre et la cour de Louis XIV (1933), 60.

252   Her marriage : Birch, II, 423–6; CSPV XXXII, 271; Motteville, IV, 256.

252–3 The French court at Fontainebleau : CSPV XXXIII, 268–75; EG, 408–9; Montpensier, III, 527.

253   Minette's first child : CSPV XXXIII, 68, 77, 84.

253–4 Henrietta returns to England in 1662 : Ferrero, 125–30.

254–5 Music in restoration England : Michael Foss, The Age of Patronage (1971), 40.

255   The penal laws and the Act of Uniformity : Ferrero, 129; John Miller, Popery and Politics in England, 1660–1688 (1973).

The Peaceful Mother : The Speech of her Majesty the Queen Mother's Palace, upon the reparation and enlargement of it, 1665.

256   Threats to the Queen Mother's Chapel : Birch, II, 455–6; HMC Hastings, II, 146.

257   Trouble over the dowry : CSPV XXXIV, 239, 280, 281; XXXV, 63, 74.

Princess Anne at Colombes : Oman, 330–1.

258   The Chevalier de Lorraine : Letters from Liselotte, ed. Maria Kroll, (1970), 38.

Henrietta visited by doctors : Birch, II, 465; EG, 413.

Her death : Birch, II, 465–7; EG, 416; Ludlow, II, 420.

259   The funeral ceremony : 'Relation de la pompe funèbre, faite en l'église de St. Denys en France pour la Reyne Mère d'Angleterre', Bib. Nat. 38153, f. 76.

The funeral oration : Oraisons Funèbres de Bossuet (1874), 36.

Index

281